# THE
# ITALIAN
# LAKES

**DAMIEN SIMONIS**
**BELINDA DIXON**

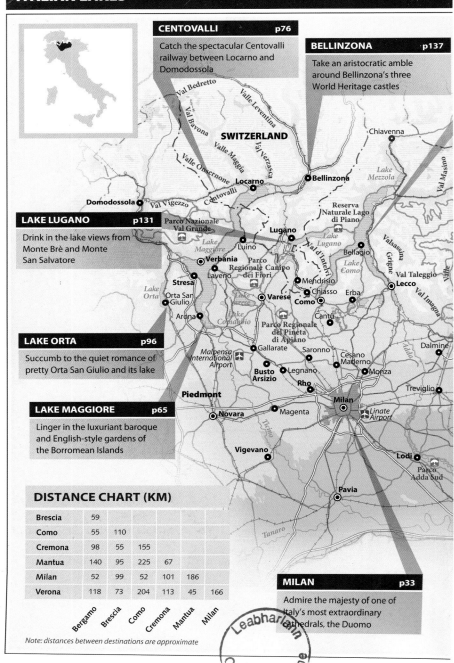

# ITALIAN LAKES

**CENTOVALLI** p76
Catch the spectacular Centovalli railway between Locarno and Domodossola

**BELLINZONA** p137
Take an aristocratic amble around Bellinzona's three World Heritage castles

**LAKE LUGANO** p131
Drink in the lake views from Monte Brè and Monte San Salvatore

**LAKE ORTA** p96
Succumb to the quiet romance of pretty Orta San Giulio and its lake

**LAKE MAGGIORE** p65
Linger in the luxuriant baroque and English-style gardens of the Borromean Islands

**MILAN** p33
Admire the majesty of one of Italy's most extraordinary cathedrals, the Duomo

## DISTANCE CHART (KM)

| | Bergamo | Brescia | Como | Cremona | Mantua | Milan |
|---|---|---|---|---|---|---|
| **Brescia** | 59 | | | | | |
| **Como** | 55 | 110 | | | | |
| **Cremona** | 98 | 55 | 155 | | | |
| **Mantua** | 140 | 95 | 225 | 67 | | |
| **Milan** | 52 | 99 | 52 | 101 | 186 | |
| **Verona** | 118 | 73 | 204 | 113 | 45 | 166 |

*Note: distances between destinations are approximate*

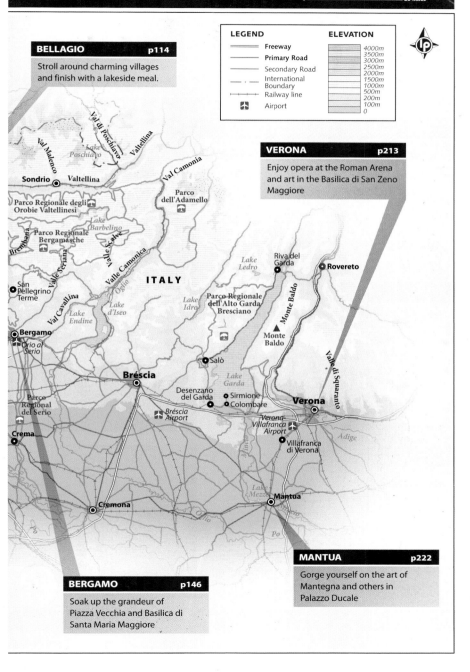

**BELLAGIO** p114

Stroll around charming villages and finish with a lakeside meal.

**LEGEND**

Freeway
Primary Road
Secondary Road
International Boundary
Railway line
Airport

**ELEVATION**

4000m
3500m
3000m
2500m
2000m
1500m
1000m
500m
200m
100m
0

0 ———— 40 km
0 ———— 20 miles

**VERONA** p213

Enjoy opera at the Roman Arena and art in the Basilica di San Zeno Maggiore

Val di Poschiavo
Val Malenco
Lake Poschiavo
Valtellina
Valtellina
Sondrio Valtellina
Val Camonia
Parco Regionale degli Orobie Valtellinesi
Parco dell'Adamello
Lake Barbelino
Parco Regionale Bergamasche
Valle Scalve
Valle Seriana
Valle Camonica
**ITALY**
Brembana
Lake Iseo
Lake d'Iseo
Lake Idro
Lake Ledro
Riva del Garda
Rovereto
San Pellegrino Terme
Oglio
Parco Regionale dell'Alto Garda Bresciano
Monte Baldo
Val Cavallina
Lake Endine
▲ Monte Baldo
**Bergamo**
Orio al Serio
Salò
Lake Garda
Valle di Squaranto
Parco Regional del Serio
**Bréscia**
Desenzano del Garda
Sirmione
Colombare
**Verona**
Verona-Villafranca Airport
Bréscia Airport
Crema
Mincio
Villafranca di Verona
Adige
Lake Mezzo
**Mantua**
Cremona
Oglio
Po
Po

**MANTUA** p222

Gorge yourself on the art of Mantegna and others in Palazzo Ducale

**BERGAMO** p146

Soak up the grandeur of Piazza Vecchia and Basilica di Santa Maria Maggiore

# INTRODUCING
# THE
# ITALIAN
# LAKES

**FORMED AT THE END OF THE LAST ICE AGE, AND A POPULAR HOLIDAY SPOT SINCE ROMAN TIMES, THE LAKES HAVE AN ENDURING, BREATHTAKING BEAUTY.**

LAKE ORTA

Lined up one after another across northern Italy and, in part, the southern Swiss canton of Ticino, the lakes each have distinct characters. Lake Garda, the largest and most easterly, is like a cross between the French Riviera and southern Italy, with its olive and lemon groves. Central Lake Como mixes charming lakeside towns, such as Bellagio, with wild mountains and forests. The western lakes of Lugano and Maggiore are dotted with pretty towns, castles and villas.

In counterpoint come the big city sophistication of Milan and artistic wonders of cities like Bergamo, Mantua and Verona, while Po valley towns hide architectural gems, and deep green valleys crawl north to the Orobie Alps.

Hikers and cyclists will find plenty to keep them occupied, from the gentle vineyard plains of the Franciacorta to lakeside mountain trails, while foodies will discover all manner of local specialities, from steaming *pizzoccheri* (buckwheat pasta) and polenta to grilled fresh lake perch, all washed down with some of Italy's finest wines.

Art, architecture, scenery, sport, food and wine – no sensory stone is left unturned around the Italian lakes.

---

**TOP** Isola San Giulio, in Lake Orta **BOTTOM LEFT** A fountain in Bergamo's Città Alta **BOTTOM RIGHT** Mantua's Palazzo Ducale, in front of the Basilica di Sant'Andrea

BERGAMO

MANTUA

LAKE LUGANO

BELLAGIO

**LAKE MAGGIORE**

TOP LEFT A view of Lake Lugano from Brè village
TOP RIGHT An Isola Bella garden, Borromean Islands
BOTTOM LEFT The grounds of Villa Melzi d'Eril, outside
Bellagio BOTTOM CENTRE Stone seats in Verona's
Roman Arena BOTTOM RIGHT Centovalli railway

**VERONA**

**CENTOVALLI**

# GETTING STARTED

DAVID TOMLINSON

## WHAT'S NEW

* The Triennale di Milano's permanent design museum (p43)

----

* BikeMi, Milan's public bicycle service (p57)

----

* Classic racing cars at Museo Mille Miglia (p167)

----

* The Museo del Ciclismo, on one of the legs of the Giro d'Italia cycle race (p116)

----

* Mussolini's Arengario in Piazza del Duomo, Milan, will host the Museo del Novecento (p42)

## CLIMATE: MILAN

Average Max/Min

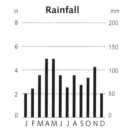

## PRICE GUIDE

|  | BUDGET | MIDRANGE | TOP END |
|---|---|---|---|
| **SLEEPING** | <€80 | €80-200 | >€200 |
| **MEALS** | <€20 | €20-45 | >€45 |
| **PARKING** | €0.50/hr | €2/hr | €20-25/day |

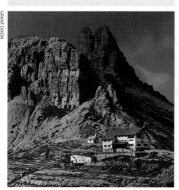

GRANT DIXON

DAVID TOMLINSON

----

**TOP** Gargnano harbour (p200), Lake Garda **BOTTOM LEFT** A *rifugio* in northern Italy's mountains **BOTTOM RIGHT** A Roman bridge over the Adige in Verona (p213) **FAR RIGHT** Galleria Vittorio Emanuele II (p47), in Milan

## ACCOMMODATION

Accommodation around Italy's lakes ranges from shoreline camping grounds, youth hostels, *agriturismi* (farm-stays) and *rifugi* (mountain huts), through to little B&Bs and hotels of all classes, to sublime comfort in lakeside villas and ultratrendy digs in the heart of metropolitan Milan. Or consider apartments, which offer the advantage of private cooking facilities. One key attraction of the lakes is the chance to enjoy some splendid views, so it is often worth paying extra for a room directly overlooking the lake of your choice. See the Accommodation chapter (p286) for listings.

## MAIN POINTS OF ENTRY

**MALPENSA AIRPORT** (www.sea-aeroportimilano.it) Most European and other international flights use Milan's Malpensa airport, 50km northwest of the city.

**LINATE AIRPORT** (www.sea-aeroportimilano.it) The majority of domestic and a handful of European flights use Milan's secondary airport, a convenient 7km from the city centre.

**ORIO AL SERIO** (☎ 035 32 63 23; www.sacbo.it) Just 4km southeast of Bergamo train station, this airport receives regular European flights and has direct transport links to Milan.

## THINGS TO TAKE

- ★ Robust shoes for walks in the hills around the lakes
- ★ A corkscrew for picnicking with marvellous wines
- ★ Mosquito repellent – a must in summer at the lakes
- ★ Warm clothes for the cool evenings and the mountains
- ★ Swimming costume for bracing bathes in the lakes

PAOLO CORDELLI

## WEBLINKS

**ITALIA** (www.enit.it) Italian tourism

**REGIONELOMBARDIA: PORTALE DEL TURISMO** (www.turismo.regione.lombardia.it) Lombardy tourism

**DISTRETTO DEI LAGHI** (http://distrettolaghi.eu) Lakes Maggiore and Orta

**PROVINCIA DI VERONA** (www.tourism.verona.it) Verona province, including Lake Garda

# FESTIVALS & EVENTS
### THE ITALIAN LAKES

## JANUARY

### CORTEO DEI RE MAGI

The three wise men hit Milan for this parade to celebrate Epiphany on 6 January (p51)

## MARCH

### MOSTRA NAZIONALE DELLA CAMELIA

Verbania gets a splash of extra floral colour in late March from a display of more than 200 varieties of camellia (p83; www.camelieinmostra.it)

## APRIL

### SETTIMANA DEL TULIPANO

Endless fields of tulips erupt in bloom on the grounds of Villa Taranto at the end of April (p80)

## MAY

### FESTIVAL DI CREMONA CLAUDIO MONTEVERDI

A month-long series of concerts in Cremona celebrates Claudio Monteverdi and other baroque-era composers (p172; www.teatroponchielli.it)

## JUNE

### GIRO D'ITALIA

The famous cycle race takes place in Bergamo's valleys and finishes in Milan (p23; www.ilgiroditalia.it)

## JULY

### ARENA DI VERONA

Verona's Roman Arena is a spectacular place for an opera season; from mid-June to the end of August (p220; www.arena.it)

### ESTIVAL JAZZ

Free open-air jazz concerts over three days in early July in Lugano (www.estivaljazz.ch)

## AUGUST

### SWISS NATIONAL DAY

Fireworks over Lake Lugano celebrate Switzerland's nationhood on 1 August

### FESTIVAL INTERNAZIONALE DI FILM

This two-week film festival in Locarno, one of Europe's most important, has been going since 1948 (p74; www.pardo.ch)

TOP Giro d'Italia racers power up a hill RIGHT Crowds in Locarno during the Festival Internazionale di Film

## SEPTEMBER

### ITALIAN F1 GRAND PRIX

Monza's historic autodrome hosts the F1 circuit (p62; www.monzanet.it)

### CENTOMIGLIA

As many as 350 vessels turn out for this prestigious sailing regatta on Lake Garda (www.centomiglia.it)

### SETTIMANE MUSICALI

Classical music from around the world is celebrated in Ascona from the end of August to mid-October (www.settimane -musicali.ch)

## OCTOBER

### MILANO MUSICA FESTIVAL

Contemporary compositions feature in a month of concerts throughout the city and at La Scala (www.milanomusica.org)

### IL PALIO DI VIGEVANO

Parades in period dress celebrate central Vigevano's glory days as a Sforza residence, on the second weekend in October (www.paliodivigevano.it)

## NOVEMBER

### FESTA DEL TORRONE

A weekend celebration of the sticky Christmas sweet *torrone* (nougat) in Cremona (p172; www.festadeltorrone cremona.it)

## DECEMBER

### FESTA DI SANT' AMBROGIO & FIERA DEGLI OBEI OBEI

The feast day of Milan's patron saint is celebrated in the city on 7 December with a large Christmas fair at Castello Sforzesco

KRZYSZTOF DYDYNSKI

# CULTURE

## TOP VILLAS

**VILLA BALBIANELLO** (p121) Dominating a wooded promontory, this villa was used as a set in *Casino Royale*

**VILLA TARANTO** (p80) A Scottish officer turned the grounds into a flourishing botanic garden

**ISOLA BELLA** (p86) The powerful Milanese Borromeo clan converted this island into a luxurious baroque fantasy

**VILLA MELZI D'ERIL** (p114) Soothing English-style gardens surround a stately home in Bellagio

**VILLA CARLOTTA** (p122) The villa bristles with statuary and its grounds with brilliant flowers and towering trees

**VILLA MONASTERO** (p126) A centuries-old magnolia dominates a dense garden surrounding the villa, which is crammed with period furniture

## THE CRADLE OF ROMANESQUE

From around the 11th century, Lombard master builders began to build churches more or less modelled on Roman basilicas. The Maestri Comacini (Como Masterbuilders) spread across Lombardy and Europe (some travelling as far as Catalonia and St Petersburg). They left lovely stone churches scattered around the lakes, with characteristic square-based bell towers. Many are modest affairs but some, like the grand Basilica di Sant'Abbondio in Como, have an undeniable majesty. In Milan, the Po Valley and plains towns from Pavia to Verona, a more imposing variant evolved. Built largely in brick and far grander than their lakeside equivalents, these churches nonetheless had in common certain key features, among them the use of the semicircle in doorways, windows and apses. For more on the architectural history of the lakes area, see p250.

GLENN VAN DER KNUFF

**TOP** Basilica di San Zeno Maggiore **BOTTOM** Villa Balbianello, on Lake Como **RIGHT** *The Last Supper*

## TOP CHURCHES

**DUOMO** (p39) Milan's Gothic masterpiece took centuries to complete.

**BASILICA DI SAN ZENO MAGGIORE** (p217) San Zeno is one of the most striking Romanesque churches in all northern Italy.

**BASILICA DI SANT'ABBONDIO** (p109) Como's towering Romanesque church boasts fine frescos.

**BASILICA DI SANTA MARIA MAGGIORE** (p148) Colleoni's Renaissance chapel was added to a Romanesque-Gothic mix in Bergamo.

ARKRELIGION.COM/ALAMY

## DON'T MISS EXPERIENCES

★ *Aperitivo* time – Snack and tipple in Milan's fashionable bars (p48)

★ Catch a ferry – Enjoy a jaunt around one of the great lakes

★ A night at the opera – Toss a coin and opt for a night of operatic grandeur at Milan's Teatro La Scala (p48) or Verona's Roman Arena (p220)

★ Buy silk – Browse in Mantero's Como silk showroom, La Tessitura (p111)

★ Discover the Città Alta – Wander the tight medieval web of Bergamo's old town (p149)

★ Art immersion – Visit the region's top art collections in Milan's Pinacoteca di Brera (p47) and Bergamo's Accademia Carrara (p149)

## WEBSITES

**IL CENACOLO VINCIANO** (www.cenacolovinciano.org) Book your visit to *The Last Supper* mural

**BORROMEAN** (www.borromeo turismo.it) Information on the Borromean Islands

**MUSEO DELLA SETA** (www .museosetacomo.com) A font of information on Como's silk history

**RUPESTRE.NET** (www.rupestre .net) Valle Camonica rock art details

**CONSORZIO LIUTAI ANTONIO STRADIVARI CREMONA** (www.cremonaliuteria .it) Information on the tradition of violin-making and modern violin-makers in Cremona

# CULTURE

MARTIN MOOS

## FINEST CASTLES

**CASTELLI DI BELLINZONA** (p138) Bellinzona's three castles form a magnificent ensemble.

**CASTELLO SFORZESCO** (p43) Milan's castle exudes little menace and is home to a series of museums.

**ROCCA D'ANGERA** (p88) This Borromeo fortress commands fine views atop a vine-layered hill.

**ROCCA DI SONCINO** (p175) The Sforza family raised this four-towered fortress in 1473.

**CASTELLO DI VEZIO** (p127) The castle ruins above Varenna are a draw for the views.

## TOP FRESCOS

**IL CENACOLO VINCIANO** (p42) Leonardo da Vinci's *Last Supper*

**BASILICA DI SAN GIULIO** (p98) Vivid depictions of saintly martyrs

**PALAZZO DUCALE** (p223) Mantegna's work is Mantua's top draw

**CHIESA DI SANTA MARIA FORIS PORTAS** (p94) Rare, pre-Romanesque frescos in a 7th-century church

**BASILICA DI SANT'ABBONDIO** (p109) An extraordinary series charting scenes from Jesus' life

**COLLEGIATA, CASTIGLIONE OLONA** (p93) The life of St John the Baptist, by Florentine master Masolino da Panicale

## RENAISSANCE ART IN LOMBARDY

The Renaissance explosion in Florence and later in Venice did not leave Lombardy and other parts of northern Italy indifferent. Andrea Mantegna was one of the first northern artists to absorb the lessons of some of Florence's finest, and went on to leave major works in Verona's Basilica di San Zeno Maggiore and the Palazzo Ducale in Mantua. Leonardo da Vinci's *Last Supper* fresco is the greatest testimony to that artist's long stint in Milan. Other Renaissance stars to work in the area include Lorenzo Lotto, Pordenone and Masolino da Panicale. For more on the region's art history, see p244.

**TOP** A statue in a Castello Sforzesco courtyard **RIGHT** *Oculus*, by Andrea Mantegna, in the Palazzo Ducale

## COMO'S SILK TRADE

The art of silk-weaving and -printing reached Italy in the 13th century. Silk-weavers appeared around Lake Como in the 14th century but the industry didn't take off until Empress Maria Theresa made Lake Como textile production duty-free. Lyon (France) and Krefeld (Germany) provided stiff competition but by the early 20th century Como was established as a centre of fine silk. Since the end of WWII (by which time Lyon and Krefeld had ceased to be active producers), Como's silk dynasties have concentrated on top-quality design and production for the world's leading fashion houses. Mass silk production in China, fierce competition and the global economic downturn are all putting pressure on these businesses. For more on Como silk, see p265.

## DOS & DON'TS

★ Italians take pride in their dress and appearance. You don't have to go as far as they do but it's easy enough to avoid fashion faux pas.

★ The standard form of greeting is a handshake. Kisses (one on each cheek, right then left) are for intimates.

★ Dress up, not down: flip-flops and T-shirts don't cut the mustard in restaurants and cafes.

★ Cover yourself when entering a church.

★ Topless bathing is not at all the norm on lake beaches.

# FOOD & DRINK

## TOP WINE AREAS

**BARDOLINO** (www.stradadelbar
dolino.com) One of the Veneto's
top reds is cultivated on Lake
Garda.

**FRANCIACORTA** (www.francia
corta.net) Spumante (sparkling)
whites and rosés have made
this wine region northwest of
Brescia a household name.

**OLTREPÒ PAVESE** (www
.vinoltrepo.it) Some 20 wines are
classified as DOC in this area
around Pavia, south of Milan.

**SOAVE** (www.ilsoave.com) The area
east of Verona produces some
of Italy's finest white wines.

**TICINO** (www.ticinowine.ch) Merlot is king in the Swiss canton.

**VALPOLICELLA** (www.valpoli
cella.it) Home of the legendary
Amarone della Valpolicella
DOC.

**VALTELLINA** (www.valtellinavini
.com) The Lombard valley boasts
two DOCGs, including the
prized Sforzato.

## WHAT'S COOKING?

Climate and history have influenced cooking
around the lakes, with boiled meats and escalopes
(a reminder of the Austrians' long presence in
Lombardy) high on the list of typical products.
Milan is an island in food terms, combining traditional tastes with cuisines imported with migrants
from around Italy (and, more recently, the world).
Restaurants around the lakes will happily prepare
seafood but prefer fresh local fish, like *persico*
(perch), and the Alpine country around the lakes
is a source of tasty cheeses. Many main courses
come with polenta, a maize-based staple that
comes as a thick yellow wedge or in a porridgelike
form, and the Po plains produce 50 types of rice,
the basis for fine risottos. For more on the delicious dishes of the region, such as the irresistible
northern *panna cotta* (literally 'cooked cream', a
creamy set dessert bathed in sauce), see p274.

**TOP** Indulge in local pastries in Milan **BOTTOM** DOC wines and picturesque countryside in Valpolicella **RIGHT** Take a break in a Milan cafe **FAR RIGHT** Sample just-caught fish on the lakes

## TOP RESTAURANTS

**CASABELLA** (p88) Elegantly prepared fish, and lake views

-----

**EL BRELLIN** (p52) Romantic, canalside spot in Milan

-----

**HOTEL LIDO ANGERA** (p90) Lake-fish sushi platters on Lake Maggiore

-----

**DA ANNETTA** (p94) Exquisite cuisine near Lake Varese

-----

**LA COLDANA** (p176) Feast in a sprawling farmhouse

-----

**LA CUCINA DI MARIANNA** (p124) Imaginative, down-home cooking

## DON'T MISS EXPERIENCES

- ★ Franciacorta – Take a drive through this undulating wine country, visiting monasteries and castles on the way (p160)

-----

- ★ Wine tasting – Tour the Costaripa winery and sample some chiaretto (p195)

-----

- ★ Soave – Sample some fine white wine at Enoteca Il Drago in the shadow of Soave's castle (p222)

-----

- ★ Tasting oil – Learn how olive oil is made, and taste test at the Frantoio Montecroce (p193)

-----

- ★ Gourmet hideaway – Head out of the way and submit your palate to pleasure at Ristorante Marconi (p77)

-----

- ★ Delicatessen – Drop by Peck, Milan's famous gourmet food store, to make some mouth-watering purchases (p53)

## TOP DROPS

**AMARONE DELLA VALPOLICELLA DOC**
A velvety red made from dried grapes

-----

**BARDOLINO SUPERIORE DOCG** An excellent, dry red

-----

**FRANCIACORTA DOCG**
Sparkling whites and rosés

-----

**SOAVE SUPERIORE DOCG**
Among Italy's best still whites

-----

**SFORZATO DI VALTELLINA DOCG** A strong, tannin-heavy nebbiolo-based red

-----

**OLTREPÒ PAVESE SANGUE DI GIUDA DOC** A sweet red known as Judas' Blood

# FOOD & DRINK

## TOP CHEESES

**STRACCHINO** Made from cow's milk extracted during the seasonal moves to and from Alpine pastures

**GORGONZOLA** A well-known cheese whose two-curd, blue-mould version is strong on the nose

**TALEGGIO** A popular soft cheese

**MASCARPONE** Used especially to make desserts

**BAGOSS** Mature and strong flavoured

**ROBIOLA** Soft-ripened cheese with a thin rind

## TOP REGIONAL DISHES

Trying out strictly local dishes is part of the fun around the lakes.

**CASONSÈI** Big egg-based ravioli (aka *casoncelli*) stuffed with meat, cheese or spinach

**GNOCCHI DI PATATE** Potato-based balls usually served in a meat or tomato sauce

**MARUBINI** Meat and cheese stuffed discs of pasta served in a broth

**PASTISSADA DE CAVAL** Horse-meat stew

**PIZZOCCHERI** Buckwheat tagliatelle

**RISOTTO** A dish with limitless variations

**SCALOPPINA ALLA MILANESE** A breaded veal escalope

## NORTH ITALIAN WINES

The lakes of northern Italy extend from eastern Piedmont across Lombardy and into the Veneto and Trentino-Alto Adige, a formidable battery of wine-growing areas. Italians love trying wines from other regions but are equally loyal to good local product. In restaurants on the Piedmont side of Lake Maggiore, you may well be served typical Piedmontese drops such as Barbera d'Asti, Dolcetto d'Alba and Barolo. Hop over the west side of the lake and it's likely to be a Lombard tipple – an Oltrepò Pavese, for example, or a Sforzato from the Valtellina. Around Verona, Valpolicella and Soave rule, OK. For more on wine, see p270.

TOP Valtellina's own *pizzoccheri* (buckwheat pasta) RIGHT Alfresco dining in Milan's Brera district (p47)

## BEYOND PASTA

Some 50 varieties of rice are grown in the Po Valley plains. Indeed, rice is the traditional *numero uno* staple in Lombardy and much of Piedmont and the Veneto: a risotto has more northern cache than pasta ever will. Sure, pasta (probably an import from more southern climes and an integral part of Italian cooking by the 17th century) abounds but you can do without it altogether. Verona is the birthplace of *gnocchi di patate* (little potato-based pasta balls), which can be served with all sorts of accompaniments. The least-known *primo* (first course) is *pizzoccheri,* a kind of buckwheat tagliatelle served with potatoes, cabbage and melted cheese, which has its origins in the Valtellina, in northern Lombardy. For more on your first course, see p277.

## RESTAURANTS WITH FABULOUS VIEWS

**GATTO NERO** (p124) High-end Italian cuisine with unfettered views over Lake Como

**LA COLLINA** (p157) Classy countryside hilltop dining

**AL BORDUCAN** (p93) A tasteful hideaway high above Varese

**RISTORANTE MILANO** (p85) Verbania's classiest eatery has a lakeside garden

**CASABELLA** (p88) Elegantly prepared fish with close-up views of Isola Superiore

**ALBERGO BELVEDERE** (p117) Romantic pergola in a village overlooking Lake Como

**ALBERGO SILVIO** (p118) Fine lake fish and sunset views just outside Bellagio

MARTIN MOOS

DAVID TOMLINSON

# OUTDOORS

## THE ITALIAN LAKES

## TOP WALKS

**GREENWAY DEL LAGO DI COMO** (p122) An easygoing 10km stroll on the west bank of Lake Como

**MONTE MOTTARONE** (p82) Opt to hike all or part of the way up or down Monte Mottarone, a superb lookout point

**CIMETTA** (p70) A gentle walk that leads to 360-degree views above Locarno; further trails abound

**DORSALE** (p116) Two-day hike (with option to follow the crests) from Brunate to Bellagio

**ANELLO AZZURRO** (p99) A pretty three-day route around Lake Orta

**VIA DEI MONTI LARIANI** (p122) A classic 130km trail along high ground above the west flank of Lake Como

## OUTDOOR PURSUITS

Both the lakes and the mountains around them offer plenty of incentives for outdoor activity. For many it will simply be a case of getting about on your own two pins. Options cover every level, from meandering in the fabulous gardens of many a lakeside villa, to short, intense upward hikes that lead to inspiring lookout points. Serious hikers can spend days trekking in the mountains between *rifugi* (mountain huts). Cycling is an excellent (and popular) way to get around the lakes, while some of the better laid-out walking trails (often one-time mule tracks) are ideal for mountain biking. Water-sport options abound, from tootling about on pedalos to sailing, windsurfing, kitesurfing, wakeboarding or just swimming. Although top ski fields lie further afield, there is no shortage of family-style spots for a day's fun in the white stuff. For more details, see p260.

DENNIS JONES

**TOP** Lake Garda seen from Monte Baldo **BOTTOM** Parasurfing on Lake Garda **RIGHT** San Siro stadium in Milan **FAR RIGHT** A catamaran on Lake Garda

## TOP PANORAMIC VIEWPOINTS

**SASSO DEL FERRO** (p89) Catch the Laveno Funivia to this marvellous viewpoint

**MONTE BALDO** (p207) For panoramic views of Lake Garda and beyond

**BRUNATE** (p111) Take the funicular high above Como

**SACRO MONTE DEL ROSARIO** (p93) A historic pilgrimage ends in a hamlet with splendid views

**MONTE GENEROSO** (p136) The best viewpoint in Ticino, with 360-degree views

## DON'T MISS EXPERIENCES

* Rifugio Menaggio – Hike up to the Rifugio Menaggio mountain hut for superb views of Lake Como and, with luck, a meal (p122)

* Windsurfing – Make the best of the Pelèr and Ora winds to sail at speed on Lake Garda (p206)

* Onno beach – Stretch out for some rays and take a brisk dip in Lake Como southeast of Bellagio (p124)

* Goooaaal! – Join Milan's *tifosi* (fans) for an afternoon's *calcio* (football) excitement at San Siro stadium (p49)

* Lake Como waterskiing – Hire your own boat and equipment for a morning's waterskiing or wakeboard fun at Lake Como's north end (p124)

## GLIDE & SURF

* Paragliding – Take to the skies at the top of Lake Maggiore's Laveno Funivia (p89) or Monte Baldo (p207)

* Kitesurfing – Head for the little-touristed north of Lake Como (p130)

* Windsurfing – Speed along Lake Garda at Torbole (p206)

* Canoeing – Push the boat out for a paddle on Lake Endine (p161)

# OUTDOORS

CURIOIMAGES SRL/ALAMY

## TOP SPORT EVENTS

**FOOTBALL** (p49; September to May) Twice a year, rivals AC Milan and Inter clash in Milan

**GIRO D'ITALIA** (opposite; May) Italy's great cycle race, runner-up in importance to the Tour de France.

**CENTOMIGLIA** (September) A forest of white sails sweeps across Lake Garda during this classic race.

**FORMULA ONE** (p62; September) Ferrari and co compete for line honours at Monza.

## A SPOT OF SKIING

Excellent skiing can be had just beyond the scope of this book, in Bormio (www.bormio.it) and around Monte Rosa (especially Macugnaga; www.macugnaga.it). For a modest family outing closer by, there are several options:

**FOPPOLO** (p263) A popular ski station in the Alpi Orobie

**MONTE MOTTARONE** (p82) Attracts families for snow and lake views

**MONTE BALDO** (p82) Offers runs above Lake Garda

**PIAN DEL TIVANO** (p116) Northeast of Como, this area has cross-country runs

**CIMETTA** (p70) Locarno folks get in some practice here

## FOOTBALL AS RELIGION

For many Lombards, the true cathedral in Milan is not the Duomo but the San Siro football stadium (p49). *Calcio* is more than a religion for many Italians, it is a raison d'être. Here, two of the country's best teams, AC Milan and FC Internazionale Milano (aka Inter), play on alternate weeks. Inter took the 2009 premier league (Serie A) trophy in 2009, leaving AC Milan (owned by Italy's ubiquitous prime minister-cum-media tycoon, Silvio Berlusconi) down the table and in financial difficulty. There is nothing as electric as when Milan's competing home sides clash in the local derby.

**TOP** Cross-country skiing in the mountains near Brescia and Bergamo **RIGHT** Mountain biking above Lake Como

## THE GIRO D'ITALIA

Around Lake Como and in the Bergamo valleys, you'll soon espy groups of weekend cyclists kitted out as champions. Just as in any elegant Milan bar, locals like to do things with class. Many follow routes that have been used as stages of the nation's great cycle race, the Giro d'Italia. Second only to the Tour de France, the Giro has drawn champions from around the world since its inauguration in 1909. The rugged Lombard territory is perfect for challenging competition, and at least one stage in the race is usually held in the mountains north of Bergamo. A speed racers' stage in Milan is tradition. Italians have dominated the Giro but, in 2009, the Russian Denis Menchov took the pink maillot.

## CYCLING ROUTES

Cycling is a great way to get around the lakes, although traffic can be heavy on popular routes on summer weekends. Some walking trails also make good mountain-biking routes.

* Dorsale - This hiking trail is ideal for a day's mountain-bike exploration (p116)

* Monte Mottarone - Rent a mountain bike for the 25km descent to Stresa (p82)

* Madonna del Ghisallo - Feel like a champion on this classic climb from Bellagio (p116)

* Monte Isola - Cycle round Lake Iseo's island (p158)

VARIO IMAGES GMBH & CO.KG/ALAMY

# FAMILY TRAVEL

ROCCO FASANO

## TOP LODGINGS

**AGRITURISMO IN LOMBARDIA** (www.lombardia.campagna mica.it) An exhaustive site on Lombard farm-stays and farm restaurants

**AGRITURISMO MUNT DE VOLT** (p294) A house in sloping, open fields (with swings) high up inland from Bellagio

**HOTEL AURORA** (p295) A hotel with kayaks, waterskiing and an aqua-trampoline in the lake waters.

**LE STANZE DEL LAGO** (p294) Handy apartments in the heart of Como

## DON'T MISS EXPERIENCES

**GARDALAND** (p212) One of Italy's top theme parks, with dinosaurs, pirate ships and roller coasters

**CANEVAWORLD** (p212) Medieval shows, an aqua park and Movieland Studios, where action-packed stunt shows are held

**SWISSMINIATUR** (p136) Countless Swiss monuments presented as kid-size replicas

**PARCO DELLA VILLA PALLAVICINO** (p81) Animals and exotic birds roam free

**AERO CLUB COMO** (p106) Take to the air in a flying boat over Lake Como

**LAGO MAGGIORE ADVENTURE PARK** (p83) Climb and abseil your way to exhaustion

## TRAVEL WITH CHILDREN

A lakeside holiday can be perfect for kids and adults. While touring the cities can become trying for smaller children, they will soon warm to the lakes, which offer an array of plannable activities. There are plenty of small beaches, ideal for lying and splashing around, and in many places you can hire pedalos, kayaks and small boats. We don't provide camping-ground information in this book, but there are plenty of options, particularly at the beaches along the south sides of Lakes Garda and Iseo. Rides on ferries and hydrofoils, as well as some of the funiculars leading to lookout points, will also thrill most children, and the occasional gelato reward is guaranteed to please.

**TOP** Splashing around in Lake Como

# CONTENTS

# THE AUTHORS

### DAMIEN SIMONIS

**Coordinating Author, Milan, Lake Maggiore & Lake Orta, Lake Como & Lake Lugano, Bergamo, Brescia & Cremona**
Damien still remembers listening to crackly shortwave Italian broadcasts on Australian midsummer nights in the '80s. His love of Italy blossomed into a university obsession. In the 1990s he lived in Milan and this guide was something of a home-coming. He has never been long absent from the *bel paese* (beautiful country), having worked on eight editions of Lonely Planet's *Italy*, as well as *Venice, Best of Venice, Florence, Tuscany* and *Sardinia.*

### BELINDA DIXON

**Lake Garda, Verona & Mantua**
Belinda first experienced the wonder that is Italy on the ubiquitous teenage month-long rail trip and has been an enthusiastic visitor ever since. This latest Lonely Planet adventure has been an absolute treat: opera, art and ferry-hopping; cheeses, truffles and wine trails. It really doesn't get much better than that.

## LONELY PLANET AUTHORS

Why is our travel information the best in the world? It's simple: our authors are passionate, dedicated travellers. They don't take freebies in exchange for positive coverage so you can be sure the advice you're given is impartial. They travel widely to all the popular spots, and off the beaten track. They don't research using just the internet or phone. They discover new places not included in any other guidebook. They personally visit thousands of hotels, restaurants, palaces, trails, galleries, temples and more. They speak with dozens of locals every day to make sure you get the kind of insider knowledge only a local could tell you. They take pride in getting all the details right, and in telling it how it is. Think you can do it? Find out how at lonelyplanet.com.

# ITINERARIES

## THE VILLAS OF LAKE COMO

### THREE DAYS // COMO TO VARENNA // 38KM

Lake Como is studded with villas and, especially, gardens of extraordinary beauty. Start in Como with **Villa Olmo** (p110) before moving up the road to **Cernobbio**

(p118), where you will need to book to get into the grounds of Villa d'Este (unless you're sleeping there!). A drive up the west bank will take you past many private mansions until you reach the promontory paradise of **Villa Balbianello** (p121), in Lenno. A short jaunt northeast will lead you to **Villa Carlotta** (p122), in Tremezzo, with statuary inside and botanical wonders outside. A ferry makes the hop from nearby Cadenabbia to **Bellagio** (p114), where two breathtaking gardens surround Villas Serbelloni and Melzi d'Eril. Another ferry heads to pretty **Varenna** (p126), home to two more villas.

ITINERARIES

## THE BEST OF LAKE MAGGIORE

### FOUR DAYS // LOCARNO TO ANGERA // 89KM

Starting in film-festival town **Locarno** (p65) and adjacent Ascona, this southbound trip leads over the Switzerland–Italy border to **Cannobio** (p79), where you might

overnight in **Hotel Pironi** (p292) before making a pilgrimage to the Sacro Monte della SS Trinità at **Ghiffa** (p80). In Verbania, time should be made for the spectacular gardens of **Villa Taranto** (p80). While here, take a boat to **Isola Madre** (p87), one of the three Borromean Islands. The others are more easily accessed from **Stresa** (p80). Behind that gentle lakeside town, hike up **Monte Mottarone** (p82) for the views, or take the cable car. Next, stop at a huge hollow statue the Borromeo clan left in **Arona** (p83), south of Stresa, and, lastly, at their fortress across the lake in **Angera** (p88).

## VERONA & THE BEST OF LAKE GARDA

### SIX DAYS // VERONA ROUND TRIP // 224KM

After a couple of days strolling magical **Verona** (p215), head across the Valpolicella wine region to **Bardolino** (p210), a fine little wine town on Lake Garda. To the

north, the road will take you through **Torri del Benaco** (p209) and fetching **Malcesine** (p206), from where you can take the cable car to Monte Baldo. An excellent stop at the top end of the lake is **Riva del Garda** (p203) and the first stop on the west bank is **Gargnano** (p200), surrounded by lemon and olive terraces. Follow this with **Gardone Riviera** (p199), home to the oddball Vittoriale degli Italiani mansion-monument. Pretty **Salò** (p197) has a dark history, while the slim **Sirmione** (p191) peninsula boasts Roman remains. From here, it's a short trip back east to Verona.

# A PO VALLEY TOUR

## SIX DAYS // CREMONA ROUND TRIP // 207KM

For something different, a tour of southern Lombardy is rich in discovery. After a full day admiring the medieval heart of **Cremona** (p169), head west for the fortress village

of **Pizzighettone** (p173), on the Adda river. Zip further west to **San Colombano al Lambro** (p270) to taste local wine before continuing to the student town of **Pavia** (p58), with its pretty old centre. Then make the excursion north to the impressive **Certosa di Pavia** (p58) and northeast to central **Lodi** (p174), which harbours a Renaissance gem in the Tempio Civico dell'Incoronata. Another 16km brings you to **Crema** (p174), a surprise packet that repays exploration. Then, head on to **Soncino** (p175), graced by a fine Sforza fortress, and take a gentle back-country drive south back to Cremona.

# CITY LINE-UP

## FIVE DAYS // MILAN TO VERONA // 182KM

The A4 motorway and railways link some of the region's main cities in a neat line. Starting in **Milan** (p33), you could take as little or long as you want to complete the

trip, perhaps taking a leisurely couple of days to wander the Lombard capital, with its **Duomo** (p39), shops and gourmet indulgence in places like **El Brellin** (p52). Exploration of **Bergamo** (p146) could take a day, punctuated with an overnight stay in **Hotel Piazza Vecchia** (p298). A short morning ride leads east to historic **Brescia** (p164), where you can explore the Roman relics and churches before heading to romantic **Verona** (p213), worth at least two days of your time, especially if you can include a night at the **opera** (p220).

ITINERARIES

# A TRIANGULAR CIRCUIT

## FIVE TO SEVEN DAYS // COMO ROUND TRIP // 108KM

The **Triangolo Lariano** (p114) is worth exploring if you're after a little-touristed area of Lake Como. The first stop out of Como should be **Torno** (p115), with its enchant-

ing lake square. **Careno** (p116) is a typical, steep village with a great eating stop (p116) and **Bellagio** (p114) is the place to spend a night or two. Use the latter as a base for ferry rides to **Tremezzo** (p122) and **Varenna** (p126). Then follow the cyclists' climb south to **Magreglio** (p116) and stop at **Lasnigo's** (p117) lovely Romanesque church, from where you can wind down to the beach at **Onno** (p124). Further south, **Civate** is the starting point for a pretty hike to a hilltop abbey (p117). Backtrack a little for a well-deserved lakeside drink at **Lecco** (p126) before returning to Como.

# A WINE MEANDER

## ONE DAY // BARDOLINO TO SOAVE // 77KM

Although it is not always easy to find wineries that open to passers-by, a wander across the wine territory east of Lake Garda can be highly pleasurable. Start in **Bardolino**

(p210), lakeside home of the eponymous wine, then head west into **Valpolicella** wine territory (p221) for **San Giorgio**, its views and Romanesque church. Nearby **Gargagnano** is home to that king of local drops, Amarone. To the north, the narrow country roads to Marano di Valpolicella take you through the heart of wine country, a lovely drive, from where you can turn southeast to Negrar, a quiet wine village, and drop down to Parona di Valpolicella. End the wine tour east in the capital of Veneto whites, castle-topped **Soave** (p222).

# MILAN

## 3 PERFECT DAYS

### ❦ DAY 1 // DISCOVERING THE DUOMO AND CENTRAL MILAN

Whether it's your first or 100th visit to Milan, a pilgrimage to the overwhelming Duomo (p39) rarely fails to impress. Head up for a rooftop view of the city centre, then set off to stroll in the Galleria Vittorio Emanuele II (p47), an eye-catching neoclassical arcade, and world-renowned 18th-century La Scala opera house (p48). From there, walk to the Castello Sforzesco (p43), where you can mix culture in the castle's museums with downtime in the Parco Sempione (p46).

### ❦ DAY 2 // SUPPER, SHOPS AND MORE SUPPER

Make sure you're booked in to admire Leonardo da Vinci's *Il cenacolo* (The Last Supper; p42) in the morning. Inspired by such beauty, a trip to the Monte Napoleone area (aka the Quadrilatero d'Oro; p43) is in order to discover the heart of high-fashion shopping, Milan style. After dropping your acquisitions off at the hotel, head to the Navigli (p48) area for a slap-up meal at El Brellin (p52) and drinks at one of the many nearby bars.

### ❦ DAY 3 // DAY TRIPPING

For a change of pace, you could squeeze in a couple of day trips out of Milan. The first would take you south to Pavia (p58), a pretty university town well worth exploring in its own right. The main attraction, however, is the extraordinary Certosa di Pavia (p59), a Renaissance monastery complex 10km north of Pavia and easily reached by local transport. Hourly buses also run southwest to Vigevano (p61), whose central Piazza Ducale (p61) is a theatrical Renaissance masterpiece.

# MILAN

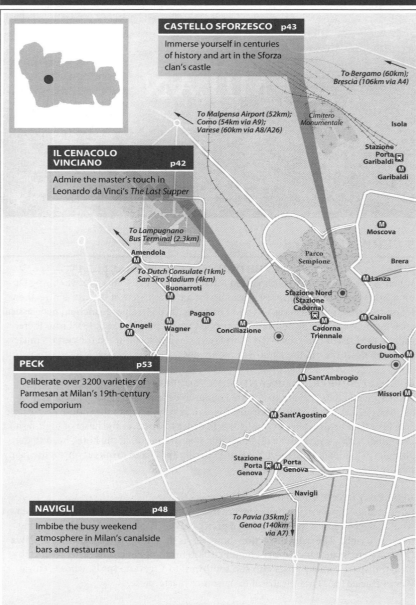

**CASTELLO SFORZESCO** p43

Immerse yourself in centuries of history and art in the Sforza clan's castle

To Bergamo (60km); Brescia (106km via A4)

To Malpensa Airport (52km); Como (54km via A9); Varese (60km via A8/A26)

Cimitero Monumentale

Isola

Stazione Porta Garibaldi

Garibaldi

**IL CENACOLO VINCIANO** p42

Admire the master's touch in Leonardo da Vinci's *The Last Supper*

To Lampugnano Bus Terminal (2.3km)

Moscova

Amendola

To Dutch Consulate (1km); San Siro Stadium (4km)

Buonarroti

Parco Sempione

Brera

Lanza

Pagano

Stazione Nord (Stazione Cadorna)

De Angeli   Wagner   Conciliazione

Cadorna Triennale

Cairoli

Cordusio

Duomo

**PECK** p53

Deliberate over 3200 varieties of Parmesan at Milan's 19th-century food emporium

Sant'Ambrogio

Missori

Sant'Agostino

Stazione Porta Genova   Porta Genova

Navigli

**NAVIGLI** p48

Imbibe the busy weekend atmosphere in Milan's canalside bars and restaurants

To Pavia (35km); Genoa (140km via A7)

MILAN

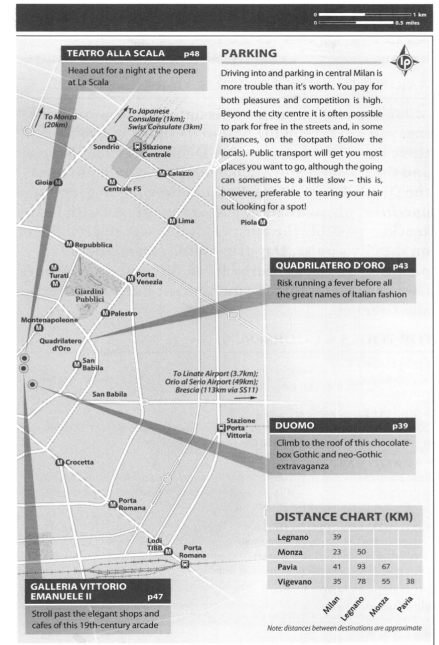

0 _____ 1 km
0 _____ 0.5 miles

## TEATRO ALLA SCALA    p48

Head out for a night at the opera at La Scala

## PARKING

Driving into and parking in central Milan is more trouble than it's worth. You pay for both pleasures and competition is high. Beyond the city centre it is often possible to park for free in the streets and, in some instances, on the footpath (follow the locals). Public transport will get you most places you want to go, although the going can sometimes be a little slow – this is, however, preferable to tearing your hair out looking for a spot!

To Monza (20km)

To Japanese Consulate (1km); Swiss Consulate (3km)

Sondrio

Stazione Centrale

Gioia

Centrale FS

Calazzo

Lima

Piola

Repubblica

Turati

Porta Venezia

Giardini Pubblici

Palestro

Montenapoleone

Quadrilatero d'Oro

San Babila

San Babila

## QUADRILATERO D'ORO    p43

Risk running a fever before all the great names of Italian fashion

To Linate Airport (3.7km);
Orio al Serio Airport (49km);
Brescia (113km via SS11)

Stazione Porta Vittoria

## DUOMO    p39

Climb to the roof of this chocolate-box Gothic and neo-Gothic extravaganza

Crocetta

Porta Romana

Lodi TIBB

Porta Romana

## GALLERIA VITTORIO EMANUELE II    p47

Stroll past the elegant shops and cafes of this 19th-century arcade

## DISTANCE CHART (KM)

| | Milan | Legnano | Monza | Pavia |
|---|---|---|---|---|
| Legnano | 39 | | | |
| Monza | 23 | 50 | | |
| Pavia | 41 | 93 | 67 | |
| Vigevano | 35 | 78 | 55 | 38 |

Note: distances between destinations are approximate

# MILAN
# GETTING STARTED

## MAKING THE MOST OF YOUR TIME

Milan is a frenetic metropolis but, with forward thinking, you can take in the best of its sights in two or three days. Standouts are the Duomo, *The Last Supper* and the Castello Sforzesco. Shoppers should not miss the Quadrilatero d'Oro. Build in time for an evening *aperitivo,* when Milanese gather for a tipple with bar snacks – possibly the most enjoyable way to get a finger on the city's pulse. Day-trip options from Milan are plentiful: as well as nearby Pavia, Vigevano and Monza (two days for all three), you can visit Bergamo, Brescia and Cremona.

## TOP TOURS & COURSES

### ❦ BOAT TOURS
Take a weekend punt along some of Milan's *navigli* (canals). ( ☎ 02 667 91 31; Alzaia Naviglio Grande 4; tours €12)

---

### ❦ GIROCITTÀ IN AUTOBUS
This three-hour tour of Milan takes in all the key sights, including a visit to Leonardo da Vinci's *The Last Supper.* ( ☎ 02 3391 0794; www.autostradale.it; tours €55)

---

### ❦ PALAZZO MARINO
Milan's town hall is housed in this grand 16th-century *palazzo,* which you can visit by free guided tour, conducted in Italian. You need to book ahead. (Map pp44-5; ☎ 02 8845 6617; 🕙 9.30am-12.30pm & 2-5pm Mon-Fri; Ⓜ Duomo)

---

### ❦ ISTITUTO EUROPEO DI DESIGN
You can embark on anything from amateur-oriented evening courses in design, the visual arts and fashion, through to year-long and three-year full-time courses. (Map pp40-1; ☎ 02 579 69 51; www.ied.edu; Via Sciesa 4; Ⓜ San Babila)

---

### ❦ ISTITUTO DI MODA BURGO
A broad range of fashion-related courses, from pattern creation to dressmaking, is available at this central Milan fashion school. (Map pp44-5; ☎ 02 78 37 53; www.imb.it; Piazza San Babila 5; Ⓜ San Babila)

---

# GETTING AWAY FROM IT ALL

The Milanese forever talk about moving away and slowing down. There are less drastic ways of taking a break from the madness.

* **Relax at aperitivo time** Wander into Bar Basso and shed your cares in favour of a cocktail and bar munchies (p54)
* **Get some green** After dodging traffic on Milan's busy streets, a restorative stroll in the Giardini Pubblici, one of the city's few green lungs, is just what the doctor ordered (p50)
* **Revel in a Renaissance setting** A train can take you to Vigevano, whose Renaissance square is like a theatre set (p61)

# ADVANCE PLANNING

If you want to make the most out of a stay in the Lombard capital, a little forward planning can make all the difference.

* **Three months before you go** Book tickets for Leonardo da Vinci's *The Last Supper* (p42) and an opera or ballet performance at the Teatro alla Scala (p48). Football fans should check the Serie A schedule to see what games are taking place at San Siro stadium (p49).
* **Three weeks before you go** Book a table at Cracco (p51) for a cracking dinner
* **One week before you go** Make any other dinner bookings for all but the most casual of restaurants
* **The day before you go** Check the weather report at *Corriere della Sera* (http://meteo.corriere.it)

# TOP RESTAURANTS

**♥ CRACCO**
A fancy chef with cooking fantasy (p51)

**♥ EL BRELLIN**
Romantic canalside spot for classic Milanese fare (p52)

**♥ L'ANTICO RISTORANTE BOEUCC**
In business since 1696 (p52)

**♥ OSTERIA LE VIGNE**
An ever popular stop in the Navigli (p53)

**♥ PIQUENIQUE**
For vegetarians and Sunday brunchers (p54)

**♥ PESCHERIA DA CLAUDIO**
Boisterous bar lunches of fresh fish (p53)

**♥ PECK ITALIAN BAR**
A gourmet store's gourmet restaurant (p53)

# RESOURCES

* **Cenacolo Vinciano** (www.cenacolovinciano.org) Book your visit to *The Last Supper* mural
* **Hello Milano** (www.hellomilano.it) Aimed at foreign visitors and residents
* **Visita Milano** (www.provincia.milano.it/turismo) The tourist office website
* **Expat Blog** (www.expat-blog.com/en/directory/europe/italy/milan) A series of blogs by expats living in Milan
* **Milano da Bere** (www.milanodabere.it, in Italian) For tips on eating, drinking and shows

MILAN

MILAN

# INTRODUCING MILAN

**pop 1.3 million**
**Home of Italy's stock exchange, an**
**industrial powerhouse and the inter-**
**nationally accepted arbiter of taste**
**in fashion and design, Milan is a**
**seething metropolis. At times it can**
**seem brash and soulless but beneath**
**the veneer is a serious sense of his-**
**tory and place. The grand Gothic**
**cathedral, the Duomo, lies at the**
**geographical heart of this one-time**
**Imperial Roman capital, and ex-**
**presses the love of beauty and power**
**that still drives the city today. Art**
**collections old and new, unparalleled**
**shopping, one of Europe's biggest**
**trade-fair complexes, sparkling night-**
**life, the prestige of opera at La Scala,**
**the mark of Leonardo da Vinci's**
**genius and endless opportunities to**
**eat the best of Lombard and Italian**
**food make Milan much more than**
**the puritanically work-obsessed city it**
**is often portrayed as.**

From its founding as a Celtic settlement, Milan (or Mediolanum – Middle
of the Plain) was always an important
crossroads. It was here that Christianity
was declared the official religion of the
Roman Empire in AD 313. As a powerful
medieval city state, Milan expanded its
power by conquest under a series of colourful (and often bloody) dynasties –
the Torrianis, the Viscontis and finally
the Sforzas. Under Spanish rule from
1525 and then the Austrians from 1713,
however, Milan lost some of its brio.
In 1860, it joined the nascent, united
Kingdom of Italy.

Benito Mussolini founded the Fascist
Party in Milan in 1919 and his lifeless
body was strung up in the same city, in
Piazzale Loreto, by the partisans who
had summarily executed him towards
the end of WWII in 1945.

Allied bombings during WWII had
destroyed much of central Milan. Treasures that survived include the Duomo,
Leonardo da Vinci's *The Last Supper*
mural, the Castello Sforzesco and the
Teatro alla Scala opera house (just). Milan was quick to get back on its feet after
the war and what still sets it apart today
is its creative streak and can-do, high-
speed cosmopolitan feel.

Armani, Versace, Prada, Dolce & Gabbana, Gucci and many more took off on
Milan's runways (although many, like
Gucci, first came to the world's attention in Florence). Fashionistas make a
pilgrimage here to shop at the designers'
flagship stores in the Quadrilatero d'Oro
(Golden Quad).

Inevitably, not all that glistens is
squeaky clean gold. In 1992 the Tangentopoli scandal broke, implicating thousands of Italian (and among them many
Milanese) politicians, officials and busi-
nesspeople. Tax evasion on a huge scale
and pay-offs to financial police were at
the heart of the investigations – fashion
designer Giorgio Armani accepted a plea
bargain following bribery charges.

One of those investigated but never
convicted is Milan's self-made media
mogul Silvio Berlusconi. He moved into
politics in the 1990s and has since been
elected prime minister three times, most
recently in 2008. The city's centre-right
mayor, Letizia Moratti (the city's first
female mayor), elected in 2006, runs a
coalition government with various
parties on the right and left.

Milan remains Italy's financial heart
and the centre of publishing, media, advertising, design and fashion. The city's
next big date with destiny is Expo2015, a
world exhibition.

Fashion and finance aside, Milan's other religion is *calcio* (football). The city is home to AC Milan and Inter, two of Italy's top teams, and passionate crowds pack San Siro stadium every Sunday (the teams alternate) in season.

## ESSENTIAL INFORMATION

**DANGERS & ANNOYANCES //** Petty theft (pickpocketing for the most part) is a problem on public transport and around the main train station, Stazione Centrale, as well as in Piazza del Duomo. Keep a close eye on your belongings at all times.

**EMERGENCIES //** 24-hour pharmacy (Map pp40-1; ☎ 02 669 09 35; Stazione Centrale; Ⓜ Centrale FS); Farmacia Carlo Erba (Map pp44-5; ☎ 02 87 86 68; Piazza del Duomo 21; ☽ 8pm-8.30am daily, plus 3-7pm Mon, 9.30am-7pm Tue-Sat; Ⓜ Duomo); Foreigners police office (Map pp44-5; ☎ 02 6 22 61; Via Montebello 26; Ⓜ Turati); Ospedale Maggiore Policlinico (Map pp40-1; ☎ 02 5 50 31, foreigners 02 5503 3137; www.policlinico.mi.it; Via Francesco Sforza 35; Ⓜ Crocetta) Hospital; Police station (Questura; Map pp44-5; ☎ 02 6 22 61; Via Fatebenefratelli 11; Ⓜ Turati)

**TOURIST OFFICES //** Milan Tourist Office (www.provincia.milano.it/turismo) Main tourist office (Map pp44-5; ☎ 02 7740 4343; lower level, Piazza del Duomo 19a; ☽ 8.45am-1pm & 2-6pm Mon-Sat, 9am-1pm & 2-5pm Sun; Ⓜ Duomo); Linate airport ( ☎ 02 7020 0443; Welcome Desk Meeting Milano; ☽ 7.30am-11.30pm); Malpensa airport ( ☎ 02 5858 0080; Welcome Desk Meeting Milano, Terminal 1; ☽ 8am-8pm); Stazione Centrale (Map pp40-1; ☎ 02 7740 4318; ☽ 9am-6pm Mon-Sat, 9am-1pm & 2-5pm Sun & holidays; Ⓜ Centrale FS) In front of platform 13.

## ORIENTATION

Central Milan's spiderweb of streets radiates from the city's geographical and spiritual heart, the Duomo.

Immediately north of the Duomo is the Quadrilatero d'Oro, Milan's designer shopping precinct. Northwest of here is the gentrified, former bohemian quarter of Brera, with narrow cobblestone streets, upmarket antique shops and alfresco cafes. The city's best nightlife is on and around Corso Como, further northwest, beyond which is the edgy Isola design district. Northeast of the Duomo is Stazione Centrale. To the Duomo's south lies the Navigli canal district. Northwest are the Castello Sforzesco and Parco Sempione.

Criss-crossing the city are Milan's four underground metro lines, and an extensive network of buses and trams. Milan's catwalk-flat terrain, however, makes it easy to cover the centre on foot.

## EXPLORING MILAN

### ❦ DUOMO // GAZE IN AWE AT MILAN'S MEDIEVAL WONDER

The cloudy Candoglian marble facade and sky-piercing spires of the city's cathedral appear out of the chaotic maze of streets – a sudden, otherworldly vision. The Duomo (Map pp44-5; ☎ 02 7202 2656; www.duomomilano.it; Piazza del Duomo; admission free; ☽ 8.30am-6.45pm; Ⓜ Duomo) may be the enduring symbol of Milan, but it's a cathedral with a chequered past. Begun by Gian Galeazzo Visconti in 1387, its ambitious design was considered impossible to build. Canals were constructed to transport marble to the centre of town, new technologies were invented to adapt to the never-before-attempted scale. There was also the matter of style. Its Gothic lines went rapidly out of fashion (it was even criticised as being 'too French'), and it took on several different looks as the years, then centuries, dragged on. The Duomo's slow construction made its name a byword for an impossible task (*fabrica del Dom* in the Milanese dialect). Indeed, much of the

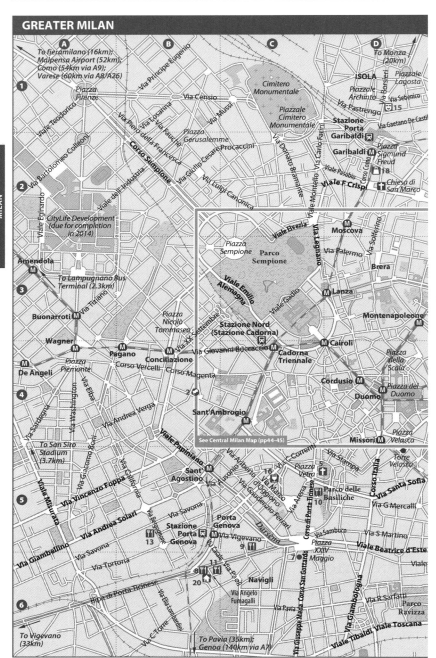

# GREATER MILAN

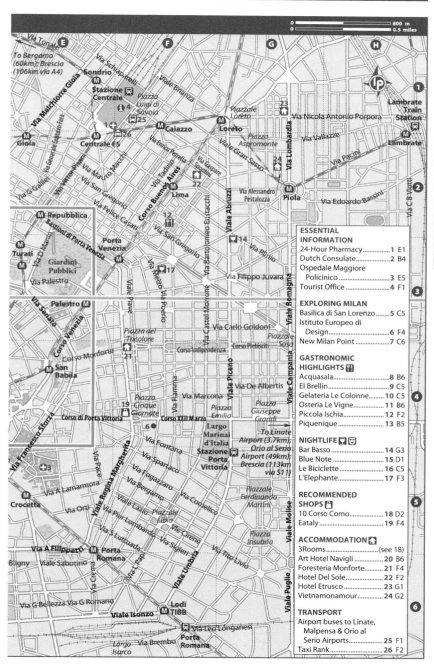

MILAN

MILAN

ornament is 19th-century neo-Gothic (carried out to the medieval specifications, with the final touches only applied in the 1960s).

Crowning it all is a gilded copper statue of the **Madonnina** (Little Madonna), the city's traditional protector. History has left its scars – the brass doors at the front bear the marks of bombs that fell nearby during WWII.

The cathedral's echoing interior is equally awe-inspiring, with 146 stained-glass windows and intricately carved pillars. Although the ceiling also appears carved, it's a trompe l'œil–painted optical illusion. High above the altar is a **nail** said to have been the one that impaled Christ's right hand on the cross. Predating the cathedral is the early-Christian baptistery, the **Battistero di San Giovanni** (admission €2; 9.30am-5.15pm Tue-Sun), accessed via a stairwell next to the main entrance. The **crypt** (admission free) displays the remains of San Carlo Borromeo, who died in 1584, in a glass casket; off to the side, the **treasury** (admission €1; 9.30am-1.30pm & 2-6pm Mon-Fri, 9.30am-1.30pm & 2-5pm Sat, 1.30-3.30pm Sun) has a small collection of liturgical vessels (interesting only to the truly dedicated).

For a close-up of the forest of spires, statuary and pinnacles – and views as far as Switzerland on a clear day – you can climb 165 steps to the **cathedral roof** (admission €5; 9am-5.45pm). Alternatively, it's a quick zip up in the **lift** (admission €8; 9am-5.30pm).

### Around the Duomo

The Duomo's surrounding plaza, the **Piazza del Duomo**, is the hub for the city's celebrations and festivities. Looking onto Piazza del Duomo (and now covered by scaffolding) is Mussolini's **Arengario** (Map pp44-5; M Duomo), from where he would *arengare* (harangue) huge crowds in the glory days of his regime. It is getting a makeover and will house the **Museo del Novecento** (Museum of the 20th Century; www .museodelnovecento.org).

### ❣ IL CENACOLO VINCIANO // PONDER THE POWER OF LEONARDO'S LAST SUPPER

Leonardo da Vinci's depiction of Christ and his dinner companions is one of the world's most iconic images. Viewing it first-hand, however, is not easy. Generally, you need to book anything from two weeks to a couple of months ahead, or take a somewhat pricey city tour (p36) that tacks on a visit. That said, if you turn up on a day when there is room, it is occasionally possible to get a ticket on the spot. On the booked day, you will be let through with groups of no more than 25 people and allowed to admire the mural for 15 minutes.

---

## TOP FIVE

### FOR ART

- ★ **Il cenacolo Vinciano** (right) – Leonardo da Vinci's Milan masterpiece

- ★ **Pinacoteca di Brera** (p47) – for stars of the Venetian Renaissance and Italian Modernists like Morandi

- ★ **Museo Poldi-Pezzoli** (p49) – Botticelli leads the way with his *Madonna and Child*

- ★ **Pinacoteca e Raccolte d'Arte** (p46) – for works by Bellini, Tiepolo, Mantegna, Correggio, Titian and Van Dyck

- ★ **Pinacoteca Ambrosiana** (p50) – solid on Italian art through the centuries

The **mural** (Map pp44-5; ☎ 02 8942 1146; www.cenacolovinciano.org; adult/EU citizen 18-25yr/EU citizen under 18yr or over 65yr €6.50/3.25/free, plus booking fee €1.50; Ⓜ Cadorna Triennale) is hidden away on one wall of Il Cenacolo Vinciano, the refectory adjoining the **Chiesa di Santa Maria delle Grazie** (Map pp44-5; Corso Magenta; ☾ 8.15am-7pm Tue-Sun). Restoration of *Il cenacolo* (The Last Supper) was completed in 1999 after more than 22 years' work. The mural was in a lamentable state after centuries of damage and decay. Da Vinci himself is partly to blame: his experimental mix of oil and tempera was applied between 1495 and 1498, rather than only over a week or so as is typical of fresco techniques. The Dominicans didn't help matters in 1652 by raising the refectory floor, hacking off a lower section of the scene, including Jesus' feet. The most damage was caused by the methods used by restorers in the 19th century, whose alcohol and cotton-wool technique removed an entire layer. Despite the painstaking restoration effort, 80% of the original colour has been lost.

Reservations must be made by phone. You'll be allotted a visiting time and a reservation number, which you present 30 minutes before your visit at the refectory ticket desk. If you turn up late, your ticket will be resold.

The ticket desk rents out audio guides (one/two people €2.50/4.50) in English. English-language guided tours (€3.25) take place at 9.30am and 3.30pm Tuesday to Sunday – again you'll need to reserve ahead.

## ♥ SHOPPING IN THE QUADRILATERO D'ORO // STRUT YOUR STUFF ON PLANET FASHION'S FINEST BLOCK

For anyone interested in the fall of a frock or the cut of a jacket, a stroll around the **Quadrilatero d'Oro** (Golden Quad; Map pp44-5; Ⓜ Montenapoleone), the world's most fabled shopping district, is on every shopper's lifetime to-do list. This quaintly cobbled quadrangle of streets may have always been synonymous with elegance and money (Via Monte Napoleone was where Napoleon's short-lived government managed loans), but the Quad's legendary fashion status belongs firmly to Milan's postwar reinvention. During the boom years of the 1950s, the city's fashion houses established ateliers in the area bounded by Via Monte Napoleone, Via Sant'Andrea, Via della Spiga and Via Alessandro Manzoni. Their customers soon followed, although it wasn't until the 1980s that 'Monte Napo' became known worldwide.

Global marquees like Dolce & Gabbana, Armani and Prada continue to gobble up street frontage and the gilding now drips down to Via Pietro Verri and Corso Venezia. Among the giants, more discreet but no less expensive boutiques ply their trade in anything from baby carriages to jewellery.

Even if you don't have the slightest urge to sling a swag of glossy carriers over your arm, the people-watching is priceless. Bespoke-suited silver foxes prowl while gazelle-limbed models lope up and down, perfecting a look of glazed detachment for the coming catwalk shows.

## ♥ CASTELLO SFORZESCO // SOAK UP CULTURE BEHIND THE BATTLEMENTS

Originally a Visconti fortress, this immense red-brick **castle** (Map pp44-5; ☎ 02 8846 3700; www.milanocastello.it; Piazza Castello; adult/senior/child €3/1.50/free, after 2pm Fri free;

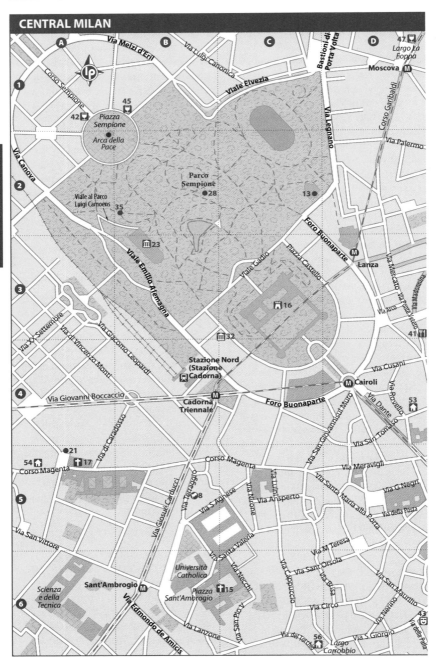

CENTRAL MILAN

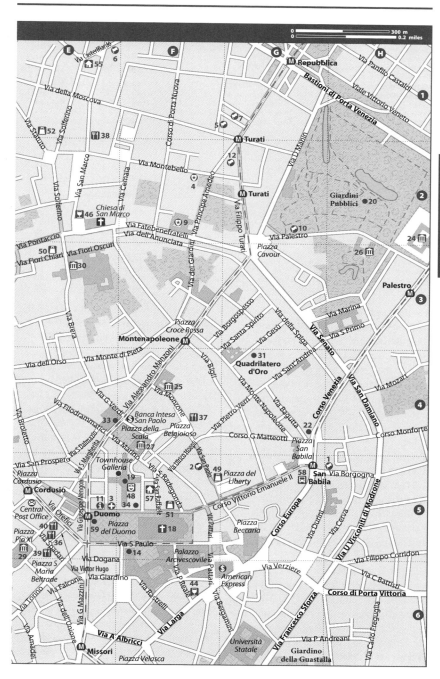

MILAN

**MILAN**

👁 castle grounds 7am-6pm or 7pm, museums 9am-5.30pm Tue-Sun; Ⓜ Cairoli) was later home to the mighty Sforza dynasty that ruled Renaissance Milan. Multitalented Leonardo da Vinci designed the castle's defences; Napoleon later had the moat drained and the drawbridges removed. Today, it shelters a series of specialised museums, all accessible on the same ticket.

Among the standouts is the **Museo d'Arte Antica**, containing Michelangelo's last, unfinished work, *Pietà Rondanini* (in the Sala degli Scarlioni). Paintings by Bellini, Tiepolo, Mantegna, Correggio, Titian and Van Dyck take pride of place in the **Pinacoteca e Raccolte d'Arte**. Milan's distant past is unearthed at the **Museo della Preistoria**, which displays local archaeological finds from the Palaeolithic era to the Iron Age. Vintage instruments, including some of the world's earliest violins, are a must-see for music lovers at the **Museo degli Strumenti Musicali**.

Sprawling over 47 hectares behind the castle, the leafy **Parco Sempione** (Map pp44-5; Ⓜ Cadorna Triennale) is graced by a neoclassical arch and the **Torre Branca** (Map pp44-5; ☎ 02 331 41 20; www.branca.it; admisson €3; 👁 9.30pm-midnight Tue & Thu, 10.30am-12.30pm, 4-6.30pm & 9.30pm-midnight Wed, 2.30-6pm & 9.30pm-midnight Fri, 10.30am-2pm, 2.30-7.30pm & 9.30pm-midnight Sat & Sun mid-Apr–mid-Oct, 10.30am-12.30pm & 4-6.30pm Wed, 10.30am-1pm, 3-6.30pm & 8.30pm-midnight Sat, 10.30am-2pm & 2.30-7pm Sun mid-Oct–mid-Apr; Ⓜ Cadorna Triennale), a 108m-tall steel tower raised in 1933, from the top of which you have a wonderful bird's-eye view of the city.

Also here is the ageing **Acquario Civico** (Aquarium; Map pp44-5; ☎ 02 8646 2051; Viale Gadio 2; www.verdeacqua.eu, in Italian; admission free; 👁 9am-1pm & 2-5.30pm Tue-Sun; Ⓜ Lanza) and **La Triennale di Milano** (Map pp44-5; ☎ 02 7243 4212; www.triennaledesignmuseum.it; Viale Emilio Alemanga 6; adult/senior/student €8/6/6; 👁 10.30am-8.30pm Tue-Sun; Ⓜ Cadorna Triennale). Regular shows in the Triennale building have championed design practice since its inception in the 1930s, but its permanent museum dedicated to Italian design was only launched late in 2007.

### ❦ PINACOTECA DI BRERA // LOSE AN AFTERNOON IN A PALAZZO OF RENAISSANCE TREASURES

Founded in the late 18th century, up-stairs from the centuries-old Brera Academy (still one of Italy's most prestigious art schools), the **Pinacoteca di Brera** (Map pp44-5; ☎ 02 8942 1146; www.brera.beniculturali.it; Via Brera 28; non-EU adult/child €10/7.50, EU adult/child €5/free; ◷ 8.30am-7.15pm Tue-Sun; Ⓜ Montenapoleone) housed the teaching aids of the day: marble and oils.

Napoleon soon added to the collection with priceless works 'borrowed' from various religious orders. Much of the bounty was 'lifted' in Venice. The roll-call of masters may include a Rembrandt, but you're here to ogle the Italians: Titian, Tintoretto and Veronese, a Caravaggio and the Bellini brothers for starters.

Much of the work has tremendous emotional clout. A Bellini *Madonna,* clad in a deep, meditative navy blue, is sad-eyed and resolute, while Mantegna's *Cristo morto nel Sepolcro e tre Dolenti* (Lamentation over the Dead Christ) is brutal and unsentimental in its violent foreshortening of Christ's corpse.

The number of pious treasures is exhausting. Take a break and see conservators at work in a climate-controlled glass box, visit the small but luminous collection of Italian Modernists, including the spirituality of Morandi, or join dreadlocked art students downstairs for a post life-drawing-class Peroni.

The surrounding neighbourhood of Brera, with its tight cobbled streets and ancient buildings, was not so long

ago a study in boho raffishness. There are still plenty of galleries and artisans' workshops but they are quickly being outnumbered by hairdressers and chichi bars.

For all that, it remains a delightful spot for gallery-hopping, shopping, drinks or dinner; Via Ponte Vetero and Via Mercato have some of Milan's best options for each.

### ❦ GALLERIA VITTORIO EMANUELE II // ADMIRE A NEOCLASSICAL WONDER OF GLASS AND IRON

Directly across from the Duomo sits a precocious feat of engineering. This soaring iron-and-glass neoclassical **arcade** (Map pp44-5; Ⓜ Duomo) links Milan's cathedral to its opera house, the Teatro alla Scala, and heralds the new industrial Italy of the late 19th century.

Despite churchlike proportions and a cruciform plan, the Galleria Vittorio Emanuele II celebrates the gleefully secular: shopping. Highly innovative for its time, the building has spawned countless imitators, right down to the glazed-roofed megamalls of today.

Architect Giuseppe Mengoni plummeted to his death on the job in 1877, just before the 14-year project was complete. To avoid such bad luck, observe Milanese tradition: head under the vast glass dome at the centre of the arcade to the mosaic of a bull, and grind your heel firmly into its testicles. Despite the mascot's daily humiliations, the Taurean spirit of luxury and gracious sloth still dominate.

Prada and Gucci and clamouring chains mix with the glove shops and milliners of old, and cafes dole out coffee and Campari to be sipped seated on century-old mosaics.

MILAN

### ♥ APERITIVO // SIP AND GRAZE IN THE CITY'S BARS

Milan may not have invented the tradition of taking an *aperitivo* – a pre-dinner drink (or two) with snacks on the house – but the Milanese have turned it into an art form. Bars all over town bring on the laden platters from 6pm. To partake, order a Negroni (a potent, slightly medicinal-tasting blend of Campari, Antico Rosso and gin) or other cocktail concoction (€6 to €12) and fight your way back to the bar or dedicated buffet table. (Occasionally you'll pay a cover charge up front that includes a drink and buffet fare, which generally works out the same.)

There are a few areas that will yield lots of choice in a small radius: Corso Sempione and Corso Como for a bit of glam or Corso Buenos Aires and Navigli for a more laid-back vibe. **Milano Tonight** (www.milano.tonight.eu) has extensive listings of new bars, and travellers can also check out **Aperonet** (www.aperonet.jimdo.com) for a weekly roster of *aperitivo* meet-ups. A perfect place to try out this pleasant evening pastime is **Bar Basso** (p54) or **Le Biciclette** (p55). For more on what to expect at *aperitivo* time, see p280.

### ♥ TEATRO ALLA SCALA // SWOON IN THE OPERA STALLS

Despite recent renovation behind the scenes (superior acoustics and bilingual libretto screens on the back of seats are some of its public face), the charm of the world's best-known opera house – also known as La Scala – remains resolutely of the 18th century.

Six stories of loggia (boxes and galleries) are bedecked in gilt and lined in crimson, and, for evening performances at least, audiences are similarly turned out. Milanese money, old and new, is deliciously on display.

If you miss out on a show, visit the **Museo Teatrale alla Scala** (Map pp44–5; ☎ 02 887 97 473; www.teatroallascala.org; Largo Ghiringhelli 1, Piazza della Scala; adult/conc €5/4; ⊙ 9am-noon & 1.30-5pm; Ⓜ Duomo) by day. Harlequin costumes and a spinet inscribed with the command 'Inexpert hand, touch me not!' hint at centuries of Milanese musical drama, on and off stage. Portraits show Rossini apparently chatting up patrons, while Verdi seems troubled by mixed reviews. Your visit can include a glimpse of the theatre's famed interior from a box and a backstage tour if you don't clash with rehearsal time.

The opera season runs from November to July but you can see theatre, ballet and concerts here year-round, with the exception of August.

You'll need perseverance and luck to secure opera tickets (€10 to €180; up to €2000 for opening night). About two months before the first performance, tickets can be bought by telephone ( ☎ 02 86 07 75; 24 hours) and online – these tickets carry a 20% surcharge. One month before the first performance, any remaining tickets are sold (with a 10% surcharge) at the **box office** (Map pp44–5; ☎ 02 7200 3744; www.teatroallascala.org; Galleria Vittorio Emanuele II; ⊙ noon-6pm; Ⓜ Duomo). On performance days, 140 tickets for the gallery are sold two hours before the show – one ticket per customer. You have to get there early to queue for this. Any remaining, unsold tickets are sold at 25% off full price. Consult the computer terminal in the La Scala box office or the website for ticket availability.

### ♥ NAVIGLI // NAVIGATE CANALSIDE BARS AND RESTAURANTS

South of the city centre, the **Navigli** (Map pp40–1; Ⓜ Porto Genova) neighbourhood is named after its most identifiable feature – *navigli* – and was, until mid-last-century, a working-class area of ancient docks, laundries and warehouses.

The Naviglio Grande (Big Canal) grew from an irrigation ditch to one of the city's busiest thoroughfares in the 1200s. Canals were the motorways of medieval Milan, and got salt, oil, cheese and wine to town in a timely fashion. More canals were built to deliver marble for constructing the Duomo; filled and paved, many of these now serve as Milan's ring roads.

After a brief desolate spell when the docks closed in the 1960s and '70s, Navigli's tangle of streets, turbid waterways and pretty iron bridges drew Milan's savvy artists and musicians. It has since lost its subversive edge but some of the city's most scenic restaurants, liveliest bars and innovative shops are still here.

On the last Sunday of every month more than 400 antique and secondhand traders set up along a 2km stretch of the Naviglio Grande. There's a fascinating mix of high-quality antiques, including paintings, glass art and antiquities.

### 🐦 FOOTBALL // SHOUT GOOOOOOOAAAAAL AT SAN SIRO
Unlike the Duomo, **San Siro stadium** (Stadio Giuseppe Meazza; off Map pp40-1; ☎ 02 404 24 32; www.sansirotour.com; Via dei Piccolomini 5, museum & tours Gate 14; museum adult/child €7/5, incl guided tour €12.50/10; ⏱ nonmatch days 10am-5pm; Ⓜ Lotto) wasn't designed to hold the entire population of Milan. On a Sunday afternoon amid 85,000 football-mad citizens, however, it can certainly feel like it.

The city's two clubs, AC Milan and FC Internazionale Milano (aka Inter), play on alternate weeks from October to May. *Tifosi* (fans) cluster at the *curva nord* (north curve) or *curva sud* (south curve) of the stadium.

**Guided tours** of the 1920s-built stadium take you behind the scenes to the players' locker rooms and include a visit to the **Museo Inter e Milan**, a shrine of memorabilia, papier-mâché caricatures of players, and film footage. The accompanying stadium tour covers the locker room, where you can gingerly rest your bum on the same bench as countless naked football legends. The museum closes 30 minutes before kick-off on match days.

Match tickets are available at the stadium or, for **AC Milan** (www.acmilan .com) matches, from **New Milan Point** (Map pp40-1; ☎ 02 8942 2711; Corso San Gottardo 2; Ⓜ Porta Genova) and branches of the Banca Intesa Sanpaolo d'Italia. For **Inter** (☎ 02 5 49 14; www.inter.it) matches, try Banca Popolare di Milano branches or Ticket One (see boxed text, p54).

Take tram 24, bus 95, 49 or 72, or the metro to the Lotto stop, from where a free bus shuttles to the stadium.

### 🐦 MUSEO POLDI-PEZZOLI // DISCOVER THE CITY'S TOP PRIVATE COLLECTION
Botticelli's *Madonna and Child* is the star attraction at the **Museo Poldi-Pezzoli** (Map pp44-5; ☎ 02 79 48 89; www.museopoldi pezzoli.it; Via Alessandro Manzoni 12; adult/child €8/5.50; ⏱ 10am-6pm Tue-Sun; Ⓜ Montenapoleone). The city's most important private collection, the museum also displays some superb porcelain, jewellery, tapestries, antique furniture and paintings. Giacomo Poldi-Pezzoli, blessed with a fortune, aristocratic connections and an obsessive streak, managed to amass an amazing collection of Renaissance treasures during his short lifetime. Inspired by the 'house museum' that was later to become London's V&A, he got busy transforming his apartment into a series

of historically styled rooms. Treasures include Pollaiuolo's profile of a woman, a triptych by Florence's Bernardo Daddi, scenes by Venice's Francesco Guardi and rare examples of old Murano glassware.

### 💗 GIARDINI PUBBLICI // TAKE A BREATH OF (RELATIVELY) FRESH AIR

Put some green space between you and Milan's madding crowds and traffic at **Giardini Pubblici** (🕑 6.30am-sunset; Ⓜ Palestro). Follow pebble paths past bumper cars and a carousel, onward past a game of kick-to-kick, kissing teens, a beer kiosk, baby prams, jogging paths and shady benches. Jump in, or just stop and smell the roses. For grey days, the charming **Museo Civico di Storia Naturale** (Natural History Museum; ☎ 02 8846 3337; Corso Venezia 55; adult/conc €3/1.50; 🕑 9am-5.30pm Tue-Sun; Ⓜ Palestro) beckons – the grand neo-Romanesque building houses dinosaurs, fossils and, they say, the largest geology collection in Europe.

### 💗 ANCIENT BASILICAS // REACH BACK DEEP INTO THE MIDDLE AGES

Two remarkable and comparatively little-visited basilicas in Milan exemplify the simple beauty of the pre-Romanesque and Romanesque styles in Lombardy (for background, see p250). The **Basilica di Sant'Ambrogio** (Map pp44-5; Piazza Sant'Ambrogio 15; Ⓜ Sant'Ambrogio), apart from being the burial place of Milan's 4th-century patron saint, St Ambrose, is a remarkable slice of Italian architectural history. Much of what you see was built between the early 11th and 12th centuries (although a lot of not always fortunate add-ons came with 19th-century 'restoration'). A delightful porticoed atrium leads the eyes to the

*a capanna* facade (called 'hut facade' because it looks like a simple hut or warehouse), with its two graceful series of arches. It is flanked by two bell towers, the oldest dating to the 9th century (there was a church on this site as early as the 4th century). The second chapel on the right contains frescos by Tiepolo. A passage off to the right of the main altar leads off to the **Sacello di San Vittore in Ciel d'Oro**, a small hall with a semicircular apse with 5th-century frescos in the dome.

Virtually ignored by everyone is the **Basilica di San Lorenzo** (Map pp40-1; Parco delle Basiliche; Ⓜ Missori). Yet, when you stumble across it, it is difficult not to be bowled over by this hotchpotch jumble of towers, lodges, apses and domes. Taken together, they look like an imaginary medieval town. Although the irregular opening hours mean you probably won't get inside, just wandering around it is a rare treat. In spite of appearances, it really is one basilica. At its heart is an early-Christian, circular structure with three attached, octagonal chapels, dating to about the 4th century. What's left of a Romanesque atrium leads to the heart of the church and before it stand 16 Roman columns nicked from an earlier pagan temple.

### 💗 PINACOTECA AMBROSIANA // BROWSE THE HALLOWED LIBRARY HALLS FOR CARAVAGGIO

Europe's first public library, built in 1609, the Biblioteca Ambrosiana was once more about intellectual ferment than quiet scholarship. It houses 75,000 volumes and 35,000 manuscripts, while upstairs the **Pinacoteca Ambrosiana** (Map pp44-5; ☎ 02 80 69 21; www.ambrosiana .it; Piazza Pio XI 2; adult/conc €8/5; 🕑 10am-5.30pm Tue-Sun; Ⓜ Cordusio) has its fair share of breakthrough works including Caravaggio's *Canestra di frutta* (Basket of Fruit), which helped launch the young painter's career and initiated Italy's ultrarealist tradition, and Leonardo da Vinci's *Musico* (Musician). The many halls are filled with mostly Italian art from the 14th to the 20th centuries, sprinkled with the occasional universally known name.

## FESTIVALS & EVENTS

La Scala's opera season opens on Milan's biggest feast day, the **Festa di Sant'Ambrogio**, on 7 December. The **Fiera degli Obei Obei** is held 7–10 December and has origins reaching to the 13th century. Other festivals to look out for:

**Corteo dei Re Magi** Legend says the remains of the three wise men are buried in Milan. Be that as it may, each year on 6 January they parade in costume from the Duomo to the Porta Ticinese.

**Carnevale Ambrosiano** The world's longest carnival, this event culminates with a procession to the Duomo; February.

**Cortili Aperti** (www.italiamultimedia.com/cortili aperti, in Italian) For one May Sunday, the gates to some of the city's most beautiful private courtyards are flung open. Print a map and make your own itinerary.

**Festa del Naviglio** Parades, music and performances; first 10 days of June.

**La Bella Estate** (www.comune.milano.it, in Italian) Concerts in and beyond town. Check the town hall website; June to August.

**La Nivola e il Santo Chiodo** Using a strange basket mechanism decorated with papier mâché clouds and angels, each September the Archbishop of Milan is lifted to the chancel roof to take hold of a nail from Christ's cross and then carry it around the inside of the cathedral. This procession first took place in 1576 in an effort to end a bout of plague.

**Milano Musica Festival** From late September to early November, La Scala and other locations host concerts of classical and contemporary orchestral music.

## GASTRONOMIC HIGHLIGHTS

Milan's generations of internal Italian immigrants have injected the cuisine of virtually every region into the lifeblood of the city, where you'll also find plenty of Lombard classics alongside a rich international selection of anything from Ethiopian to sushi. Milan's clutch of Michelin-starred chefs cook up some of Italy's most sophisticated food. Smart spots gather around the streets near Piazza del Duomo and plenty of options dot the Navigli area. Reservations are a good idea and essential for top-end establishments.

### ☙ ACQUASALA €€

Map pp40-1; ☎ 02 8942 3983; www.acquasala .it, in Italian; Ripa di Porta Ticinese 71; meals €30-35; ⓨ Tue-Sun; Ⓜ Porta Genova

The nostalgic and mostly Puglian dishes here are wonderful comfort food. Try crisp, baked rice with mussels and potatoes, or *orecchiette* (Puglian earshaped pasta) with various accompaniments, including a horsemeat sauce. You might precede with a soup like *moscardini in zuppa con cipolla rossa* (tiny octopuses with red onion). Meat dishes dominate the mains – anything from horsemeat sausages to Tuscan T-bone steaks.

### ☙ CRACCO €€€

Map pp44-5; ☎ 02 87 67 74; www.ristorante cracco.it; Via Victor Hugo 4; meals from €100; ⓨ Mon-Sat; Ⓜ Duomo

Star chef Carlo Cracco keeps the Milanese in thrall with his off-the-wall inventiveness. Cherry-wood boiserie on the walls and creamy lighting are neutral enough to allow you to concentrate on your food.

MILAN

## HOME CHIC HOME

Milan is the world's capital of fashion for the home. The latest innovations are unveiled each April at the five-day **Salone Internazionale del Mobile** (International Furniture Fair; www.cosmit.it) at the **fieramilano** (off Map pp40-1; www.fieramilano.it; Strada Statale del Sempione 28, Ⓜ Rho-Fiera) fairground in Rho. It has been wowing interior design aficionados since 1961.

Art and design intertwine at the city's ground-breaking contemporary galleries. Leading the pack is **Padiglione d'Arte Contemporanea** (PAC; Map pp44-5; ☎ 02 760 09 085; www.comune.milano.it/pac; Via Palestro 14; adult/senior/student €5/3/3; ◷ 2.30-7.30pm Mon, 9.30am-7.30pm Tue-Wed & Fri-Sun, 9.30am-10.30pm Thu; Ⓜ Palestro), which mounts experimental exhibits in all media. Retro items at **Studio Museo Achille Castiglioni** (Map pp44-5; ☎ 02 7243 4231; Piazza Castello 27; ◷ tours 10am, 11am & noon Tue-Sun; Ⓜ Cadorna Triennale) range from the streetlight-turned-pendulum Arco floor lamp to early examples of Alessi's gadget wizardry; tours are free (bookings required) with prepurchased Triennale di Milano ticket (p46).

At newsstands, look out for the magazines *Domus* (www.domusweb.it) and *Casabella*, both founded in 1928 by Gio Ponti, considered the architect of Italian design.

---

The *risotto al sedano, rapa, tartufo nero e caffè* (with celery, turnip, black truffle and coffee) is unlike any traditional northern Italian rice dish you may have stumbled across elsewhere. Let the waiters do the thinking by ordering one of the tasting menus (€130 and €160).

### 🍴 EL BRELLIN €€

Map pp40-1; ☎ 02 5810 1351; www.brellin.com; cnr Vicolo dei Lavandai & Alzaia Naviglio Grande 14; meals €40-45; ◷ 7pm-2am Mon-Sat, 12.30-3pm Sun; Ⓜ Porta Genova

Set around a 1700s public canal laundry, El Brellin's candlelit garden is a romantic spot for homemade pasta and classic Milanese specialities like saffron risotto. Or roll up your sleeves to dig into a *cazzoeula* (pork rib chops, skin and sausage stew) with polenta or a *rustin negaà* (roast loin veal) with baked potatoes. The Sunday brunch buffet tables are laden with cured meats, spinach-and-ricotta lasagne, whole smoked salmon, and homemade desserts.

### 🍴 GELATERIA LE COLONNE €

Map pp40-1; ☎ 02 837 22 92; Corso di Porta Ticinese 75; ice creams €2-3; ◷ 12.30pm-1.30am Mon-Thu, 12.30pm-2am Fri & Sat, 3pm-1am Sun; Ⓜ Porta Genova

Come here for artisan ice cream in wild flavours such as rice, amaretto or orange blossom, and specials like Huehuetenango coffee from Guatemala.

### 🍴 L'ANTICO RISTORANTE BOEUCC €€€

Map pp44-5; ☎ 02 7602 0224; www.boeucc .com, in Italian; Piazza Belgioioso 2; meals €60-80; ◷ lunch & dinner Mon-Fri, lunch Sun; Ⓜ Duomo

Set in the basement of the grand-looking neoclassical Palazzo Belgioioso, Milan's oldest restaurant has been regaling diners since 1696. Vaulted dining rooms and service reminiscent of more regal times lend your evening meal a sense of theatre. From *crespelle al prosciutto* (a kind of cross between pasta and crêpe with ham) you might move on to a *trancio di salmone al pepe verde* (slice of salmon with green pepper). The Milanese writer

Alessandro Manzoni (see p239) lived just across the square.

### ☙ LATTERIA €€

Map pp44–5; ☎ 02 659 76 53; Via San Marco 24; meals €25-30; ☉ Mon-Fri; Ⓜ Moscova

If you can snare a seat in this tiny and ever-popular restaurant, you'll find old favourites like *spaghetti alla carbonara* mixed in with chef Arturo's own creations, such as *polpettine al limone* (little meatballs with lemon) or *riso al salto* (risotto fritters) on the ever-changing, mostly organic, menu.

### ☙ OSTERIA LE VIGNE €€

Map pp40–1; ☎ 02 837 56 17; Ripa di Porta Ticinese 61; meals €25-30; ☉ Mon-Sat; Ⓜ Porta Genova

A perennially popular Navigli eatery, this place is hard to beat for value. The muted cream decor, combined with dark wooden furniture and low lighting, make it instantly likeable. Perusal of the menu will reveal such options as *straccetti di pasta fresca con pollo* (strips of fresh pasta with chicken).

### ☙ PECK ITALIAN BAR €€

Map pp44–5; ☎ 02 869 30 17; www.peck.it; Via Cesare Cantù 3; meals €35-45; ☉ 7.30am-8.30pm Mon-Sat; Ⓜ Duomo

Peck's spacious, orange-tinted dining room lets quality produce shine with staples like risotto and roasts done with

fresh ingredients. Suits especially like to pull up an elegant black chair and settle in to savour, say, the *riso mantecato con pere e Taleggio* (creamed rice with pears and Taleggio cheese), followed by a tender *vitello tonnato con verdure grigliate* (veal in a tuna sauce with grilled vegetables). Bow-tied waiters dispense wine by the glass. The kitchen is open from 11am.

### ☙ PESCHERIA DA CLAUDIO €€

Map pp44–5; ☎ 02 805 68 57; www.pescheriada claudio.it, in Italian; Via Ponte Vetero 16; meals €25-30; ☉ 11am-8pm Mon, 9am-9.30pm Tue-Sat; Ⓜ Cairoli

Join the savvy suits for a power lunch or early dinner of *pesce crudo* (raw fish). Plates loaded with marinated tuna, mixed salmon, tuna and white fish with pistachios, or lightly blanched octopus 'carpaccio' are consumed standing around the horseshoe bar, around which are stands displaying the fishmonger's produce. It's a wonder there is any fish left over to sell to shoppers at this self-proclaimed 'fishmonger to the Milanese' after the lunchtime melee.

### ☙ PICCOLA ISCHIA €€

Map pp40–1; ☎ 02 204 76 13; www.piccolaischia .it; Via Giovanni Battista Morgagni 7; pizzas €8-15, meals €30; ☉ lunch & dinner Mon-Tue & Thu-Fri, dinner Sat & Sun; Ⓜ Lima

Walls covered in murals of *la bella Napoli* don't always guarantee authenticity but

## FEELING PECKISH

Forget *The Last Supper*: gourmets head to the food and wine emporium **Peck** (Map pp44–5; ☎ 02 802 31 61; www.peck.it; Via Spadari 7-9; ☉ 3-7.30pm Mon, 8.45am-7.30pm Tue-Sat; Ⓜ Duomo). This Milanese institution opened its doors as a deli in 1883. The Aladdin's cave–like food hall is smaller than its reputation suggests, but what it lacks in space it makes up for in variety, with some 3200 variations of Parmigiano-Reggiano (Parmesan) at its cheese counter, just for starters. Other treasures include an exquisite array of chocolates, pralines and pastries; freshly made gelato; seafood; caviar; pâtés; a butcher, and fruit and vegetable sellers; truffle products; olive oils and balsamic vinegar.

MILAN

here you'll recognise the real thing. The Campanian potato croquettes, *arancini* (rice-stuffed pastries) and zucchini blossoms do nicely for starters but the main attraction is the pizzas.

### ☙ PIQUENIQUE €€

Map pp40-1; ☎ 02 4229 7225; www.piquenique .it, in Italian; Via Bergognone 24; meals €30; ☺ lunch Mon, lunch & dinner Tue-Sat, noon-3pm brunch Sun; Ⓜ Porta Genova

Wander in past the adverts plastered at the entrance into what is a cross between a country-house setting and oh-so-homey alternative East London eatery and wine bar. All the tables, chairs and linen are different, in a deliberately higgledy-piggledy way, floors are of exposed timber and linen ranges from gingham to chintsy. Veggie options include couscous dishes but there's something for everyone, largely using organic products. The design crowd descends for brunch on Sunday.

## NIGHTLIFE

Milanese bars are generally open until 2am or 3am, and virtually all serve *aperitivi* (see p48). The Navigli canal district, the cobbled backstreets of Brera, and swish Corso Como and its surrounds are all great areas for a drink. The tourist office stocks several entertainment guides in English: *Milano Mese, Hello Milano* (www.hellomilano .it) and *Easy Milano* (www.easymilano .it). The free Italian newspapers distributed on the metro are also handy for what's-on listings.

### ☙ BAR BASSO

Map pp40-1; ☎ 02 2940 0580; www.barbasso .com; Via Plinio 39; ☺ 9am-2am Wed-Mon; Ⓜ Piola

This elegant corner bar is home of the *sbagliato*, the Negroni made with prosecco instead of gin, as well as *mangia e bevi* (eat and drink), involving a supersized goblet of strawberries, cream and *nocciola* ice cream and a large slug of some kind of booze. Plonk into a green velvet seat with tipple and snacks. Huge mirrors hang off the walls, reflecting light from the chandeliers. Black-tie waiters dart about serving cocktails (€10) as cool jazz rhythms waft over.

### ☙ BHANGRA BAR

Map pp44-5; ☎ 02 3493 4469; www.bhangrabar milano.com; Corso Sempione 1; admission free-€6; ☺ 7pm-midnight Wed & Thu, 7pm-2am Fri, 10pm-2am Sat, 7-10pm Sun; Ⓜ Moscova

Bhangra Bar is famous for its cushions and couscous-and-curry *aperitivo* buffet, served with a side of African percussion on Friday. Indeed, music and other cultural happenings constitute a fairly steady diet – expect anything from jazz nights to chilled trip-hop with the option of a little shiatsu massage between cocktails. The place is divided into three spaces – one huge and the other more intimate – with enough Indian decor to make you wonder whether you haven't wandered into a temple.

## SCORE TICKETS

Tickets for concerts, sporting events and the theatre can be booked online through **Ticket One** ( ☎ 892 101; www .ticketone.it) or **Ticket Web** ( ☎ 199 158158; www.ticketweb.it). In person, you can get tickets for concerts at **Ricordi Media-store** (Map pp44-5; ☎ 02 8646 0272; www .ricordimediastores.it, in Italian; Galleria Vittorio Emanuele II; Ⓜ Duomo) and **FNAC** (Map pp44-5; ☎ 02 72 08 21; fnac@ticketweb.it; Via della Palla 2; Ⓜ Missori).

## ❤ BLUE NOTE

Map pp40-1; ☎ 899 700022; www.bluenote
milano.com; Via Borsieri 37; tickets €23-30; ⏲ concerts 9pm & 11pm Tue-Fri, 9pm & 11.30pm Sat, 9pm
Sun; Ⓜ Garibaldi

The Blue Note hosts top-class jazz acts
from around the world, the perfect accompaniment to any tipple. You could
make a night of it here by coming for
dinner. Tickets are available by phone,
online or at the door from 7.30pm.
There's also a popular easy-listening
Sunday brunch (€35 per head).

## ❤ G-LOUNGE

Map pp44-5; ☎ 02 805 30 42; www.glounge.it; Via
Larga 8; ⏲ 7.30am-9.30pm Mon, 7.30am-2am Tue-
Sun; Ⓜ Missori

By day, this former Fascist hang-out/
billiard hall does lunches with a view of
the Torre Velasca; by night it's
caipirinhas and chill-out tunes in this
fashionable corner bar with red backlit
shelves laden with bottles. Some call
G-Lounge a straight-friendly gay bar,
others a gay-friendly straight bar. We
just call it fun.

## ❤ LE BICICLETTE

Map pp40-1; ☎ 02 5810 4325; Via Torti 4; ⏲ 6pm-
2am Mon-Sat, 12.30pm-2am Sun; Ⓜ Sant'Agostino

Once a bike warehouse and now one
of the best *aperitivo* bars in Milan, Le
Biciclette is a hip place, tucked down
a narrow lane, where cocktails meet
minimalist decor. Dinner is an option
here and the walls are hung with ever-
changing displays of contemporary
art. Evidence of its former life includes
glassed-in bicycle memorabilia.

## ❤ L'ELEPHANTE

Map pp40-1; ☎ 02 2951 8768; Via Melzo 22;
⏲ 6pm-2am Tue-Sun; Ⓜ Porta Venezia

The arty-alternative crowd
mixed as its killer cocktails: g
and straight, locals and visitors
setting is equally eclectic: no two
are alike and the dominating colours are
black, metallic grey and shades of deep
purple.

## ❤ LIVING

Map pp44-5; ☎ 02 331 00 84; www.livingmilano
.com; Piazza Sempione 2; ⏲ 8am-2am Mon-Fri,
9am-2am Sat & Sun; Ⓜ Moscova

Living has one of the city's prettiest settings, with a corner position and floor-
to-ceiling windows overlooking the Arco
della Pace. The bounteous *aperitivo*
spread and expertly mixed cocktails
draw crowds of smart-casual 20- and
30-somethings.

## ❤ N'OMBRA DE VIN

Map pp44-5; ☎ 02 659 96 50; www.nombradevin
.it; Via San Marco 2; ⏲ 9am-midnight Mon-Sat;
Ⓜ Montenapoleone

This *enoteca* (wine bar) is set in a cute
three-storey house, once an Augustine
refectory attached to the nearby Chiesa
di San Marco. The bar retains a catholic
approach to wine, which can be sampled
at the street-level bar or in the spacious
basement. Tastings can be had all day
and you can also indulge in food such
as *carpaccio di pesce spade agli agrumi*
(swordfish carpaccio prepared with
citrus) from a limited menu.

## ❤ RADETZKY

Map pp44-5; ☎ 02 657 26 45; Corso Garibaldi 105;
⏲ 8pm-1am; Ⓜ Moscova

Fabulous banquette and window seating
make this one of the most popular places
on this stylish, largely pedestrianised
strip for an *aperitivo* or long Sunday
session (well, it started with brunch…).
The tanned, tarted-up crowd spills from

MILAN

## ACCOMMODATION

Finding a room in Milan (let alone a cheap one) isn't easy, particularly during the fashion weeks, furniture fair and other exhibitions, when rates skyrocket.

Services you'd take for granted, such as breakfast, sometimes command an additional fee. There may not be any public areas such as a bar or lounge, and wi-fi and bar fridges are never a given. Here are four highlights; more Milan accommodation can be found from p288.

★ **Vietnamonamour** (p290) Asian-style B&B

★ **Antica Locanda Leonardo** (p289) Antique charm in 19th-century residence

★ **Antica Locanda Solferino** (p289) Understated Brera boutique beauty

★ **3Rooms** (p289) Plush comfort in hip fashion villa

this corner hang-out on to the street (where there's a handful of lounges) and adjacent little square. Inside, the creamy coloured walls are bedecked with playful paintings and Doric columns rise from the grey slate floors.

## RECOMMENDED SHOPS

### ❤ 10 CORSO COMO
Map pp40-1; ☎ 02 2900 2674; www.10corsocomo .com; Corso Como 10; Ⓜ Garibaldi
It might be the world's most hyped 'concept shop', but Carla Sozzani's selection of desirable things (Lanvin ballet flats, Alexander Girard wooden dolls, a demi-couture frock by a designer you've not read about *yet*) makes 10 Corso Como a tempting shopping experience. Next to the gallery upstairs is a bookshop

with art and design titles, Bruno Munari children's books, magazines and a large music department.

### ❤ EATALY
Map pp40-1; ☎ 02 9287 0066; www.eataly.it; 1st fl, Coin Bldg, Piazza Cinque Giornate; Ⓜ San Babila
Eataly, an outlet of Italy's Turin-based Slow Food movement, aims to keep the food supply chain simple, ensuring reasonable prices on artisan and small-producer lines of wine, cheese, pasta, oils and even tuna.

### ❤ FERRARI STORE
Map pp44-5; ☎ 02 7631 6077; www.ferraristore .com; Piazza del Liberty 8; Ⓜ San Babila
Formula One fans can make a pit stop here at the largest of Italy's Ferrari outlets, spanning three floors of cool toys, accessories and racing wear. There are two Ferrari stores at Malpensa airport too.

### ❤ GALANTE VISCONTI
Map pp44-5; ☎ 02 8699 8876; www.galante visconti.com; Via Fiori Chiari 2; Ⓜ Lanza
The handmade creations here are deluxe but have a rock-and-roll edge. Rough-beaten pink gold surrounds deep-pink tourmalines in delicate, ancient-looking earrings, and diamond-clad circles swivel on rings evoking the innards of pre-industrial machinery.

### ❤ LA RINASCENTE
Map pp44-5; ☎ 02 8 85 21; www.rinascente.it; Piazza del Duomo; Ⓜ Duomo
Italy's most prestigious department store doesn't let the fashion capital down – come for Italian diffusion lines, French lovelies and LA upstarts. The basement also hides an amazing homewares department. Take away edible souvenirs from the 7th-floor food market (and peer across to the Duomo while you're at it).

♥ **LA VETRINA DI BERYL**
Map pp44–5; ☎ 02 65 42 78; Via Statuto 4;
Ⓜ Moscova

Barbara Beryl's name was known to cultists around the world way before 'Manolo' became a byword for female desire. Stumbling upon this deceptively nondescript shop is like chancing upon the shoe racks at a *Vogue Italia* photo shoot. Edgier pieces from Prada, Marc Jacobs and Costume National are joined by practically certifiable eccentrics like Paul Harden.

# TRANSPORT

## TO/FROM THE AIRPORT

**MALPENSA AIRPORT //** Most European and other international flights use **Malpensa airport** (www.sea-aeroportimilano.it), 54km northwest of the city. The 40-minute **Malpensa Express** (☎ 199 151152; www.malpensaexpress.it; adult/child €11/5.50) train serves Stazione Nord every 30 minutes. **Malpensa Shuttle** (☎ 02 5858 3185; www.malpensa-shuttle.com; adult/child €7/3.50) coaches depart from Piazza Luigi di Savoi (Map pp40–1), next to Stazione Centrale, every 20 minutes from 5am to 10.30pm, taking 50 minutes to the airport. A **taxi** would cost at least €65.

**LINATE AIRPORT //** The majority of domestic and a handful of European flights use the more convenient **Linate airport** (www.sea-aeroportimilano.it), 7km east of the city centre. From Milan's Piazza Luigi di Savoia, **Starfly** (☎ 02 5858 7237) runs buses to

Linate airport (adult/child €4.50/2.50, 25 minutes) every 30 minutes from 5.40am to 9.35pm. Local **ATM bus 73** (€1, 20 minutes) runs from Piazza San Babila (Map pp44–5), on the corner of Corso Europa, every 10 to 15 minutes from 5.35am to 12.35am.

**ORIO AL SERIO AIRPORT // Autostradale** runs buses every 30 minutes between 4am and 11.30pm from Piazza Luigi di Savoia to Orio al Serio airport, near Bergamo (adult/child €8.90/4.45, one hour). **Orio Shuttle** (www.orioshuttle.com; adult/child €8/3, one hour) is similar, running every 30 to 60 minutes between 4am and 11.15pm.

## GETTING AROUND

**BICYCLE // BikeMi** (www.bikemi.it) is a public bicycle system with stops all over town. Get passes online or by dropping into the ATM Info Point (below).

**PUBLIC TRANSPORT //** Milan's public transport is run by ATM (☎ 800 808181; www.atm-mi.it). The metro consists of four underground lines (red MM1, green MM2, yellow MM3 and blue Passante Ferroviario), which run from 6am to midnight. A ticket costs €1 and is valid for one metro ride or up to 75 minutes' travel on ATM buses and trams. You can buy a 10-ride pass for €9.20 or unlimited one-/two-day tickets for bus, tram and metro for €3/5.50. Tickets are sold at metro stations, tobacconists and newsstands around town, but you can't buy them on board. Tickets must be validated on trams and buses. Free public transport maps are available from the **ATM Info Point** (Map pp44–5; ⏲ 7.45am-7.15pm Mon-Sat) inside the Duomo metro station.

MILAN

### ECOPASSING

Milan's city council introduced the Ecopass in 2008, in an attempt to combat traffic congestion and air pollution. Cars entering the designated central zone between 7am to 7pm Monday to Friday must display an Ecopass ticket. Prices vary from €2 to €10 depending on the pollution rating of what you're driving. Licence-plate classifications are listed on the Ecopass website (you're exempt if your home country doesn't enforce the system, or confused if it does). The pass can be bought online or from ATM shops, tobacconists and newsagents. The scheme goes on holiday with the rest of Milan in August. For information, contact **Ecopass** (☎ 02 02 02; www.comune.milano.it/ecopass, in Italian); an English fact sheet can be downloaded from the website. Honestly, though, you should have little reason to want to drive around the restricted area anyway – take a tram or the metro.

**TRAIN //** **Trenitalia** (www.trenitalia.it) has regular trains from Stazione Centrale (Piazza Duca d'Aosta) to Venice (€25.20, 2½ hours), Florence (€39.90, two hours), Turin (€21.90, one hour 20 minutes) and Rome (€67.50, 3½ hours) and more. International services run to/from Switzerland and France. **Ferrovie Nord Milano** (FNM; www.ferrovienord.it, in Italian; Piazza Luigi Cadorna) trains from Stazione Nord connect Milan with Como (€3.60, one hour, half-hourly). Regional services to many towns northwest of Milan are more frequent from Stazione Porta Garibaldi.

**BUS //** Most national and international buses start and terminate at Lampugnano bus terminal (Lampugnano metro station), about 5km west of central Milan. The bulk of Italian national services are run by **Autostrade** (☎ 02 7200 1304; www.autostrade.it), which has a ticket office at the main tourist office (p39).

**CAR & MOTORBIKE //** The A1, A4, A7 and A8 autostradas converge from all directions on Milan.

**PARKING //** Street parking costs €1.50 per hour in the city centre (€2 per five hours after 7pm). To pay, buy a SostaMilano card from a tobacconist, scratch off the date and hour, and display it on your dashboard. Underground car parks charge €2.50 for the first half-hour and between €1 and €3 per hour after that.

**TAXI //** As elsewhere in Italy, hailing taxis is futile – they don't stop. Head for a taxi rank or call ☎ 02 40 40, ☎ 02 69 69 or ☎ 02 85 85. The average short city ride will cost €10.

# AROUND MILAN

· · · · · ·

## PAVIA

**pop 70,200**

First impressions of Pavia are deceiving, as its pretty old town is encircled by an industrial-agricultural belt. Pavia's cobbled streets and piazzas buzz with students from the ancient university and are a refreshing change from the hubbub of Milan, 30km north. Half a day is ample.

Until the 11th century, Roman Pavia rivalled Milan as the capital of the Lombard kings, who left behind a Romanesque basilica. Legacies of the battle-plagued years that ensued include medieval watchtowers, a domed cathedral, and the 15th-century Castello Visconteo. To the north lies Pavia's highlight, the Carthusian monastery Certosa di Pavia.

## ESSENTIAL INFORMATION

**TOURIST OFFICE //** **Tourist Office** (☎ 0382 59 70 01; www.turismo.provincia.pv.it, in Italian; Piazza Petrarca 4; ◷ 8.30am-noon & 2-5pm Mon-Fri)

## EXPLORING PAVIA

❦ OLD TOWN // MEANDER THROUGH THE OLD UNIVERSITY TOWN
**Castello Visconteo**
Looming over the old town is the forbidding **Castello Visconteo**, built in 1360 for Galeazzo II Visconti. It now houses the **Musei Civici** (☎ 0382 30 48 16; www.museicivici.pavia.it, in Italian; Viale XI Febbraio 35; adult/EU senior & child to 18yr €6/free; ◷ 9am-1.30pm Tue-Sun Jul-Aug & Dec-Feb, 10am-6pm Tue-Sun Mar-Jun & Sep-Nov). Intriguing collections include archaeological, ethnographic and art collections, plus displays on medieval Pavia, the Renaissance, the Risorgimento (the Italian reunification period) and a section on Somalia (once an Italian colony).

**An Ancient University**
Christopher Columbus and inventor of the electric battery, Alessandro Volta, are two illustrious graduates of the **Università degli Studi di Pavia** (University of Pavia; ☎ 0382 98 11; www.unipv.it; Corso Strada Nuova 65). Founded as a school in the 9th century, it became a university in 1361. You can wander around the grounds and courtyards when the university is open. The stately campus

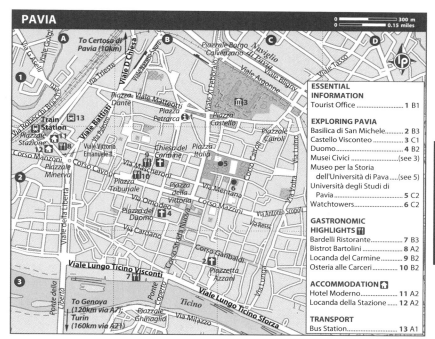

PAVIA

To Certosa di Pavia (10km)

To Genoa (120km via A7); Turin (160km via A21)

**ESSENTIAL INFORMATION**
Tourist Office ........................... **1** B1

**EXPLORING PAVIA**
Basilica di San Michele........... **2** B3
Castello Visconteo ................. **3** C1
Duomo...................................... **4** B2
Musei Civici ...........................(see 3)
Museo per la Storia
  dell'Università di Pava .....(see 5)
Università degli Studi di
  Pavia ................................... **5** C2
Watchtowers........................... **6** C2

**GASTRONOMIC HIGHLIGHTS**
Bardelli Ristorante.................... **7** B3
Bistrot Bartolini ....................... **8** A2
Locanda del Carmine............. **9** B2
Osteria alle Carceri.............. **10** B2

**ACCOMMODATION**
Hotel Moderno....................... **11** A2
Locanda della Stazione ...... **12** A2

**TRANSPORT**
Bus Station............................ **13** A1

MILAN

houses the small **Museo per la Storia dell'Università di Pavia** ( ☎ 0382 98 47 09; Corso Strada Nuova 65; admission free; ☷ 2-5pm Mon, 9am-noon Wed & Fri), on its history. Other university collections can only be seen, if at all, by appointment.

### Churches & Watchtowers
Crowning the town centre is the immense dome of Pavia's red-brick **Duomo** (Piazza del Duomo; ☷ 8am-noon & 3-7pm), which is Italy's third-largest cathedral. Leonardo da Vinci and Donato Bramante contributed to the design of the cathedral, which was begun in 1488 but not completed until the 19th century. In 1989, its bell tower collapsed, killing four people.

Barbarossa was crowned Holy Roman Emperor in 1155 at the **Basilica di San Michele** (Piazzetta Azzani 1), built in the Romanesque style in 1090.

More than 100 medieval watchtowers once dotted the old town; the trio of **watchtowers** on Piazza di Leonardo da Vinci and a couple scattered elsewhere in the city are all that remain.

### ♥ CERTOSA DI PAVIA // BEHOLD A RENAISSANCE AND GOTHIC MARVEL
One of the Italian Renaissance's most notable buildings is the splendid **Certosa di Pavia** (Pavia Charterhouse; ☎ 0382 92 56 13; www .certosadipavia.com; Viale Monumento; admission by donation; ☷ 9-11.30am & 2.30-5.30pm Tue-Sun). Gian Galeazzo Visconti of Milan founded the monastery, 10km north of Pavia, in 1396 as a private chapel and mausoleum for the Visconti family. Construction proceeded in stop-start fashion until well into the 16th century, making this a prime example of the switch from Gothic to Renaissance.

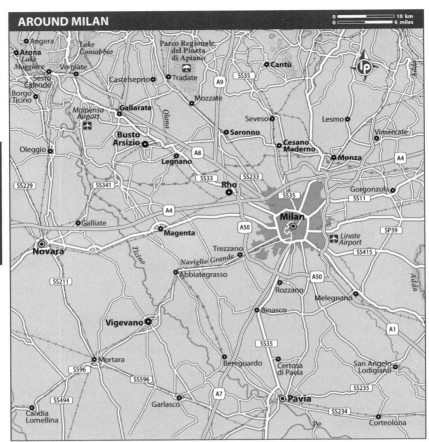

While the airy interior is indeed pre-dominantly Gothic, the exterior is almost entirely a creature of the Renaissance. The church is fronted by a spacious courtyard and flanked by a small cloister, which itself leads on to a much grander, second cloister, under whose arches are 24 cells, each a self-contained living area for one monk. Several cells are open to the public. In the former sacristy is a giant sculpture, dating from 1409 and made from hippopotamus teeth, including 66 small bas-reliefs and 94 statuettes. In the chapels you'll find frescos by, among others, Bernardino Luini and the Umbrian master, Il Perugino.

**Sila** ( ☎ 199 153155; www.sila.it, in Italian) bus 175 (Pavia–Binasco–Milano) links the bus station with **Pavia bus station** (Via Trieste) and Certosa di Pavia (15 minutes, at least seven daily).

## GASTRONOMIC HIGHLIGHTS

There is no shortage of places to eat well in Pavia, something that might induce you to hang about a little longer (perhaps staying for lunch and dinner).

### ☙ BARDELLI RISTORANTE €€

☎ 0382 2 74 41; www.bardellipv.it; Viale Lungo Ticino Visconti 2; meals €35-45; ☽ Mon-Sat

This beautiful old frescoed riverside mansion, with its glassed-in winter garden and courteous staff, serves up *risotto mantecato la serre* (creamed risotto with asparagus and saffron) and filling Lombard meat mains, washed down with regional tipples.

### ☙ BISTROT BARTOLINI €€

☎ 0382 53 84 49; Viale Vittorio Emanuele II 29; meals €40-45; ☽ dinner Sat, lunch & dinner Sun-Fri

Located in the Hotel Moderno, this bistro is an elegant gourmet gem for creative variations on good northern Italian cooking. Risotto can hardly fail to be on the menu, and here it is done in Bonarda wine and accompanied by pasta with salami and beans, a strange but successful mix. And what about the *coscia d'anatra croccante con verdure glassate* (crunchy duck leg with glazed vegetables)?

### ☙ LOCANDA DEL CARMINE €€

☎ 0382 2 96 47; www.locandadelcarmine.com; Piazza del Carmine 7a; meals €35-40; ☽ lunch & dinner Mon-Fri, dinner Sat

Sharing the square with the like-named church (which you can admire if you snare one of the handful of outside spots) the Locanda del Carmine has a cheerful dining area. You could do much worse than order up a succulent *tagliata di scottona lombarda* (a cut of Lombard beef best eaten rare – the slivers of fat in the meat enrich the flavour).

### ☙ OSTERIA ALLE CARCERI €€

☎ 0382 30 14 43; www.osteriaallecarceri.it; Via Marozzi 7; meals €30; ☽ lunch & dinner Mon-Fri, dinner Sat

Down a narrow lane off Corso Cavour and next door to the one-time town prison after which it takes its name, this inviting *osteria* (wine bar and eatery) offers tables stamped with prison numbers, grilled meats and such openers as *linguine Cocco con guanciale, carciofi, semi di pappavero e ricotta di pecora* (pasta with pork cheek meat, artichokes, poppy seeds and sheep's ricotta).

## TRANSPORT

**TRAIN //** Plenty of direct trains link Pavia train station with Milan's Centrale station (from €3.05, 23 to 40 minutes).

# VIGEVANO

**pop 59,000**

A graffiti-covered suburban train clatters 35km southwest out of Milan's Porta Genova station through residential and light-industrial districts, and then across flat farmland criss-crossed by canals to Vigevano, a dormitory satellite town.

Doesn't sound promising, but wait! A 10-minute walk from Vigevano's train station is one of the most beautiful town squares in Lombardy. When it passed under the control of Milan's Viscontis, Vigevano was little more than fort. By the time the Sforzas came to power, it had become a sumptuous residence for Milan's rulers.

## EXPLORING VIGEVANO

### ☙ PIAZZA DUCALE & CASTELLO SFORZESCO // ADMIRE THE DUKES' SQUARE AND CASTLE

Ludovico Il Moro ordered the creation of **Piazza Ducale**, a magnificent square that is a triumph of the Renaissance. The grand porticoed buildings that line the

**MILAN**

square are covered with frescos. At the east end, the eye-catching concave baroque facade of the **Duomo** (cathedral) lends the square a striking theatrical touch.

A broad stairway leads southwest off the square to the **Castello Sforzesco** (admission free; ⊙ 8.30am-7pm Mon-Fri, 8.30am-8pm Sat & Sun & holidays Apr-Sep, 9am-6pm Mon-Fri, 9am-7pm Sat & Sun & holidays Oct-Mar), which was largely raised in the course of the 14th century. The main buildings, long neglected, are likely to be closed for years of restoration work. Visitors have access to the grounds inside the outer walls and the **Torre di**

**Bramante** (admission free; ⊙ 10am-12.30pm & 2.30-5pm Sat & Sun & holidays), a watchtower designed by Renaissance architect Donato Bramante (some claim that Bramante and Leonardo da Vinci together designed Piazza Ducale).

Above the former stables in the castle's outer walls you'll find the **Museo della Calzatura** (Footwear Museum; ☎ 0381 693 39 52; adult/student/child under 12yr €2.50/1/free; ⊙ 10am-1pm & 2-6pm Tue-Sat, 10am-1pm & 2-6pm Sun & holidays). Vigevano was long a centre of shoe production and knew its golden age in the 1950s and '60s, when many of Italy's great designers manufactured

---

## ∼ WORTH A TRIP ∼

Known to many as home of a classic European Formula One track (where high-speed races have been held annually in September since 1950), **Monza** (pop 121,000) is generally overlooked by visitors to Milan. Aside from the **racetrack** ( ☎ 039 2 48 21; www.monzanet .it; Via Vedano 5, Parco di Monza; admission €40; ⊙ 9am-1pm & 2-6pm Mon-Fri Dec-Feb), which you can actually drive on most days in winter, history and architecture buffs are also rewarded.

The Gothic **Duomo** (Piazza Duomo), with its white and green banded facade (largely the result of 19th-century restoration), contains a key early-medieval treasure, the **Corona Ferrea** (Iron Crown), so called because legend has it that it was fashioned from, among other things, one of the nails with which Christ was crucified. Emblazoned with precious jewels and gold leaf, the crown is said to date to the 5th century AD and may have belonged to Rome's Ostrogoth rulers and later the Lombards. Charlemagne saw it as a symbol of empire and he was not alone. Various Holy Roman Emperors, including Frederick I (Barbarossa) and Napoleon had themselves crowned with it. The crown is on show in the chapel dedicated to the Lombard queen Theodolinda (see p234). The **Museo Serpero** ( ☎ 039 32 34 04; www .duomomonza.it; Piazza del Duomo; adult/student/senior €8/6/6 with Corono Ferrea; ⊙ 9am-1pm & 2-6pm Tue-Sun), attached to the Duomo, contains one of greatest treasures of religious art in Europe. Among the gems are Queen Theodolinda's own crown and a curious Lombard sculpture of a hen and seven chicks in silver and gold.

A stroll in the **Giardini Reali** (admission free; ⊙ 7am-8pm Apr-Oct, 7am-6.30pm Nov-Mar), the southern end of the immense Parco di Monza, will bring you to the **Villa Reale**, built from 1777 to 1780 as a viceregal residence when Lombardy was still under Habsburg Austrian rule. Modelled on Vienna's Schönbrunn palace, it fell into disuse in the 20th century. It is now being restored.

Regular trains connect Milan's Porta Garibaldi station with Monza (€1.65, 15 to 20 minutes), 23km to the north, making this an easy half-day trip.

their shoes here. On show are all sorts of items, from Pope John XXIII's papal slippers to a snazzy pair of shoes that belonged to dictatorial fashion victim Benito Mussolini.

### 🍴 IL GHISIO // SAMPLE CREATIVE CUISINE IN CONTEMPORARY SETTING

A short stroll west of the train station, this modern-looking **restaurant** (☎ 0381 8 77 41; www.ilghisio.it; Via della Madonna degli Angeli 21; meals €40-45; ☺ Tue-Sat & lunch Sun) dominated by red and white decor (and a tad overlit) has spacious dining areas. Exquisite first courses include *soffici di ricotta, gamberi rossi, carciofi a pomodorino confit* (ricotta pasta with red shrimps, artichokes and cherry-tomato confit), followed by something like a *filetto d'anatra al burro di cacao, patate allo zenzero e salsa al prosciutto crudo e noci* (duck filet with cocoa butter, ginger potatoes and a sauce of raw ham and nuts).

## FESTIVALS & EVENTS

**Il Palio di Vigevano** (www.paliodivigevano .it) For a couple of days, central Vigevano reverts to its glory days as a Sforza residence, with day- and night-time parades in period dress and other activities in Piazza Ducale and the Castello; second weekend in October.

## TRANSPORT

**TRAIN //** There are hourly trains from Milan's Porta Genova train station (€2.70, 35 minutes). You can also pick up buses here from Pavia (€3.05, 40 minutes).

# LAKE MAGGIORE & LAKE ORTA

## 3 PERFECT DAYS

### 🐦 DAY 1 // ISLAND-HOP THE BORROMEAN ISLANDS
It is worth catching a ferry (with an all-day ticket) from Stresa or Baveno to Isola Bella (p86) in order to marvel at the baroque wealth of the Borromeo family's island pleasure palace and gardens. Once saturated by all this richness, it's possible to transfer to Isola Superiore (p87) for lunch at one of this Fishermen's Island's restaurants. Then the perfect completion to this experience of the Borromean Islands is to enjoy an afternoon on Isola Madre (p87). For an extra treat, sleep on Isola Superiore (p292).

### 🐦 DAY 2 // ASCEND MOTTARONE AND DISCOVER ROMANTIC LAKE ORTA
The splendid views of lakes and Alps can be seen by driving, hiking, or taking the funicular from the belle époque lakeside town of Stresa to Monte Mottarone (p82). Then it's worth heading down the other side to enchanting little Lake Orta (p96) and its star village, Orta San Giulio, a quintessential romantic spot and the perfect base for local exploration, in particular of Isola San Giulio and the *sacro monte* (holy mountain).

### 🐦 DAY 3 // RIDE THE CENTOVALLI RAILWAY TO LOCARNO
It's possible to enjoy a string of mountain valley villages by catching a train in Stresa bound for Domodossola, which is the starting point for the scenic Centovalli railway trip (p76) through a string of mountain valley villages to Locarno (p70). You can then explore this elegant film-festival town and its pretty lakeside neighbour, Ascona, for the rest of the day. From there, you can head south back over the Italian border to reach captivating Cannobio (p79), one of the most enticing places to stay overnight on Lake Maggiore.

# LAKE MAGGIORE

· · · · · ·

**Lake Maggiore is one of the first impressions that many first-time visitors to Italy get to experience. By train or by road, travellers traversing the Alps from Switzerland at the Simplon Pass wind down from the mountains and sidle up to this enormous finger of blue beauty. The star attractions are the Borromean Islands, which, like a fleet of fine vessels, lie at anchor at the Borromean Gulf's (Golfo Borromeo) entrance, an incursion of water between the lake's two main towns, Stresa and Verbania.**

More than its siblings to the east, Lake Como and Lake Garda, Lake Maggiore has retained a belle époque air. All three have mesmerised foreign visitors down the centuries but Lake Maggiore became a popular tourist destination in the late 19th century after the Simplon Pass was opened.

Locarno (scene of one of Europe's top film festivals) and Ascona, at the northern Swiss end, and Stresa, in the southwest, have long been beloved of northern Europeans seeking the soothing waters and gentle climate of the broad lake. The climate helps a multitude of colourful plants to flourish and trees thrive in a series of extraordinarily rich gardens on islands, in villas and botanic gardens.

The Piedmontese western shore is the more attractive; it's sprinkled with picturesque villages, and circled with palms and cypresses. The shoreline drive along the SS34 and SS33 (in that order heading south) is delightful. The eastern, Lombard shore is less well groomed but contains a handful of gems well worth searching out.

## TRANSPORT

**BOAT //** Ferries and hydrofoils around the lake are operated by **Navigazione Lago Maggiore** (☎ 800 551801; www.navigazionelaghi.it, in Italian), which has its main ticket office in Arona. Services are drastically reduced in autumn and winter. The only car ferry connecting the western and eastern shores for motorists sails between Verbania Intra and Laveno. Ferries run every 20 minutes; one-way transport costs from €6.90 to €11.50 for a car and driver or €4.30 for a bicycle and cyclist. One-day return tickets from key points at the Italian end of the lake to the towns (including Locarno) on the Swiss side are available from March to October. Adults/children pay from €15.50/8.80 to €21.50/11.80 depending on their departure port. Services are drastically reduced in autumn and winter. Limited day passes cost Sfr13.80 on the Swiss side. The Sfr24 version is valid for the entire Swiss basin.

# LOCARNO & AROUND

With its palm trees and much vaunted 2300 hours of sunshine a year, Locarno has attracted northern tourists to its warm, Mediterranean-style setting since the late 19th century. The lowest town in Switzerland and the most striking one on Lake Maggiore, it seemed like a soothing spot to host the 1925 Locarno Conference where treaties were signed to bring peace to Europe after WWI.

## ESSENTIAL INFORMATION

**TOURIST OFFICES // Locarno Tourist Office** (☎ 091 791 00 91; www.maggiore.ch; Largo Zorzi 1; ◷ 9am-6pm Mon-Fri, 10am-6pm Sat & holidays, 10am-1.30pm & 2.30-5pm Sun mid-Mar–Oct, 9.30am-noon & 1.30-5pm Mon-Fri, 10am-noon & 1.30-5pm Sat Nov–mid-Mar) Ask about the Lago Maggiore Guest Card and its discounts.

*(Continued on page 70)*

LAKE MAGGIORE & LAKE ORTA

# LAKE MAGGIORE & LAKE ORTA

## GETTING AROUND

Driving around Lakes Maggiore and Orta presents particular challenges on summer weekends, when roads congest with day trippers from Milan and beyond. The A26 motorway feeds you into the area around Stresa and close to Lake Orta from Milan, while the A8 leads to Varese from Milan. They are usually fluid. Otherwise you must be prepared for dense traffic along the lakes at weekends and around Varese daily. Parking is generally possible and metered in towns like Locarno, Stresa, Verbania and Varese.

### VALLE MAGGIA    p78

Explore one of the most picturesque valleys in southern Switzerland

### PARCO NAZIONALE VAL GRANDE    p84

Penetrate a deep wilderness only a short way from Lake Maggiore

### BORROMEAN ISLANDS    p86

Discover paradise on earth in the islands' villas and gardens

0    15 km
0    10 miles

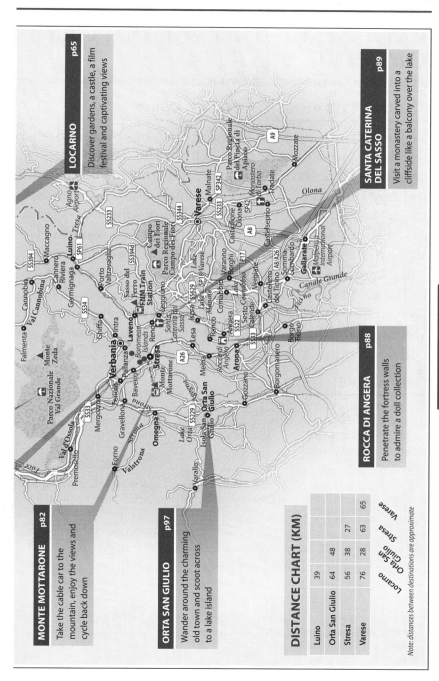

**LOCARNO**   p65

Discover gardens, a castle, a film festival and captivating views

**SANTA CATERINA DEL SASSO**   p89

Visit a monastery carved into a cliffside like a balcony over the lake

**ROCCA DI ANGERA**   p88

Penetrate the fortress walls to admire a doll collection

**MONTE MOTTARONE**   p82

Take the cable car to the mountain, enjoy the views and cycle back down

**ORTA SAN GIULIO**   p97

Wander around the charming old town and scoot across to a lake island

LAKE MAGGIORE & LAKE ORTA

## DISTANCE CHART (KM)

| | Locarno | Orta San Giulio | Stresa | Varese |
|---|---|---|---|---|
| Luino | 39 | | | |
| Orta San Giulio | 64 | 48 | | |
| Stresa | 56 | 38 | 27 | |
| Varese | 76 | 28 | 63 | 65 |

Note: distances between destinations are approximate

# LAKE MAGGIORE & LAKE ORTA GETTING STARTED

## MAKING THE MOST OF YOUR TIME

**Key points around Lake Maggiore can be covered in a few days, and should be topped by at least one night on serene Lake Orta, to the west. The most spectacular sights include the Borromean Islands, adorned with baroque palaces and overflowing gardens, and the sentinel castle above Angera. Flower enthusiasts will want to visit Verbania's Villa Taranto. More castles await in Locarno and, more spectacularly, Bellinzona, at the Swiss end of the lake. A rewarding day out from Locarno would see you explore the Valle Maggia. Panoramic viewpoints abound, including Monte Mottarone, Laveno and the cliffside Santa Caterina del Sasso monastery.**

## TOP TOURS

### ❦ FERRARI DRIVING TOUR

Red Travel proposes four-day driving holidays around Lake Maggiore, Lake Como and Milan in latest-model Ferraris, staying in luxury hotels and eating in top restaurants. (www.red-travel.com)

### ❦ CENTOVALLI TRAIN

The Centovalli train, which trundles across numerous viaducts past villages along the deep valley between Locarno and Domodossola, is a scenic thrill. (www.centovalli.ch)

### ❦ BIRD'S-EYE VIEW BICICÒ STYLE

Combine a helicopter ride over Lake Maggiore with a mountain-bike descent of Monte Mottarone. The two-day package includes hiking the lake's back country. (www.bicico.it)

### ❦ GUIDED STROLL AROUND LAKE ORTA

The Ecomuseo del Lago d'Orta e Mottarone organises walks around Lake Orta. It offers a mountain-bike version too. (www.lagodorta.net)

### ❦ SCENIC WALKING TOUR IN CANDOGLIA MARBLE QUARRIES

Parco Nazionale Val Grande guides lead summer tours to the Candoglia marble quarries. (www.parcovalgrande.it)

# GETTING AWAY FROM IT ALL

Visitors tend to concentrate in Stresa and the Borromean Islands, Locarno and Ascona, while Orta San Giulio fills with Milanese day-trippers on weekends.

★ **Ticino's western valleys** Sneak northwest from Locarno and follow a series of captivating back-country valleys (p76)

★ **Sacro Monte della SS Trinità** Walk or drive to this shady haven high above the town of Ghiffa (p80)

★ **Parco Nazionale Val Grande** Hike in a near-pristine mountain reserve (p84)

★ **Castelseprio & Torba** Seek out the quiet remains of a fortified Lombard settlement (p93)

# TOP FRESCOS

Many historic locations contain fabulous frescos, artistic remnants with centuries of history, in some cases remarkably well preserved. The cream range from pre-Romanesque to wonderful Florentine Renaissance:

★ **Basilica di San Giulio, Isola San Giulio** The 12th-century church on Lake Orta's island is jammed with vibrant frescos depicting saints (p98)

★ **Collegiata, Castiglione d'Olona** Florentine master Masolino da Panicale carried out a series on the life of St John the Baptist in 1435 (p93)

★ **Chiesa di Santa Maria Foris Portas, Castelseprio** A modest Lombard church contains lively pre-Romanesque frescos that may date to the 7th century (p93)

★ **Santa Caterina del Sasso** The church in this former monastery is filled with well-preserved frescos (p89)

# TOP RESTAURANTS

❦ **CASABELLA**
Elegantly prepared fish with close-up lake views (p88)

❦ **DA ANNETTA**
Exquisite Italian cooking near Lake Varese (p94)

❦ **HOTEL LIDO ANGERA**
Lake-fish sushi platter amid greenery (p90)

❦ **IL SOLE**
High-end gourmands' delight on Lake Maggiore (p90)

❦ **OSTERIA CHIARA**
Bucolic atmosphere in sophisticated Locarno (p75)

❦ **RISTORANTE MARCONI**
Foodies' paradise in a remote village (p77)

❦ **RISTORANTE MILANO**
Verbania's classiest eating option (p83)

❦ **RISTORO OLINA**
Creative zest in the heart of timeless Orta San Giulio (p99)

# RESOURCES

★ **Borromeo** (www.borromeoturismo.it) All you need to know about the Borromean Islands

★ **Lago Maggiore** (www.lagomaggioreturismo .it) General information on Lake Maggiore

★ **Lago d'Orta** (www.lagodortaturismo.it) General information on Lake Orta

★ **Varese Land of Tourism** (www.varese landoftourism.it) Varese province resource, including Lake Maggiore's east bank

LAKE MAGGIORE & LAKE ORTA

(Continued from page 65)

## EXPLORING LOCARNO & AROUND

----------------------------------------

### ❦ SANTUARIO DELLA MADONNA DEL SASSO // MAKE A PILGRIMAGE HIGH ABOVE TOWN

Overlooking the town, this sanctuary was built after the Virgin Mary supposedly appeared in a vision to a monk, Bartolomeo d'Ivrea, in 1480. There's a small **museum** (☎ 091 743 62 65; Via del Santuario 2; adult/student & child Sfr2.50/1.50; ☽ 2-5pm), a **church** (☽ 8am-6.45pm) and several rather rough, near lifesized statue groups (including one of the Last Supper) in niches on the stairway. The best-known painting in the church is *La fuga in Egitto* (Flight to Egypt), painted in 1522 by Bramantino.

Contrasting in style are the naive votive paintings by the church entrance, where the Madonna and Child appear as ghostly apparitions in life-and-death situations.

A funicular runs every 15 to 30 minutes from the town centre (Sfr4.50 up, Sfr6.60 return) past the sanctuary to Orselina, but the 20-minute walk up is not all that demanding (take Via al Sasso off Via Cappuccini) even though it is a chapel-lined path known as the Via Crucis.

### ❦ OLD TOWN // GET LOST IN LOCARNO'S BACKSTREETS

Stride out and about the Italianate piazzas and arcades, and admire the Lombard houses. There are some interesting churches. Built in the 17th century, the **Chiesa Nuova** (New Church; Via Cittadella) has a dizzyingly ornate baroque ceiling. Outside, left of the entrance, stands a giant statue of St Christopher with disproportionately tiny feet. The 16th-century **Chiesa di San Francesco** (Piazza

---

### DAY TRIP

**Lake Maggiore Express** (www.lagomaggioreexpress.com; adult/child €30/15) is a picturesque day trip under your own steam (no guide) that includes train travel from Arona or Stresa to Domodossola, from where you get a charming little train to Locarno in Switzerland and a ferry back from Locarno to Stresa. The two-day version (adult/child €36/18) is perhaps better value if you have the time. Tickets are available from Navigazione Lago Maggiore (p65).

---

San Francesco) has frescos by Baldassare Orelli, while the **Chiesa di Sant'Antonio** is best known for its altar to the *Cristo morto* (Dead Christ). A fortified castle, **Castello Visconteo** (☎ 091 756 31 70; Piazza Castello; adult/student Sfr7/5; ☽ 10am-noon & 2-5pm Tue-Fri, 10am-5pm Sat & Sun Apr–mid-Nov), dating from the 15th century and named after the Visconti clan who long ruled Milan, today houses a museum with Roman and Bronze Age exhibits. Locarno is believed to have been a glass-manufacturing town in Roman times, which accounts for the strong showing of glass artefacts in the museum. This labyrinth of a castle, whose nucleus was raised around the 10th century, also hosts a small display (in Italian) on the 1925 Locarno Treaty. The castle changed hands various times and was occupied by the Milanese under Luchino Visconti in 1342. Taken by French forces in 1499, the castle and town of Locarno eventually fell to the Swiss confederation in 1516.

### ❦ CIMETTA // BE WHISKED UPWARDS FOR JAW-DROPPING VIEWS

From the Orselina funicular stop, a cable car goes to **Cardada** (☽ 8am-8pm Jun-Sep, 9am-

6pm Mon-Thu, 8am-8pm Fri-Sun Mar-May & Oct-Nov), and then a chairlift soars to **Cimetta** (www .cardada.ch, in Italian & German; return adult/senior/6-16yr/under 6yr Sfr33/25/11/free; 9.15am-12.30pm & 1.30-4.50pm daily Mar-Nov) at 1672m. You can engage in some gentle hikes at Cardada

and Cimetta. At the former, make for the promenade suspended above the trees, at the end of which is a lookout point with 180-degree views over the city, Lake Maggiore and the valleys beyond. The geological observation point at Cimetta goes one

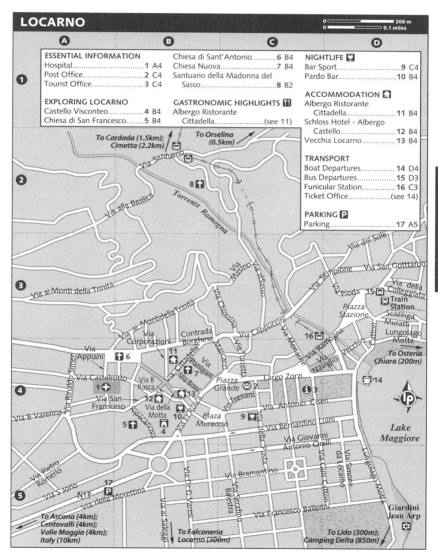

## LOCARNO

0 — 200 m
0 — 0.1 miles

**ESSENTIAL INFORMATION**
Hospital.................................1 A4
Post Office..........................2 C4
Tourist Office.....................3 C4

**EXPLORING LOCARNO**
Castello Visconteo................4 B4
Chiesa di San Francesco........5 B4

Chiesa di Sant'Antonio...........6 B4
Chiesa Nuova........................7 B4
Santuario della Madonna del
   Sasso..................................8 B2

**GASTRONOMIC HIGHLIGHTS**
Albergo Ristorante
   Cittadella.....................(see 11)

**NIGHTLIFE**
Bar Sport.............................9 C4
Pardo Bar.........................10 B4

**ACCOMMODATION**
Albergo Ristorante
   Cittadella......................11 B4
Schloss Hotel - Albergo
   Castello........................12 B4
Vecchia Locarno..............13 B4

**TRANSPORT**
Boat Departures..............14 D4
Bus Departures.................15 D3
Funicular Station.............16 C3
Ticket Office.................(see 14)

**PARKING**
Parking............................17 A5

LAKE MAGGIORE & LAKE ORTA

# LAKE MAGGIORE & LAKE ORTA

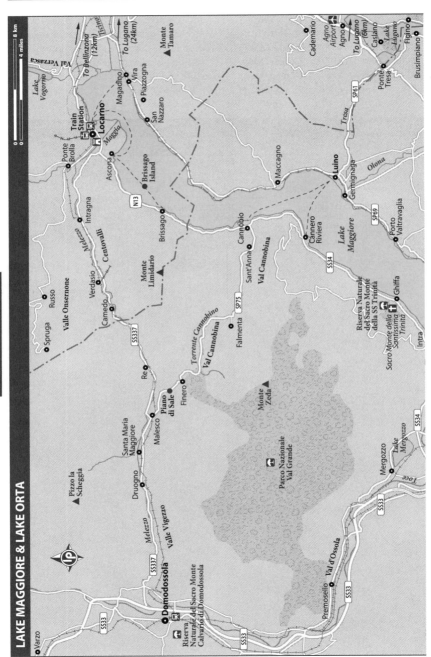

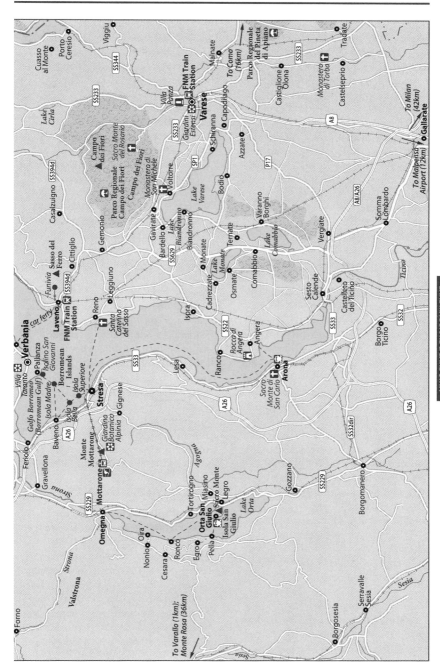

better, with 360-degree views. The mountain is sliced up by walking trails (paths are marked) that can have you stomping along from 1½ to four or so hours, depending on the trails you choose. Longer routes lead into the Valle Maggia and Val Verzasca (see p77). Cimetta is a popular launch spot for paragliders. If you want to have a go with an instructor in a tandem flight, contact **Volo Libero Ticino** (www .cvlt.ch). On the web page is a list of qualified instructors and details for contacting them. Locals get in a little ski practice up here in winter.

### ☙ ASCONA // INVESTIGATE LOCARNO'S LAKESIDE TWIN

A phalanx of pretty pastel-hued houses sides up to the placid lakefront in Ascona (population 5430), Locarno's smaller twin across the Maggia river delta. Behind them, a tangle of little streets makes for pleasant wandering, with plenty of eateries and bars to distract you. Walking paths file up into the green hills around the town from the southern end of the waterfront. The late 19th century saw the arrival of 'back to nature' utopians, anarchists and sexual libertarians from northern Europe in Ascona. Their aspirations and eccentricities are the subject of the **Museo Casa Anatta** ( ☎ 091 785 40 40; www. monteverita.org; Via Collina 78; adult/student & senior Sfr6/4; ☺ 3-7pm Tue-Sun Jul & Aug, 2.30-6pm Tue-Sun Apr-Jun & Sep-Oct) on Monte Verità (take the small bus to Buxi from the post office; Sfr1). All sorts of characters, including Hermann Hesse, dropped by to look at the goings-on. A ferry runs from Locarno to Ascona (20 minutes, Sfr8.70 one way).

### Museum of Modern Art

The **Museo Comunale d'Arte Moderna** ( ☎ 091 759 81 40; www.museoascona.ch; Via Borgo 34; adult/concession Sfr7/5; ☺ 10am-noon & 3-6pm

Tue-Sat, 4-6pm Sun), in Palazzo Pancaldi, includes paintings by artists connected with the town, among them Modernist painters such as Paul Klee, Ben Nicholson, Alexej Jawlensky and Hans Arp.

### Papal College

The **Collegio Papio** (Via Cappelle), now a high school, boasts a fine Lombard courtyard and includes the 15th-century **Chiesa Santa Maria della Misericordia**, decorated with medieval frescos.

### ☙ ISOLE DI BRISSAGO // CARESS YOUR SENSES IN ISLAND GARDENS

The Ticino authorities could not have chosen a more enchanting spot to locate some botanic gardens. On **Isole di Brissago** ( ☎ 091 791 43 61; www.isolebrissago.ch; adult/child Sfr8/2.50; ☺ 9am-6pm Apr-Oct), you can visit one of the two specks of green, San Pancrazio. Renowned for its spring-blooming rhododendrons, camellias and azaleas, the garden (which contains some 1500 species of plants) is rich in subtropical plants from as far off as Southeast Asia and South America. The mild climate here makes this possible. Ferries run from Locarno (35 minutes), Ascona (15 minutes) and other points at the Swiss end of Lake Maggiore. The last one back to Ascona and Lorcano leaves at 6.10pm.

### FESTIVALS & EVENTS

**Festival Internazionale di Film** (International Film Festival; ☎ 091 756 21 21; www.pardo.ch; Via Ciseri 23, CH-6600 Locarno) For two weeks in August (and going strong since 1948), the cinema world descends on Locarno. Cinemas are used for screenings during the day, but at night, films are shown on a giant screen in Piazza Grande.

**Settimane Musicali** (www.settimane-musicali .ch) International classical music festival held annually in Ascona since 1946 from the end of August to mid-October.

# ACCOMMODATION

Accommodation is especially abundant in Stresa and Verbania, both of them launch pads for the Borromean Islands and the latter home to the sumptuous Villa Taranto. There is also a fair choice in Locarno and Ascona. The more popular west side of the lake has a smattering of options along its length. The quieter east bank has fewer choices. Possibly the most romantic hotel locations are Isola Superiore (one of the Borromean Islands), Orta San Giulio on Lake Orta, Cannobio on Lake Maggiore and the *sacro monte* (holy mountain) outside Varese.

A selection of accommodation around Lakes Maggiore and Orta follows; many more options can be found from p291.

* **Castello Seeschloss** (Ascona, p291) A 13th-century castle-turned-hotel

* **Hotel Pironi** (Cannobio, p292) A frescoed house near the lake in old Cannobio

* **Albergo Verbano** (Isola Superiore, p293) A peaceful island getaway with a century of history

* **Al Borducan** (Sacro Monte, Varese, p293) A tasteful hilltop hideaway

## GASTRONOMIC HIGHLIGHTS

### ALBERGO RISTORANTE CITTADELLA // LOCARNO €€
☎ 091 751 58 85; Via Cittadella 18; meals Sfr40-55; ⌚ Tue-Sun

This is the place to go if you enjoy fine fish and seafood – the elegant upstairs section, with leather-backed chairs and broad, round tables draped in impeccable white linen, does not serve anything else. Downstairs in the trattoria, the atmosphere is more relaxed and the menu not quite so focused on the aquatic. You can grab a pizza from Sfr6 to Sfr8.50.

### ANTICA OSTERIA VACCHINI // ASCONA €€€
☎ 091 791 13 96; Contrada Maggiore 23; meals Sfr70; ⌚ Mon-Sat

Diners find no shortage of pasta, meat and fish options in this old-time eatery (with an outdoor section located across the lane). The house special is *piodadella della Vallamaggia,* a set of three kinds of cold meats with three matching sauces, salad and fries – a filling and tasty summer option. Inside, you can take a seat in the grand 17th-century dining hall.

### OSTERIA CHIARA // LOCARNO €€€
☎ 091 743 32 96; Vicolo della Chiara 1; meals Sfr70-80; ⌚ Tue-Sat

Tucked away on a cobbled lane, this has all the cosy feel of a *grotto* (a typical Ticino country eatery, which is half carved out of stone). Sit at granite tables beneath the pergola outside or at the timber tables by the fireplace inside, and enjoy chunky pasta and mostly meaty mains. From the lake, follow the signs up Vicolo dei Nessi.

## NIGHTLIFE

### BAR SPORT // LOCARNO
Via della Posta 4; ⌚ 8am-1am Mon-Fri, 10am-1am Sat, 2pm-1am Sun

A fairly run-of-the-mill place by day, this rough-and-tumble bar with the red-walled dance space out the back and beer garden on the side is an extremely popular hang-out with Locarno's nightowls. There are a few other bars in the vicinity.

**♥ PARDO BAR // LOCARNO**
☎ 091 752 21 23; www.pardobar.com; Via Motta 3;
🕒 4pm-1am daily
With its background music, scattered timber tables (a couple of computers on one) and wine and cocktails on offer, Pardo Bar attracts a relaxed and mixed crowd.

## TRANSPORT

**CAR //** The SS34 road from Verbania follows Lake Maggiore north to Locarno. From Lugano, follow the A2 motorway north and take the Locarno turn-off.

**PARKING //** There is cheap street parking (Sfr3 for 10 hours) along Via della Morettina.

**BOAT //** Lake Maggiore boats (see p65) call in at the wharf equidistant from Piazza Grande and Piazza Stazione in Locarno and at Ascona.

**TRAIN //** Trains run every one to two hours from Brig (Sfr51, 2½ to three hours), passing through Italy (bring your passport). Change trains at Domodossola. Various trains reach Locarno from Zürich (Sfr57, three to 3½ hours) and other locations in central and northern Switzerland, mostly via Bellinzona (off Map pp66–7).

**BUS //** Postal buses to the western valleys leave from outside Locarno train station. Bus 31 from Locarno's train station and Piazza Grande stops at Ascona's post office, with departures every 15 minutes (Sfr2.80).

# TICINO'S WESTERN VALLEYS

The valleys ranging to the north and west of Locarno teem with grey-stone villages, gushing mountain streams, cosy retreats, traditional *grotti* and endless walking opportunities.

## EXPLORING TICINO'S WESTERN VALLEYS

**♥ CENTOVALLI // TAKE THE 'HUNDRED VALLEYS' TRAIN**
The 'hundred valleys' is the westward valley route from southern Ticino to Domodossola in Italy, known on the Italian side as Valle Vigezzo (which is an access route to the Parco Nazionale Val Grande, see p84).

A picturesque **train** (www.centovalli.ch; one way adult/child under 6yr/6-16yr Sfr32/free/16) clatters along the valley, trundling across numerous precarious-looking viaducts, from Locarno for Domodossola (or vice versa). There are up to 11 departures a day; the journey is one hour and 50 minutes. Take your passport.

By car, the route is slightly less exhilarating but you have greater flexibility to stop and explore on the way. The road winds west of Ponte Brolla (4km from Locarno) in a string of tight curves, high on the north flank of the Melezzo stream. The quiet towns with their stone houses and heavy slate roofs, mostly high above the road and railway line on either side of the valley, make tranquil bases for mountain hikes. Among the best stops are **Verdasio**, **Rasa** and **Bordei**. Rasa is only accessible by cable car from Verdasio.

At **Re**, on the Italian side, there is a procession of pilgrims on 30 April each year, based on a tradition that originated when a painting of the Madonna was reported to have started bleeding when struck by a ball in 1480. More startling than the legend is the bulbous basilica built in the name of the Madonna del Sangue (Madonna of the Blood) in 1922–50.

From Re, the route passes through a series of picturesque villages. Valle Vigezzo is also locally known as the Valley of the Painters. An art school was established in **Santa Maria Maggiore** in the 19th century, and many houses and chapels are gaily adorned with frescos. The road and train line end in **Domodossola**, a frontier town on the train line that links Milan with Geneva.

### ❤ VAL VERZASCA // FOLLOW THE EMERALD STREAM

Located about 4km northeast of Locarno, this rugged 26km valley snakes north past the impressive Vogorno dam, fed by the gushing Verzasca (Green Waters) river. Just beyond Lake Vogorno, look to the left and you will see the picture-postcard hamlet of **Corripo** seemingly pasted on to the thickly wooded mountain flank. To reach it you cross the **Gola Verzasca**, a scintillating gorge. About 5km upstream, **Lavertezzo** is known for its narrow, double-humped, Roman-esque bridge (rebuilt from scratch after the 1951 floods destroyed it) and natural pools in the icy stream. Be careful, as storms upstream can turn the river into a raging torrent in no time. Another 12km takes you to **Sonogno**, a once abandoned hamlet at the head of the valley that has been resuscitated largely due to tourism.

### ❤ RISTORANTE MARCONI // DELIGHT IN A GOURMET HIDEAWAY IN THE MOUNTAINS

Just 16.5km north of Domodossola, the village of **Crodo** hides **Ristorante**

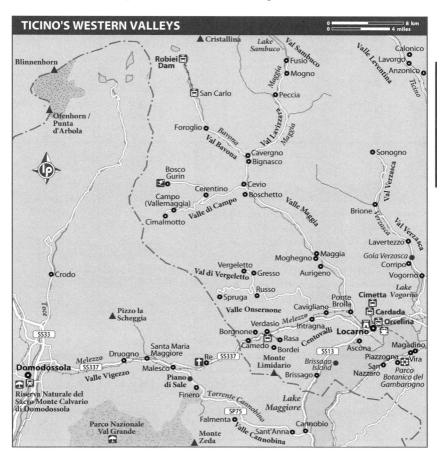

TICINO'S WESTERN VALLEYS

LAKE MAGGIORE & LAKE ORTA

**Marconi** (☎ 0324 61 87 97; www.ristorantemarconi
.com, in Italian; Via Pellanda 21; meals €30; ☺ Wed-
Mon). In a simple but welcoming stone
house, you will be regaled with fine food.
Antipasti and first courses are an early
indication of the creativity you can expect
from chef Denis Croce. You might hesitate between the *polpo con tampone di
patata e limone* (fresh octopus with potato and lemon) or the *orecchioni di pasta
all'uovo con ricotta profumata agli agrumi
e salsa alle triglie* (ear-shaped pasta filled
with citrus-touched ricotta and a mullet
sauce). A limited selection of mains follows. Tasting menus are an option, the
cheese platters are a dairy fan's delight
and it offers kids' dishes for around €6.
For dessert (all homemade) you can opt
for a mixed platter or plump for, say, the
sinful *semifreddo alle stecche di vaniglia
Tahiti con salsa di cioccolata Guanaja*,
basically a soft creamy vanilla dessert
smothered in a rich chocolate sauce.

## TRANSPORT

**CAR //** Your own transport is by far the most flexible
way to get around the valleys.

**BUS //** Postal buses to the western valleys leave from
outside Locarno train station. For instance, buses operate to Sonogno from Locarno as often as once hourly
(Sfr17.60, 70 minutes). Regular buses run from Locarno
to Cevio and Bignasco (Sfr15.80, 50 minutes), from
where you make less regular connections into the side
valleys. In Valle Maggiore, a bus runs four times a day
from Bignasco to San Carlo (Sfr10.80, 30 minutes), from
April to October.

## LAKE MAGGIORE WEST BANK

This section follows Lake Maggiore's
west bank from the Swiss border south.
The high point is without doubt a visit to
the Borromean Islands (dealt with separately in the following section), but there
is plenty of interest along the way.

---

### ∼ WORTH A TRIP ∼

The broad Valle Maggia follows the Maggia river from Ponte Brolla (4km northwest of
Locarno) – the valley's **tourist office** (☎ 091 753 18 85; www.vallemaggia.ch) is in **Maggia**. Visit
**Aurigeno**, a village known for its colourful frescos. At **Cevio**, where the valley splits,
12km northwest of Maggia, admire the colourful facade of the 16th-century **Pretorio**,
covered with local ruling families' coats of arms, and old-town mansions. A short, signposted walk away are *grotti* (cellars carved out of great blocks of granite). At Cerentino,
the road forks – the right fork leads 5.5km along hairpin bends to **Bosco Gurin**, a minor
ski centre and high pasture village, where the main language is German. The left fork
from Cerentino leads up the 8km-long **Valle di Campo** along a winding forest road to
another upland valley. The prettiest of its towns is **Campo**, with its Romanesque bell
tower. Back in Cevio, the Valle Maggia road continues 3km to Bignasco. Turn west for
the **Val Bavona**, the valley's prettiest area. A road follows a mountain stream through
narrow meadows set between rocky walls to a series of irresistible hamlets. **Foreloin**
is dominated by a waterfall (a 10-minute walk away), and is home to **Ristorante La
Freda** (☎ 091 754 11 81; meals Sfr50; ☺ Apr-Oct). Sit by a crackling fire for *stinko di mailer* (pork
shank), served with the best polenta you are likely to taste. Just after San Carlo, a **cable
car** (adult/child return Sfr20/10; ☺ mid-Jun–early Oct) rides up to the **Robiei dam** and nearby
lakes – a great spot for hiking.

## ESSENTIAL INFORMATION

**TOURIST OFFICES // Arona Tourist Office** ( ☎ 0322 24 36 01; Piazzale Duca d'Aosta; ⏱ 9.30am-12.30pm Mon-Wed, 9.30am-12.30pm & 3-6pm Thu-Sat); **Cannobio Tourist Office** ( ☎ 0323 7 12 12; www.procannobio.it; Via Giovanola 25; ⏱ 9am-noon & 4.30-7pm Mon & Wed-Sat, 9am-noon Sun & holidays); **Stresa Tourist Office** ( ☎ 0323 3 13 08; Piazza Marconi 16; ⏱ 10am-12.30pm & 3-6.30pm mid-Mar–mid-Oct, 10am-12.30pm & 3-6.30pm Mon-Fri, 10am-12.30pm Sat mid-Oct–mid-Mar); **Verbania Tourist Office** ( ☎ 0323 50 32 49; www.verbania-turismo.it; Corso Zanitello 6-8; ⏱ 9am-1pm & 3-6pm Mon-Fri) is on the waterfront in Verbania Pallanza and has accommodation details. Check www.visitstresa.com too.

## EXPLORING LAKE MAGGIORE WEST BANK

### ☙ CANNOBIO // BASE YOURSELF IN AN ELEGANT LAKE TOWN

Just 5km south of the Swiss border, **Cannobio's** (population 5120) toytown, cobblestone streets are impossibly quaint. Nicely set apart from the busier towns to the north and south, it is a dreamy place with a special magic and makes for a charming lake base. Most beguiling of all is the east-facing waterfront promenade. Its central stretch, the elongated **Piazza di Vittorio Emanuele III** (closed off at its north end by the Bramante-style Santuario della Pietà church), has pastel-hued houses that overlook the pedestrian-only flagstone square across to the hills of the east shore. There's no shortage of places to enjoy breakfast here, bathed in the morning sun. A series of restaurants and cafes occupy the houses' ground floors and spill on to the square. Wandering the web of lanes that makes up the old town is a pleasant way to while away your time, although specific sights are few and far between. You can take sailing and windsurfing lessons at **Tomaso Surf & Sail** ( ☎ 0323 7 22 14; www.tomaso.com; Via Nazionale 7), next to a patch of gritty beach at the village's northern end. You can also hire small sailing boats here (at €120 a day).

### ☙ VAL CANNOBINA // CYCLE ALONG A TWISTING MOUNTAIN VALLEY

The narrow, scenic SP75 road winds its way 28km, following the surging Torrente Cannobino stream, into the heavily wooded hills west of Cannobio to reach **Malesco** in Valle Vigezzo (the Italian side of the Centovalli, see p76). One way to discover its villages, poking out here and there from the forest, is to hire a mountain bike in Cannobio from **Cicli Prezan** ( ☎ 0323 7 12 30; www.cicliprezan.it; Viale Vittorio Veneto 9; mountain bike per hr/day €4/14). Just 2.5km along the valley from Cannobio, in Sant'Anna, the Torrente Cannobio forces its way powerfully through a narrow gorge known as the **Orrido di Sant'Anna**, crossed at its narrowest part by a cute Romanesque bridge, and can be viewed from a restaurant (p84). A series of stone villages lines the valley, rarely visited by tourists. About 7km further up the valley, a steep 3km side road consisting of hairpin bends leads up to the central valley's main town, **Falmenta** (666m – they say the town's priest would like to have 1m added to or subtracted from the official figure). About 150 people live here (most work over the border in Switzerland) and many of the houses are holiday residences owned by Germans. It's pleasant to wander around and worth a lunch stop (p83). About 6km east of Malesco, the old road has been replaced by two tunnels. On the abandoned stretch is a memorial to partisans killed in a German ambush in October 1944. For a brief period, this area belonged to the so-called Repubblica d'Ossola, a chunk of partisan-controlled territory that fell to occupying German forces when they marched into Domodossola on 14 October after months of fighting (see also p84).

### ☙ GHIFFA'S SACRED MOUNT // REST AT A HOLY, SHADY SANCTUARY

Ghiffa is a blip of a village 4km northeast of Verbania. The main reason for stopping is to make a minor pilgrimage 3km inland and uphill (by road – a stone-paved walking trail is a little shorter and steeper) to the **Sacro Monte della Santissima Trinità**. This holy mount was laid out in the mid-17th century but apparently it was not completed. The lovely tree-filled sanctuary, including its church and a couple of chapels (not to mention the handy restaurant) is sited within a small nature reserve and provides a balcony view over Lake Maggiore below (albeit partly obscured by the thick foliage). One chapel on the walking path (about 100m away) was completed but, presumably, a series of them, running all the way downhill, was originally planned. Hikers have plenty of paths to choose from around here. The **Via delle Genti**, an historic walking path that has connected Switzerland and northern Italy via the St Gotthard pass for centuries, passes by here (it's almost a 1½-hour walk to Verbania). Other signed walking paths abound – for more information, ask at Verbania's tourist office (p79).

### ☙ VERBANIA // SEE FLOWERS BLOOM AT VILLA TARANTO

**Verbania** (population 30,940), the biggest town on the lake, is split into three

districts. Verbania Pallanza, the middle chunk, is the most interesting of the three, while Verbania Intra has a pleasant enough waterfront and handy car ferries to Laveno on the lake's east bank. Pallanza's highlight is the grounds of the late-19th-century **Villa Taranto** ( ☎ 0323 40 45 55; www.villataranto.it; Via Vittorio Veneto; adult/child €9/5.50; ☺ 8.30am-6.30pm Mar-Sep, to 5pm Oct). In 1931 royal archer and Scottish captain Neil McEacharn bought the Normandy-style villa from the Savoy family after spotting an ad in the *Times*. He planted some 20,000 species over 30 years, and today it is considered one of Europe's finest botanic gardens. The main entrance path is a grand affair, bordered by a strip of lawn and a cornucopia of colourful flowers. Depending on when you visit, the experience will differ. The winding dahlia path, for instance, shows off blooms from more than 300 species from June to October. In April and May, the dogwood and related flowers run riot. In the hothouses you can admire extraordinary, equatorial water lilies. The villa itself is not open to the public. Boats stop at Pallanza and at the landing stage in front of the villa. Just west of the villa and its grounds is the mess of streets and lanes that constitutes the old heart of Pallanza, nice for a little aimless strolling. The waterfront road, Via Vittorio Veneto, has a jogging and cycling path that follows the lakefront, which is especially pretty around the little port and the nearby **Isolino San Giovanni**, a wooded islet moored just off the shore.

### ☙ STRESA // TAKE A BELLE ÉPOQUE STROLL

Perhaps of all Lake Maggiore's towns, **Stresa** (population 5180) maintains the most belle époque air, along with a ringside view of sunrise over the lake.

The town's easy access from Milan has made it a favourite for artists and writers since the late 19th century. Hemingway was one of many who visited; he arrived in Stresa in 1918 to convalesce from a war wound. A couple of pivotal scenes towards the end of his novel *A Farewell to Arms* are set at the **Grand Hôtel des Iles Borromées**, the most palatial of the historic hotels (others include the Grand Hotel Bristol and the Regina Palace) garlanding the lake. People still stream into Stresa to meander along its promenade and explore the little hive of cobbled streets in its old centre (especially pleasant for a coffee break is shady **Piazza Cadorna**). The little pebble beach just west of the main ferry dock is good for a sunbathe.

### ❤ PARCO DELLA VILLA PALLAVICINO // SAY HELLO TO THE ANIMALS

Barely 1km southeast of central Stresa along the SS33 main road, exotic birds and animals roam relatively freely at the child-friendly **Parco della Villa Pallavicino** ( ☎ 0323 3 15 33; www.parcozoopallavicino

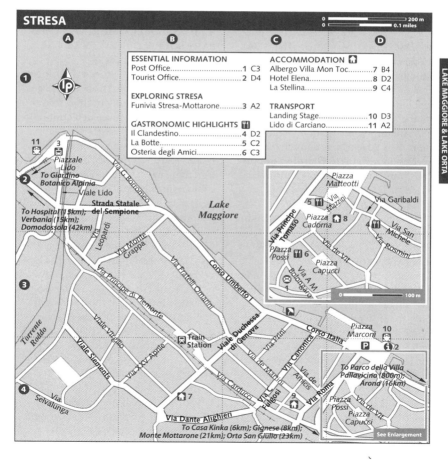

STRESA

0 ─── 200 m
0 ─── 0.1 miles

ESSENTIAL INFORMATION
Post Office.............................1 C3
Tourist Office.........................2 D4

EXPLORING STRESA
Funivia Stresa-Mottarone.........3 A2

GASTRONOMIC HIGHLIGHTS
Il Clandestino.........................4 D2
La Botte.................................5 C2
Osteria degli Amici..................6 C3

ACCOMMODATION
Albergo Villa Mon Toc...........7 B4
Hotel Elena............................8 D2
La Stellina............................9 C4

TRANSPORT
Landing Stage.......................10 D3
Lido di Carciano...................11 A2

.it, in Italian; adult/child €9/6; ☻ 9am-6pm Mar-Oct). Some 40 species of animal, including llamas, Sardinian donkeys, flamingos, toucans keep everyone amused.

### ☙ MONTE MOTTARONE // ENJOY ALPINE VIEWS AND SUB-ALPINE FLORA

The mountain that rises about halfway between Stresa and Lake Orta provides a full day's diversion for everyone. Walkers, skiers, botany fans and sightseers are all catered for.

Captivating views of the lake unfold during a 20-minute cable-car journey on the **Funivia Stresa-Mottarone** (☎ 0323 3 02 95; www.stresa-mottarone.it; Piazzale Lido; return adult/child €17.50/11; ☻ departs every 20min 9.30am-5.30pm May-Oct) to the top of 1491m-high Monte Mottarone. On a clear day you can see Lake Maggiore, Lake Orta, several other smaller lakes and Monte Rosa, on the Alpine border with Switzerland.

At the Alpino midstation (803m), more than 1000 Alpine and sub-Alpine species flourish in the **Giardino Botanico Alpinia** (☎ 0323 3 02 95; www.giardinoalpinia .it; adult/child €2/1.50; ☻ 9.30am-6pm Apr-Oct), a botanic garden dating from 1934.

The mountain itself offers good **biking trails** as well as **walking** opportunities. **Bicicò** (☎ 0323 3 03 99; www.bicico.it) rents out mountain bikes at the lower Stresa cable-car station. Rates include a helmet and road book detailing a 25km panoramic descent (about three hours, of which only about 30 minutes require slight ascents, thus making it accessible to pretty much anyone who can ride a bike) from the top of Mottarone back to Stresa. A one-way trip with a bike on the cable car to Alpino/Mottarone costs €7/10.

Walkers can ask at the cable-car station for a free copy of *Trekking on the Slopes of Mount Mottarone,* which outlines a two-hour walk from Stresa to the Giardino Botanico Alpinia and a four-hour walk to the top of Mottarone.

Skiing Mottarone's gentle slopes is limited to five green and two blue slopes, making it good for beginners. Gear can be hired from the station at the top of Mottarone. The **skipass** (www.mottaroneski .it; return adult/child €23/17.50) includes the cost of the cable car and you can hire gear at the top. Since 2008 it has been possible to ski in summer too: on a green synthetic-grass piste unrolled from June to September. For €15, you can hire the necessary gear and use the slope all day.

### ☙ MUSEO DELL'OMBRELLO E DEL PARASOLE // DISCOVER LOCAL UMBRELLA HISTORY

Those driving to Mottarone or Orta San Giulio (for Lake Orta) from Stresa could stop in Gignese (8km out from Stresa) for the intriguing **Museo dell'Ombrello e del Parasole** (Umbrella and Parasol Museum; ☎ 0323 20 80 64; Via Panorama Golf 2; admission €2.50; ☻ 10am-noon & 3-6pm Tue-Sun). The building is nothing to write home about but the contents are original. Some folks in these parts once made a living from handmade parasols and umbrellas, and later small-scale industrial production. The parasol became an indispensable part of ladies' fashion in the mid-19th century, as Romanticism dictated that my fair lady had indeed to be fair. This passion for pallor wore off only from the 1920s onwards. The museum has more than 1000 items, of which only a part is on show. Starting with tiny parasols from the 1850s, the gamut runs to more-modern umbrellas up until about the time of WWII. It is startling what work once went into these items, with carved ivory handles, printed silk covers and intricate lace decoration for fancier ones.

## ❤ LAKE MAGGIORE ADVENTURE PARK // THRILLS, SPILLS AND LAKE VIEWS

Heading 4km north of Stresa brings you to **Baveno** (population 4860), an attractive lakeside town with shady promenade, the lovely 11th-century Romanesque **Chiesa di SS Gervaso e Protaso**, good ferry links to the Borromean Islands, and a fistful of hotels and eateries. Aside from a stroll here, the real attraction for those with energy to burn (or kids with same) is the **Lake Maggiore Adventure Park** ( ☎ 0323 91 97 99; www.sport-fun.info; Strada Cavalli 18, Baveno; full course adult/child €22/15; ☺ 10am-4pm Mar-May & Sep-Oct, 10am-11pm Jul-Aug). Thrills and spills include suspension courses, an artificial climbing wall, a trampoline 'acro-jump', and a cycling course with jumps. Its cafe has stunning lake views from the patio. The park is located just north of Baveno and south of Feriolo.

## ❤ ARONA // CLIMB INSIDE A SAINTLY BRONZE STATUE

It was in **Arona** (population 14,370), 20km south of Stresa, that the son of the Count of Arona and Margherita de' Medici, who would go on to be canonised San Carlo Borromeo (1538–84), was born. In 1610 he was declared a saint and his cousin, Federico, ordered the creation of a *sacro monte,* with 15 chapels lining a path uphill to a church dedicated to the saint. The church and three of the chapels were built, along with a special extra atop the **Sacro Monte di San Carlo** (admission €4; ☺ 9am-12.30pm & 2-6.15pm daily Apr-Sep, Sat & Sun only Oct, 9am-12.30pm & 2-4.30pm Sat & Sun Mar & Nov-Dec): a hollow, 35m bronze-and-copper statue of the saint. Commonly known as the Sancarlone (Big St Charles) or the Colosso di San Carlo (St Charles Colossus) and erected between 1614 and 1698, it can be climbed, affording a spectacular view from the top. You climb spiral stairs to a platform surrounding the giant's feet. There you will be handed a miner's-type helmet and wait in a queue to head up. It's a bit of a vertiginous ascent and children under six years old are not allowed up. To reach this hill, with nice views over the south end of Lake Maggiore and across to the Rocca di Angera (p88), walk or drive about 2km west from Piazza del Popolo, Arona's most charming piazza. The broad square with its little marina, sits pretty on the lake and offers several restaurants and cafes for a post-Sancarlone break.

## FESTIVALS & EVENTS

**Mostra Nazionale della Camelia** (www .camelieinmostra.it) Twice a year, in spring and autumn, a splash of extra floral colour comes to Verbania Pallanza with a display of more than 200 varieties of camellia in the gardens of Villa Giulia ( ☎ 0323 55 62 81; Corso Zanitello 8) or Villa Rusconi-Clerici (www.villarusconiclerici .it; Via Vittorio Veneto) or both. Dates vary, but you are looking at a weekend in late March and late November. **Settimana del Tulipano** In the last week of April, tens of thousands of tulips erupt in magnificent multicoloured bloom in Verbania's Villa Taranto.

## GASTRONOMIC HIGHLIGHTS

### ❤ CIRCOLO FALMENTA // FALMENTA €€

☎ 338 383 9867; meals €30-35; ☺ Tue-Sun Head along pedestrian Via Roma in this high valley town and you emerge in the church square. The post office building hides, on the first floor, this one-time social centre turned simple eatery. You can wander in anytime and Carlo will prepare something (if you are not in a rush). Otherwise, it's better to call the day before and he'll get in the ingredients of a fish- or meat-grill feast. Ask him what he can do and what it will cost, then sit back and wait. You can sit inside or pull up a plastic chair and table in the square, and admire the endless-valley view.

### ❦ GROTTO SANT'ANNA // ORRIDO SANT'ANNA €€

☎ 0323 7 06 82; Via Sant'Anna; meals €30-35; ☽ Tue-Sun Apr-Jun & Sep-Oct, daily Jul-Aug
This Ticino-style grotto overlooks the thundering gorge that is the Orrido di Sant'Anna. Granite tables and benches located under a thick-leaved pergola provide a ringside seat to this natural

phenomenon. If you can take your eyes off the water, dig into a dish of *fagottini di asparagi e ricotta su crema di gamberi* (pasta stuffed with asparagus and ricotta on a creamy, prawn bed), followed perhaps by grilled lake-whitefish or oven-cooked lamb.

### ❦ IL CLANDESTINO // STRESA €€

☎ 0323 3 03 99; Via Rosmini 5; meals €30; ☽ Wed-Mon
An elegant, corner dining room decorated with parquet floors, creamy white linen, soft music and a largely seafood

## PARCO NAZIONALE VAL GRANDE

A wooded wilderness set amid a little-visited stretch of the Italian Alps, the **Parco Nazionale Val Grande** ( ☎ 0324 8 75 40; www.parcovalgrande.it) offers the chance to dive into nature that is far removed from the more domesticated beauty of the lakes, yet geographically it is only a short distance (Verbania is barely 10km away from its southeastern edge). Declared a park in 1992, it covers 150 sq km.

Never more than sparsely inhabited by farmers in search of summer pastures for cattle and loggers, the area has been largely free of human inhabitants since the 1940s. The last of them were partisans who fought the Germans in the latter half of WWII. (In June to October 1944, 5000 German troops moved against 500 partisans holed up in the Val Grande, killing 300 of them and destroying farms across the area.) All around the park, however, are villages of neighbouring valleys, which allow for a peaceful stopover.

The lower Val Grande is dominated by chestnut trees, which give way to beech trees further up. Milan's Duomo had a special licence to log here from the 14th century. Wood was needed in the Candoglia marble quarries, to float the marble on canals to Milan and for use in scaffolding.

The virtual total absence of humans in the park today makes it unique in Italy, and safe ground for animals. Most numerous is the chamois, and Peregrine falcons and golden eagles can be spotted.

Information centres are located in five villages surrounding the park. The handiest for those staying around Lake Maggiore are Intragna and Cicogna (both near Verbania), the latter actually inside the park boundary. They tend to open only in spring and summer – call the main number for opening hours. Walks into the park will bring you to some majestic locations but as a rule should be done with local guides. Extremely basic, unstaffed refuges where you can sleep (if you have your own sleeping bag) dot the park. They come with a stove and wood for heating, and little else. Otherwise, some much easier *sentieri natura* (nature paths) have been staked out. Routes are available at the information centres and on the website.

menu, Il Clandestino is worth searching out. Some dishes have a Sicilian touch, as evidenced by the source of the raw materials. A nice starter would be *scampi e gamberi di Sicilia nel raviolo di farro biologico* (Sicilian prawns and scampi in a big raviolo of organic pasta). It does some excellent lake-fish dishes too, but no red meat.

### ❦ IL CORTILE // CANNERO RIVIERA €€

☎ 0323 78 72 13; www.cortile.net; Via Massimo d'Azeglio 73; meals €35-45; ☒ Thu-Tue

Just a few metres back from the lake in the town of Cannero Riviera (7km south of Cannobio), the Courtyard is what it says it is: a tranquil courtyard inside a charmingly decked out hotel. The menu fairly bristles with original takes on northern Italian classics, such as the *risotto al brut di Franciacorta con dadolata di scamorza affumicata* (risotto done in Franciacorta sparkling wine with cubes of smoked scamorza cheese) or the *scaloppa di foie gras su riso nero di Venere e lamelle di tartuffo* (foie gras escalope in black rice and truffle shavings).

### ❦ LA BOTTE // STRESA €€

☎ 0323 3 04 62; Via Mazzini 6; meals €25; ☒ Fri-Wed

Polenta is at the heart of this Piedmontese trattoria's business. This is a good one to look for on cooler days, as it serves up all sorts of regional dishes that will warm the cockles of your heart. The location is an unchanged traditional *osteria* just in from the lakefront, with simple, dark timber furniture and decades of accumulated baubles hanging on the walls. The *lavarello spaccato alla piastra alle erbe fini* (a tasty boned and grilled whitefish in herbs) is a light option, or

opt for the heavy artillery with *filettini di vitello con fonduta di Gorgonzola* (little veal filets in a Gorgonzola cheese melt).

### ❦ LO SCALO // CANNOBIO €€€

☎ 0323 7 14 80; www.loscalo.com; Piazza Vittorio Emanuele III 32; meals €60-70; ☒ lunch & dinner Wed-Sun, dinner Tue

For an elegant and romantic dinner, it is hard to beat this lakefront high-flyer. The setting is perfect, and inside Lo Scalo is as tempting as being outside on the square is. Candlelit intimacy is assured. Start with delicate *tagliolini neri, seppioline, zucchine e filetti di pomodoro* (thin ribbon pasta with cuttlefish, zucchini and sliced tomato) and proceed to anything from lake fish in an almond crust to roast guinea fowl (*faraona*).

### ❦ OSTERIA DEGLI AMICI // STRESA €

☎ 0323 3 04 53; Via Anna Maria Bolongaro 33; pizzas €4.50-9, meals €25

You may need to queue (it's always packed), but it's worth it to dine under vines on one of Stresa's most delightful terraces in the centre of town, set just off pedestrianised Via Mazzini. If it's a little cool for sitting outside, the indoor dining room, with its canary-yellow paint job and round tables, is an equally good setting for getting stuck into a pizza.

### ❦ RISTORANTE MILANO // VERBANIA PALLANZA €€€

☎ 0323 55 68 16; Corso Zanitello 2; meals €60-80; ☒ lunch & dinner Wed-Sun, lunch Mon

It is difficult to imagine a prettier setting for a meal. Antique-filled Ristorante Milano sits off its own shady gravel-and-lawn garden where a handful of tables are set up and birdsong provides the background music. It overlooks Verbania Pallanza's cute port and Isolino San

Giovanni. The cuisine is broadly Italian, such as *gamberi di Sicilia con crema di ceci* (Sicilian prawns in chickpea cream) and *coregone affumicato con salsa di mele* (smoked lake whitefish in apple sauce).

## TRANSPORT

**CAR //** Coming from Milan, take the A8/A26 motorway, following signs for Gravellona. To follow the lake road, exit the autostrada at Castelleto del Ticino. From there, the SS33 hugs the shore to Arona, Stresa and Baveno. From Feriolo, the SS34 continues the lakeside run to the Swiss border (where it becomes route 13 to Locarno and beyond).

**PARKING //** Parking in Arona, Stresa and Verbania can require patience and is mostly metered.

**TRAIN //** Stresa is on the Domodossola–Milan train line. Domodossola (€3 to €7.60), 30 minutes northwest, is on the Swiss border, from where the train line leads to Brig and on to Geneva.

**BUS //** Buses leave from the waterfront at Stresa for destinations around the lake and elsewhere, including Milan, Novara and Lake Orta. The daily Verbania–Milan intercity bus service operated by **SAF** ( ☎ 0323 55 21 72; www.safduemila.com, in Italian) links Stresa with Arona (€2; 20 minutes), Verbania Pallanza (€2; 20 minutes) and Verbania Intra (€2; 25 minutes), all €2; and Milan (€6.70, 1½ hours).

**BOAT //** Boats connect Stresa with Arona (one way adult/child €7.40/4, 40 minutes), Angera (€7.40/4, 35 minutes), Baveno (€4.90/2.80, 20 minutes) and Verbania Pallanza (€6.30/3.50, 35 minutes).

# BORROMEAN ISLANDS

Forming Lake Maggiore's most beautiful corner, the Borromean Islands (Isole Borromee) can be reached from various points around the lake, but Stresa and Baveno offer the best access. Three of the four islands – Bella, Madre and Superiore (aka dei Pescatori) – can all be visited, but tiny San Giovanni is off limits.

## TOP FIVE

**GARDENS**

★ **Isola Bella** (below)

★ **Isola Madre** (opposite)

★ **Villa Taranto** (p80)

★ **Villa della Porta Bozzolo** (p89)

★ **Giardino Botanico Alpinia** (p82)

## EXPLORING THE BORROMEAN ISLANDS

❦ **ISOLA BELLA // SWOON BEFORE THE PALACE AND ITS GARDENS**
Isola Bella took the name of Carlo III's wife, the *bella* Isabella, in the 17th century, when its centrepiece, **Palazzo Borromeo** ( ☎ 0323 3 05 56; www.borromeoturismo.it; adult/child €12/5; ⏱ 9am-5.30pm Apr–mid-Oct), was built for the Borromeo family. It's hard to imagine that, prior to its construction, the island was little more than a chunk of rock inhabited by a handful of hardy fishing families. To this day, only 16 people live year-round on the island, but in summer the place looks like a scene from the Normandy landings of 1944, with countless vessels ferrying battalions of visitors to and fro. Construction of the villa and gardens was thought out in such a way that the island would have the vague appearance of a vessel, with the villa at the prow and the gardens at the rear.

Well-known guests have included Napoleon and Josephine in 1797 (you can see the bed they slept in), and Prince Charles and Princess Di in 1985. Presiding over 10 tiers of terraced gardens, the baroque palace remains private property. In summer, the family who owns it moves in and occupies the 2nd and 3rd floors (off limits to visitors), totalling a mere 50-odd rooms. Visitors can see the ground and 1st floors, the latter also known as the 'noble' floor. As was typical in such mansions, the noble floor was largely one of representation, including guestrooms, ballrooms, studies and reception halls. Beneath a 23m-high ceiling in the Salone Grande (part of the ballroom) is a 200-year-old wooden model of the palace and island.

### Picture Gallery

A separate €4 ticket gains access to the recently reopened **Galleria dei Quadri** (Picture Gallery), a hall in which the walls are covered from top to bottom with 130 paintings of the Borromeo collection. There seems to be little rhyme or reason to the arrangement and the more closely you scan the walls, the more likely you are to see pieces by several Old Masters, including Rubens, Titian, Paolo Veronese, Andrea Mantegna or José Ribera (Spagnoletto). Elsewhere in the building are scattered further works of art, as well as Flemish tapestries and sculptures by Antonio Canova.

Below, a 3000-year-old fossilised boat is displayed behind glass in the cool palace *grotti*. The grottoes are studded with pink marble, lava stone, and pebbles from the lakebed. White peacocks, whose fanned feathers resemble bridal gowns, strut about the gardens, considered one of the finest examples of a baroque Italian garden design. A combined ticket covering admission to the Borromeo and Madre palaces (on Isola Madre) costs €16.50/7.50 per adult/child.

### 🐾 ISOLA MADRE // ADMIRE AN ENGLISH GARDEN AND THE COUNTESS' DOLLS

All of Isola Madre is taken up by the 16th- to 18th-century **Palazzo Madre**

( ☎ 0323 3 05 56; adult/child €10/5, Mar–Oct). The gardens were even ish than those of Palazzo Borrome Isola Bella. In late June 2006, howeve a tornado struck the island, uprooting many of the island's prized palms and other plants. Nevertheless, this English-style botanic garden is full of interest, with azaleas, rhododendrons, camellias, eucalypts, banana trees, hibiscus, fruit orchards, an olive grove and much more. The palace itself was unscathed by the 2006 storm: interior highlights include Countess Borromeo's doll collection, a neoclassical puppet theatre designed by a scenographer from Milan's La Scala, and 'horror' theatre with a cast of devilish marionettes. A combined garden-and-palazzo ticket costs €16.50/7.50 per adult/child.

### 🐾 ISOLA SUPERIORE (PESCATORI) // ABSORB THE ATMOSPHERE OF A FISHING ISLAND

Tiny 'Fishermen's Island', with an absence of souvenir stalls, retains much of its original fishing-village atmosphere. About 50 people live here full-time. Apart from an 11th-century apse and a 16th-century fresco in the charming **Chiesa di San Vittore**, there are no real sights. Many visitors make it their port of call for lunch, and some brave souls take a dip in the waters on its north side. Restaurants cluster around the boat landing, all serving grilled fish fresh from the lake from around €15. On some days in spring and autumn, abundant rainfalls can lift the lake's level a fraction, causing minor flooding on the island. The houses are built with this in mind, with entrance stairs facing internal streets and they're high enough to prevent water entering the houses.

## GASTRONOMIC HIGHLIGHTS

### ❦ CASABELLA // ISOLA SUPERIORE (PESCATORI) €€

☎ 0323 3 34 71; Via del Marinaio 1; meals €40; ⊙ Feb-Nov

With room for about 40 people, this spot is warmly recommended by locals. Lots of timber panelling, well spread-out tables and fine white linen abound, and some sort of lake view is inevitable from almost wherever you sit. Better still, it has a handful of tables set up outside that overlook the water. The menu is rich in variety, with a good stock of lake-whitefish on order. For those who don't want to leave, it has two rooms.

### ❦ ELVEZIA // ISOLA BELLA €€

☎ 0323 3 00 43; www.elvezia.it; Isola Bella; meals €30-35; ⊙ Wed-Sun Mar-Oct, Fri-Sun Nov-Feb

With its rambling rooms, fish-themed portico and upstairs pergola and balcony dining area, this is the best spot on the island for home cooking. It serves pastas including ricotta-stuffed ravioli, various risottos and a hearty lasagne, as well as lake fish such as *coregone alle mandorle* (lake-whitefish in almonds). Booking ahead is essential for winter dinners.

## TRANSPORT

**BOAT //** Ferries chug to the islands from Stresa (the main dock), Lido di Carciano (by the Stresa–Mottarone cable car) and Verbania Pallanza. Isola Bella and Isola Superiore are close to Stresa, while Verbania Pallanza is handier for Isola Madre. Services connect them all but more regular half-hourly runs connect Stresa, Isola Bella, Isola Superiore and Baveno. Depending on which island you are heading for and from where, one-way tickets cost from €2.90 to €4.40. Return tickets are double. A day ticket (€9.80) allows unlimited travel between Stresa, Baveno, Isola Bella and Isola Superiore (aka dei Pescatori). A day ticket including these islands and Isola Madre costs €12 . More expensive one-day passes include admission to the various villas.

# LAKE MAGGIORE EAST BANK

## ESSENTIAL INFORMATION

**TOURIST OFFICES // Laveno Tourist Office** (☎ 0332 66 87 85; Piazza Italia 6; ⊙ 9.30am-1pm & 2.30-5pm Tue-Sun) Walkers should ask for the free Via Verde Varesina map (1:35,000), with various hiking trails marked.

## EXPLORING LAKE MAGGIORE EAST BANK

### ❦ ROCCA DI ANGERA // CHECK OUT THE DOLLS IN A FORTRESS

The chunky medieval **Rocca di Angera** (Map pp72–3) fortress lords it over the town of Angera in no uncertain terms. From a distance, it is the first thing one sees. Inside is the 12-room **Museo della Bambola** (Doll Museum; ☎ 0331 93 13 00; adult/child €7.50/4.50; ⊙ 9am-5.30pm Apr–mid-Oct), displaying the Borromeo family's priceless collection of dolls. What better place for them than this towering, fairy-tale castle with its high, crenellated walls atop a rocky outcrop? Modest vineyards cling to the slopes around it. The Borromeo clan bought it from Milan's Visconti family in 1449. Various rooms and halls open on to the courtyard, among them the awe-inspiring Sala della Giustizia (Hall of Justice), with its overarching vault and lively 13th-century frescos. From the tower you have breathtaking views. The doll collection counts more than 1000 items, while a separate collection of French and German mechanical dolls and figurines (dating from 1870 to 1920) becomes highly amusing when they are set in sometimes noisy motion. A combined ticket including Isola Bella and Isola Madre is adult/child €20/10. The easiest way up is by car (signposted from the centre of Angera). By foot, fol-

LAKE MAGGIORE & LAKE ORTA

low the signs from Piazza Parrocchiale. The rest of Angera repays a stroll too. The shady waterfront is speckled with villas and old fishing families' houses.

### ❦ MUSEO EUROPEO DEI TRASPORTI // ALL ABOARD TRICYCLES AND STEAM TRAINS

Just outside the tranquil lake town of **Ranco** lurks this eccentric **Museo Europeo dei Trasporti** (European Transport Museum; ☎ 0331 97 51 98; Via Alberto 99, Ranco; admission free; ⏱ 10am-noon & 3-6pm Tue-Sun), fun for anyone who likes machines and it's potentially a great distraction for kids. Collection items stretching from the 1800s include a tricycle, various horse-drawn carriages from around Europe and beyond, a double-decker horse-drawn tram from Milan and a strange wind-powered tram with sail (which generally had to be dragged along by horses or oxen). Among the various steam-train locomotives and cars, there is one that was put at the personal disposal of the composer Giuseppe Verdi. Among the buses is a wonderful 1912 Fiat. Also on show are cable cars, hot-air balloons and the recreation of a Milan metro stop.

### ❦ SANTA CATERINA DEL SASSO // VISIT A CLIFFSIDE MONASTERY

The monastery of **Santa Caterina del Sasso** (admission free; ⏱ 8.30am-noon & 2.30-6pm) is one of the most spectacularly located such places in northern Italy. Clinging to the high rocky face of the southeast shore of Lake Maggiore, it is reached by a spiralling stairway (a lift is being built too) from 60m above. First news of this convent came in the 13th century, when Dominican friars founded it, and bits were tacked on subsequently down the centuries. It was abandoned in the course of the 20th century. You enter by a por-

tico overlooking the lake, pass through the south monastery and a small courtyard (with an 18th-century winepress), which leads into another Gothic portico. A 16th-century fresco series depicting the *Danza macabra* (Dance of Death) can still be made out on its upper level. Finally you reach the church, fronted by a four-arch portico. The church is a curious affair; it's actually the cobbling together of a series of 13th- and 14th-century chapels that form an oddly shaped whole. Inside, you behold a carnival of frescos, among them the Christ Pantocrator in the Cappella di San Nicola, the first chapel on the right upon entering. Ferries from Stresa (return €5.80) call here irregularly. Otherwise, by car or bus it's 6.5km south of Laveno (watch for the signs for Leggiuno and then a sign for the convent, 1km in off the main road).

### ❦ LAVENO FUNIVIA // TAKE IN THE VIEW OR GO HANG-GLIDING

Laveno is a pleasant enough lakeside town but the main reason for coming is to take the **Funivia** (adult/child €9/6.50; ⏱ 10.30am-6pm Mon-Sat, 10am-6.30pm Sun & holidays), which whisks you up to a panoramic beauty spot 949m above sea level, in the shadow of the **Sasso del Ferro** peak (1062m). The views over the lake and beyond to the Alps are breathtaking. Does that all seem a bit bland? Extreme-sports enthusiasts can approach **Icaro 2000** (☎ 0332 64 83 35; www.icaro2000.com; basic hang-gliding course €900) about doing a hang-gliding course here, as the terminus of the Funivia is a popular launch spot for hang-gliders.

### ❦ VILLA DELLA PORTA BOZZOLO // CALL BY A 17TH-CENTURY NOBLE HOME

In the unassuming town of **Casalzuigno**, about 9km east of Laveno, generations of

nobles have swanned about the magnificent gardens of **Villa della Porta Bozzolo** ( ☎ 0332 62 41 36; www.fondoambiente.it; adult/
child €5/2.50; ☺ 10am-6pm Wed-Sun Mar-Sep, to 5pm
Wed-Sun Oct-Feb), completed in 1690. The
grand, two-storey building, surrounded
by various outbuildings, has a calm, self-
assured feel. Inside, the ballroom and
upstairs gallery are richly decorated with
frescos. The cool, dark library, with its
18th-century walnut book cabinets, is
only open on Sundays. Outside, fine Italianate gardens create a pleasing world of
natural harmony.

### ❧ MARKET DAY IN LUINO // JOIN THE SHOPPING CROWDS FROM AFAR

The otherwise dull town of Luino becomes something of a consumers' mad-
house on the day of the **mercato** (market;
☺ 8.30am-4.30pm Wed). This is no ordinary
local flea market but rather an enormous
bazaar. The records show that an important weekly market was first held here in
1535. Today more than 350 stands are
set up in the old town centre, with everything from local cheese to second-hand
fashion on sale. Bargain-hunters come
from as far away as the Netherlands and
it is madness if you try to get in here with
a vehicle (unless you arrive very early).
Extra ferry services from the other side
of the lake are put on and either way, it
is probably best to approach Luino by
public transport (trains and buses travelling up and down the lake are another
option).

### ❧ PARCO BOTANICO DEL GAMBAROGNO // SWOON AMID THE SPRING FLOWERS

In the hills above Vira, about 8km north
of the Switzerland–Italy border and
16.5km southeast of Locarno spread the
heady gardens of the **Gambarogno Botanic Gardens** ( ☎ 091 795 18 66; www.parco
botanico.ch; admission Sfr5; ☺ daily). Hundreds of
types of azalea, camellia, magnolia, rho-
dodendron and other spring and summer
flowers fill the air with their vivid colours
and intoxicating perfumes. The owners
sell plants too. Simply wander in at any
time (there seems to be no real closing
time) and pop a Sfr5 coin into the box at
the entrance (it works on a trust system),
then wander around. The gardens are
located at the north end of the village of
Piazzogna. From Locarno, you need to
take a ferry to Magadino and pick up a
local bus to Piazzogna, from where it is a
short walk. The trip takes 45 minutes. By
car, head for Piazzogna from either Vira
or San Nazzaro (about 2.5km either way).

## GASTRONOMIC HIGHLIGHTS

### ❧ HOTEL LIDO ANGERA // ANGERA €€

☎ 0331 93 02 32; www.hotellido.it; Viale Libertà 11;
meals €45; ☺ lunch & dinner Tue-Sun, dinner Mon
If you like fresh lake fish then this is the
place to come and indulge. Set right on
the lake and surrounded by greenery, this
hotel-restaurant serves up an original
sushi platter of Lake Maggiore fish as a
starter, followed by a mix of classical local
dishes with a contemporary spin, especially in the pleasing presentation. The wine
list is broad, including products from all
over the country. Grab a table by the large
windows, gaze over the lake and enjoy.

### ❧ IL SOLE // RANCO €€€

☎ 0331 97 65 07; www.ilsolediranco.it; Piazza Venezia 5; meals €80-100; ☺ Wed-Sun
Aside from the transport museum (p89),
the main thing to do in Ranco is call by
this fantastic restaurant, with its lake
views, beautiful garden and even better grub. Some local critics consider it

among the best in Italy. It's difficult to choose: a risotto with Parmesan froth? Or perhaps the heavenly light *fritto misto* (mixed fried fish and seafood)? Leave the thinking up to staff and opt for one of the tasting menus at €80. Oh, and it has rooms too.

## TRANSPORT

**CAR //** The A26 tollway from Milan arrives at the south end of Lake Maggiore at Sesto Calende. From there you exit and follow the SP69 north (it becomes the SS394 at Luino).

**BOAT //** Ferries call in at all the lakeside stops mentioned in this section. This can be slow-going but some runs are handy, like the Stresa ferry to Santa Caterina del Sasso and the car ferry linking Laveno with Verbania Intra (on the western shore).

**TRAIN //** Trains from Milan serve the east shore of Lake Maggiore. FNM trains from Milan (Cadorna station) arrive in Laveno via Varese.

**BUS //** Local buses shuttle up and down the east bank of the lake. For Santa Caterina del Sasso, jump on one of the buses running between Laveno and Ispra.

# VARESE & AROUND

· · · · · ·

**Spread out between Lakes Maggiore and Como province, Varese and the area around it has several remarkable surprises in store for the curious traveller. Its treasures include the beautiful gardens of the city's modest imitation of Versailles, a series of three small lakes and the extraordinary 17th-century *sacro monte,* a kind of pilgrim's Via Crucis that leads you to magnificent views and fine food at a great height. It is well worth cutting inland away from the shores of Lake Maggiore to investigate.**

# ESSENTIAL INFORMATION

**TOURIST OFFICE // Varese Tourist Office** ( ☎ 0332 28 36 04; www.vareseturismo.it, www .vareselandoftourism.it; Via Carrobbio 2; ⏲ 9.30am-12.30pm & 2.30-5pm Mon-Thu, 9am-12.30 Fri & Sat)

# EXPLORING VARESE & AROUND

### ♟ PALAZZO ESTENSE // VISIT THE 'VERSAILLES OF MILAN'

Spread out to the south of the Campo dei Fiori hills, **Varese** is a prosperous provincial capital. From the 17th century, nobles and the rich, many from Milan, began to build second residences around the historic centre. Of these, the most sumptuous is the **Palazzo Estense**, completed in 1771 for Francesco III d'Este, the Austrian-appointed governor of the Duchy of Milan. From Via Sacco, the main entrance, you'd hardly know what it was, as the main graceful facade actually looks south onto the beautiful Italianate **Giardini Estensi** ( ⏲ 8am-dusk). The building now belongs to the town hall and cannot be visited, but anyone may swan through the entrance into the gardens, punctuated by ponds and, hidden on a rise behind Villa Mirabello, is a giant cedar of Lebanon. Villa Mirabello and its gardens, now fused with the Giardini Estensi, was once a separate property.

**Villa Mirabello** houses the city's main **museum** ( ⏲ 10am-12.30pm & 2-6pm Tue-Sun Jun-Oct, 9.30am-12.30pm & 2-5.30pm Nov-May), of which only a modest section with Roman remnants is open.

To get to the Palazzo Estense from the train stations, make your way down Via Vittorio Veneto into **Piazza Monte Grappa**, itself fascinating for history and architecture buffs. The square was

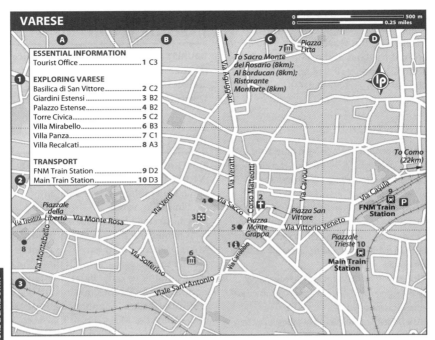

completely remade in grand Fascist fashion in 1935. Most extraordinary is the **Torre Civica**, an enormous and somehow menacing clock tower at whose base flowers an *arengario* (a balcony from which Mussolini and co could harangue the populace). It has an almost sci-fi quality about it. From there, it's a 100m walk to Palazzo Estense. Villa fans could round off by walking half a kilometre from Via Sacco to the 17th-century **Villa Recalcati**, now seat of the provincial government. You can wander around the outside of the building.

### Varese's Old Centre
North off Piazza Monte Grappa, the delightful pedestrianised Corso Matteotti signals the western boundary of the tiny old centre, at whose heart rises the baroque **Basilica di San Vittore** (Piazza San Vittore). The surrounding tangle of lanes makes for a pleasant meander, dotted with several eateries and cafes.

### 💚 VILLA PANZA // COMBINE ART WITH A VILLA VISIT
In a hilly part north of Varese's centre, where the high walls of private residences close in narrow, winding streets and lanes, **Villa Panza** ( ☎ 0332 28 39 60; Piazza Litta 1; adult/child €8/3, park only adult/child €2/free; ☺ 10am-6pm Tue-Sun) throws open its doors to visitors. The villa, which enjoys beautiful views of the Alps from its extensive gardens, was donated to the nation in 1996. Part of that donation was an intriguing art collection, mostly monochrome canvases by American post-WWII artists, scattered about the opulent rooms and halls of the villa. One of the finest rooms is the 1830 Salone

Impero (Empire Hall), with heavy chandeliers and four canvases by American David Simpson (born 1928). More can be seen in the outbuildings *(rustici)*, which are also used for temporary art exhibitions. The gardens, a combination of 18th-century Italianate and early-19th-century English style make for a lovely meander before or after the art.

### ♥ A SACRED MOUNT // CLIMB A COBBLED TRAIL AND FIND REWARD

The medieval hamlet of Santa Maria del Monte (880m), with a sanctuary devoted to Our Lady, was long a site of pilgrimage for the faithful. Then, at the beginning of the 17th century, the Church and Lombardy's Spanish rulers came up with the idea of creating a sacred way to lead up to this sacred mount, **Sacro Monte del Rosario** ( ☎ 0332 28 46 24; www.sacromonte.va.it), one of a dozen or so built in the 16th and 17th centuries in Lombardy and Piedmont. The result is a cobbled, 2km climb (the starting point is at 585m). Fourteen chapels dotted along the way are representative of the mysteries of the Rosary (hence the name). The interval between each is supposed to give you time to recite 10 Hail Mary prayers. Anyone silly enough not to bring water can relax. At the end of the climb there is ample reward. You can drink in the magnificent views with a well-deserved beer on the terrace of **Ristorante Monforte** ( ☎ 0332 22 70 27; Via del Santuario 74; ☻ Wed-Mon).

The *sacro monte,* 8km north of Varese, is inside the Parco Regional Campo dei Fiori, a patch of thickly wooded hills. After the views, the hamlet is worth exploring too. Its tight lanes will lead you to several hotels and a funicular to get back down, but which operates only on weekends, holidays and daily in sweltering August. It is also possible to drive up to the back side of the *sacro monte* this way (but that would be cheating). Many folks make the sacrifice of climbing up in the evening for a romantic evening meal at the *stile liberty* (Italian art nouveau) **Al Borducan** ( ☎ 0332 22 29 16; www.borducan.com; meals €45; ☻ Thu-Tue). Inside is a fine dining room of elegant simplicity, with timber furniture, cream linen and artful tile floor. The terrace is great for sipping a wine. Proceed inside to the circular dining room and grab a table with views over Varese's lakes. Mains tend to be meaty. Homemade tagliatelle in rabbit stew might tempt you.

### ♥ CASTIGLIONE OLONA // ENTER THE FLORENTINE RENAISSANCE

The nondescript modern town of Castiglione Olona, 8km south of Varese off the SP42 road, contains a quite extraordinary gem. The old centre was largely rebuilt under the auspices of its most favoured son, Cardinal Branda Castiglioni (1350–1443) in Florentine Renaissance style. Via Branda leads from the central square up to the **Collegiata** (admission €6.50; ☻ 10am-6pm Tue-Sat Apr-Oct, 10am-1pm & 2.30-5pm Tue-Sun Nov-Mar), a church that contains the town's masterpiece. Inside its baptistery, Florentine master Masolino da Panicale carried out a series of frescos on the life of St John the Baptist in 1435.

### ♥ CASTELSEPRIO & TORBA // DISCOVER A LOMBARD FORT, MONASTERY & CHURCH

Spread out in peaceful woods about 1.5km outside the village of Castelseprio is the ancient archaeological site of Sibrium, a Lombard *castrum* (fortified settlement) with remains of fortress walls, various churches and towers. As long ago as the 5th or 6th century AD, the

Lombards began erecting a fort on this site. By the 7th century it was a small town, with its Basilica di San Giovanni, houses and watchtowers. Along with six other Lombard sites up and down the Italian peninsula, Castelseprio and Torba have been proposed as a combined Unesco World Heritage site.

Four kilometres away by road, but a short walk from the **Parco Archeologico di Castelseprio** ( ☎ 0331 820438; www.beni culturali.it; Via Castelvecchio 1513; admission free; ⊗ 8.30am-7.20pm Tue-Sat, 9.30am-6.20 Sun & holidays), is the **Monastero di Torba** ( ☎ 0331 82 03 01; www.fondoambiente.it; admission adult/child €3.50/2.50; ⊗ 10am-6pm Wed-Sun Mar-Sep, to 5pm Wed-Sun Oct–mid-Dec & Feb), which started life as a forward watchtower for the *castrum* (it was the only one to remain intact). It was then turned into the centrepiece of a Benedictine convent and adorned with rare frescos.

A short walk west from the Monastero di Torba is the **Antiquarium** ( ⊗ 2.45-5.15pm Sun & holidays), a small repository of objects and documents on the site. To get to the archaeological park take a leafy 1.5km drive from Castelseprio village. The church is 200m from the parking area and information office. Torba is about 1.5km drive northeast from the village.

### ❧ CHIESA DI SANTA MARIA FORIS PORTAS // FRESCOS IN A ROMANESQUE SETTING

Outside the walls, the small pre-Romanesque **Chiesa di Santa Maria Foris Portas** (Holy Mary Outside the Gates; admission free; ⊗ 8.30am-2.30pm & 5.30-7pm Sat, 9.45am-2.30pm & 5.30-6pm Sun & holidays), was built around the 7th century. Inside in the apse are some remarkable frescos depicting scenes from the infancy of Jesus Christ and dominated by an image

of Christ Pantocrator. Art historians tend to think these were painted in Lombard times but some believe they are from the Carolingian period (8th or 9th century). Either way, they are a rare and vivid ray of pre-Romanesque artistic beauty. The realism, life and colour of the human figures seems to owe something to classical art of ancient times, not at all like the stiff and, to some eyes, childlike religious art of the Romanesque period, still several centuries away.

## GASTRONOMIC HIGHLIGHTS

### ❧ DA ANNETTA // CAPODILAGO €€€

☎ 0332 49 02 30; www.daannetta.it; Via Fé 25; meals €60-70; ⊗ lunch & dinner Thu-Mon, lunch Tue Sep-Jul

When this place opened in 1928, its owners couldn't have guessed it would have such a long life. The broad menu offers all sorts of tempting goodies, starting with the *fagottini di pasta rossa, ricotta, pesto, olive e crema di burrata* (red pasta bundles stuffed with ricotta, pesto, olives and mozzarrella-style cream), which you might follow with a tender *carrè d'agnello scozzese al forno, cipolle di Tropea, e riduzione al pinot nero* (oven-cooked Scottish lamb *carrè* with fine onions and pinot nero reduction). From Varese, head for Schiranna (see opposite) and veer southeast on the SP1 for Capodilago. Take Via Bodio into the centre of the village.

### ❧ VECCHIO MULINO // CADREZZATE €€€

☎ 0331 95 31 79; Via Solferino 376; meals €50; ⊗ Wed-Sun

Close to Lake Monate and perfect for a romantic dinner for two, the Old Mill offers an enticing setting and equally good food. Low lighting at dinners adds to the atmosphere as your *gnocchi di ceci con lenticchie e briciole del salume di mezzanotte* (chickpea gnocchi served with lentils and snippets of cold meats) appears. A limited selection of meat and fish mains follows. Leave room for the homemade desserts.

## TRANSPORT

**CAR //** The fastest way to Varese is on the A8 motorway from Milan. Otherwise, you must expect slow-going on almost all other roads. Traffic is fairly heavy everywhere, especially on the SP342 east to Como.

**TRAIN //** Regular but sluggish trains leave from Milan's Porta Venezia and Porta Garibaldi stations for Varese (€4.60, 55 minutes to one hour 20 minutes). Some of these continue to Laveno on Lake Maggiore. FNM trains (www.ferrovienord.it) run from Milan's Stazione Nord to Varese (and one to Laveno) via Voltorre and Gemonio.

**BUS //** Local buses fan out from Varese to most towns around the province. Local city bus C runs from various stops around central Varese to the *sacro monte*.

## DRIVING TOUR: THREE LAKES & A CLOISTER

**Distance: 55km**
**Duration: half-day**

The trio of lakes to Varese's south make for a pleasant and easy driving tour that could be done in as little as half a day (or combined with a tour of Varese and the nearby *sacro monte* as a full-day trip) from **Varese** itself. From Villa Recalcati (p91), take the signposted road to Lake Varese, which heads southwest out of Varese to the lake at **Schiranna**, where you could park and go for a gentle walk along **Lake Varese's** shore. Together with Lake Comabbio, it was heavily polluted by the chemical industry in the 1970s. The water is much cleaner now,

LAKE MAGGIORE & LAKE ORTA

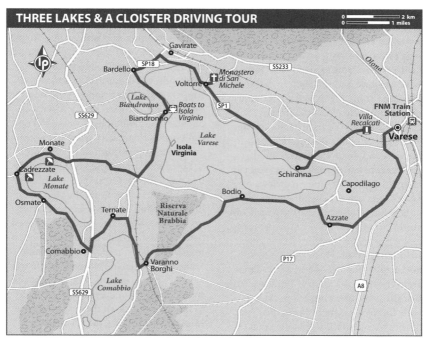

THREE LAKES & A CLOISTER DRIVING TOUR

but bathing is still not allowed. An odd side effect of the pollution is that no one much has built houses around either lake, giving them a fresh, uncluttered feel.

From Schiranna, follow the SP1 west to **Voltorre**, just short of Gavirate. As you enter Voltorre, a sign to the right leads straight to the **Monastero di San Michele** ( ☎ 0332 73 14 02; www.chiostrodivoltorre .it; ☺ 10am-1pm & 2-7pm Tue-Sun). The attraction is the pretty, little Romanesque cloister, three sides dating to the 12th century and the fourth, with brick arches atop its columns, to the 13th century. In the former monastery itself there are frequently temporary exhibitions.

A few kilometres further west, past **Gavirate** (whose old centre boasts several impressive nobles' *palazzi*), take the tiny SP18 for Bardello and then Biandronno, from where boats service the heavily wooded **Isola Virginia**, an islet in the lake, in summer. You can go for a wander and get snacks at the island's only restaurant.

From Biandronno, head west for **Lake Monate** and the eponymous town, **Monate** (home to a late-Romanesque church and peaceful, little beach). This lake was spared the industrial rampage of the 1970s and is the prettiest of the three. A couple of kilometres south, **Cadrezzate** has more beaches (you can hire pedalos) and some nice views of Lake Monate and Lake Maggiore. You pass through Osmate en route for **Comabbio** (where you'll find 11th-century castle ruins), on the third of the lakes, **Lake Comabbio**. From there, you head north along the lake's east bank. There are some nice views from **Varanno Borghi** and some pleasant parkland with children's swings along the lake between Varanno Borghi and Ternate.

Minor roads lead to the south bank of Lake Varese, where you turn east. A 1km southward detour from the eastern end of the lake is **Azzate**, a pretty village whose centre is dotted with several villas and a couple of churches. From there, it's a quick trip back north to Varese.

# LAKE ORTA
· · · · · ·

**Enveloped by thick, dark-green woodlands, tranquil Lake Orta (aka Lake Cusio) could make a perfect elopers' getaway. At 13.4km long by 2.5km wide, it's separated from its bigger and better-known eastern neighbour, Lake Maggiore, by Monte Mottarone. The focal point of the lake is the captivating medieval village of Orta San Giulio (population 1170), often referred to simply as Orta.**

If it's romance you want, come during the week and you'll have the place largely to yourself. On spring and summer weekends, good-natured groups of day trippers from Milan and beyond descend on the place, creating plenty of atmosphere, but crowding the town out. You can't blame them: it's perfect for a day out and a long Sunday lunch.

You could drive right around the lake in a day. Outside Orta, specific sights are few and far between. The ride along the largely flat, east bank of the lake is the best for lake views, while on the west bank, the main road runs mostly high up in the hills and out of sight of the lake. Some out-of-the-way villages on the west bank are fun to explore, however. Roads stretch away from the lake on either side to the mountains. To the east is Monte Mottarone (p82). To the northwest stretches the beautifully wild and little-visited Valstrona.

## ESSENTIAL INFORMATION

**TOURIST OFFICES // Main Tourist Office**
(☎ 0322 90 51 63; www.comune.ortasangiulio.no.it; Via Panoramica; ⏲ 9am-1pm & 2-6pm Wed-Sun Apr-Oct, 9am-1pm & 2-6pm Wed-Fri, 8am-12.30pm & 1.30-5pm Sat & Sun Nov-Mar) for information on the whole lake area; **Pro Loco** (☎ 0322 9 01 55; Via Bossi 10; ⏲ 11am-1pm & 2-6pm Mon & Wed-Fri, 10am-1pm & 2-6pm Sat & Sun) in the Comune (Town Hall) Bldg, for town information.

## EXPLORING LAKE ORTA

❤ **ORTA SAN GIULIO // WANDER THE STREETS OF THE LAKE'S PRETTIEST TOWN**
There's something magic about rising early and heading for a coffee on Piazza Mario Motta, gazing across at the sun-struck Isola San Giulio in the early morning quiet.

At the north end of the square, a squat, fresco-enlivened structure sitting atop pillars like giant stilts, the Palazzotto, was once the seat of a local council and now

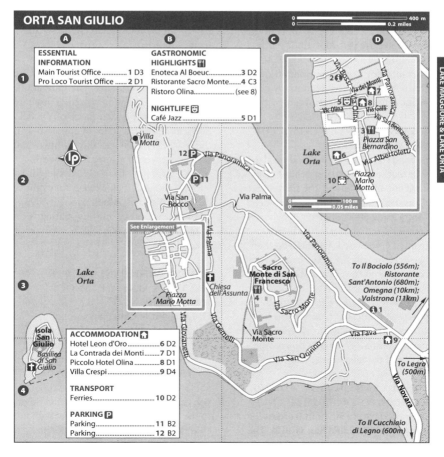

LAKE MAGGIORE & LAKE ORTA

occasionally opens for temporary exhibitions. The square burbles with local life on market day (Wednesday). Orta San Giulio has centuries of history and rewards aimless strolling. The main street is shop- and eatery-lined Via Olina (later Via Bossi and Via Gippini), which straggles north from the square. A series of uneven lanes branches off it to the lake, while others wiggle their way inland. Via Gippini finally changes name to Via Ettore Motta on its way past the lakeside Villa Motta – a pleasant waterside wander.

### Legro

About 3km from central Orta, Legro seems bent on redirecting some of the attention Orta gets to itself. If you arrive by train, you are in Legro. Take the opportunity for a quick wander around to study the murals that lend many of the village's houses a cheerful tone.

### ❧ SACRO MONTE // CLIMB THE HOLY MOUNTAIN

Beyond the lush gardens and residences that mark the hill rising behind Orta is a kind of parallel 'town', the *sacro monte*. From Piazza Mario Motta, Salita della Motta leads up a cobbled hill between centuries-old houses to the baroque-fronted Chiesa dell'Assunta and then bends right (south) to the cemetery and back right up the Sacred Mountain, with its 20 chapels scattered about, each dedicated to recounting a part of the biography of St Francis of Assisi. Some boast wonderful frescos while others are more modest affairs. The views down over Orta and the lake are captivating.

### ❧ ISOLA SAN GIULIO // ADMIRE FRESCOS & STROLL IN SILENCE

Anchored barely 500m in front of Piazza Mario Motta is **Isola San Giulio**. The island is dominated by the 12th-century **Basilica di San Giulio** ( 9.30am-6.45pm Tue-Sun, noon-6.45pm Mon Apr-Sep, 9.30am-noon & 2-5pm, 2-5pm Mon Oct-Mar), full of vibrant frescos that alone make a trip to the island worthwhile. They mostly depict saints (and sometimes their moment of martyrdom – St Laurence seems supremely indifferent to his roasting on a grate).

The church, island and mainland town are named after a Greek evangelist, Giulio, who's said to have rid the island of snakes, dragons and assorted monsters in the late 4th century. His remains lie in the crypt. Regular ferries (see Transport, p100) run from Orta San Giulio's waterfront. More-expensive private launches (€4 one way) also run, departing when there are sufficient passengers to warrant the five-minute crossing. The footpath encircling the island makes for a peaceful stroll, hence its popular name of Via del Silenzio. Indeed, a series of aphorisms on the wonders of silence (all very fine when screaming school groups have the run of the place) have been placed along the way. If you walk it clockwise, they now call it the Via della Meditazione, with a whole load of other multilingual signs to inspire you on your search for inner peace.

### ❧ WEST BANK // INDULGE IN GENTLE WALKS AND SNOOP AROUND RONCO

Heading out of **Omegna**, a not unattractive town at the head of the lake (and quite lively on Thursday morning, market day), the road (follow the signs for Varallo) quickly takes you up high and out of view of the lake. At Nonio, you can follow a steep, minor road down to the lake at **Oira**, a tiny hamlet with a church, boat landing and lakeside pizzeria. A few km further south, at Cesara, turn east for Egro. The 4km country road leads you past the half-abandoned stone hamlet of Grassona before reaching **Egro**. From this quiet, stone village a wooded walking trail leads down to the lakeside town of **Pella** (about 45 minutes). As you descend, you have views across Isola San Giulio and the lake. High above Pella you may detect a small chapel built in a seemingly impossible outcrop of rock. More interesting is the narrow road that leads 3km north of Pella to **Ronco**, a little gem of a village, all dark-stone houses huddled around a grid of teensy lanes and facing the lake.

### ❦ WALKING CIRCUIT // WALK AROUND LAKE ORTA

Known locally as the **Anello Azzurro** (Blue Ring), the circuit walk of the entire lake can take about three days at a leisurely pace. Starting at Orta and heading south, you are looking at about 14km to Pella, about 13km the following day to Omegna and another 14km back from Omegna to Orta. The recommended kick-off point is *sacro monte* in Orta. Readers of Italian can get a closer route description at www.lagodorta.net, where all sorts of other ideas on walks in the area are presented.

### ❦ VALSTRONA // LOSE YOURSELF IN A HIGH MOUNTAIN VALLEY

West out of Omegna, 14km of winding valley road follow a deep river gorge (some locals bring their own equipment for a little white-water fun on weekends), the Torrente Strona, on a verdant, meandering course northwest to the settlement of **Forno** (850m). The object of the trip is essentially to dive into the splendid scenery, which becomes more dramatic the higher you climb. Keep your eyes open for majestic spring waterfalls and snowcapped mountains (most of the year) in the background.

From Forno, a 3km track leads west to the Campello Monti, mountain pasture land that was inhabited in the 13th century by the Walser community. The Walsers, speakers of a German dialect from the Upper Valais area of southern Switzerland, migrated to various parts of southern Switzerland, Austria and northern Italy over the Middle Ages. In the 13th century they arrived here. To this day, they maintain their dialect and a scattering of their traditional timber farmhouses.

## GASTRONOMIC HIGHLIGHTS

### ❦ AGRITURISMO CUCCHIAIO DI LEGNO // LEGRO €€

☎ 0322 90 52 80; Via Prisciola 10; set menu €25; ⏲ dinner Thu-Sun

A 500m stroll beyond the train station, this honest-to-goodness *agriturismo* restaurant (no guestrooms) cooks up delicious local dishes including risotto, fish straight out of the lake, and salami and cheese from the surrounding valleys. Dine alfresco on the vine-draped patio overlooking the herb-planted garden. It really is like being at someone's house. It's about 800m from the Orta–Miasino train station.

### ❦ ENOTECA AL BOEUC // ORTA SAN GIULIO €

☎ 339 584 00 39; Via Bersani 28; meals €15-20; ⏲ Wed-Mon

Enter this candlelit stone cavern that has been around since the 16th century. In its present incarnation, you will be served light meals to be savoured with fine wines by the glass (eg a velvety

Barolo for €8). Choose between a *tris di bruschette* (three different kinds of toast with topping), sausage, platters of cheese and cold meats or a Piedmontese favourite, *bagna caüda* (a hot dip made of butter, olive oil, garlic and anchovies in which you bathe vegetables).

### ✿ IL BOCCIOLO // ORTA SAN GIULIO €€

☎ 0322 9 03 02; Via Domodossola 26; meals €30; ⊗ Thu-Tue

About 1km north of Orta San Giulio, Il Bocciolo sits on a rise affording sweeping views west over the lake. You can enjoy this from outdoor tables or retreat inside, where one of the dining areas has a comforting fireplace for chillier days. A set-lunch menu (€12) is an option. A word of warning: the place often opens only for lunch.

### ✿ RISTORANTE SACRO MONTE // SACRO MONTE €€

☎ 0322 9 02 20; Parco Naturale Sacro Monte; meals €30; ⊗ Wed-Mon

Amid the chapels dedicated to St Francis of Assisi on the *sacro monte,* this low-slung restaurant with its slate roof is a welcoming spot for a broad range of pasta, risotto and mainly meat main courses. The timber-floored dining areas are warm and inviting. The cooking is largely Piedmontese, with a few broader Italian touches. Wines too, lean to the excellent drops produced in Piedmont.

### ✿ RISTORANTE SANT'ANTONIO // TORTIROGNO €€

☎ 0322 91 19 63; meals €25-30; ⊗ Wed-Sun

Got a hankering for grilled fish straight out of the lake? Or seafood? Situated about 1.5km north of Orta on the main road, this is a simple, family-run place

with a handful of seats outside by the lake, and a small, bustling dining room. While the occasional meat dish appears, fish is the name of the game.

### ✿ RISTORO OLINA // ORTA SAN GIULIO €€

☎ 0322 90 56 56; Via Olina 40; meals €30-35; ⊗ Thu-Tue

The whiteness of the furniture, decor and light can seem a bit much, especially if you're looking for a typical lowlit trattoria. Don't be put off. This place offers a broad range of imaginative dishes that combine creativity with excellent products. Service is thoughtful. You might start with the slightly sweet-and-sour *gnocchi di castagne e zucca con crema di radicchio scottato* (chestnut and pumpkin gnocchi in a radish cream).

## NIGHTLIFE

### ✿ CAFFÈ JAZZ

☎ 333 923 25 22; Via Olina 13; ⊗ 11am-12.30am Tue-Sun

This trendy bar accentuated with low lighting and a nice assortment of wines by the glass is at its liveliest on spring and summer weekends when Milanese urbanites seeking some nocturnal entertainment on their getaway lend the place a touch of capital-city ambience. The internal courtyard out back is a grand open space.

## TRANSPORT

**CAR //** The most direct way to reach Orta from Milan or other distant location is to follow the A26 tollway and exit at Meina for the south end of the lake or Gravellona Toca for the north end.

**PARKING //** In Orta San Giulio, almost all parking is metered or in garages. You pay up to €1.50 an hour or €8 a day in metered areas, or €2 and €10 respectively in garages.

**BOAT //** Navigazione Lago d'Orta ( ☎ 0322 84 48 62) runs boats to numerous lakeside spots from its landing stage on Piazza Mario Motta, including Isola San Giulio (one way/return €1.80/2.50), Omegna (€4/6), Pella (€2.20/4) and Ronco (€2.80/4). A day ticket for unlimited travel on the whole lake costs €7.50.

**TRAIN //** Orta Miasino train station is a 3km walk from the centre of Orta San Giulio. It is on the line from Novara to Domodossola and trains stop at all the towns on the east shore of the lake. From Milan, there are trains from Stazione Centrale (change at Novara) every two hours or so (€5.40, two hours). Between March and October, a little tourist train (one way/return €2.50/4; ☒ Thu-Tue) shuttles between the town centre, *sacro monte* and the train station approximately every half hour.

**BUS //** Only intermittent bus services serve the west bank towns. From June to September, three buses a day run between Stresa and Orta (€3.50).

LAKE MAGGIORE & LAKE ORTA

# LAKE COMO & LAKE LUGANO

## 3 PERFECT DAYS

### 🌣 DAY 1 // FROM COMO TO CERNOBBIO

Take an early funicular up to Brunate (p111) to catch views of the city and lake under the rising sun's rays. Back in Como, explore the old centre, making time for the Duomo and to see the remarkable frescos in Basilica di Sant'Abbondio (p109). It's then time for lunch at Osteria del Gallo (p112), after which you can head 7km around the lake to Cernobbio (p118), to admire the pretty lakeside villas, followed by a drive up to Monte Bisbino (p119), arriving in time for sunset views over the lake. You could finish with a splendid meal at Gatto Nero (p124).

### 🌣 DAY 2 // FERRY YOURSELF TO BELLAGIO AND VILLA CARLOTTA

Catch a ferry from Como to Bellagio (p114), where you could take a room and spend the morning discovering the gardens of two fine villas, and the topsy-turvy beauty of the town itself. Lunch could follow at Albergo Silvio (p118) before taking a car ferry to Cadenabbia for an afternoon visit to nearby Tremezzo's Villa Carlotta (p122). Car ferries returning to Bellagio run late into the evening.

### 🌣 DAY 3 // VARENNA'S VILLAS AND A SERENE ABBEY

From Bellagio, jump on another car ferry to Varenna (p126), a rival in beauty to Bellagio. You could spend the bulk of a day here, especially if you include a walk up to the Castello di Vezio (p127) to gaze back down on Varenna. Those with wheels can easily head north for the medieval hamlet of Corenno Plinio (p127) and, just further on, the lovely Abbazia di Piona (p128), where you can stay if you don't want to turn back.

# LAKE COMO

• • • • • •

In the shadow of the snow-covered Rhaetian Alps and hemmed in on both sides by steep, verdant hillsides, Lake Como (aka Lake Lario) is the most spectacular and least visited of the three major lakes. Shaped like an upside-down Y, measuring around 160km in squiggly shoreline, it's littered with villages, including exquisite Bellagio and Varenna. Where the southern and western shores converge is the lake's main town, Como. Lecco, the other large town on the lake, sits where the southern shore meets the less-explored eastern shore.

Among the area's siren calls are some extraordinarily sumptuous villas, often graced with paradisiacal gardens. The mountainous terrain means that opportunities for taking bird's-eye views of the lake and its towns are numerous. Much of the area has a wild feel, especially with its extravagantly luxuriant greenery. Como long ignored tourism, confident of the wealth generated by the silk business. As foreign competition in that sector began to bite deeper, interest in developing tourism grew from the mid-1990s. Still, the figures speak for themselves. While 1.5 million overnight stays were registered in Lake Como hotels in 2008, Lake Maggiore had 12 million and Lake Garda 23 million. For that reason alone, the lake and its surrounding area offer the traveller the chance to enjoy a real sense of discovery.

## TRANSPORT

**Navigazione Lago del Como** (☎ 031 57 92 11, 800 55 18 01; www.navigazionelaghi.it; Piazza Cavour) Ferries and hydrofoils operated by this Como-based company criss-cross the lake, departing year-round from the

## TOP FIVE

### LAKE VIEWS

**Rifugio Menaggio** (p122) A couple of hours' hiking is rewarded with Lake Como views.

**Monte Bisbino** (p119) A winding 17km drive leads to wonderful vistas over Lake Como, the Lombard plains and Alps.

**Brunate** (p111) Take the funicular high above Como.

**Castello di Vezio** (p127) A castle lookout for eagle-eye views of Varenna.

**Cima Sighignola** (p182) Italy's Balcony affords views as far west as the Matterhorn.

jetty at the north end of Piazza Cavour. Single fares range from €1.90 (Como–Cernobbio) to €10 (Como–Lecco). Return fares are double. Hydrofoil fast services entail a supplement of €1.10 to 3.90, depending on the trip.

**Car ferries** (see p118) connect Bellagio with Varenna and Cadenabbia. A whole host of other tickets is available, including those for day cruises with lunch and those that include admission to lakeside villas.

## COMO

**pop 83,170**

With its charming historic centre, Como sparkles year-round. Within its remaining 12th-century city walls, the beautiful people of this prosperous city whisk about from shop to cafe, sweeping by the grandeur of the city's cathedral, villas and the loveliness of its lakeshore with admirable insouciance. The days since the Milanese conquered Como's forces in 1127 and ordered the destruction of all walls and buildings save its churches are long gone. Indeed, the locals seem quite indifferent to folks from the Lombard capital.

Como built its wealth on the silk industry and it remains Europe's most important producer of silk products. You can buy silk scarves and ties for a fraction of

LAKE COMO & LAKE LUGANO

(Continued on page 109)

# LAKE COMO & LAKE LUGANO

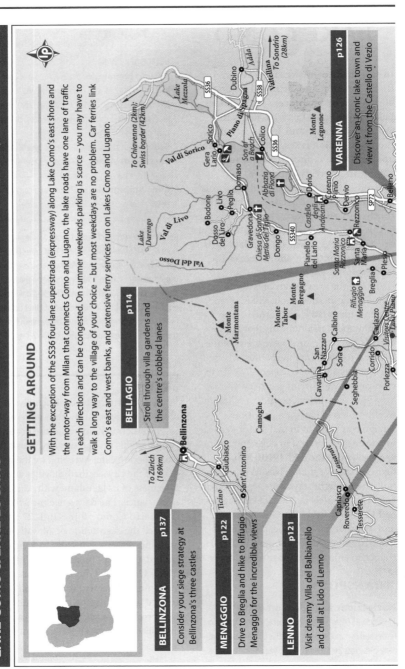

## GETTING AROUND

With the exception of the SS36 four-lane superstrada (expressway) along Lake Como's east shore and the motor-way from Milan that connects Como and Lugano, the lake roads have one lane of traffic in each direction and can be congested. On summer weekends parking is scarce – you may have to walk a long way to the village of your choice – but most weekdays are no problem. Car ferries link Como's east and west banks, and extensive ferry services run on Lakes Como and Lugano.

### BELLAGIO    p114

Stroll through villa gardens and the centre's cobbled lanes

### VARENNA    p126

Discover an iconic lake town and view it from the Castello di Vezio

### BELLINZONA    p137

Consider your siege strategy at Bellinzona's three castles

### MENAGGIO    p122

Drive to Breglia and hike to Rifugio Menaggio for the incredible views

### LENNO    p121

Visit dreamy Villa del Balbianello and chill at Lido di Lenno

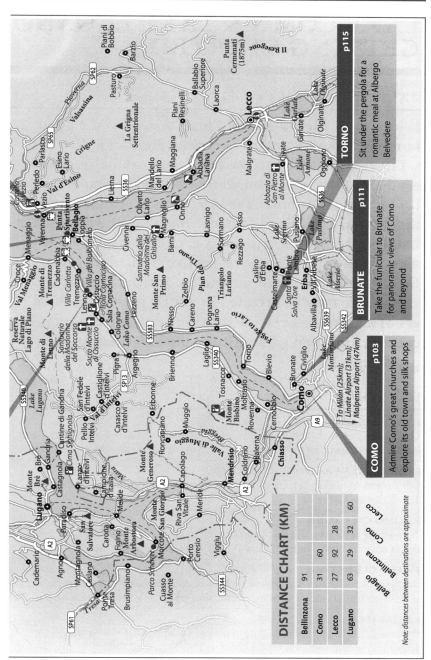

**DISTANCE CHART (KM)**

| | Bellinzona | Como | Lecco |
|---|---|---|---|
| Bellinzona | 91 | | |
| Como | 31 | 60 | |
| Lecco | 27 | 92 | 28 |
| Lugano | 63 | 29 | 32 | 60 |

*Note: distances between destinations are approximate*

**COMO** p103
Admire Como's great churches and explore its old town and silk shops

**BRUNATE** p111
Take the funicular to Brunate for panoramic views of Como and beyond

**TORNO** p115
Sit under the pergola for a romantic meal at Albergo Belvedere

# LAKE COMO & LAKE LUGANO GETTING STARTED

## MAKING THE MOST OF YOUR TIME

**Lake Como, the wildest and least visited of the great Lombard lakes, is full of surprises. Remarkable villas set in awe-inspiring parks are laced around the southern half of the lake. You could take in the major ones (in Bellagio, Varenna, Tremezzo and Cernobbio) in three days. Como and Lugano, the main town on sister Lake Lugano, are worth a day each (especially for the views at the end of their respective funicular rides). Gourmands can combine fine food with wonderful views once they've invested in a little planning. Walkers of all levels can stride into surprisingly untouched country and then gain altitude for breathtaking panoramas.**

## TOP TOURS

### ☙ LAKE COMO CYCLING

A local cycling enthusiast will take you on one-day mountain-bike tours of Lake Como – or around Lombardy, into Switzerland and even to Rome. (www.lakecomocycling.com; tours €120)

### ☙ GIRO DELLE FRAZIONI DI BELLAGIO

A three-hour guided walk takes you around Bellagio and surrounding hamlets. (tours €10; ⊙ 9.15am Mon May-Sep)

### ☙ COMO CITY TOUR

Discover the main monuments of the old heart of Como on this two-hour walking tour of central Como, run by Mondo Turistico. (www.mondoturistico.it; tours €8)

### ☙ AERO CLUB COMO

The Aero Club Como offers seaplane flights around Lake Como, from short flights over its southern half to longer jaunts to Lake Lugano. (☎ 031 57 44 95; www.aeroclubcomo.com)

### ☙ DORSALE

This two-day hike goes from Brunate to Bellagio, skirting little-visited villages. A challenging variant climbs along the crests. (p116)

# GETTING AWAY FROM IT ALL

Tourists concentrate in Como, Lugano, Bellagio, Varenna, Cernobbio and around Tremezzo. Beyond, you'll nary see a one.

* **Val d'Intelvi** Explore the quiet towns and trails of this valley, away from Lake Como's busy west bank; they lead you into rugged, one-time smugglers' country between Lakes Como and Lugano (p120)

* **Interior** Venture on a tour of the interior of the Triangolo Lariano, which leads you to Romanesque churches and splendid walking trails (p114)

* **Onno** Go where only locals know – the sunny pebble beach at Onno, between Bellagio and Lecco (p124)

* **Deep North** Corenno Plinio is a seemingly untouched medieval hamlet on the northeastern shore – flashback in time (p127)

# FESTIVALS & EVENTS

Although Como stages various cultural events throughout the year, Lugano and Bellinzona have some outstanding annual events that are worth being around for if you can time a visit to coincide with them.

* **Lugano Festival** (www.luganofestival.ch) A series of classical-music concerts held from April to May in Lugano's Palazzo dei Congressi

* **Estival Jazz** (www.estivaljazz.ch) Open-air jazz concerts fill the Lugano air with bright sounds for three days in July

* **Piazza Blues Festival** (www.piazzablues .ch) This July festival in Bellinzona is a four-day international blues extravaganza

# TOP RESTAURANTS

☙ **ALBERGO BELVEDERE**
Romantic pergola in a lakeside village (p117)

☙ **ALBERGO SILVIO**
Fine lake fish and views at sunset (p118)

☙ **BOTTEGONE DEL VINO**
Matching fine wines to classic Ticino cooking (p135)

☙ **GATTO NERO**
Doyen of high-end Italian cuisine (p124)

☙ **LA CUCINA DI MARIANNA**
Down-home lakeside cooking (p124)

☙ **OSTERIA ANGOLO DEL SILENZIO**
Classy dining in a rustic ambience (p112)

☙ **OSTERIA DEL GALLO**
Timeless classic for scrumptious lunch (p112)

☙ **SALE E TABACCHI**
Hidden gem in a hill hamlet (130)

# RESOURCES

* **Bellagio** (www.bellagiolakecomo.com) All you need to know about Bellagio
* **Comunità Montana – Triangolo Lariano** (www.triangololariano.it, in Italian) Information on the Triangolo Lariano area
* **Lago di Como** (www.lakecomo.org) Como province tourism website
* **Lugano** (www.lugano-tourism.ch) Lugano's official website
* **Provincia di Lecco** (www.turismo.provincia .lecco.it, in Italian) For the low-down on Lake Como's east bank.

LAKE COMO & LAKE LUGANO

COMO

LAKE COMO & LAKE LUGANO

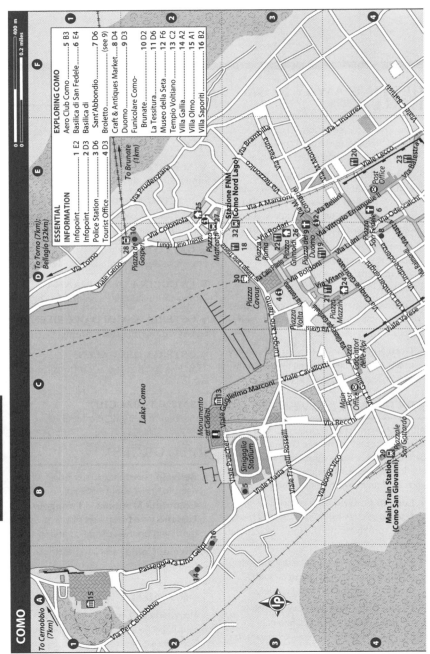

**ESSENTIAL INFORMATION**

| | |
|---|---|
| Infopoint.................... | 1 E2 |
| Infopoint.................... | 2 D3 |
| Police Station.......... | 3 D6 |
| Tourist Office.......... | 4 D3 |

**EXPLORING COMO**

| | |
|---|---|
| Aero Club Como.................. | 5 B3 |
| Basilica di San Fedele.......... | 6 E4 |
| Basilica di Sant'Abbondio...... | 7 D6 |
| Broletto.......................... | (see 9) |
| Craft & Antiques Market...... | 8 D4 |
| Duomo.......................... | 9 D3 |
| Funicolare Como-Brunate...... | 10 D2 |
| La Tessitura.................... | 11 D6 |
| Museo della Seta.............. | 12 F6 |
| Tempio Voltiano................ | 13 C2 |
| Villa Gallia.................... | 14 A2 |
| Villa Olmo.................... | 15 A1 |
| Villa Saporiti................ | 16 B2 |

To Cernobbio (7km)

To Torno (7km); Bellagio (32km)

To Brunate (1km)

Lake Como

Via Per Cernobbio

Via Torno

Viale Geno

Via Prudenziana

Via Colonióla

Lungo Lario Trieste

Piazza del Gasperi

Piazza Matteotti

Stazione FNM (Como Nord Lago)

Via A Manzoni

Via Brambilla

Via Recchi

Via I Insurrex

Viale Lecco

Via I Ballestra

Post Office

Via Odescalchi

Piazza San Fedele

Via Vittorio Emanuele II

Via Bellini

Piazza del Duomo

Via Garimoldi

Via Rodari

Via Luini

Piazza Roma

Piazza Cavour

Lungo Lario Trento

Piazza Volta

Via Cairo Plinio

Via Boldoni

Via Vitani

Piazza Mazzini

Viale Varese

Viale Cavallotti

Via Gallio

Main Post Office

Piazza Cacciatori delle Alpi

Viale Masia

Viale Fratelli Rosselli

Via Borgo Vico

Monumento ai Caduti

Viale Guglielmo Marconi

Viale Puecher

Sinigaglia Stadium

Passeggiata Lino Gelpi

Main Train Station (Como San Giovanni)

Piazzale San Gottardo

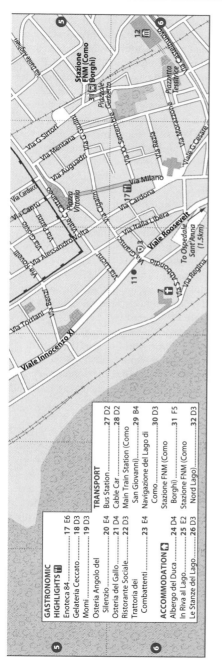

GASTRONOMIC
HIGHLIGHTS 🍴
Enoteca 84..............................17 E6
Gelateria Ceccato.................18 D3
Momi.........................................19 D3
Osteria Angolo del
 Silenzio...............................20 E4
Osteria del Gallo..................21 D4
Ristorante Sociale................22 D3
Trattoria dei
 Combattenti......................23 E4

ACCOMMODATION 🏠
Albergo del Duca...................24 D4
In Riva al Lago.......................25 E2
Le Stanze del Lago...............26 D3

TRANSPORT
Bus Station............................27 D2
Cable Car................................28 D2
Main Train Station (Como
 San Giovanni)....................29 B4
Navigazione del Lago di
 Como....................................30 D3
Stazione FNM (Como
 Borghi)................................31 F5
Stazione FNM (Como
 Nord Lago)..........................32 D3

*(Continued from page 103)*

what is charged at boutiques internationally (see p111). This town is a lovely spot for an aimless wander, punctuated with coffee and drink stops, especially in Piazzas Cavour, Volta and San Fedele.

## ESSENTIAL INFORMATION

**EMERGENCIES //** **Ospedale Sant'Anna** ( ☎ 031 58 51; Via Napoleona 60) Hospital; **Police station** ( ☎ 031 31 71; Viale Roosevelt 7)
**TOURIST OFFICES //** **Tourist Office** ( ☎ 031 26 97 12; www.lakecomo.org; Piazza Cavour 17; 🕙 9am-1pm & 2.30-6pm Mon-Sat year-round, 9.30am-1pm Sun Jun-Sep); **InfoPoint** (Bus station; 🕙 10.30am-12.30pm & 2.30-6pm Mon & Wed-Fri, 10am-8pm Sat, Sun & holidays); **InfoPoint** (Via Maestri Comacini; 🕙 10.30am-12.30pm & 2.30-6pm Tue-Fri, 10am-1pm & 2-6pm Sat, Sun & holidays).

## EXPLORING COMO

💚 **GOING TO CHURCH //** **ADMIRE ROMANESQUE FRESCOS AND GOTHIC GRANDEUR**
About 500m south of the city walls and just beyond busy and rather ugly Viale Innocenzo XI, is the remarkable 11th-century Romanesque **Basilica di Sant'Abbondio** (Via Regina; 🕙 8am-6pm). Aside from its proud, high structure and impressive apse decorated with a beautiful geometric relief around the outside windows, the highlight is the remarkable fresco series inside the apse. Depicting scenes from the life of Christ, from the Annunciation to his burial, they were restored to their former glory in the 1990s. A university occupies what was once the cloister. To get a closer glimpse of the apse exterior, amble into its grounds.

### Basilica di San Fedele
The circular layout of the originally 6th-century **Basilica di San Fedele** (Piazza San

LAKE COMO & LAKE LUGANO

Fedele; ◷ 8am-noon & 3.30-7pm), with three naves and three apses, has been likened to a clover leaf. Its 16th-century rose window and precious 16th- and 17th-century frescos add to its charm. The facade is the result of a 1914 remake but the apses are the real McCoy, featuring some eye-catching sculpture on the right side. A **craft and antiques market** (Piazza San Fedele; ◷ 9am-7pm Sat) fills the piazza in front of the basilica.

## Duomo

Although largely Gothic, elements of Romanesque, Renaissance and baroque styles can also be seen in Como's fancy, marble-clad **Duomo** (cathedral; Piazza del Duomo; ◷ 7am-noon & 3-7pm). The cathedral was built between the 14th and 18th centuries, and is crowned by a high octagonal dome. Next door, the polychromatic **Broletto**, or medieval town hall, is unusual in that it butts right up against the church and is rather overwhelmed by it – a singular defeat for laicisation.

### ❦ VILLA OLMO // STROLL LAKESIDE, SWIM, THEN INDULGE IN A COCKTAIL

Set grandly facing Lake Como, the sandy-coloured, statue-topped, neoclassical facade of **Villa Olmo** (◷ 9am-8pm Tue-Thu, 9am-10pm Fri-Sun during exhibitions) is one of Como's landmarks. It owes its name to a giant elm that once grew in the gardens and was, they say, mentioned by Pliny the Younger in his writings. The building was started in 1728 by the Odescalchi family, related to Pope Innocent XI. If there's an art exhibition inside, you will get to admire the grand ballroom, at the heart of the long building. Otherwise, this mini-Versailles may well be locked up, but that won't stop you from having a jog around the **gardens** (◷ 8am-11pm late Apr-Sep, 8am-7pm Oct-late Apr), Italianate facing the lake and English-style at the rear.

Almost as nice as the gardens is the lakeside stroll to get there. From the stadium, follow Passeggiata Lino Gelpi along the water. You pass a series of mansions and villas (and their gardens) along the way, including **Villa Saporiti** (late 18th century) and the adjacent **Villa Gallia** (17th century), both now part of the provincial government.

A summertime bonus is the **Lido di Villa Olmo** (Via Per Cernobbio 2; ◷ 9am-7pm mid-May–Sep), an open-air swimming pool and lakeside bar, complete with sand and umbrellas.

### ❦ MUSEO DELLA SETA // SEE THE HEAVY MACHINES THAT WEAVE THE SMOOTHEST FABRIC

Housed in the bowels of the predictably ugly 1970s buildings of the Istituto Tecnico Industriale di Setificio textile technical school (where tomorrow's silkmakers and designers learn their trade), the **Museo della Seta** (Silk Museum; ☎ 031 30 31 80; www.museosetacomo.com; Via Castelnuovo 9; adult/child €8/2.60; ◷ 9am-noon & 3-6pm Tue-Fri) unravels the town's silk history, with early dyeing and printing equipment on display. A wander around takes you through the entire process of producing silk. Explanations start with the humble

## ART TALKS

If you speak Italian, a handy service for those wanting to know more about certain central city sights is **Speak Art**. Call ☎ 031 25 22 25 from your mobile phone and you key in the code posted on the information panel at the sight (eg 14, Piazza San Fedele) for some extended description. These calls can be a trifle expensive from non-Italian mobile phones.

## SWITCHED ON

The lakeside **Tempio Voltiano** ( ☎ 031 57 47 05; Viale Guglielmo Marconi; adult/senior/child €3/1.50/free; ⌚ 10am-noon & 3-6pm Tue-Sun Apr-Oct, 10am-noon & 2-4pm Nov-Mar) was built in 1927 in memory of Como-born inventor of the battery, Alessandro Volta (1745–1827). The singular, circular landmark is more significant for what it represents than for its slim contents. In 1800 Volta invented the Voltaic battery, which preceded the electric battery – an invention that would later be refined and revolutionise people's daily life.

silkworm and how it is raised (no longer the case in Italy, which imports raw silk mainly from China) through to the creation of bundles and reels of silk, and on to the dyeing and production of finished products.

### ❦ LA TESSITURA // BROWSE FOR SILK IN MANTERO'S MEGASTORE

Mantero, one of the biggest names in Como silk, runs **La Tessitura** ( ☎ 031 32 16 66; www.latessitura.com; Viale Roosevelt 2; ⌚ 11am-9pm Tue-Sat), a large-scale outlet-style store and warehouse on the site of what was, from the early 1980s to 2004, its factory (with 90 looms). Mantero had opened that factory on the site of a late-19th-century silk factory. If you can print and weave it, you'll find it here. For shopping breaks, you can pause at the on-site Loom Café. The place is more than just a silk supermarket – multimedia screens help you learn more about the history and production of silk.

### ❦ BRUNATE // TAKE THE HIGH GROUND ABOVE COMO

Como is flanked to the east and west by steep and thickly wooded hills (scarred in part by the spread of residential housing). A ride up to the quiet residential village of **Brunate**, which seems to float above Lake Como – it sits at 720m above sea level – is repaid by exhilarating views.

Northeast along the waterfront from central Como, the **Funicolare Como-Brunate** ( ☎ 031 30 36 08; www.funicolarecomo .it; Piazza de Gasperi 4; one way adult/child €2.50/1.65, return €4.35/2.75; ⌚ 6am-midnight mid-Apr–mid-Sep, to 10.30pm mid-Sep–mid-Apr) was built in 1894. It takes just seven minutes to reach Brunate (quicker than the switchbacks that you can take by car).

Brunate's baroque **Chiesa di San Andrea** (Piazza della Chiesa), with its faded pink exterior and giant bell peeking out of the bell tower, is hard to miss. In **San Maurizio**, a steep 40-minute walk (the first stage of the Dorsale hike, see p116) from Brunate's funicular stop, scale 143 steps to the top of the lighthouse, built in 1927 to mark the centenary of Alessandro Volta's death. The Como tourist office can provide a map with various suggested walks around Brunate.

## GASTRONOMIC HIGHLIGHTS

### ❦ ENOTECA 84 €€

☎ 031 27 04 82; Via Milano 84; meals €25-30; ⌚ lunch & dinner Fri & Sat, lunch only Mon-Thu

Down one side of this minuscule locale are lined-up tables; down the other are shelves groaning under the weight of tightly packed bottles of fine wine. The menu changes often, and ranges from platters of cold meats and cheeses to such Lombard classics as *pizzoccheri artigianali* (handmade buckwheat tagliatelle) or *pappardelle agli asparagi e porri con panna fresca* (broad-ribbon pasta with asparagus and leeks in fresh cream).

### ❦ GELATERIA CECCATO €

☎ 031 2 33 91; Palace Hotel, Lungo Lario Trieste 16; gelato €1.50-4; ⏲ 9am-midnight

For generations, Comaschi have turned to Ceccato for their Sunday afternoon gelato and then embarked on a ritual *passeggiata* (walk) with the dripping cones along the lakeshore. You can do no better than imitate them: order a creamy stracciatella (chocolate chip) or perhaps a mix of fresh fruit flavours and head off for a relaxed promenade along the lakefront.

### ❦ MOMI €€

☎ 031 26 78 46; www.ristorantemomi.it; Via Pietro Boldoni 3; meals €25-35; ⏲ lunch & dinner Mon-Sat, lunch Sun, cafeteria 9am-7.30pm daily

On the 5th floor of the Coin supermarket building, this bright, trendy eatery offers a little of everything. While enjoying rooftop views, indulge in sweet pastries, savoury snacks and drinks at any time during the day. Meal options are broad. From a set lunch (€23) you can stray over a selection of Italian and Mediterranean dishes – anything from *zuppa di bio-legumi misti con vero brodo di cappone* (organic vegetable soup with capon broth) to a slew of vegetarian, fish and meat mains.

### ❦ OSTERIA ANGOLO DEL SILENZIO €€

☎ 031 337 21 57; Viale Lecco 25; meals €35-40; ⏲ lunch & dinner Wed-Sun, dinner Tue

The Corner of Silence is set on a very noisy street, but it still manages to live up to its name inside, where the succession of dining rooms are quiet enough. On warm days, the rear garden is even more pleasant. Locals mix with the occasional celeb hoping to pass off unobserved while digging into a steaming plate of *tagliatelle nere con gamberi e seppie* (black

tagliatelle with shrimps and cuttlefish) or a succulent and fancily presented *petto d'anatra al pepe rosa* (duck breast cooked with pink pepper).

### ❦ OSTERIA DEL GALLO €€

☎ 031 27 25 91; Via Vitani 16; meals €25; ⏲ lunch Mon-Sat

This ageless *osteria* (wine bar serving food) is a lunchtime must. Cheerful green and white gingham is draped over the little timber tables. All around are shelves of wine and other goodies. The menu is recited by staff (in French if you wish) and might include a first of giant ravioli stuffed with mozzarella and topped with tomatoes, followed by lightly fried filets of *agone*, a local lake fish. Lunch is roughly from noon until 3pm. Otherwise, pop by for a glass of wine.

### ❦ RISTORANTE BELLAVISTA €€

☎ 031 22 10 31; Piazza di Bonacossa 2, Brunate; meals €35; ⏲ Wed-Mon

Ride the cable car up to Brunate to dine in this peaceful historic villa with great views over the lake. In the old town centre, the place is essentially one dining room with an adjoining terrace for summertime al fresco dining. As in many restaurants in Brunate, the menu reflects local traditions, with plenty of game meat in autumn and mains accompanied by polenta. A reasonable slew of pasta first courses include lip-smacking *tagliolini al sugo di cervo* (pasta in deer stew).

### ❦ RISTORANTE SOCIALE €€

☎ 031 26 40 42; Via Rodari 6; meals €25; ⏲ Wed-Mon

Once attached to a nearby theatre, the Sociale is a local institution. The present location has a pleasant downstairs dining area with reasonably packed tables

LAKE COMO & LAKE LUGANO

and, upstairs, a dining room sporting an outsized baroque fireplace and walls enlivened by frescos. In addition to the menu, the waiter will announce a constantly changing series of dishes of the day. Cooking is hearty and no-nonsense, ranging from *risotto trevisana* (with chicory) to huge Milanese *scaloppine* (veal escalopes).

♥ **TRATTORIA DEI COMBATTENTI** €
☎ 031 27 05 74; Via Balestra 5/9; meals €20;
🕑 Wed-Mon
Set off a lovely cobblestone lane just inside the old city walls, this popular trattoria is housed in the building of the Italian retired servicemen's association. You can sit inside at timber tables with muted decor, in an inner courtyard or the sunny gravel yard at the front. Opt for an *insalatone* (€9) if you want a 'big salad', or the €14 set lunch. Grilled meats take a prominent place, which you might precede with *chitarra ai frutti di mare* (chunky seafood spaghetti).

## TRANSPORT

**BUS** // **ASF Autolinee** (SPT; ☎ 031 24 72 47; www.sptlinea.it, in Italian) operates buses around the lake. Key routes include Como–Colico (€5.10, 1½ hours, three to five daily) via the west shore; Como–Bellagio (€2.75, 70 minutes, roughly hourly); and Como–Erba–Lecco (€2.75, one hour, almost hourly). Further afield, buses link Como with Bergamo (€4.40, 2¼ hours, up to six daily).

**CAR** // Traffic in and around Como tends to be intense. From Milan, take the A9 motorway and turn off at Monte Olimpino. The SP342 leads east to Lecco and west to Varese. The roads around the lake are narrow and, on weekends especially, can be hair-raising.

**PARKING** // Most parking is metered in Como and there are several covered car parks. Competition for spaces is intense.

**TRAIN** // Como's main train station (Como San Giovanni) is served from Milan's Stazione Centrale or Porta Garibaldi (€3.60 to €8.50 depending on type of train, 40 to 60 minutes, at least hourly) that continue into Switzerland. If travelling between Como and Lugano or Bellinzona, take the regional trains (on the Ticino side, look for the S10 train), as the long-distance trains

## ACCOMMODATION

Finding vacant rooms around Lakes Como and Lugano can be problematic in key places (Como, Bellagio, around Tremezzo and Varenna especially) from July to August and, to a lesser extent, at Easter. At these times it is wise to book ahead. At other times, generally you should not encounter too many problems if you just turn up.

Around Lake Como especially, apartment hire is popular if you are staying for a week or more and want a stable base. See p287 for some initial website search options. Also check out www.lakecomo.org.

In the mountains around the lakes, several mountain huts *(rifugi)* are scattered about for hikers. They open in summer only.

★ **Hotel La Pergola** (Bellagio, Pescallo, p295) A former convent that has lovely rooms overlooking a quiet corner of Lake Como

★ **Relais Regina Teodolinda** (Laglio, p296) A gorgeous lakefront villa

★ **Albergo Conca Azzurra** (Piona, p296) Great-value rooms; many include balconies and fine views

★ **Le Stanze del Lago** (Como, p294) Comfortable apartments in central Como, a stone's throw from the lake

between Milan and Zürich cost more. Trains from Milan's Stazione Nord (€3.60, one hour, hourly) use Como's lakeside Stazione FNM (aka Como Nord Lago).

# TRIANGOLO LARIANO

They call the stretch of territory between Como and Lecco in the south and Bellagio in the north the Triangolo Lariano (Lake Lario Triangle), a mountainous and crumpled territory that is jammed with a surprising variety of landscapes. From the high and exhilarating 32km coast road between Como and Bellagio to quiet inland villages, there's plenty to discover.

The pearl is Bellagio, suspended like a pendant on the promontory where the lake's western and eastern arms split and head south. Hidden from view along the Como–Bellagio road are enchanting lakeside villages, like Torno and Careno (which get no direct sunlight in winter). The sunnier 22km eastern branch, between Bellagio and Lecco, is an easier, pretty drive.

## ESSENTIAL INFORMATION

**TOURIST OFFICES // Bellagio Tourist Office** ( ☎ 031 95 02 04; Piazza Mazzini; ☺ 9am-12.30pm & 2.30-5pm Mon-Tue & Thu, 9am-1pm Wed, 9am-1pm & 3-6pm Fri & Sat); **PromoBellagio** ( ☎ 031 95 15 55; www.bellagiolakecomo.com; Piazza della Chiesa 14; ☺ 9.30am-1pm Mon, 9.30am-12.30pm & 1.30-4pm Wed-Fri), housed in an 11th-century watchtower.

## EXPLORING THE TRIANGOLO LARIANO

🌿 **BELLAGIO // SURROUND YOURSELF IN EXUBERANT GARDENS AND A PICTURE-POSTCARD TOWN**
It's impossible not to be smitten by **Bellagio's** (population 3020) waterfront

of bobbing boats, its maze of steep stone staircases, red-roofed and green-shuttered buildings, dark cypress groves and rhododendron-filled gardens. Like the prow of a beautiful vessel, it sits at the crux of the inverted Y that is Lake Como; the Como and Lecco arms of the lake wash off to port and starboard. Wander out of the old town centre to **Punta Spartivento** and gaze north up the third arm towards the Alps. In Roman times, Pliny had one of his favourite villas here.

The lavish gardens of **Villa Serbelloni** ( ☎ 031 95 15 55; Via Garibaldi 8; adult/child €8.50/4.50; ☺ tours 11am & 3.30pm Tue-Sun Apr-Oct) cover much of the promontory on which Bellagio sits. Visits are by guided tour only and numbers are limited; tickets are sold 10 minutes in advance at the small **information office** (Piazza della Chiesa 14) near the church. The villa has seen plenty of the great and the good swing by: Austria's Emperor Maximilian I, Ludovico il Moro and Queen Victoria, to name a few.

Garden lovers can also stroll the magnificent grounds of neoclassical **Villa Melzi d'Eril** ( ☎ 339 457 38 38; www .giardinidivillamelzi.it; Via Per Carcano, Lungo Lario Manzoni; adult/child €6/4; ☺ 9.30am-6.30pm Mar-Nov), built in 1808 for one of Napoleon's associates, and coloured by flowering azaleas and rhododendrons in spring. The gardens, adorned with statues scattered about, were the first English-style park on Lake Como. Other villas, closed to the public, are in this vicinity as well.

Walks around the town lead off to various hamlets, such as **Pescallo**, a small one-time fishing port about 1km from the centre. Several Romanesque churches can also be seen, above all the

**Basilica di San Giacomo** (Piazza della Chiesa) in central Bellagio, built in the 12th century by master builders from Como. Another church is the 11th-century **Chiesa di Santa Maria** in Loppia, only visible from the outside. Bellagio is hardly a secret. On summer weekends, bewildered foreign tourists are over-whelmed by hordes of day trippers up from Milan. Try to come midweek if you want a modicum of peace. It makes a nice base for ferry trips to other loca-tions on the lake, in particular Varenna, on Lake Como's east shore.

**☞ TORNO // SEEK OUT A LAKE BALCONY AND THE HOLY NAIL**
Spread around a point in the jagged shore, **Torno** is a lovely stop just 7km from Como – it is easy to understand why Hermann Hesse fell in love with it when he visited in 1913. The lakeside Piazza Casartelli, fronted by three restaurants and the **Chiesa di Santa Tecla** (a baroque remake of the Romanesque original), the tiny port and shady trees complete the picture of this front-row seat on the lake. About a 10-minute walk northeast around the point is the Romanesque-Gothic

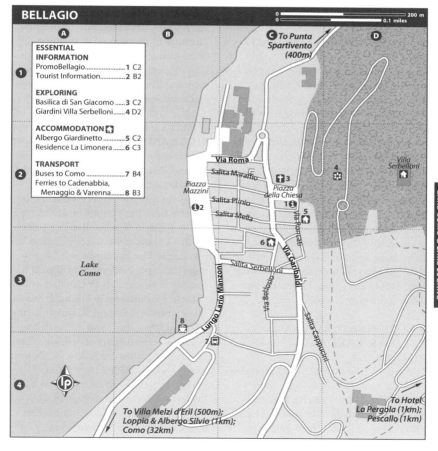

BELLAGIO

0 — 200 m
0 — 0.1 miles

**ESSENTIAL INFORMATION**
PromoBellagio.....................1 C2
Tourist Information..............2 B2

**EXPLORING**
Basilica di San Giacomo .....3 C2
Giardini Villa Serbelloni....4 D2

**ACCOMMODATION**
Albergo Giardinetto ............5 C2
Residence La Limonera ......6 C3

**TRANSPORT**
Buses to Como ......................7 B4
Ferries to Cadenabbia,
  Menaggio & Varenna........8 B3

To Punta Spartivento (400m)

Via Roma
Salita Maraffio
Piazza Mazzini
Salita Plinio
Salita Mella
Piazza della Chiesa
Via Roncati
Via Garibaldi
Via Bellagio
Salita Serbelloni
Salita Cappuccini
Lungo Lario Manzoni
Villa Serbelloni

Lake Como

To Villa Melzi d'Eril (500m); Loppia & Albergo Silvio (1km); Como (32km)

To Hotel La Pergola (1km); Pescallo (1km)

LAKE COMO & LAKE LUGANO

Chiesa di San Giovanni. It holds what is purported to be a holy nail from the cross of Jesus Christ, left behind by a German crusading bishop in the 11th century. About 1.5km further east along the lake, Villa Pliniana was built in the 16th century (and therefore did not belong to the Plinys) and is one of the oldest ones located on the lake (Lord Byron stayed here and Percy Shelley thought about buying it). It may open to the public in 2010. An intermittently flowing fountain occasionally gushes from under the building into the lake. The phenomenon was observed by the Plinys and, much later, by Leonardo da Vinci.

### ❦ CARENO // BLINK AND YOU'LL MISS IT

About 1.5km south of the town of Nesso, **Careno** is signposted but, if you blink, you'll miss it. This tiny, lakeside hamlet looks like an inverted triangle from the opposite shore, with its church, the Romanesque **Chiesa di San Martino**, at the bottom. Satisfaction with discovery and a shady, lakeside stroll should be followed by a meal at the charming **Trattoria al Porto** ( ☎ 031 91 01 95; Via al Pontile 26; meals €15-20; ☻ Tue-Sun). With its oddly shaped balcony-pergola just above the ferry landing, this place is a hit with Como folks in the know and specialises in lake fish. The bus stop for Careno is between Km15 and Km16 . Head down the steep, stone stairs from the road.

### ❦ MADONNA DEL GHISALLO // CYCLISTS, MAKE YOUR PILGRIMAGE

In the high-country village of **Magreglio** (497m), 7km south of Bellagio, stands a simple 17th-century church known as the **Santuario della Madonna del Ghisallo**. The road up has frequently been

included as a classic stage of the Giro d'Italia cycle race, and is known to professional and amateur cyclists alike. The sanctuary long ago became a symbolic finishing line for cyclists, who began leaving mementoes there. The place's importance for two-wheeled enthusiasts was such that Pope Pius XII declared the Madonna del Ghisallo the patron of cyclists. The gifts and tokens left at the sanctuary down the years became so numerous that it was decided to open the nearby **Museo del Ciclismo** ( ☎ 031 96 58 85; www.museodelghisallo.it, in Italian; Via Gino Bartali 4; adult/child €5/3; ☻ 9.30am-5.30pm Tue-Fri, 9am-6pm Sat & Sun Apr-Oct, 10am-5pm Tue-Sat, 9.30am-5.30pm Sun Nov-Mar) to contain the overflow. The museum is devoted to all aspects of the business of cycling, with 100 film clips of great moments in Italian cycling, memorabilia (including many bicycles) and temporary exhibitions.

### ❦ HIKES // PATHFIND ON THE RIDGE AND ROYAL WAY

Hiking options abound in the Triangolo Lariano. The classic trail is known as the **Dorsale** (Ridge) and zigzags for 31km across the interior of this mountainous country from the Brunate funicular station to Bellagio. The standard trail takes about 12 hours and is usually done in two stages. The standard route follows mule trails, presents no particular difficulties to moderately fit ramblers and is also ideal for **mountain biking**. It passes along rivers and around mountain peaks, largely skirting the towns until arriving at San Giovanni, a part of Bellagio. The more adventurous can follow the Dorsale Creste trail, which follows a series of mountain crests. Several mountain huts *(rifugi)* are dotted along the way, and you'll find a couple of accommodation options at **Pian del Tivano**, roughly halfway along the trail. You can do a little cross-country skiing (sci di fondo) here in winter. From the 17th century until the early 1900s, when the coast road from Como to Bellagio was completed, travellers used the 32km **Strada Regia** (Royal Way), a partly stone-paved path that links various villages on the west coast of the Triangolo Lariano from Torno to Lezzeno. The easiest stretch connects Torno and Pognana Lario (about five hours), while the stage from Pognana to Lezzeno via Nesso (or Careno) branches into mountainous back country between villages. Other walking trails abound. Ask at the main Como tourist office (p109) for the fine Carta dei Sentieri (Trail Map, 1:25,000) produced by the Comunità Montana Triangolo Lariano.

### ♣ ABBAZIA DI SAN PIETRO AL MONTE // DO PENANCE AND CLIMB A STAIRWAY TO HEAVEN

Birdsong and the rush of a mountain stream will put some pep into your step as you make the pilgrimage to the Romanesque **Abbazia di San Pietro al Monte** (St Peter on the Mount). Medieval monks seemed to have had both a thing about punishing themselves and a love of good views. From the upper streets (park at Via del Pozzo) of sprawling hillside **Civate** (330m), 5km southwest of Lecco, it's a beautiful but uphill 30- to 40- minute walk (for the moderately unfit) on way-marked stone trail No 10. The trail passes fields and then winds up into dense woods before reaching a clearing where this abbey has stood (at 663m) since the 11th century. If the walk seems like penance the reward may seem close to heaven. The curious two-part Benedictine abbey (which you will probably only be able to admire from outside) is in an idyllic setting that affords views south over **Lake Annone**, one of a string of peaceful lakes along the Como–Lecco road. The first building is an enchanting chapel dedicated to St Benedict, a squat affair with apses protruding from three sides. The main building rises behind. A restored staircase leads up to a unique semicircular pronaos on two levels, which accesses the eastern apse (there is an apse at each end of the church). If you're lucky and it's open, you'll find medieval frescos depicting mostly Old Testament scenes inside.

## GASTRONOMIC HIGHLIGHTS

### ♣ ALBERGO BELVEDERE // TORNO €

☎ 031 41 91 00; Piazza Casartelli 3; meals €20; ☽ Wed-Mon Mar-Dec

At the south end of Torno's lakeside square, this old-time hotel restaurant has a bucolic touch, with timber tables and walls dripping with black-and-white photos. In the warmer months, it is opened out to a series of terrace tables, shaded by the twisting branches of a linden tree that, since 1987, has been patiently cultivated sideways to form a pergola. From here you can see Como's Villa Olmo and the lights of Cernobbio. Lake fish and meat options feature prominently.

---

## ROMANESQUE

Architecture buffs might want to search out the sprinkling of fine Lombard Romanesque churches scattered about the Triangolo Lariano. Among the lakeside villages, Careno (**Chiesa di San Martino**), Bellagio (**Basilica di San Giacomo**) and Torno (**Chiesa di San Giovanni**) stand out for their well-preserved churches. Inland, among the most important are those in Lasnigo (**Chiesa di San Alessandro**), Barni (**Chiesa di San Pietro**) and Rezzago (**Chiesa di SS Cosmo e Damiano**).

🍴 **ALBERGO SILVIO // BELLAGIO €€**
☎ 031 95 03 22; www.bellagiosilvio.com; Via Carcano 12; meals €25-30; ⊗ Mar–mid-Nov & Christmas week
Operating since 1919, this place must be getting something right to achieve the seemingly unanimous acclaim. Simple food offerings at reasonable prices combine with lovely views west over the lake. From the pergola garden outside, you also espy the Romanesque Chiesa di Santa Maria of Loppia in among the cypresses. You might start with a *riso e filetto di pesce* (rice with lemon juice and Parmesan cheese, topped by filets of the day's lake catch), followed by a *frittura leggera di luccio* (light fry-up of pike chunks). It's 1km south of the centre of Bellagio above Loppia, which you can walk down to from here along an overgrown stairway.

## TRANSPORT

**CAR //** The roads are mostly narrow and winding and can be dense with traffic on weekends especially. Watch out for groups of cyclists too.

**PARKING //** Especially on weekends, parking can be near impossible in the villages along the coast between Como and Bellagio. In Bellagio itself, there is a fair amount of meter parking (€1.50 an hour). It gets a little easier in inland locations and down the coast from Bellagio to Lecco (except in Onno and other beach locations on summer weekends).

**BUS //** Small buses rattle more or less hourly from Como to Bellagio (€2.75, 70 minutes). Other buses serve inland destinations.

**BOAT //** Regular car ferries link Bellagio to Varenna and Cadenabbia (€3.60, 10 minutes). A small car and driver pay €8.30 each way.

# LAKE COMO WEST BANK

By not having the mountains block the light, the western shore gets the most sunshine on the lake. For this reason, it's lined with the most lavish villas, where high-fliers from football players to film stars reside. The shore stretches 75km from Como north to Sorico at the lake's tip; from here you can continue north along an Alpine valley to Chiavenna and, 40km further, cross into Switzerland.

## ESSENTIAL INFORMATION

**TOURIST OFFICES // Menaggio Tourist Office** ( ☎ 0344 3 29 24; www.menaggio.com; Piazza Garibaldi 3; ⊗ 9am-12.30pm & 2.30-6pm Mon-Sat, 10am-4pm Sun Apr-Oct, 9am-12.30pm & 2.30-6pm Mon-Tue & Thu-Sat Nov-Mar); **Tremezzo Tourist Office** ( ☎ 0344 4 04 93; Via Statale Regina; ⊗ 9am-noon & 3.30-6.30pm Wed-Mon Apr-Oct).

## EXPLORING LAKE COMO WEST BANK

🍴 **CERNOBBIO // GASP AT THE WEALTH OF THE VILLAS**
The shoreline of Cernobbio, a graceful town 5km north of Como (and now melded to it with residential districts), is laced with a series of fine villas fronting the water. Inland, towards the Swiss frontier a few kilometres west, was once fairly industrialised. This is a source of wealth for those lucky residents located down by the lake. It's probably true that half of Cernobbio's visitors come by in the hope of spotting George Clooney at one of its central cafes (he lives about 10km up the road in Laglio), especially since scenes from *Ocean's 12* were shot here.

### Villa d'Este
The other half of visitors are intent on beholding the gardens of **Villa d'Este** ( ☎ 031 34 81; www.villadeste.it; Via Regina 40; ⊗ 10.30-11.30am & 3.30-4.30pm Mar-Nov), a 16th-century palace that now houses a luxury hotel. The gardens burst with spring

colour – rhododendrons, camellias, hy-drangeas, oleanders, azaleas and jasmine bushes. Among the many grand trees is a venerable plane tree more than 500 years old, but wisteria, pines, palms, cypress, magnolias and many more also thrive. Since 2004 the hotel restaurant has had its own vegetable and herb garden. You can visit only in groups of no fewer than 10 people by prior booking.

### Villa Erba

The 19th-century **Villa Erba** ( ☎ 031 34 91; www.villaerba.it; Largo Luchino Visconti 4) has been turned into a congress centre, sporting a somewhat incongruous modern glass structure plonked down near the villa. That said, business generated has al-lowed the creation of a museum inside the villa. It is open only for organised visits that are booked ahead. Several other villas are scattered about, but gen-erally they are closed to the public. One you may find open occasionally (ask at the tourist office) is **Villa Pizzo** ( ☎ 031 51 12 62; Via Regina 46).

### Villa Bernasconi

One of the most outstanding *stile liberty* (Italian art nouveau) villas in the lakes area, **Villa Bernasconi** (www.villabernasconi .eu; Via Regina 7), was built by successful textile merchant Davide Bernasconi in 1906. It bears all the classic elements, with use of ceramics, stained class, wrought iron and, a comparative nov-elty, cement. The floral relief decora-tion on the exterior displays silkworms, moths and mulberry leaves – a direct advertisement of where Bernasconi's wealth came from. Town Hall has re-stored much of the long-abandoned interior of the building, which may be open for exhibitions in 2010.

❦ MONTE BISBINO // HIT THE HIGH ROAD FOR FABULOUS VIEWS

Following signs out of central Cernob-bio, take a scenic drive that winds 17km up through the residential villages behind Cernobbio to **Monte Bisbino** (1325m), a fabulous lookout spot. You won't need to wait to reach the mountain for great views – at every turn on the way up, you look back down on the lake from a different angle. After a seemingly endless series of switchbacks on an in-creasingly narrow road that, in its latter stages, is enclosed by a canopy of thick woods, you emerge at the top. Climb the stairs to where the TV antennas are (and where you may find a bar open if you're lucky) and then take in views of the Como end of the lake, the Lombard plain to Milan and as far off as the Swiss Alps (including the Jungfrau) on a clear day.

❦ MOLTRASIO & LAGLIO // PEEK AT MORE VILLAS, GEORGE CLOONEY AND A ROMANESQUE CHURCH

The lower lakeside road (Via Regina Vecchia) skirts the lakeshore out of Cernobbio and past a fabulous row of 19th-century villas (all private property) around **Moltrasio**. Winston Churchill holidayed in one (Villa Le Rose) just after WWII and another is owned by the Versace fashion dynasty. Gianni Versace, who was murdered in Miami Beach, Florida, in 1997, is buried in the village cemetery. Near **Villa Passalacqua** (www .thevillapassalacqua.com), which is sometimes used for events, is a lovely, little 11th-century Romanesque church, the **Chiesa di Sant'Agata**, which houses some intriguing frescos (if you get lucky and find it open). A few kilometres north, the villa-lined hamlet of **Laglio** is home to *Ocean's* star George Clooney (he lives in **Villa Oleandra**). In both places, stop anywhere, clatter down the cobblestoned lanes and stairs to the lake, gawp at the villas as best you can and dream about how making it big in Hollywood could transform your life.

### ❦ PIGRA // RIDE HIGH FROM ARGEGNO TO PIGRA

The departure point into the mountains is **Argegno** on the **Funivia Argegno-Pigra** ( ☎ 031 81 08 44; one way/return €2.50/3.40; ⏱ 8.30am-noon & 2.30-6.30pm, shorter hours in winter). The cable car (about 300m north of Piazza Roma) makes the five-minute climb to the 860m-high village of **Pigra** every 30 minutes. You won't be disappointed on arrival. From the square where the cable car arrives and from the grounds of the tiny Chiesa di Santa Margherita, the views back down over the lake are beautiful. Pigra itself warrants some wandering along its centuries-old lanes and stairways.

### ❦ VAL D'INTELVI // GET LOST IN A BACK FRONTIER VALLEY

Argegno is the main entry point into the Val d'Intelvo, picturesque hill country where various villages are dotted about between Lakes Como, Piano and Lugano. A web of minor roads is spun out across the area and you need your own vehicle to get about. The main road, the SP13, leads 9km from Argegno to **San Fedele d'Intelvi**, the main town. Before entering San Fedele, take the road south to Casasco d'Intelvi and on to **Erbonne** (963m) a frontier hamlet that, until the 1970s, was a key crossing point for smugglers. Desperate locals known as *spalloni* resorted to smuggling products from Switzerland to stave off poverty. It seems hard to imagine that a few kilometres from the

glories of Lake Como's noble pleasure domes, these rural folk had been living in such misery just a few decades ago. Pitted against them were the Guardia di Finanza, a kind of customs police. Their former tiny barracks in Erbonne, now possibly the smallest museum in Italy (the **Museo della Guardia di Finanza e del Contrabbando**) is stuffed with uniforms, and other reminders of this strange game of cat and mouse – you simply peer in through the glass door. A footpath and bridge lead five minutes' walk out of the village over the valley that marks the border with Switzerland. Wander back and forth at will. There's also a great place to eat (p125).

### ❦ CIMA SIGHIGNOLA // ENJOY THE VIEW FROM THE BALCONY OF ITALY

For extraordinary views west over Lake Lugano and (on a clear day) as far as the Alpine peaks of Monte Rosa and the Matterhorn, head for this high point 6km of winding road northwest of Lanzo d'Intelvi, itself 6km west of the San Fedele d'Intelvi, the main town in the Val d'Intelvi. The vista from what is also known as the **Balcone d'Italia** (1320m) is slightly spoiled by the huge clump of concrete of a never completed cable car, but this shouldn't deter you. Below lies all of Lugano, its lake and mountain peaks and, beyond, you can make out part of Lake Maggiore, Varese, the Alps and the Lombard plains.

### ❦ ISOLA COMACINA // FEAST ON LAKE COMO'S ONLY ISLAND

Once the site of a Roman fort and medieval settlement, Lake Como's only island forms its own little bay with the mainland. When the Lombards invaded northern Italy, the island held out as a

Byzantine redoubt, and slowly filled with houses and churches, the whole known as Cristopolis. They even say the Holy Grail was deposited here for a time. The medieval settlement was razed by Como in 1169 as punishment for its loyalty to Milan. Today, as silent witness to this terrible event, lie the scant ruins of the Romanesque **Chiesa di Sant'Eufemia** and, next to it, the more solid remnants of the triple apse of a pre-Romanesque **church** at the north end of the island, about a five-minute stroll from the boat landing. Since 1947 **Locanda dell'Isola** ( ☎ 0344 5 50 83; www.comacina.it; set menu €62) has been serving the same abundant set menu on the south side of the island, characterised by a round of nine vegetables, cold meats, trout, chicken, cheese and dessert. To finish off, brandy is burned in a huge pot to ward off the excommunication of the island declared by the Bishop of Como back in the 12th century. Or you could just have a beer at **Bar La Botte**, just below the restaurant and with a gravel lakeside terrace. There's a **Boat Service** ( ☎ 031 82 19 55) that shuttles from a landing on Piazza Matteotti in Sala Comacina (€6 return by day, €7 return to restaurant by night) between 9am and 10pm, with a final return service leaving at midnight.

### 🌱 SACRO MONTE DI OSSUCCIO // SOOTHE THE SPIRIT AND DRINK IN THE VIEWS

High above the hamlets that make up the village of Ossuccio, a series of 14 chapels (built from 1635 to 1714) dedicated to the Mysteries of the Rosary lead to the **Sacro Monte di Ossuccio** (Santuario della Madonna del Soccorso; www.comunicare.it/ofmcap/luoghi/ossuccio.htm, in Italian), one of several such devotional paths created in the 17th century in Lombardy and Piedmont (the only one on Lake Como) and included in a World Heritage listing. The 20-minute climb along the cobblestone lane is worth it more than anything else for the matchless views that it offers over olive groves, the Isola Comacina and the lake beyond. At the top, you reach the Santuario della Madonna del Soccorso, which houses a 14th-century sculpture of Our Lady to which miraculous powers were long attributed. From Ossuccio, drive up to Piazza Papa Giovanni XXIII, where the pilgrim path begins. You'll find the **Trattoria del Santuario** ( ☎ 0344 5 63 11; meals €25-30; 🕙 Wed-Mon) at the top. Keen walkers could proceed uphill (about two hours for the moderately fit) to reach the splendid Romanesque **Chiesa di San Benedetto**, at the heart of a picture-postcard setting. Down in Ossuccio itself, the main road runs past the tiny 11th-century **Chiesa dei SS Giacomo e Filippo**, whose unique, lollipop-shaped Romanesque bell tower is something of a symbol of Lake Como.

### 🌱 VILLA BALBIANELLO // TREAD IN JAMES BOND'S SHADOW VIA A VILLA AND A BEACH

Located just 1km outside **Lenno**, this was where scenes from 2006's James Bond remake, *Casino Royale,* and *Stars Wars Episode II* were shot; it is one of the most dramatic locations on Lake Como (if not the world). Built by Cardinal Angelo Durini in 1787, **Villa Balbianello** ( ☎ 0344 5 61 10; www.fondoambiente.it; Via Comoedia 5, Località Balbianello; villa & gardens adult/child €11/6, gardens only adult/child €5/2.50; 🕙 gardens 10am-6pm Tue & Thu-Sun mid-Mar–mid-Nov) was used for a while by Allied commanders at the tail end of WWII. It is set amid florid gardens on a promontory. The sculpted gardens, which seem to drip off the high promontory like sauce off a melting ice-cream cone, are the perfect place for hopelessly romantic elopers to spend a day. Visitors are only allowed to walk the 1km path (amid vegetation so florid as to seem Southeast Asian) from the Lenno landing stage to the estate on Tuesday and at weekends. On other days, you have to take a **taxi boat** ( ☎ 333 410 38 54; return per person €6) from Lenno. If you want to see the villa, you must join a guided tour (generally conducted in Italian) by 4.15pm.

### ❤ LIDO DI LENNO // GET CHILLED AT THIS SUMMERTIME BEACH SCENE

Summer evenings in Lenno take on a hedonistic hue at the **Lido di Lenno** ( ☎ 0344 5 70 93; www.lidodilenno.com; Via Comoedia 1; ☺ 10am-3.30am daily May-Sep). People from near and far converge on this artificial sandy beach, located virtually next to the path and boat pier for Villa Balbianello, to enjoy food from the grill, cocktails (€6 to €8) and a (brief) dip in the chilly, clear waters of the lake. Access to the beach is €4; access to the bar is free. It may close earlier midweek if there are too few customers.

### ❤ VILLA CARLOTTA // IMAGINE A PRINCESS'S LIFE IN TREMEZZO

Tremezzo (population 1300) is high on everyone's list for a visit to the 17th-century, waterfront **Villa Carlotta** ( ☎ 0344 4 04 05; www.villacarlotta.it; Via Statale Regina 2; adult/senior & student/child €8/4/free; ☺ 9am-6pm Apr-Oct, 9-11.30am & 2-4.30pm mid-Mar–Easter & end Oct–mid-Nov), whose botanic gardens are filled with colour in spring from orange trees knitted into pergolas and some of Europe's finest rhododendrons, azaleas and camellias. The villa, strung with paintings, sculptures (some by Antonio Canova) and tapestries, takes its name from the Prussian princess who was given the place in 1847 as a wedding present from her mother. Upstairs, rooms with period furniture provide an insight into the life of the princessly. You too can swan from the Salotto Impero (Empire Room) to Carlotta's bedroom and wonder what it must have been like to hit the hay after a hard day at the villa. It is a short walk southwest of the Cadenabbia car ferry stop.

### ❤ STUNNING VIEWS // HIKE TO A MOUNTAIN HUT ABOVE MENAGGIO

Three km north of Cadenabbia, **Menaggio** (population 3260) has a cute cobblestone old centre, a useful tourist office and a ferry stop. The central square overlooking the lake has a couple of cafes that are perfect for lake-gazing and people-watching. Addicts of panoramic

## COMO WALKS

The west bank of Lake Como offers widely diverse walking possibilities. For one suggested strolling route of 10km between Cadenabbia and Colonno, to the south, have a look at **Greenway del Lago di Como** (www.greenwaydellago.it). For something altogether more challenging, you could head inland and get onto the **Via dei Monti Lariani**, a 130km trail from Cernobbio in the south to Sorico in the north. Keeping largely to high ground well above the lake, the journey is punctuated by mountain huts (rifugi) and the occasional village where you can find accommodation. Reckon on six days to do the walk comfortably. The trail is part of the 6000km Sentiero Italia marked out by the Club Alpino Italiano, and it's one of the most popular among hikers in Lombardy.

views who happen to have their hiking boots with them could take a minor road out of Menaggio for Plesio and then follow a walking trail (park in the hamlet of Breglia) for about two hours to the **Rifugio Menaggio** ( ☎ 0344 3 72 82; www.caimenaggio .it, in Italian; ☉ Sat, Sun & holidays mid-Jun–mid-Sep), where you can sleep and get hot meals. At 1383m altitude, the views down over the lake are ample reward for the climb. Plenty of other walking routes wind off from the refuge.

### ❧ LAKE PIANO // SLINK OFF DOWN THE BACK ROAD TO LUGANO

Menaggio is the jumping-off point for Lake Piano in Val Menaggio, a remote valley connecting Lake Como with Lake Lugano, which straddles the Italy–Switzerland border to the west. Placid Lake Piano is protected by the **Riserva Naturale Lago di Piano**. Three marked nature trails, 4km to 5.3km long, encircle the lake, and the **visitors centre** ( ☎ 0344 7 49 61; www.riservalagodipiano.it, in Italian; Via Statale 117, Piano di Porlezza; ☉ 9am-noon Mon, Tue & Sat, 2-4pm Wed May-Oct), on the lake's northern shore, rents out mountain bikes (€2.50 per hour) and row boats (€7 per hour), and arranges guided visits on foot (€5 per person per half-day or €8 per person per full day).

### ❧ SANTA MARIA REZZONICO // ADMIRE A CASTLE AND FLOP ON THE BEACH

Beyond Menaggio, the northern stretch of the lake is known as the Alto Lario (Upper Lario). It is far less touristed than other more illustrious points along the lake but holds some enticing secrets. At **Rezzonico**, an extension of Santa Maria, some 6km north of Menaggio, is a quiet pebble beach with wooden fishingfolk's seats lined up along it. To find it (when travelling north from Menaggio), follow the signs to Santa Maria and then, just before a tunnel on the SS340, a side road to Rezzonico. This brings you to a 13th-century stone **castle**, built by the Della Torre clan and largely intact (closed to the public). Around it, stone stair paths lead downhill to porticoed houses right to the lake's edge. A path marked Via al Lago to the castle's left winds past grey-stone houses and lush green gardens to the beach.

### ❧ GRAVEDONA & AROUND // ADMIRE A MASTERPIECE OF COMO ROMANESQUE

Behind a gently curved bay on the lake is where **Gravedona** (population 2670) spreads out. Towards the southern end stands a unique and beautiful Romanesque church, the late-12th-century **Chiesa di Santa Maria del Tiglio** (Piazza XI Febbraio). Square-based and with apses protruding on three sides, the structure has an unusual bell tower (probably added later), octagonal at the top, that rises from the centre of the facade. Inside, high arched galleries allow in sunlight at the top of the church. Colourful remnants of frescos dating to the 14th and 15th centuries depict, among other things, the Last Judgment. The heavy wooden crucifix is a fine example of Romanesque carving.

### Peglio & Livo

A 6km road winds out of Gravedona up to the plateau town of **Peglio** (650m), whose **Chiesa di Sant'Eusebio** offers wonderful views of the lake and plains around Gravedona. The church boasts 17th-century frescos. About 2km further, just beyond the hamlet of Livo, the 15th-century **Chiesa di San Giacomo** is also graced with frescos and offers a more restricted lake view.

## LAKE BEACHES

With the exception of an unkempt stretch at the lake's northern end around Gera Lario, beaches around Lake Como tend to be of the grey pebble variety. That doesn't stop locals getting out for a bracing dip and sunbathe. At some of the more popular ones, sun lounges are set out and you'll find summertime bars. Restaurants and pizzerias are never far off. Among the nicer stretches are the beach at **Rezzonico** (p123) on the west bank, a series of strands at **Onno** (about halfway down the road between Bellagio and Lecco) and the strip at **Abbadia Lariana** on the east shore, north of Lecco.

### ❦ WATER SPORTS // GRAB YOUR OWN ZODIAC AND WATERSKI

Although possible at various points around the lake, boat hire is popular at the north end of the lake, with several outlets at Dongo, Gravedona and Domaso, which is 3km northeast of Gravedona. At **Comolakeboats** ( ☎ 333 401 49 95; www.comolakeboats.it; Via Antica Regina 26, Domaso) you can hire your own zodiac (expect to pay €80 for two hours) as well as organise to do waterskiing (€55 for 30 minutes) and wakeboarding (€50 for 30 minutes). For an extra charge, it can also provide instructors.

## GASTRONOMIC HIGHLIGHTS

### ❦ BARCHETTA // ARGEGNO €€

☎ 031 82 11 05; www.ristorantebarchetta.it, in Italian; Piazza Roma 2; meals €25-30; ⏱ Tue-Sun
One of a couple of good restaurants based on this square overlooks the lake. The 'Little Boat', appropriately enough, specialises in lake fish and, come autumn, dishes using mushrooms and

truffles. A few tables are scattered along the footpath, but dining inside is a more refined experience. The food is fabulous. Start with the *gnocchi zola e rucola* (gnocchi with strong Gorgonzola cheese and rocket) and follow with an abundant *misto pesce di lago* (a mixed grill of lake fish).

### ❦ GATTO NERO // ROVENNA (CERNOBBIO) €€€

☎ 031 51 20 42; www.il-gatto-nero.it, in Italian; Via Monte Santo 89; meals €60-70; ⏱ lunch & dinner Wed-Sun, dinner Tue
Finding your way up the narrow labyrinth is a challenge, but the effort is repaid on arrival. Try to book a front-row table for the unobstructed view of the lake far below in this locally renowned eatery far above central Cernobbio. The dining rooms, with dark-tile floors, plenty of timber and low lighting, are pure romanticism. If it's on the menu, the risotto with fresh lake perch, a local classic, is particularly delicate in flavour. The huge scales by the entrance are not used for weighing guests on the way out.

### ❦ LA CUCINA DI MARIANNA // CADENABBIA €€

☎ 0344 4 31 11; www.lamarianna.com; set menus €30-45, light menu €18, children's menu €12; ⏱ Tue-Sun
With its shady terrace jutting out over the water, this is about the most romantic spot you could choose to eat around the Cadenabbia area. Marianna cooks by theme, so if Tuesday is Venice day (with salted cod pâté and stewed cuttlefish), Thursday is Garden day, with lots of veggies. So there's no hassle ordering. Food servings are copious and of good quality, and there's no pretence at going beyond a down-home feel.

### ❦ OSTERIA DEL VALICO // ERBONNE €€

☎ 031 83 01 74; meals €25; ✆ Wed-Mon Jun-Sep, Sat, Sun & holidays Oct-May

The frontier village of Erbonne has had an eatery for more than 100 years. It has moved from house to house, snaking up in its present charming location since 2000, which has timber floors and a porch. Guests sit at a handful of tables, with ceramics built into the wood, for simple local fare, such as *pizzoccheri* followed by polenta served with pork, liver or local cheeses. When you've had your fill, ask for a grappa (a huge bottle hangs from the ceiling at the bar) or an Amaro Gratta il Culo (Scratch Your Arse Amaro, a herbal liquor) to digest it all.

### ❦ TAVERNA BLEU // SALA COMICINA €€

☎ 0344 5 51 07; www.tavernableu.it; Via Puricelli 4; meals €25-30; ✆ Wed-Mon

Known all over the lake for its fine fish dishes, the Blue Tavern is in a lovely spot down from the main road at lake level. Sit in the shady gravel-and-grass garden by the canary-yellow building that hosts indoor dining and a charming hotel. Eat à la carte or opt for the four-course set menu (€40), which includes a tasty mixed vegetable dish, a *risotto con burro e parmigiano* (with butter and Parmesan) and a melt-in-the-mouth filet of lake perch.

### ❦ TRATTORIA DEL FAGIANO // TOSNACCO €€

☎ 031 29 00 00; www.trattoriadelfagiano.it, in Italian; Via Roma 54; meals €25; ✆ lunch & dinner Wed-Sun, lunch Mon

A short climb above the SS340 road and Moltrasio, you'll stumble across this easygoing, family affair. The Pheasant serves no-nonsense local food (fish features highly, but several meat dishes are on offer too) in a good-natured, rambunctious atmosphere. Booking is strongly advised for Friday, Saturday and Sunday nights, as the place is a local favourite and often packed to the rafters. On weekdays, it has a sensational set menu (excluding drinks) for just €7.50. From the square, you even get a glimpse of the lake.

### ❦ TRATTORIA LA VIGNETTA // SALA COMICINA €€

☎ 0344 344 70 55; www.lavignetta.it; Via Monte Grappa 32; meals €30-35; ✆ Wed-Mon

A five-minute uphill walk along a jasmine-perfumed residential lane, this hotel restaurant sits atop a little rise. Inside, the timber-panelled dining room with its antique wooden tables is a lovely setting for perfectly oven-cooked fish, perhaps preceded by a creamy risotto. The *rombo* (turbot), prepared with cherry tomatoes, olives and giant Sicilian capers, is especially good. On a balmy evening, take a table in the gravel garden outside and admire the surrounding greenery.

## TRANSPORT

**CAR //** Traffic along the west shore of Lake Como can be intense at the best of times and choked on summer weekends. The SS340 road runs some way inland and is characterised largely by tunnels. This is for moving around quickly. More picturesque at the southern end (between Cernobbio and Brienno) is the old Via Regina shore road.

**PARKING //** Parking is restricted or metered in town centres and can be difficult on summer weekends and holidays.

**BUS //** Buses run the length of the lake from Como to Colico: Como to Menaggio takes about an hour 10 minutes; from there you change for Colico (another hour). Buses stop in most towns en route. Services between Como and Cernobbio run often and take 10 to 15 minutes.

**BOAT //** Regular car ferries (every half hour through most of the day) cross from Cadenabbia to Bellagio (€3.60 per adult or €8.60 per small car and driver).

# LAKE COMO EAST BANK

Lake Como's eastern shore has a wilder feel to it than the more illustrious west. Little touristed, it hides three gems that alone justify the effort. Back-country drives take you still further off the beaten track. The main town is **Lecco** (population 47,330), with a shady and gently winding waterfront and a pleasant nucleus of pedestrian streets, but little of specific interest.

## ESSENTIAL INFORMATION

**TOURIST OFFICES //** **Lecco Tourist Office** ( ☎ 0341 29 57 20; www.turismo.provincia.lecco.it; Via Nazario Sauro 6; ❧ 9am-1pm & 2.30-6pm); **Varenna Tourist Office** ( ☎ 0341 83 03 67; www.varenna

italy.com; Via del IV Novembre 7; ❧ 10am-12.30pm & 3-5.30pm Tue-Sat, 10am-12.30pm Sun Apr-Sep, to 5pm Sat Oct-Mar); **Valtellina Tourist Office** ( ☎ 0342 45 11 50; www.valtellina.it; Piazzale Bertacchi 77, Sondrio; ❧ 9am-12.30pm & 3.30-6.30pm Mon-Fri, 9am-noon Sat).

## EXPLORING LAKE COMO EAST BANK

### ❦ VARENNA // ADMIRE VILLA GARDENS AND ROMANESQUE FRESCOS

**Varenna** (population 850), a beguiling village bursting with florid plantlife, exotic flowery perfumes and birdsong, is a short ferry ride away from its rival in postcard beauty, Bellagio (p114). Its pastel-coloured houses defy the standard laws of physics, seemingly gripping for all they're worth to the steep slopes that rise from the lake. High above the lake, the SP72 road passes two luxurious villas and the town's main square, Piazza San Giorgio, before skooting on north. A series of lanes-cum-stairways slithers down the hill past bunched-up houses to the lake. About halfway down, and parallel to the SP72 is Main St, Varenna; the narrow, pedestrian-only Via XX Settembre.

**Villas**

Those arriving by ferry land at Piazzale Martiri della Libertà. From there, a 15- to 20-minute stroll follows the shore south and cuts up to Piazza San Giovanni and the town's main attractions, **Villa Cipressi** ( ☎ 0341 83 01 13; Via IV Novembre 18-22; adult/child €3/1.50; ❧ 9am-7pm Mar-Oct), now a luxury hotel, and, 100m further south, **Villa Monastero** ( ☎ 0341 29 54 50; www.villa monastero.eu; Via IV Novembre; villa & gardens adult/senior/child 7-13yr/child under 7yr, €6/4/1/free, gardens only adult/senior/child €4/2/1/free; ❧ gardens 9am-6pm daily, villa 9am-1pm & 2-6pm Sat, Sun & holidays Mar-Oct), a former convent turned into a

## MANZONI

A slow learner at school, Alessandro Manzoni (1785–1873) became an Italian icon as the country's greatest 19th-century novelist. Born into a family from Barzio, outside Lecco in Valsassina, Manzoni led a life of relative ease, with revenue from farmlands in Lombardy. Thus freed up, he devoted considerable time to writing his magnum opus, *I promessi sposi* (The Betrothed), an epic novel set in fictional plague times and at the same time a thinly veiled expression of Italian nationalism at a time when the country was largely under foreign control. He wrote in what he hoped to express as a standard national Italian language, based largely on Tuscan, abandoning his own Milanese dialect. He died three years after Italy achieved his dream of unity and independence.

vast residence by the Mornico family from the 17th to the 19th centuries. In both cases, a stroll through the magnificent gardens, which reach down to the lake, is a balm to the senses. A wander through Villa Monastero is a lesson in how well the other half can live – in the room that fronts the bathroom, the walls are covered in finely engraved Spanish leather to protect the walls from humidity! Magnolias (including one specimen in front of the villa said to be up to 400 years old), camellias and yucca trees are among the villas' floral wonders.

### Church

Much overlooked in all the excitement about Varenna's villas are the lovely 14th-century frescos, somewhat damaged but nevertheless full of colour, tucked inside the tiny Romanesque **Chiesa di San Giovanni Battista** (Piazza San Giovanni). Opening times are hit-and-miss.

### ♥ VEZIO'S VIEWS // BEHOLD VARENNA FROM A HIGH-CASTLE EYRIE

The SP65 mountain road winds away 3km eastward from the north exit of Varenna into the hills to the hamlet of **Vezio** (thought by some to have Etruscan origins), dominated by the ruins of the 13th-century **Castello di Vezio** ( ☎ 348 824 2504; www.castellodivezio.it; admission €4; ⌚ 10am-6pm). From this one-time fortified watchtower (part of a chain of such towers erected along the lake in the Middle Ages and, in this case, the successor to older forts since Roman times), gaze down upon Varenna and over the lake. An old **mule path** from the Olivedo (north end) part of Varenna also leads up here – it's about a 30-minute puff uphill. A demonstration of falconry is thrown

in at about 4.30pm – otherwise you can see the raptors sitting in the shade before the castle walls. The SP65 beyond makes for a pretty drive into the **Val d'Esino**, through the villages of Perledo, Esino Lario and **Parlasco** (which has tarted itself up with more than a dozen frescos on the walls of its stone houses), where it runs into Valsassina (p128).

### ♥ BELLANO // THE 'ORRIDO' IS MORE SPECTACULAR THAN HORRID

Once an industrial centre, **Bellano** (5km north of Varenna) is a sleepy lakeside town with a singular sight: the **Orrido** ( ☎ 0341 82 11 24; adult/child €3.50/3; ⌚ 10am-1pm & 2.30-7pm Apr-Sep, 8.45-10pm Jul-Sep, 10am-12.30pm & 2.30-5pm Oct-Mar), which is a powerful waterfall where the river Pioverna thunders down between tight, rock walls before flowing out through the town into the lake. The power of the falls has hammered out weird shapes in the rock walls, topped by vegetation so thick that you could be forgiven for thinking you're in Asia. The silly part is all the model dinosaurs they have scattered about the place.

### ♥ CORENNO PLINIO // CLAMBER AROUND A LAKESIDE MEDIEVAL MARVEL

Located about 6km north of Bellano, this spot is a bite-sized taste of another era. Even the main square, Piazza Garibaldi, is roughly cobblestoned and it is plain from its warped nature that nothing much has changed here down the centuries. Many of the deep-grey, stone houses are still occupied, their inhabitants carefully tending garden plots that give the huddled hamlet flashes of bright colour. On the square, the 14th-century **Chiesa di Tommaso Beckett** competes for attention with the neighbouring **Castello** degli Andreani, built around the same time. Frescos inside the church were uncovered during restoration work that was done in 1966. Two stout, crenellated towers stand guard over the castle, which is closed to visitors. A series of uneven stone stairways tumbles between the tightly packed houses to the shoreline, one ending up at a tiny port (with space for nine motorboats and a family of ducks).

### ❦ ABBAZIA DI PIONA // MEDITATE ON THE MONKS' CHOICE OF LOCATION

About 3km short of Colico, a side road (half of it cobblestoned) leads 2km from the SP72 road to the **Abbazia di Piona** ( ☎ 0341 94 03 31; www.cistercensi.info/piona, in Italian; ⏱ 7am-7.30pm), a Cistercian abbey that has a marvellous setting on a promontory stretching out into the lake. There is evidence that a small chapel was built here in the 7th century. The present church is a Romanesque gem that the Cluniac order raised. The church and its 13th-century frescos are attractive, but the star (aside from the setting) is the 13th-century, irregularly shaped cloister, a rich example of transitional style from Romanesque to Gothic; it's an oasis of peace. The monks who live here today enjoy incomparable views west over the lake to Gravedona and the snowcapped peaks behind it and to the north.

### ❦ VALSASSINA // TAKE A BACK-VALLEY DETOUR

It doesn't occur to too many people to follow this 33km back-valley route between Lecco to Bellano. If you've driven up or down the coast one way, this drive along the **Valsassina** (www.valsassina.it, in Italian) is an alternative for the return trip. From Lecco, the SP62 road switches back

## HIKING

Waymarked walking paths (look for the red-and-white signs with path numbers or similarly coloured paint splotches) criss-cross the Parco della Grigna Settentrionale. Some trails include challenging *vie ferate* (where iron railings or other aids have been installed for climbing) and others require mountaineering experience. The Lecco tourist office can provide brochures, but you should seek proper hiking maps scaled at 1:25,000 in local bookshops before undertaking the more challenging walks.

and forth, affording priceless views of the Lecco end of Lake Como over your shoulder. These views are finally cut off by the Grigne mountain range, whose highest peak is **La Grigna Settentrionale** (2408m). The core of this area constitutes the **Parco della Grigna Settentrionale** (www.parks.it/parco.grigna.settentrionale). From Lecco, you cannot fail to notice the jagged crest of **Il Resegone**, a broad-spined mountain with what look like dangerously pointy teeth (the highest of which is Punta Cermenati, at 1875m). About 9km northeast of Lecco, at Ballabio Superiore, a turn-off west sees you ascend about 8km of switchbacks through wooded country to **Piani Resinelli**. Again, you do this mainly for the views. The arrival point is made up of a small settlement, highland fields and woods, backed by bare rockfaces. It is a starting point for several hiking trails.

Some 15km northeast of Lecco, the village of **Barzio** is important above all as the birthplace of Alessandro Manzoni (p126). Nearby, **Pasturo** retains something of its medieval feel and is a starting point of a hiking trail to the Grigna Settentrionale summit. The first part, from

Via Cantellone, sidles along a bubbling brook and makes for an effortless stroll in its initial stages. Locals enjoy some modest downhill and cross-country skiing in winter at **Piani di Bobbio**, just outside Barzio.

### ☙ VALTELLINA // EXPLORE AN ALPINE WINE REGION

From the north end of Lake Como, the **Valtellina** cuts a broad swathe of a valley (at whose centre runs the Adda river) eastward between the Swiss mountain frontier to the north and the Alpi Orobie mountains to the south. Much of its steep, northern flank is carpeted by the vineyards (mostly the nebbiolo grape variety) that produce such coveted drops as Sforzato (Sfurzat). You can largely skip the valley towns, but a detour to the hillside wine villages is worthwhile. Two points of reference are **Ponte in Valtellina**, 8km east of Sondrio, and **Teglio** (with a cute Romanesque church), 8km further east. The brisk climb up among the vineyards affords sweeping views across the valley. Calling in at village cafes or restaurants gives you a look into local life far from any tourist trail. And

what better way to taste Valtellina reds than by calling into any local trattoria?

The prettiest town along the valley floor is **Tirano**, terminus for trains arriving from Milan via Lake Como and others arriving from Switzerland. At its east end is the quiet old town, with winding lanes next to the gushing Adda. About 1.5km west of the centre stands the proud **Renaissance Santuario della Madonna** church.

### ☙ VAL MASINO // SNAKE UP TO AN ALPINE WALL AND THERMAL BATHS

A lovely 17km road, the SP9, leads north up **Val Masino** from a point 7km east of Morbegno in the Valtellina valley. Almost immediately when you leave the traffic, car dealerships and megamarkets of the valley floor behind, you can discover thickly wooded hills, the surging Masino river and snowcapped Alps. From Valmasino town, 9km north of the valley floor, the scenery takes on an Alpine hue. From San Martino, 2km on, take the left fork. A series of switchbacks (watch for some staggering waterfalls) brings you to **Bagni di Masino**, the end

LAKE COMO & LAKE LUGANO

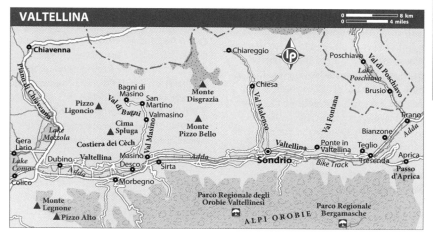

of the road, with an old-time spa hotel (see p296) that is an experience in itself. Surrounded by fir trees and granite mountains you feel you could touch, the spot has a bracing wilderness feel. Properly equipped hikers can trudge off into the Alps from here along marked trails.

### ♥ WINDSURFING & KITESURFING OFF GERA LARIO // CATCH THE SUMMER SOUTH WINDS

Local and foreign kitesurfers favour the steady south winds (from April to October) at the north end of Lake Como. There's not an awful lot else to do around here, as the town of Gera Lario is dead quiet. For surfers, there's a small sandy beach, plenty of parkland in which to rig up, and parking space. Beginners could approach **Son of a Beach** ( ☎ 389 463 78 73; www.windsurf-colico.com, in Italian; Via Sacco 49), a windsurfing school in nearby Colico. Beginners' courses start at €110 for two days.

## GASTRONOMIC HIGHLIGHTS

### ♥ ANTICA OSTERIA CASA DI LUCIA // LECCO €€

☎ 0341 49 45 94; Via Lucia 27; meals €30; ☺ lunch & dinner Mon-Fri, dinner Sat

Some claim that this 18th-century house is the one Alessandro Manzoni had in mind as Lucia's place in his 19th-century blockbuster, *I promessi sposi* (The Betrothed). Lucia would love to wander in here now for the grilled *missoltini* with polenta, lake fish and homemade pasta. It's a bit of a hike from the centre, in a district known as Acquate, but everyone can point the way to this classic.

### ♥ SALE E TABACCHI // MAGGIANA €€

☎ 0341 73 37 15; Piazza San Rocco 3; meals €25-30; ☺ lunch & dinner Wed-Sun, lunch Mon

Tucked away in the hamlet of Maggiana, signposted 3km uphill from lakeside Mandello del Lario (home to the legendary Moto Guzzi motorcycle manufacturer), an eatery that has appeared in countless Italian good-food guides could hardly be better disguised. The post office, bar and tobacco store also has a modest dining room situated off to one side, filled with dark timber tables. In the summer months, lake fish dominates the menu. Try the perch risotto. Just behind the restaurant is a medieval watchtower, where they say Holy Roman Emperor Frederick Barbarossa stayed in 1158 – too soon for him to try the risotto.

### ♥ VECCHIA VARENNA // VARENNA €€

☎ 0341 83 07 93; www.vecchiavarenna.it; Contrada Scoscesa 10; meals €35-40; ☺ Tue-Sun Feb-Dec

Of the handful of lakeside-dining options in Varenna, this is the best. Dine on risotto prepared with pears and Taleggio cheese, or choose from mains of lake fish, duck breast or, say, a *tagliata di struzzo con radicchio e noci* (ostrich steak with chicory and nuts). A dozen tables are set up in an enclosed terrace suspended over the water.

## TRANSPORT

**CAR //** The SS36 fast highway, mostly a series of inland tunnels, is for those in a hurry between Lecco and Colico. If you want to *see* the lake, follow the SP72 road. The main inland road along the Valsassina mountain valley is the SP62 between Lecco and Bellano. The SS36 and then SP342 roads lead west 29km from Lecco to Como.

**PARKING //** Parking in central Lecco and Varenna is metered. In the latter it be can tough finding a space in summer.

**TRAIN //** Trains from Milan run to Lecco (€3.60, 40 minutes) and call in at all towns on the east shore of the lake before swinging east at Colico into the Valtellina (heading as far east as Tirano, where Swiss trains connect on a scenic line north to St Moritz). Note that Piona station is in Colico, not at the Abbazia Piona. Trains link Lecco with Bergamo (€2.75, 45 minutes).

**BUS //** Regular buses connect Lecco with Como. Others run up the shoreline to Colico, but it is often just as easy to take the train.

# LAKE LUGANO

· · · · · ·

**Shared in fits and starts by Italy and the Swiss canton of Ticino, Lake Lugano (aka Lake Ceresio) has in common with its bigger neighbour, Lake Como, a dramatic mountain scenery, especially at its northern end, around Lugano. The city of Lugano itself is a busy banking centre and set prettily between soaring hills on either side. Accessed by a short train ride north, the three castles of Bellinzona are an extraordinary sight, which are justifiably included on Unesco's World Heritage lists.**

## TRANSPORT

**Società Navigazione del Lago di Lugano** ( ☎ 091 971 52 23; www.lakelugano.ch) Boats are operated by this company. Example return fares from Lugano are Melide Sfr22.60, Morcote Sfr31.40 and Ponte Tresa Sfr39. If you want to visit several places, buy a pass: Sfr40/60 for one/three days and Sfr71 for one week (reduced fares for children).

**Lugano Regional Pass** (adult pass 3-/7-day Sfr92/108, child pass 3-/7-day, Sfr58/50) Gives free travel on Lake Lugano, and on regional public transport in and around Lugano (including the funiculars up to Monte Brè and Monte San Salvatore). It also gives free or discounted rides on the area's cable cars, rack-and-pinion railways, as well as half-price transport to and around Locarno and on Lake Maggiore. Available for 2nd class only, issued from around Easter to October, purchase from tourist offices, railway stations and local travel agencies.

# LUGANO

**pop 49,720**

The largest city in Switzerland's Ticino canton (but not its capital), Lugano squeezes itself around the heights that close in Lake Lugano at its northern end. Switzerland's third-biggest banking centre (after Geneva and Zürich), it is a prosperous city chosen by a not indifferent number of Milanese as their main residence. Lugano offers a pretty, if small, old centre and a handful of churches and museums to visit but, above all, it has a splendid natural setting to explore (starting with funicular rides up to steep hills to enjoy marvellous views). Somewhat somnolent in winter, it sparkles to life in summer, when its piazzas, cafes, bars and restaurants fill to bursting with a Mediterranean-style joie de vivre.

## ESSENTIAL INFORMATION

**EMERGENCIES //** Ospedale Civico ( ☎ 091 811 61 11; Via Tesserete 46) Hospital north of the city centre.

**TOURIST OFFICE //** Tourist Office ( ☎ 091 913 32 32; www.lugano-tourism.ch; Municipio Bldg, Riva Giocondo Albertolli; ☼ 9am-7pm Mon-Fri, to 5pm Sat, 10am-5pm Sun & holidays Apr-Oct, 9am-noon & 2-5.30pm Mon-Fri, 10am-12.30pm & 1.30-5pm Sat Nov-Mar). There is also a tourist information booth at the main railway station ( ☼ 2pm to 7pm Monday to Saturday).

## ORIENTATION

Lugano's train station stands above and to the west of the Centro Storico (Old Town). Take the stairs or the funicular (Sfr1.10, open 5.20am to 11.50pm) down to the centre, a patchwork of interlocking piazzas. The most important one, Piazza della Riforma, is presided over by the

# LUGANO

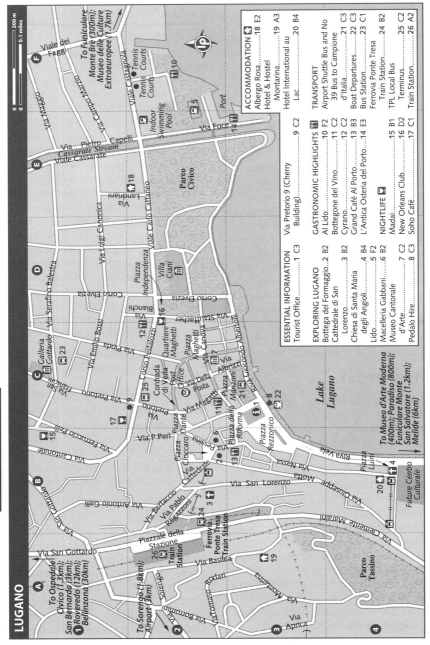

**ESSENTIAL INFORMATION**
Tourist Office..................................1 C3

**EXPLORING LUGANO**
Bottega del Formaggio.....2 B2
Cattedrale di San
  Lorenzo...........................3 B2
Chiesa di Santa Maria
  degli Angioli................4 B4
Lido.....................................5 F2
Macelleria Gabbani.........6 B2
Museo Cantonale
  d'Arte..............................7 C2
Pedalo Hire.......................8 C3

Via Pretorio 9 (Cherry
  Building)........................9 C2

**GASTRONOMIC HIGHLIGHTS**
Al Lido...............................10 F2
Bottegone del Vino.........11 C2
Cyrano..............................12 C2
Grand Café Al Porto.......13 B3
L'Antica Osteria del Porto....14 E3

**NIGHTLIFE**
Madai................................15 B1
New Orleans Club...........16 D2
Soho Café.........................17 C1

**ACCOMMODATION**
Albergo Rosa...................18 E2
Hotel & Hostel
  Montarina.....................19 A3
Hotel International au
  Lac..................................20 B4

**TRANSPORT**
Airport Shuttle Bus and No
  39 Bus to Campione
  d'Italia...........................21 C3
Boat Departures..............22 C3
Bus Station......................23 C1
Ferrovia Ponte Tresa
  Train Station.................24 B2
TPL Local Bus
  Terminus........................25 C2
Train Station....................26 A2

1844 neoclassical Municipio (town hall). East of the Cassarate stream, is the **Lido**, with beaches, pool, pedalos and a cool brunch location, Al Lido (p134).

## EXPLORING LUGANO

### ❦ OLD TOWN & CHURCHES // TAKE A WALK AND INSPECT FINE FRESCOS

Wander through the porticoed lanes woven around the busy main square, Piazza della Riforma (even more lively when the Tuesday and Friday morning markets are held), which is an excellent spot to linger over a cappuccino and paper. The simple Romanesque **Chiesa di Santa Maria degli Angioli** (St Mary of the Angels; Piazza Luini; ⏲ 7am-6pm) contains two frescos by Bernardino Luini dating from 1529. Covering the entire wall that divides the church in two is a grand, didactic illustration of the Crucifixion. The closer you look, the more scenes of Christ's Passion are revealed, along with others of him being taken down from the cross and his resurrection. The power and vivacity of the colours are astounding. Less alive is Luini's depiction of the Last Supper on the left wall.

Below the train station, the early 16th-century **Cattedrale di San Lorenzo** (St Lawrence Cathedral; ⏲ 6.30am-6pm) boasts a Renaissance facade and contains some fine frescos and ornately decorated baroque statues.

### ❦ MUSEUMS & GALLERIES // GET AN INJECTION OF ART

The **Museo Cantonale d'Arte** (Cantonal Art Museum; ☎ 091 910 47 80; www.museo-cantonale -arte.ch, in Italian; Via Canova 10; adult/student Sfr7/5, special exhibitions Sfr10/7; ⏲ 2-5pm Tue, from 10am Wed-Sun) celebrates, above all, the work of modern artists (mostly 19th- and 20th-century masters) from the Ticino region. That said, the broad collection is by no means closed to other artists of the same period and occasionally takes you aback with works by such greats as Pierre-Auguste Renoir, Edgar Degas and Camille Pissarro.

### Museum of Modern Art

There's creativity from the cutting edge at the **Museo d'Arte Moderna** (Modern Art Museum; ☎ 058 866 72 14; www.mdam.ch; Riva Antonio Caccia 5; adult/student & senior/15-18yr/11-14yr Sfr12/8/5/3; ⏲ 9am-7pm Tue-Sun). Housed in Villa Malpensata, it is one of the city's main art spaces and puts on a busy programme of temporary exhibitions.

### Museum of Non-European Cultures

About 1.7km from central Lugano, in Villa Heleneum, is the **Museo delle Culture Extraeuropee** ( ☎ 058 866 69 09; www. lugano.ch/museoculture, in Italian; Via Cortivo 24-28; adult/senior & student 17-25yr/child to 16yr Sfr12/8/ free; ⏲ 10am-6pm Tue-Sun). The brew of tribal relics from far-off countries includes a collection of masks and statues soaked in sexuality. Much of the material was collected in Africa. Thousands of photos and a collection of small films from expeditions carried out by the Nodari family, which has lent its collections to the museum, provide fascinating insights into the locations they travelled through. Take bus 1. The city is planning the opening of a major arts centre, the **Centro Culturale della Città di Lugano**, for around 2013.

### ❦ FUNICULARS // GET A BIRD'S-EYE LAKE VIEW

For such a view of Lugano and the lake, head for the hills. The **funicular** ( ☎ 091 971 31 71; www.montebre.ch, in Italian; one way/return Sfr14/20, Swiss Pass valid; ⏲ Mar-Dec) from Cassarate (walk or take bus 1 from central Lugano) scales Monte Brè (925m). From Cassarate, a first funicular takes you to Suvigliana (free up, Sfr1.60 down) to connect with the main funicular. Or take bus No 12 from the main post office to Brè village and walk about 15 minutes.

From Paradiso, the **funicular** (☎091 985 28 28; www.montesansalvatore.ch, in Italian; one way/return Sfr19/26; ⊙ mid-Mar–early Nov) to Monte San Salvatore operates from mid-March to mid-November. In addition to the views, the walk down to Paradiso or Melide is an hour well spent.

### ☙ MACELLERIA GABBANI // SEARCH SAMPLES OF LUGANO'S BEST PRODUCTS

You'll find it hard to miss the giant sausages hanging out the front of the irresistible **Gabbani delicatessen** (☎091 911 30 80; www.gabbani.com; Via Pessina 12). The Gabbani family has been regaling Lugano with fine and mostly local food products since anyone can remember. Just wandering by this higgledy piggledy–stuffed shop overwhelms the senses. The same people operate a tempting cheese shop, the **Bottega del Formaggio**, across the road at No 13. Between them, they are *the* gourmet shop–stop in town.

## FESTIVALS & EVENTS

**Lugano Festival** (www.luganofestival.ch, in Italian) Lugano takes in some classical tunes during this festival from April to May in the Palazzo dei Congressi.

**Estival Jazz** (www.estivaljazz.ch) Free open-air concert that occurs in early July (plus two days in Mendrisio at the end of June).

**National Day** The lake explodes in a display of pyrotechnical wizardry around midnight on 1 August, to celebrate Switzerland's national day.

**Blues to Bop Festival** (www.bluestobop.ch, in Italian) Free open-air music festivals including this one runs for three days runs over the last three days of August.

## GASTRONOMIC HIGHLIGHTS

### ☙ AL LIDO €€

☎ 091 971 55 00; www.allidobar.com, in Italian; Viale Castagnola; brunch Sfr36.50; ⊙ brunch 11am-6pm; dinner Wed-Sat

All the beautiful people from far and wide (and that means a fair-sized Milan contingent) crowd Lugano's lakeside-beach restaurant for its especially popular Sunday buffet brunch. There are several cold and warm buffets to choose from, making for well-fed customers. Chilled music wafts in the background and staff and punters alike seem eager to add to the sensation of a summer beach

## MARIO BOTTA IN THE PINK

Lugano's star architect, Mario Botta (born 1943 in nearby Mendrisio) may be best known for his work abroad (such as San Francisco's Museum of Modern Art, the Kyobo Tower in Seoul and restoration of the La Scala opera theatre in Milan), but he has left an indelible mark on and around Lugano. The 12-storey **Casino** in Campione d'Italia is one example. Botta seems to have a thing about right angles and the colour pink. Located in the centre of Lugano, his landmarks include the **BSí** (Via San Franscini 12), a series of interconnected monoliths formerly known as the Banca del Gottardo; the pink brick office block at **Via Pretorio 9** (known to locals as the Cherry Building because of the cherry tree planted on the roof); and the roof of the TPL local bus terminal on Corso Pestalozzi. At night it is illuminated…in light pink.

day in more southern climes. It also does a Wednesday evening version, **Lunar** (☽6.30pm-1am), for the same price and with a DJ thrown in.

### ♥ BOTTEGONE DEL VINO €€€
☎ 091 922 76 89; Via Magatti 3; meals Sfr60-70; ☽Mon-Sat
Favoured by the local banking brigade at lunchtime, this is a great place to taste fine local wines over a well-prepared meal. The menu changes daily and might include a *filetto di rombo al vapore* (steamed turbot fillet) or ravioli stuffed with fine Tuscan Chianina beef. Much depends on what's available in the markets. Knowledgeable waiters will suggest the perfect Ticino tipple.

### ♥ GRAND CAFÉ AL PORTO €€
☎091 910 51 30; www.grand-cafe-lugano.ch; Via Pessina 3; meals Sfr80; ☽8am-6.30pm Mon-Sat
This timeless old cafe, which began life in 1803, has several fine rooms for dining too. Timber ceilings, low lighting and a tempting pastry selection at the bar are already good reasons for popping by. On the food front, menu proposals change every month. Be sure to take a look at the frescoed and wood-panelled Cenacolo Fiorentino, once a monastery refectory.

### ♥ L'ANTICA OSTERIA DEL PORTO €€
☎091 971 42 00; www.osteriadelporto.ch, in German & Italian; Via Foce 9; mains Sfr22-39; ☽Wed-Mon
Set back from Lugano's sailing club in what was once a customs station for goods arriving from the lake, this is the place for savouring local fish and Ticinese dishes. It's hard to resist the *grigliata mista di pesci di mare e crostacei* (mixed fish and shellfish grill). The terrace overlooking the Cassarate stream is

pleasant, or opt for lake views. You can also simply pop by the wine bar.

## NIGHTLIFE

### ♥ MADAI
☎091 922 56 37; www.luganodinotte.ch, in Italian; Via Ferruccio Pelli 13; ☽7pm-3am Wed-Sat
This is a cool cocktail bar with reddish hues, lounges and dance music, and it's in this central Lugano dance location, making it one of the most popular night spots in town. At 10pm the *aperitivo* phase gives way to a club-style ambience, with some of the boys agog at the go-go girls who are swaying on the bar, and everyone else gets into some serious swaying of their own.

### ♥ SOHO CAFÉ
☎091 922 60 80; Corso Pestalozzi 3; ☽7am-1am Mon-Fri, 4pm-1am Sat
So that's where they are! All those good-looking Lugano townies crowd in to this long, orange-lit bar for cocktails. Chilled DJ music creates a pleasant buzz. The problem might be squeezing through to the bar to order your Negroni.

## TRANSPORT

**AIR //** **Agno airport** (☎ 091 612 11 11; www .lugano-airport.ch) Has a handful of flights to/from Geneva and Zürich. A shuttle bus runs from Piazza Manzoni (one way/return Sfr10/18) and the train station (Sfr8/15).

**CAR //** From Milan, the A9 autostrada via Como becomes the A2 after the border at Chiasso and proceeds through Lugano to Bellinzona and central Switzerland.

**PARKING //** Parking is mostly metered in central Lugano.

**TRAIN //** Trains run to Melide (Sfr3.40, six minutes). For Morcote, get bus 431 at Piazza Rezzonico (30 to 35 minutes).

**BUS //** Lugano is on the same road and rail route as Bellinzona. All postal buses leave from the main bus depot at Via Serafino Balestra. One goes to Menaggio, on Lake Como, via Porlezza. Local bus 1 runs from Castagnola in the east through the centre to Paradiso, while bus 2 runs from central Lugano to Paradiso via the train station. A single trip costs Sfr1.20 to Sfr2 (ticket dispensers indicate the appropriate rate) or it's Sfr5 for a one-day pass. The main local bus terminus is on Corso Pestalozzi.

# AROUND LAKE LUGANO

The tourist office has guides to some of the best lakeside walks.

## EXPLORING AROUND LAKE LUGANO

### ❧ GANDRIA // LAKESIDE WALKS AND SMUGGLERS' TALES

**Gandria** is a compact village almost dipping into the water. They say the glacier that formed this part of the lake dug so deep that the lake waters here actually reach below sea level! A popular trip is to take the boat from Lugano and walk back along the shore to Castagnola (around 40 minutes), where you can visit Villa Heleneum or Villa Favorita or both, or simply continue back to Lugano by foot or bus 1. Across the lake from Gandria is the **Museo delle Dogane Svizzere** (Swiss Customs Museum; ☎ 091 923 98 43; admission free; ☽ 1.30-5.30pm late-Mar–early Oct), at Cantine di Gandria, and accessible by boat. It tells the history of customs (and, more interestingly, smuggling) in this border area. On display are confiscated smugglers' boats that once operated on the lake.

### ❧ MONTE GENEROSO // ASCEND THE MOUNTAIN FOR THE GENEROUS VIEWS

The fine panorama provided by this summit (1701m) includes lakes, Alps and the Apennines on a clear day. Indeed, it is a 360-degree sweeping view and it is easily the most spectacular viewpoint in all of the Canton of Ticino – the clearer the conditions, the further you can see. It's possible to make out Milan and key points in the Swiss Alps, such as Monte Rosa, the Matterhorn and the Jungfrau. You don't even need to climb to enjoy this sight. To get here, take a boat (except in winter), train (Sfr5.60, 17 minutes) or car to Capolago. From there, jump on the rack-and-pinion **train** (☎ 091 630 51 11; www.montegeneroso.ch, in Italian; adult/6-16yr/under 5yr return Sfr39/19.50/free; ☽ up to 10 a day Apr-Oct & early Dec-early Jan).

### ❧ MONTAGNOLA // TRACK DOWN HERMANN HESSE

The German novelist Hermann Hesse (1877–1962) chose to live in this small town in 1919 after the horrors of WWI had separated him from his family. As crisis followed crisis in Germany, topped by the rise of the Nazis, he saw little reason to return home. He wrote some of his greatest works here, at first in an apartment in Casa Camuzzi. Nearby, in Torre Camuzzi, is the **Museo Hermann Hesse** (☎ 091 993 37 70; www.hessemontagnola.ch; Torre Camuzzi; adult/student & senior/child under 12yr Sfr7.50/6/free; ☽ 10am-12.30pm & 2-6.30pm Tue-Sun Mar-Oct, 10am-12.30pm & 2-6.30pm Sat & Sun Nov-Feb). Personal objects, some of the thousands of watercolours he painted in Ticino, books and other odds and ends help recreate something of Hesse's life. From Lugano, get the Ferrovia Ponte Tresa train to Sorengo and change for a postal bus (Sfr3.40, 20 minutes).

### ❧ MELIDE // DISCOVER THE TINY VERSION OF SWITZERLAND

Melide is a bulge of shore from which the A2 motorway slices across the lake. The main attraction is one that is bound to be a hit with most kids (and a few kids in grown-ups' clothes). **Swissminiatur** ( ☎ 091 640 10 60; www.swissminiatur.ch; Via Cantonale; adult/senior/child Sfr15/13/10; ✆ 9am-6pm mid-Mar–mid-Nov) is a miniature wonderland where you'll find 1:25 scale models of more than 120 national attractions. It's the quick way to see Switzerland in a day. Castles, such as the Château de Chillon in Montreux, vie for attention with the occasional foreign interloper – such as the Duomo in Milan.

### ♥ MORCOTE // ASCEND TO A HIGH HAMLET AND PEACEFUL PARKS
With its narrow cobblestone lanes and endless nooks and crannies, this peaceful former fishing village (population 740) clusters at the foot of Monte Abostora on Lake Lugano. Narrow stairways lead to **Chiesa di Santa Maria del Sasso**, a 15-minute climb. Views are excellent and the church has frescos (16th century) and carved faces on the organ. From there, continue another 15 minutes upstairs to **Vico di Morcote**, a pleasant high-altitude hamlet. About 5km further is Carona, which is worth a visit for the **Parco Botanico San Grato** (admission free).

### Parco Scherrer
Four hundred metres left (west) from the boat stop, **Parco Scherrer** ( ☎ 091 996 21 25; adult/student & senior/child 6-10yr/child under 6yr Sfr7/6/2/free; ✆ 10am-5pm mid-Mar–Oct, to 6pm Jul-Aug) offers a bustling range of architectural styles, including copies of famous buildings and generic types (eg Temple of Nefertiti, Siamese tea house). It's all set in subtropical parkland.

### ♥ MERIDE // DELVE INTO PREHISTORY AT THE FOSSIL MUSEUM
It's of specialised interest, but for those who are keen on prehistory, Meride,

situated about 15km south of Lugano and just west off the A2 motorway, is worth a stop. The **Museo dei Fossili** (Fossil Museum; ☎ 091 646 37 80; www.montesangiorgio.ch; admission free; ✆ 8am-6pm) displays vestiges of the first creatures to inhabit the region – reptiles and fish dating back more than 200 million years. It may sound dry, but the finds are important enough to warrant Unesco recognition of the area around nearby Monte San Giorgio (1096m), where they were uncovered, as a World Heritage–listed site. According to Unesco, the mount is the 'single best known record of marine life in the Triassic period'. And the museum is set in a gracious old building with a courtyard lined by colonnaded galleries.

Near the town is a circular **nature trail**. You can reach Meride from Lugano by taking the train to Mendrisio and then the postal bus (Sfr11).

## BELLINZONA

**pop 16,980**
Placed at the conversion point of several valleys leading down from the Alps, Bellinzona is visually unique. Inhabited since neolithic times, it is dominated by three grey-stone, medieval castles that have attracted everyone from Swiss invaders to painters like William Turner. Turner may have liked the place, but Bellinzona has a surprisingly low tourist profile, in spite of its castles forming one of Switzerland's 10 World Heritage–listed sites. The rocky, central hill upon which rises the main castle, Castelgrande, was a Roman frontier post and site of a Lombard defensive tower, and was later developed as a heavily fortified town controlled by Milan. The three castles and valley walls could not

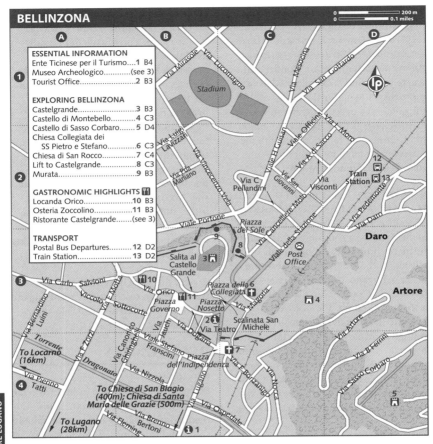

**BELLINZONA**

0 _____ 200 m
0 _____ 0.1 miles

ESSENTIAL INFORMATION
Ente Ticinese per il Turismo....**1** B4
Museo Archeologico............(see 3)
Tourist Office......................**2** B3

EXPLORING BELLINZONA
Castelgrande..........................**3** B3
Castello di Montebello..........**4** C3
Castello di Sasso Corbaro......**5** D4
Chiesa Collegiata dei
    SS Pietro e Stefano............**6** C3
Chiesa di San Rocco................**7** C4
Lift to Castelgrande................**8** C3
Murata....................................**9** B3

GASTRONOMIC HIGHLIGHTS
Locanda Orico......................**10** B3
Osteria Zoccolino................**11** B3
Ristorante Castelgrande.......(see 3)

TRANSPORT
Postal Bus Departures..........**12** D2
Train Station......................**13** D2

stop the Swiss German confederate troops from overwhelming the city in 1503, thus deciding Ticino's fate for the following three centuries.

## ESSENTIAL INFORMATION

**TOURIST OFFICES //** **Tourist Office** ( ☎ 091 825 21 31; www.bellinzonaturismo.ch; Piazza Nosetto; ☺ 9am-6pm Mon-Fri, to noon Sat) In the restored Renaissance Palazzo Civico (Town Hall); **Ente Ticinese per il Turismo** ( ☎ 091 825 70 56; www. ticino.ch; Villa Turrita, Via Lugano 12; ☺ 8.15am-noon & 1.30-5.30pm Mon-Fri).

## EXPLORING BELLINZONA

### ❤ CASTLES // CLAMBER ABOUT THE CITY'S DEFENCE WORKS

The city's three imposing castles are the main drawcard. Read up on them at www.bellinzonaunesco.ch. To visit all three, get a general ticket (adult/concession Sfr10/4), valid indefinitely.

### Castelgrande

Dating from the 6th century, **Castelgrande** ( ☎ 091 825 81 45; Monte San Michele; admission to grounds free; ☺ 9am-10pm Tue-Sun, 10am-

LAKE COMO & LAKE LUGANO

6pm Mon) is the biggest fortification and is in the town centre. You can walk (head up Scalinata San Michele from Piazza della Collegiata) or take the lift, buried deep in the rocky hill in an extraordinary concrete bunker-style construction, from Piazza del Sole.

### Archaeological Museum
The castle's **Museo Archeologico** (adult/ concession Sfr5/2; ☺ 10am-6pm mid-Mar–Oct, 10am-5pm Nov–mid-Mar) has a modest collection of finds from the hill dating to prehistoric times. More engaging is the display of 15th-century decorations taken from the ceiling of a former noble house in central Bellinzona. The pictures range from weird animals (late-medieval ideas on what a camel looked like are curious) to a humorous series on the 'world upside down'. Examples of the latter include an ox driving a man-drawn plough and a sex-crazed woman chasing a chaste man. The uncomfortable black seats you sit on for the 12-minute audiovisual on the castle's history were designed by Mario Botta (see p134) and cost around Sfr1000 a pop! After wandering the grounds and the museum, head west along the **Murata** (Walls; admission free; ☺ 9am-7pm Apr-Sep, 10am-5pm Oct-Mar).

### Castello di Montebello
Slightly above the town, **Castello di Montebello** ( ☎ 091 825 13 42; Salita ai Castelli; castle admission free, museum adult/concession Sfr5/2; ☺ castle 8am-8pm mid-Mar–Oct, museum 10am-6pm mid-Mar-Oct) has a smaller museum that continues the study of medieval Bellinzona. From here it's a 3.5km climb uphill to **Castello di Sasso Corbaro**. At this point, you should be too exhausted to explore the grounds. Lucky you – there are none. The castle hosts temporary

exhibitions ( ☎ 091 825 59 06; adult/concession Sfr5/2; ☺ 10am-6pm mid-Mar–Oct).

### ♥ CHURCHES // CONTEMPLATE SOME FINE FRESCOS
Wandering south from the train station, you will first see the **Chiesa Collegiata dei SS Pietro e Stefano** (Piazza della Collegiata; ☺ 8am-1pm & 4-6pm), a Renaissance church with baroque touches and rich in frescos inside. More immediately eye-catching is the **Chiesa di San Rocco** (Piazza dell'Indipendenza; ☺ 7-11am & 2-5pm), with its huge fresco of St Christopher, and a smaller one of the Virgin Mary and Christ. Similarly decorated is the 14th-century **Chiesa di San Biagio** (Piazza San Biagio; ☺ 7am-noon & 2-5pm), the difference being that these frescos are not 20th-century restorations.

Situated west over the railway line is the **Chiesa di Santa Maria delle Grazie** (Via Convento; ☺ 7am-6pm), a 15th-century church with an extraordinary fresco cycle (recently restored after being damaged by fire in 1996) of the life and death of Christ. The centrepiece is a panel depicting Christ's Crucifixion.

### FESTIVALS & EVENTS
**Rabadan** (www.rabadan.ch) Bellinzona's rowdy carnival starts on a Thursday seven-and-a-half weeks before Easter Sunday.
**Piazza Blues Festival** (www.piazzablues.ch) Four days of international blues are brought to the city in summer. Entry is free except to the main stage on the last two days (Sfr15); June/July.

### GASTRONOMIC HIGHLIGHTS
#### ♥ CASTELGRANDE €€€
☎ 091 826 23 53; www.castelgrande.ch; Castelgrande; meals Sfr80-100; ☺ Tue-Sun
It's not often you get the chance to eat inside a Unesco World Heritage–listed

site. The medieval castle setting alone is enough to bewitch you. The restaurant itself is an elegant mix of classic and modern tastes, including white linen and black leather chairs. Cuisine is a mix of Ticino and Italian, with flights of inventive fantasy. You could start with pasta or *asparagi verdi in salsa di formaggio dei nostri alpeggi e foglie di culatello Zibello* (green asparagus drenched in a sauce made of local Alpine cheeses and thin flakes of ham). You can opt for a set dinner menu at Sfr68 or go all out with a tasting menu at Sfr138.

### ☙ LOCANDA ORICO €€€

☎ 091 825 15 18; www.locandaorico.ch; Via Orico 13; meals Sfr70-80; ☽ Tue-Sat

Behind the lace curtains in this low-slung temple to good food, you come across such creations as *gnocchetti di patate alla zucca in una dadolata di camoscio in salmì* (little pumpkin gnocchi in jugged chamois meat). This might be followed by *coda di rospo arrostito intera, aromatizzata ai datterini e ai capperini di Pantelleria, ventaglio di patates rattes dorate* (roast monkfish, seasoned with little dates and capers from Pantelleria and accompanied by lightly roasted potatoes). The setting is rustic, with timber ceiling beams and wooden furniture.

### ☙ OSTERIA ZOCCOLINO €€

☎ 091 825 06 70; Piazza Governo 5; meals Sfr30-40; ☽ Mon-Sat

A photographer runs this slightly chaotic but cheery eatery that fills with voluble locals, especially at lunchtime. You never quite know what to expect here: a set lunch of Indian food, concerts on Thursday nights…and you may find it opens at night only if it has enough bookings. Don't worry, there are several alternatives along Via Teatro and Via Orico. But this place is an original spot and unusually easy on the hip pocket.

## TRANSPORT

**TRAIN //** Bellinzona is on the train route connecting Locarno (Sfr8.20, 20 to 25 minutes) and Lugano (Sfr11.80, 26 to 30 minutes). It is also on the Zurich–Milan route.

**BUS //** Postal buses for destinations around the region depart from beside the train station.

**CAR //** The A2 motorway from Lugano passes through here.

**PARKING //** Most of the town centre is pedestrianised or has metered parking only.

LAKE COMO & LAKE LUGANO

# BERGAMO, BRESCIA & CREMONA

## 3 PERFECT DAYS

### 🏵 DAY 1 // MAKE A NEST IN MEDIEVAL BERGAMO
Like an eagle's eyrie, the Città Alta (Upper Town) of Bergamo (p146) sits a world apart, looking down almost with condescension on the great Lombard plains to the south. Discover its lanes, the Renaissance Piazza Vecchia (p146), the medieval Basilica di Santa Maria Maggiore (p148), the Venetian defensive walls and La Rocca fortress (p149). The Città Alta is jammed with fine eateries (p149) and several romantic places to sleep over (p297).

### 🏵 DAY 2 // A GRAND PLAINS TOUR
There are plenty of options in the Lombard plains south of Bergamo. You could make a whistle-stop tour of Brescia (p164) for its old centre and Roman ruins, then shoot south to Cremona (p169) to enjoy the magnificent Piazza del Comune and its monuments and search out some of the city's violin-makers. On the return leg to Bergamo, scoot by Pizzighettone (p173) for its impressive fortress walls and then make for either Lodi (p174) or Crema (p174), both with pleasing old centres and outstanding churches.

### 🏵 DAY 3 // HEAD FOR THE HILLS
North of Bergamo, various valleys lead into the pre-Alpine hills and mountains of the Alpi Orobie, while routes east head to Lake Iseo (p158), whose jewel is the island of Monte Isola. Hill valley highlights include San Pellegrino Terme (p156), of mineral water fame; Ardesio (p156) and its pretty centre; Branzi (p156) and its hill walks to glacial lakes; Valbondione (p156) and the nearby Serio waterfalls; and, simply, the chance to admire some beautiful mountain country.

# BERGAMO, BRESCIA & CREMONA

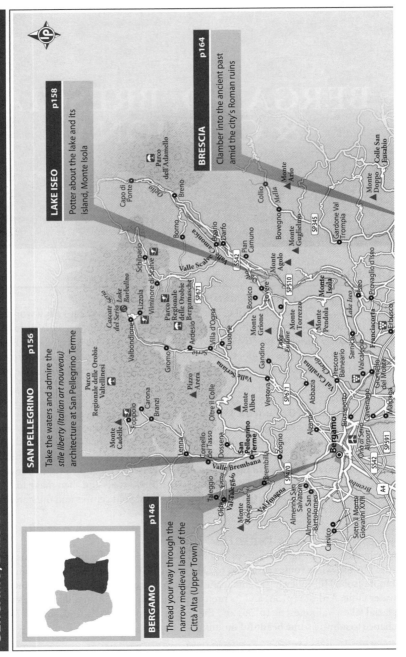

**SAN PELLEGRINO** p156

Take the waters and admire the *stile liberty* (Italian art nouveau) architecture at San Pellegrino Terme

**BERGAMO** p146

Thread your way through the narrow medieval lanes of the Città Alta (Upper Town)

**LAKE ISEO** p158

Potter about the lake and its island, Monte Isola

**BRESCIA** p164

Clamber into the ancient past amid the city's Roman ruins

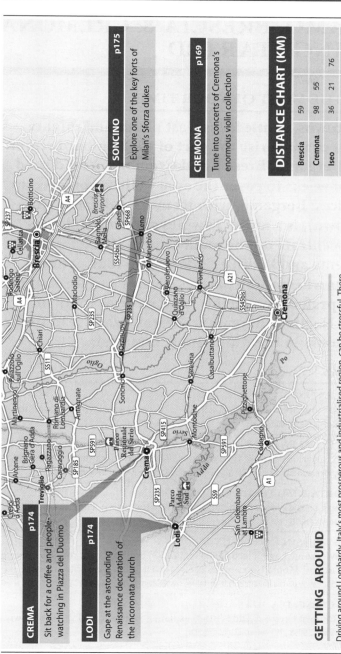

**CREMA**   p174

Sit back for a coffee and people-watching in Piazza del Duomo

**LODI**   p174

Gape at the astounding Renaissance decoration of the Incoronata church

**SONCINO**   p175

Explore one of the key forts of Milan's Sforza dukes

**CREMONA**   p169

Tune into concerts of Cremona's enormous violin collection

## DISTANCE CHART (KM)

|  | Bergamo | Brescia | Cremona | Iseo |
|---|---|---|---|---|
| Brescia | 59 | | | |
| Cremona | 98 | 55 | | |
| Iseo | 36 | 21 | 76 | |
| Lodi | 52 | 88 | 77 | 95 |

Note: distances between destinations are approximate

## GETTING AROUND

Driving around Lombardy, Italy's most prosperous and industrialised region, can be stressful. There are several traffic choking points – the area west of Bergamo is especially bad. Traffic is more fluid on the plains around Cremona, Lodi and Crema, and generally not a problem in the valleys north of Bergamo. Parking is not an option in the historic centres of Bergamo, Brescia or Cremona, but you can usually find metered parking in the immediate vicinity. Parking is fairly easy in smaller towns.

# BERGAMO, BRESCIA & CREMONA GETTING STARTED

## MAKING THE MOST OF YOUR TIME

**Medieval towns, gentle lakes, vast plains and mighty mountains characterise the part of the Lombard region taking in Bergamo, Brescia and Cremona. You'd need a couple of weeks to cover the area well, so you need to make choices. Bergamo, with its medieval Città Alta (Upper Town), is a must. Townies and church lovers might concentrate on the main centres (Brescia, Cremona, Crema and Lodi); an alternative tour of plains settlements will turn up palaces, castles and forts. Wine buffs may prefer touring the Franciacorta, south of Lake Iseo. North of Bergamo, several valleys lead to the great outdoors in the Alpi Orobie mountains.**

## TOP TOURS

### BERGAMO CENTRO STORICO

A guided two-hour tour around the Città Alta reveals some of the stories behind the facades. (www.bergamoguide.it; adult/child €10/free; tours 3pm Wed & Sun)

### CITTÀ D'ARTE DELLA PIANURA PADANA

Tours (in Italian) in various parts of the Po plains. Be sure to check out the three-day tour of Bergamo, Brescia and Lake Iseo. (www.circuitocittadarte.it, click on Pacchetti Turistici)

### FRANCIACORTA & VALTELLINA TOUR

Target Travel offers a six-day tour of the Franciacorta wine region, Lake Iseo and Valtellina. (www.targettravel.it)

### GIRO DELLE TRE ISOLE

Barcaioli and Navigazione Lago d'Iseo (☎ 035 97 14 83) both run boat tours of varying duration to and around Monte Isola and its islets, as well as longer jaunts around Lake Iseo (€5.50 to €15). (www.barcaiolimonteisola.it, in Italian; www.navigazionelagoiseo.it)

### VILLAGGIO CRESPI D'ADDA

Guided walking tours of Crespi d'Adda (p154) explain how this model workers' town came into being. (☎ 02 9098 7191; www.villaggiocrespi.it)

# GETTING AWAY FROM IT ALL

Bergamo, Brescia and Cremona are fairly tranquil but if you still find them too urban, there's no problem fleeing.

* **Hills** Numerous valleys lead north from Bergamo towards the Alpi Orobie mountains; stop in the occasional curious town far from the tourist trails (p155)

* **Wine country** Take a leisurely tour of the Franciacorta (p160) area south of Lake Iseo, topped by a slap-up meal at the Ristorante Gualtiero Marchesi (p163)

* **Lake** Relatively little-known Lake Iseo is a peaceful escape (p158)

* **Rock drawings** The Valle Camonica hides some extraordinary cave drawings (p162)

# WINNING WINES

* **Botticino** A small area 9.5km east of Brescia, where reds are made using barbera and marzemino grapes

* **Cellatica** Another tiny area just north-west of Brescia, where reds are produced from the same grapes as in Botticino

* **Franciacorta** South of Lake Iseo is this area celebrated for its sparkling white and rosé wines; look out also for *satèn*, a blanc de blanc almost exclusively made of chardonnay grapes (p160)

* **San Colombano al Lambro** Family-run wineries produce small quantities of surprising reds and whites from a tiny enclave 15km south of Lodi

* **Valcalepio** This up-and-coming area east of Bergamo produces merlot–cab sauv blends and a good white (p161)

# TOP RESTAURANTS

* **HOSTERIA '700**
Lombard cuisine beneath frescoed vaults (p172)

* **LA COLDANA**
Inventive cooking in a sprawling farmhouse (p176)

* **LA COLLINA**
Good dining on the hill (p157)

* **OSTERIA AL BIANCHI**
Timeless locale for braised donkey (p168)

* **OSTERIA AI SANTI**
Hearty Italian dishes from across Italy (p151)

* **RISTORANTE GUALTIERO MARCHESI**
A high temple of modern Italian cuisine (p163)

# RESOURCES

* **Brembana Valley** (www.vallebrembana.org) Information on the valley, accommodation, food and more

* **Rupestre.net** (www.rupestre.net) Valle Camonica rock art details

* **Sentiero delle Orobie** (www.sentierodelle orobie.it, in Italian) Walking trails in the Alpi Orobie mountains

* **Strada del Vino Franciacorta** (www .stradadelfranciacorta.it) Walking and cycling routes through Franciacorta wine country

* **Lago d'Iseo** (www.lagodiseo.org, in Italian) All-round website on Lake Iseo

BERGAMO, BRESCIA & CREMONA

# BERGAMO
· · · · · ·

**pop 115,800**

**Split into a sprawling lower town and a captivating, historical hill town, this eastern Lombard city offers a wealth of art and medieval, Renaissance and baroque architecture, a privileged position overlooking the southern plains, breathtaking views and some fine dining. Bergamo is one of northern Italy's most intriguing cities.**

The city's defining feature is a double identity. The ancient hilltop Upper Town (Città Alta) is a tangle of tiny medieval streets, embraced by 5km of Venetian walls. The main street is full of well-stocked *enoteche* (wine bars) and *alimentari* (grocery stores). A funicular carries you from the western edge of the upper town up to the quaint quarter of San Vigilio, which offers stunning views. In the plains below sprawls the Lower Town (Città Bassa).

It is thought Gauls and Etruscans had some sort of presence here, though they left nothing behind to indicate permanent settlement. The Romans, on the other hand, left a deeper mark. The hill settlement of Bergamo is strategically placed on a lonely rise south of the Lombard pre-Alps between the Brembo and Serio river valleys and was no doubt appreciated not only as a trade centre but handy lookout position over the vast Lombard plains to the south. As was typical in Roman settlements, the main roads were the intersecting *decumanus* (east–west road; Via Gombito) and *cardo* (north–south road; today Via Lupo and Via San Lorenzo).

Although Milan's skyscrapers to the southwest are visible on a clear day,

historically Bergamo was more closely associated with Venice, which controlled the city for 350 years until Napoleon arrived. Medieval Bergamo was an industrious (textiles and metals) town that was incorporated into the Venetian empire in 1428, remaining under the domination of the Serenissima (Venetian Republic) until the latter's fall to Napoleon in 1797.

## ESSENTIAL INFORMATION

**EMERGENCIES // Ospedale Riuniti** (off Map p147; ☎ 035 26 91 11; Largo Barozzi 1) Hospital; **Police station** (Map p147; ☎ 035 27 61 11; Via Alessandro Noli 26).

**TOURIST OFFICES // Lower Town Tourist Office** (Map p147; ☎ 035 21 02 04; www .turismo.provincia.bergamo.it; Piazzale Marconi; ⏱ 9am-12.30pm & 2-5.30pm Mon-Fri) Province-wide information, including Alpine activities; **Upper Town Tourist Office** (Map p150; ☎ 035 24 22 26; www.turismo.provincia.bergamo.it; Via Gombito 13; ⏱ 9am-12.30pm & 2-5.30pm) Housed in a 12th-century family watchtower at the crossroads of what were once the Imperial Roman roads to Milan, Brescia and Como.

## EXPLORING BERGAMO

### ♥ PIAZZA VECCHIA // IMBIBE THE RENAISSANCE VIBE AND TOWER VIEWS

The Upper Town's beating heart is the cafe-clad Piazza Vecchia (Old Square; Map p150), lined by elegant architecture that is a testament in stone and brick to Bergamo's long and colourful history. Le Corbusier apparently found it the 'most beautiful square in Europe' – good thing they didn't let him try out any of his ideas on it. Had he done so, he'd have been following a certain precedent. The Renaissance square was created by bulldozing the huddle of medieval housing that once stood there.

The white porticoed building on Via Bartolomeo Colleoni, which forms the northern side of the piazza, is the **Palazzo Nuovo**. Designed in 1611 by a brilliant architectural mind from Vicenza, Vincenzo Scamozzi (1548–1616), it was not actually completed until 1928. Long the seat of the town hall, it has been a library since 1873. Diagonally opposite, on the northwest side of the square, the **Palazzo del Podestà** was long home to Venice's representative in Bergamo.

Turn south and you face the imposing arches and columns of the **Palazzo della Ragione**, built in the 12th century. The lion of St Mark is a reminder of Venice's long reign here. It's an early 20th-century replica of the 15th-century original, which was torn down when Napoleon took over in 1797. The windows and balcony, of the same period and with a distinctly Venetian flavour, are original. Note the sun clock in the pavement beneath the arches and the curious Romanesque and Gothic animals and busts decorating the pillars of the arches.

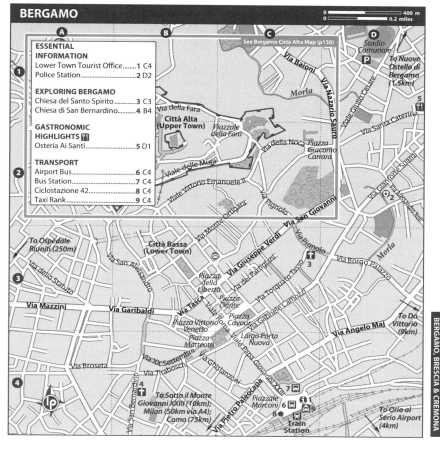

BERGAMO, BRESCIA & CREMONA

## 48 HOURS IN BERGAMO

### SUNNY DAY

Walk the length and breadth of the Città Alta (Upper Town), visiting **La Rocca** (opposite) and its gardens and then continuing to the **citadel** (opposite) to catch the funicular up to San Vigilio for still better views. Back in the Città Alta, you can walk along stretches of the Venetian defensive walls and head down into the Città Bassa (Lower Town) along Via della Noca. When down there, you could continue southwest along Via San Tomaso and then roughly southeast along Via Pignolo, one of the more eye-catching streets of the older part of the Lower Town. Catch a bus or funicular back to the Città Alta to cap the day with a climb to the top of the **Torre del Campanone** (below) for beautiful views in the late-afternoon light.

### RAINY DAY

If you're holed up in the Città Alta on a wet day, you can indulge in the great indoors, starting with the **Basilica di Santa Maria Maggiore** (below) and working your way through the museums of the **citadel** (opposite) and **La Rocca** (opposite). Several cafes along Via Gombito can be used as in-between-museum sanctuaries. At lunch, you might tarry a little longer than usual at the **Vineria Cozzi** (p152), savouring the wines.

Across the square from the palace, the colossal, square-based **Torre del Campanone** (Tower of the Big Bell; admission €3; 9.30am-1pm & 2-5.30pm Tue-Fri, 9.30am-1pm & 2-7.30pm Sat & Sun mid-Mar–Oct, by reservation Mon-Sat Nov–mid-Mar) tolls the old 10pm curfew. Originally raised in the 12th century and partly used as a jail in the 14th, it has undergone numerous alterations. In 1486, cheerful citizens lit a bonfire atop the tower to celebrate a religious holiday. Oddly, they didn't foresee that this would lead to the timber roof catching and burning to a crisp, leading to one of the many renovations. Lighting fires is no longer allowed but you can take a wheelchair-accessible lift to the top, from where there are splendid views. For €5 you get entry to the tower and other sights around the city, including La Rocca (opposite).

♥ **PIAZZA DEL DUOMO // ADMIRE A VENETIAN MERCENARY'S GLORIOUS MAUSOLEUM**
Tucked in behind the secular buildings of Piazza Vecchia, Piazza del Duomo

(Map p150) is the core of Bergamo's spiritual life. Roman remains were discovered during renovations of the modest and mostly baroque **Duomo** (☎ 035 21 02 23; 7.30-11.45am & 3-6.30pm). A rather squat maroon cathedral, it has a brilliant white facade.

A great deal more intriguing is the originally Romanesque **Basilica di Santa Maria Maggiore** (☎ 035 22 33 27; 9am-12.30pm & 2.30-6pm Apr-Oct, 9am-12.30pm & 2.30-5pm Mon-Fri, 9-12.30am & 2.30-6pm Sat, 9am-12.45pm & 3-6pm Sun Nov-Mar) next door. Begun in 1137, it is quite a mishmash. To its whirl of Romanesque apses (on which some external frescos remain visible), Gothic additions were slapped on. Influences seem to come from afar, with dual-colour banding (black and white, and rose and white) typical of Tuscany and an interesting trompe l'œil pattern on part of the facade. What most stands out, however, is the busy Renaissance addition known as the **Cappella Colleoni** (☎ 035 21 00 61; 9am-12.30pm & 2-6.30pm Mar-Oct, 9am-12.30pm & 2-4.30pm Tue-Sun Nov-Feb), which was tacked on to the side facing the square between 1472 and 1476. It was built as a magnificent mausoleum-cum-chapel for the Bergamese mercenary commander Bartolomeo Colleoni (c 1400–1475), who led Venice's armies in campaigns across northern Italy. He lies buried inside in a magnificent tomb. Venetian rococo master Giambattista Tiepolo (1696–1770) did some of the frescos below the central dome.

Detached from the main body of the church is the octagonal **baptistery** built in 1340 but plonked in its present spot in 1898.

### ♥ CITY WANDERING // MEANDER THE STREETS OF THE CITTÀ ALTA

The defensive hulk of Bergamo's **citadel** (Map p150), in the western corner of the Città Alta, is balanced by **La Rocca** (Map p150; ☎ 035 24 71 16; Piazzale Brigata Legnano; adult/child €3/free; ☼ 9.30am-1pm & 2-5.30pm Tue-Fri year-round, 9.30am-7pm Sat & Sun Jun-Sep), an impressive fortress whose round tower dates from Bergamo's days as a Venetian outpost. The citadel was built during Visconti rule but greatly altered under the Venetians. It now houses a couple of modest museums, while La Rocca houses part of the city's history museum and is surrounded by a park with lovely views over lower Bergamo. Connecting the two fortresses, Via Bartolomeo Colleoni and Via Gombito are lined with all sorts of curious shops and eateries. Getting lost in the neighbouring lanes is a pleasant way to pass the time, poking your nose into nooks and crannies as you go. Wander along the perimeter streets of the old town too, for rewarding panoramas from numerous points around the city's Venetian-era defensive walls.

### ♥ ART GALLERIES // GET TO KNOW ITALY'S OLD MASTERS

Just east of the old city walls is one of Italy's great art repositories, the **Accademia Carrara** (Map p150; ☎ 035 39 96 40; www.accademiacarrara.bergamo.it; Piazza Giacomo Carrara 82a; adult/child €2.60/free; ☼ 10am-1pm & 2.30-5.30pm Tue-Sun). Founded in 1780, it contains an exceptional range of Italian masters. Raphael's *San Sebastiano* is a highlight, but other artists represented include Botticelli, Canaletto, Mantegna and Titian. To get here on foot from the Upper Town, pass through **Porta di Sant'Agostino** and down Via della Noca. At the time of writing it was closed for restoration (until at least 2010) but a selection of its masterpieces was on show in Palazzo della Ragione (p147) in the Città Alta.

On the opposite side of the square is the **Galleria d'Arte Moderna e Contemporanea** (GAMeC; Map p150; ☎ 035 27 02 72; www.gamec.it; Via San Tomaso 53; admission free; ☼ 10am-1pm & 3-7pm Tue-Sun), which displays the academy's small permanent collection of modern works by Italian artists such as Giacomo Balla, Giorgio Morandi, Giorgio de Chirico and Filippo de Pisis. A contribution from Vassily Kandinksy lends an international touch. Admission prices and opening hours vary for temporary exhibitions.

# GASTRONOMIC HIGHLIGHTS

### ♥ ANTICA HOSTERIA DEL VINO BUONO €

Map p150; ☎ 035 24 79 93; Piazza Mercato delle Scarpe, Città Alta; meals €20; ☼ dinner Tue, lunch & dinner Wed-Sun

Feast on typical dishes like cheese-sprinkled *casoncelli* (homemade pasta cushions filled with a spicy sausage

BERGAMO, BRESCIA & CREMONA

# BERGAMO CITTÀ ALTA

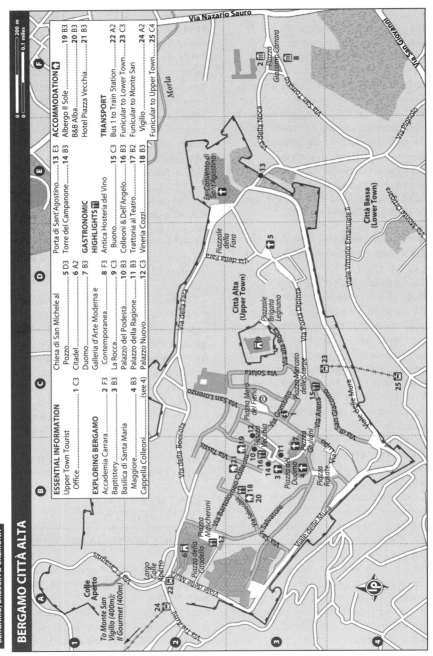

**ESSENTIAL INFORMATION**

Upper Town Tourist
Office .................................. 1 C3

**EXPLORING BERGAMO**

Accademia Carrara ............. 2 F3
Baptistery ............................ 3 B3
Basilica di Santa Maria
Maggiore ........................... 4 B3
Cappella Colleoni .......... (see 4)

Chiesa di San Michele al
Pozzo .................................. 5 D3
Citadel................................. 6 A2
Duomo................................. 7 B3
Galleria d'Arte Moderna e
Contemporanea................ 8 F3
La Rocca............................... 9 C3
Palazzo del Podestà......... 10 B3
Palazzo della Ragione...... 11 B3
Palazzo Nuovo.................. 12 C3

Porta di Sant'Agostino......13 E3
Torre del Campanone........14 B3

**GASTRONOMIC
HIGHLIGHTS**

Antica Hosteria del Vino
Buono................................15 C3
Colleoni & Dell'Angelo......16 B3
Trattoria al Teatro..............17 B2
Vineria Cozzi......................18 B3

**ACCOMMODATION**

Albergo Il Sole ....................19 B3
B&B Alba..............................20 B3
Hotel Piazza Vecchia..........21 B3

**TRANSPORT**

Bus 1 to Train Station .........22 A2
Funicular to Lower Town....23 C3
Funicular to Monte San
Vigilio...............................24 A2
Funicular to Upper Town....25 C4

meat and laced with a buttery sage sauce) followed by a plate of *stinco al forno con polenta* (baked beef shank with polenta) at this authentic inn. A typical Bergamese antipasto served up here is *schisöl* (polenta cooked with cheese and mushrooms).

### ❤ COLLEONI & DELL'ANGELO €€€

Map p150; ☎ 035 23 25 96; www.colleonidellangelo .com; Piazza Vecchia 7, Città Alta; meals €50-60, tasting menus €75; ☾ Tue-Sun

Piazza Vecchia provides the ideal backdrop to savour inventive local cuisine. Grab an outside table in summer or opt for the noble 15th-century interior, with its polished tile floors, rich linen, occasional fresco and the odd suit of armour standing about. Meals range from takes on strictly local dishes through to more generally Italian dishes and occasional use of products from further afield. Try the *ravioloni ripieni di Bagoss alle foglie di basilico fritto e vitello glassato* (big dumplings filled with Bagoss cheese with fried basil leaves and veal glazing).

### ❤ DA VITTORIO €€€

Off Map p147; ☎ 035 68 10 24; www.davittorio.com; Via Cantalupa 17, Brusaporto; set menus €70-140; ☾ Thu-Tue, closed 3 weeks Aug

Bergamo's acclaimed Vittorio is set in a country house 9km east of town and is up there with the best restaurants in Italy, not the least on account of its truffle dishes (a special truffle menu can cost €280). The guiding thought behind the cuisine is the subtle use of the freshest possible seasonal products to create local dishes with inventive flair. Why not succumb to a *maialata* (more or less literally a 'pig out'), with six courses of porcine pleasure?

### ❤ IL GOURMET €€

Off Map p150; ☎ 035 437 30 04; www.gourmet -bg.it; Via San Vigilio 1, Città Alta; meals €45; ☾ Wed-Mon

Run by two wine buffs, this gourmet's haven is hidden away in San Vigilio, a few minutes' stroll beyond the Upper Town's western walls. The 18th-century mansion's shady terraces (one with panoramic views) and artful Bergamese and Mediterranean cuisine make it worth seeking out for a meal. You may like it enough to enquire about accommodation in one of the 10 rooms.

### ❤ OSTERIA AI SANTI €€

Map p147; ☎ 035 22 50 49; www.aisantibergamo .com; Via Santa Caterina 90a, Città Bassa; meals €30-35; ☾ lunch & dinner Mon-Fri, dinner Sat

Lurking at the edge of the lower old town in a cheerful orange house, Ai Santi is a popular local eatery that is regularly packed. Dishes range across Italy, from Tuscany to Puglia. Of the latter, the *orecchiette con pesce spada, melanzane viola e mentuccia* (ear-shaped pasta with swordfish, purple eggplant and mint) is hard to ignore. You could follow with cod, steak or *caciocavallo fritto con zucchine al pepe nero di Sarawak* (a provolone-style cheese fried with zucchini sprinkled in black pepper from Sarawak).

### ❤ TRATTORIA AL TEATRO €€

Map p150; ☎ 035 23 88 62; Piazza Mascheroni 3, Città Alta; meals €30-35; ☾ Tue-Sun

For simple home cooking, this is a good bet. Located in a centuries-old building at the west end of the Città Alta, this family-run spot has a limited but constantly changing menu of local dishes. Choose from the handful of *primi* and *secondi* first and second courses), with such local classics as *casoncelli alla bergamasca* (big egg-based ravioli stuffed with meat, cheese

## IN SEARCH OF LORENZO LOTTO

One of the great names of the late Venetian Renaissance, Lorenzo Lotto worked for 12 years in and around Bergamo from 1513. Today, three of his works remain in situ in three churches scattered about the city. Seeing them is largely a matter of luck – finding these churches open is hit-and-miss. Just off Via Porta Dipinta at the eastern end of the Città Alta (Upper Town), the diminutive **Chiesa di San Michele al Pozzo** (St Michael at the Well; Map p150; Via Porta Dipinta) is home to a chapel filled with a cycle of paintings known as the *Storie della Vergine* (Stories of the Virgin Mother), starting with her birth and culminating with the scene of her visiting Elisabeth (her cousin and soon-to-be mother of St John the Baptist). In two churches in the Città Bassa (Lower Town), the **Chiesa del Santo Spirito** (Church of the Holy Spirit; Map p147; Via Torquato Tasso) and **Chiesa di San Bernardino** (Map p147; Via San Bernardino), one can observe how Lotto treats in quite different fashion the same subject in altarpieces dedicated to the *Madonna in trono e santi* (The Madonna Enthroned with Saints). The latter is done with great flair and freedom, full of vivid colour, while the former seems more subdued.

or spinach), followed perhaps by a *filetto ai ferri* (a grilled beef filet) or an *ossobuco con piselli* (sliced shin of veal with peas).

### ♥ VINERIA COZZI €€

Map p150; ☎ 035 23 88 36; www.vineriacozzi.it; Via Bartolomeo Colleoni 22, Città Alta; meals €35-45; ☺ Thu-Tue

Things have changed little since the original wine dealer started up here in 1848. Elegant little tables with delicate wrought-iron-backed chairs and a parchment-yellow paint scheme ensure a welcoming atmosphere and seem much as they were all those years ago. You can taste from the extensive wine list by the glass, and dine inside or in the tiny courtyard. Several pasta and rice options lead the way, and you might follow with a rabbit done in local Valcalepio red wine. The desserts, with a slightly modern touch, are all homemade.

## TRANSPORT

**AIR //** **Orio al Serio** ( ☎ 035 32 63 23; www .sacbo.it), 4km southeast of Bergamo train station, has regular flights to/from the UK and other European desti-

nations. **ATB** ( ☎ 035 23 60 26) buses to/from Orio al Serio airport depart every 20 minutes from Bergamo bus and train stations (€1.70, 15 minutes). Direct buses also connect the airport with Milan and Brescia.

**TRAIN //** One or two trains run every hour between Milan (not all call at Stazione Centrale) and Bergamo (€4.20, 50 to 65 minutes). Every 30 to 60 minutes a train runs to/from Brescia (€3.60, one to 1½ hours). Change there for Cremona or Mantua.

**BICYCLE //** **Ciclostazione 42** (Map p147; ☎ 389 5137313; www.pedalopolis.org; Piazzale Marconi; per day €10; ☺ 7.30-11.30am & 4-7.30pm Mon-Fri), just outside the train station, rents out bikes.

**BUS //** ATB's bus 1 connects the train station with the funicular to the Upper Town and Colle Aperto (going the other way not all buses stop right at the station but at the Porta Nuova stop). From Colle Aperto, either bus 21 or a funicular continues uphill to San Vigilio. Buy tickets, valid for 75 minutes' travel on buses, for €1 from machines at the train and funicular stations or at newspaper stands. The main bus station for provincial services is across Piazzale Marconi from the train station.

**CAR //** From Milan or Brescia, take the A4 motorway and follow the Bergamo exits.

**PARKING //** Traffic is restricted in the Città Alta, although you can approach and find limited parking outside the city walls. Otherwise, use metered parking or car parks in the Lower Town.

BERGAMO, BRESCIA & CREMONA

# DRIVING TOUR: CASTLE CIRCUIT & THE GOOD POPE

**Distance: 105km**
**Duration: one day**

The plains south of Bergamo are dotted with interesting towns and villages, some of them dominated by castles and palaces that stand as eloquent testament of their colourful history. Most of the places mentioned following can be reached by bus from Bergamo.

Take the SS42 east out of Bergamo, or drop south to the A4 motorway and head a short way east, turning south at the Seriate exit, taking the SP498 provincial road for **Cavernago**, a village presided over by one of several forts built by the mercenary commander Bartolomeo Colleoni (see p149). Known as the **Castello Colleoni** (Martinengo; ☎ 035 95 89 66), this turreted, stone hulk looms up on the right as you trundle south into Cavernago. It was raised in the Middle Ages but substantially overhauled in the 17th and 18th centuries. You can peak through slits at the entrance to see the frescoed gallery around the courtyard.

Barely 3km southwest, on a farming estate, lies the crenellated brickwork **Castello di Malpaga** (☎ 035 840 00 03; Piazza Marconi, Malpaga; ☽ 3-6pm Sun & holidays Feb-Nov), another Colleoni residence. He had the original 14th-century castle expanded, turning the original defensive walls into a kind of interior courtyard by adding various outhouses and walls around its entire perimeter. Some original frescos still remain in place.

Picking up the SP498 again, you wind up in **Romano di Lombardia** after 12.5km. The **Rocca** (Piazza della Rocca 1) is a castle built just beyond the old town under Milan's Visconti clan in classic Lom-

bard fashion, its four high walls topped by square-based towers at each corner. Partly overgrown with greenery and its plaster in dire need of some patching up, it houses a library and offices. You can wander into the courtyard in office hours – note the fresco of the lion of St Mark, showing that for some time Venice was in control here.

From Romano, the next objective is **Caravaggio**. Aside from the impressive **Chiesa dei Santi Fermo e Rustico** (Piazza San Fermo; ☽ 7am-noon & 3-6.30pm), with its brick Gothic facade, fine frescos and imposing 16th-century bell tower, and its claim to fame as the birthplace of the like-named artist, the town's main attraction lies along a tree-lined boulevard about 1.5km southwest of the centre. The **Santuario della Madonna di Caravaggio** (☎ 0363 35 71; www.santuariodicaravaggio.org; Viale Papa Giovanni XXIII; ☽ 7am-noon & 2-5pm) is a grandiose building started at the orders of Filippo Maria Visconti, Duke of Milan, after an alleged sighting on this spot of the Virgin Mary in 1432. With its fine dome and richly decorated 18th-century interior, it remains a major object of pilgrimage today.

A short hop northwest brings you to **Treviglio**, a city of some 25,000 inhabitants, at whose centre rises the **Collegiata di San Martino** (Piazza Luciano Manara; ☽ 7.30-11.30am & 2.30-6pm), a brick Gothic church with a deep baroque makeover (the facade seems to have been slapped on with Play-Doh) and typically impressive tower. A minor country road leads northeast out of Treviglio for **Brignano Gera d'Adda**, home to one of several Visconti castles in the area. Now a baroque residence jammed with frescos and backed by an overgrown garden, the **Palazzo Visconti** (Via Vittorio Emanuele II) is undergoing renovation. Barely 3km southeast, in

BERGAMO, BRESCIA & CREMONA

**Pagazzano**, stands yet another Visconti castle ( ☎ 0363 81 46 29; www.castellodipagazzano.it; Piazza Castello; ☺ 9am-noon & 2-6pm 1st & 3rd Sun of month), this one decidedly more fortress-like and surrounded by a (filled) moat. The museum inside recounts rural life and includes a 1736 wine press.

**Crespi d'Adda**, some 20km northwest along various country roads, is a perfect example of the workers' town and factory built by enlightened industrialists in various parts of Europe in the late 19th century. Here, the Crespi textile dynasty built cotton mills (which only closed

in 2004), modest but pleasant housing for employees (pretty little two-storey houses with garden), a rather boisterous castle for the family and various services (from church to school). The whole was declared a World Heritage Site in 1995. The **village** ( ☎ 02 9098 7191; www.villaggiocrespi.it) is still inhabited so there are no formal visiting hours. If hunger strikes, make for **Osteria da Mualdo** ( ☎ 02 9093 7077; www.osteriadamualdo.it; Via Privata Crespi 6; meals €55; ☺ lunch & dinner Tue-Sat, lunch Sun). Set in a renovated farmhouse with plenty of timber and exposed stonework adding to the

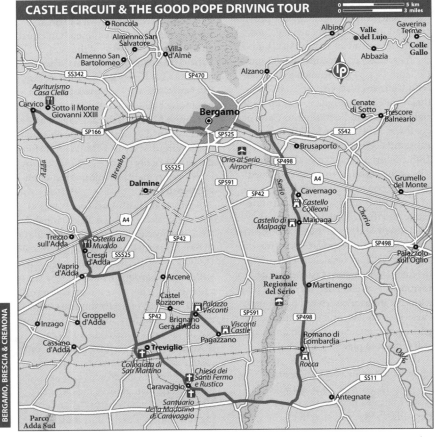

CASTLE CIRCUIT & THE GOOD POPE DRIVING TOUR

charm, it offers melt-in-the-mouth pasta and such house specialities as *maialino da latte croccante laccato al miele* (crispy suckling pig basted in honey).

From Crespi, follow the Adda river north 15km to Carvico. Two kilometres east is **Sotto il Monte Giovanni XXIII**. Angelo Roncalli was born in 1881 in this hamlet, which, as its name suggests, lies at the foot of a vineyard-draped mount that is topped by a medieval tower. No one could have guessed that, in 1958, he would become Pope John XXIII. In his five years as pontiff, he changed the face of the Catholic Church through the Vatican II Council reforms. You can visit his humble birthplace in the centre of town and a small museum set up in a house he used on summer holidays as cardinal. There are several places to get a bite, including the **Agriturismo Casa Clelia** ( ☎ 035 79 91 33; www.casaclelia.com; Via Corna 1/3; set lunches €15, meals €30-35; ☺ Tue-Sun). This working farm has rooms and offers such goodies as risottos and stuffed rabbit. Many of the ingredients are organic. Dine in centuries-old rooms or under the pergola in summer.

From here, it is an 18km drive east back into Bergamo along the SP166.

# BERGAMO'S VALLEYS

· · · · · ·

**The series of tranquil valleys that works its way like a hand of bony fingers into the mountains north of Bergamo couldn't provide a greater contrast to the traffic-choked roads just south of the city and west towards Milan.**

The hills north of Bergamo rise up to the status of mountains in the Alpi Orobie (Orobie Alps), which throw up a mix of jagged peaks, gentler, snow-covered slopes, thickly wooded dales and open high-country pasture. All sorts of little gems await discovery, from the Cascate del Serio waterfall outside Valbondione to the medieval stone hamlets of Cornello dei Tasso and Gromo. Serious hikers have endless opportunities to take in fresh air in the Alpi Orobie (see p261).

## EXPLORING BERGAMO'S VALLEYS

### ♣ FROM THE BERGAMO HILLS TO TALEGGIO // ROMANESQUE BEAUTY AND REMOTE CHEESE COUNTRY

From Bergamo's Città Alta, several minor roads lead through the pleasant **Colli di Bergamo** (Bergamo Hills) and drop down into plains around Almenno San Salvatore (follow the SP470) road. Sitting in the country between this town and **Almenno San Bartolomeo** is a wonderful example of early Lombard Romanesque, the circular **Chiesa di San Tomè** ( ☺ 2.30-6pm Sat, 10am-noon & 2.30-6pm Sun & holidays). The exterior of this unusual stone church boasts some pleasing decorative patterns. The play of circular and semicircular spaces inside is testimony to the fine aesthetic sensibility of medieval builders.

A possible driving route from Almenno San Salvatore would lead 5.5km northeast along the SP470 and then north up the SP24 into the Val Brembilla. North of the town of Brembilla, the wooded hill country makes for a fine scenic drive that brings you back to the SP470 through the little-visited **Val Taleggio**, home to one of Lombardy's signature cheeses. The valley passes through the 3km-long **Gola dell'Enna**, a narrow rocky gorge at the bottom of which surges the Enna river.

### ♥ SAN PELLEGRINO TERME // THE SOURCE OF SAN PELLEGRINO MINERAL WATER

They first started bottling lightly sparkling mineral water in **San Pellegrino Terme**, 25km north of Bergamo along the Valle Brembana, at the beginning of the 19th century. Thermal baths tourism began late that century and local investors decided to spend big on new facilities in the early 1900s, creating the massive, seven-storey Grand Hotel (1904) and the exuberant Casinò Municipale (1907). They face each other over the Brembo river and together form a treasure chest of *stile liberty* (Italian art nouveau). The Casinò Municipale, especially, is full of whimsical detail. The facade bears reliefs and sculptures of mythological figures and naturalistic forms (from laurel leaves to beetles), as well as two giant, wrought-iron lampholders. Both buildings could only be seen from the outside at the time of writing, as restoration work progresses to restore them to their original glory.

### ♥ CORNELLO DEI TASSO // STUMBLE INTO A TIMELESS MEDIEVAL VILLAGE

Eight kilometres north of San Pellegrino Terme, **Cornello dei Tasso** (signposted off the SP470) is a compact time warp, a golden stone medieval hamlet high above the Brembo river that seems to have stood still, unconcerned by the passing of the centuries. You can park down near the main road and climb a pretty path (with great valley views). The heavy stone houses seem to huddle together, and the main lane is shielded from the elements by a series of protective vaults.

### ♥ NORTHERN VALLE BREMBANA // EXPLORE SCENIC MOUNTAIN ROUTES AND WALKING BASES

From Cornello dei Tasso, the valley road proceeds north and splits deltalike into a series of valleys, some of which culminate in small winter ski towns, such as Foppolo, in the Alpi Orobie. Hikers should note **Branzi** and **Carona**, which can make bases for walks up to a series of glacial lakes. Scenic-drive enthusiasts might opt for a different route, a minor road linking the Valle Brembana with the Valle Seriana via the villages of **Dossena** and **Oltre il Colle**. Territory ranges from dense forest to some fine open views north to the Orobie mountains from around Oltre il Colle.

### ♥ VALLE SERIANA // FROM GUSHING BAROQUE TO THUNDERING WATERFALLS

As you wind out of Bergamo to the northeast, the Valle Seriana starts as a broad affair, pierced by a busy road (the SP671) and lined with towns and some industry.

Along the way, 25km northeast of central Bergamo, the town of **Gandino** is well worth a stop for its impressive **Basilica di Santa Maria Assunta** (Piazza della Emancipazione; ☾ 8am-noon & 3-6pm), a baroque beauty with a richly decorated interior atop a sloping square.

Back on the main SP671 road, things continue much as before. Then, quite suddenly, it all changes at **Ardesio**. The gushing Serio river is crowded in by lush green mountains and traffic drops to a trickle. Three kilometres north of Ardesio, **Gromo** is a charming little medieval hamlet, with twisting lanes and stone houses topped by slate roofs.

Another 12km leads you north to **Valbondione**, a town used as a base by hikers and winter-sports enthusiasts. The highlight here is a 2½-hour hike to the **Cascate del Serio**, a triple cascade of 300m that constitutes one of Europe's tallest waterfalls. Follow signs for the nearby **Rifugio Curó** ( ☎ 0346 4 40 76; www .antoniocuro.it), which sits at 1915m near a pretty glacial lake and offers beds and meals. Check ahead for opening times. A 7km drive along a series of hairpin bends leads east up to **Lizzola**, another hiking base at 1256m, with magnificent views of the surrounding mountains and back south down the valley.

# GASTRONOMIC HIGHLIGHTS

### ❦ CÀ BIGIO // SAN PELLEGRINO TERME €€
☎ 0345 2 10 58; www.bigio.info; Via Papa Giovanni XXIII 60; meals €40

The Bigio family invented that archetypal Bergamese dessert, *polenta e osei* (cakes filled with jam and cream, topped with sweet polenta and chocolate birds). At their restaurant, though, it's the savouries that will win you over. Grab a table at the back for views up through the garden to the Casinò Municipale and order a dish of *tortelli di patate cuore morbido al formaggio d'Alpe Grass de Rost e tartufo nero* (potato pasta packets with a 'soft heart' of cheese and black truffle). A main to follow could be a *filetto di maialino avvolto nello speck e cotto nel fieno* (suckling pig filet wrapped in a kind of salted, smoked ham and cooked in hay).

### ❦ LA COLLINA // ALMENNO SAN BARTOLOMEO €€€
☎ 035 64 25 70; www.ristorantecollina.it; Via Ca'Paler 5; meals €50-60; ✆ Wed-Sun

With several dining areas, an outdoor pergola for summer meals, and a privi-

leged position overlooking the surrounding territory, La Collina (aptly, The Hill), is a stylish setting for carefully prepared and beautifully presented Lombard cooking with international flair. First courses range from fish ravioli to a risotto that changes with the caprices of the chef. Meat dominates the next stage and can range from tongue to a melt-in-the-mouth chunk of sirloin in orange and juniper, served with a savoury-sweet fruit salad.

### ❦ POSTA AL CASTELLO // GROMO €€
☎ 0346 4 10 02; www.postalcastello.it; Piazza Dante Alighieri 3; meals €25-30; ✆ Tue-Sun

Spread about inside what remains of the one-time castle at the heart of Gromo, the various rooms (some with frescos) have a convivial air. Mushrooms are the speciality and you'll find them in many of the dishes, starting with the *zuppa di funghi* (mushroom soup) or *la delizia del Posta* (a kind of cheese-and-mushroom pancake). You can get away from them, though, by opting for something like the *tagliata al romasmarino* (juicy beef slab in rosemary).

### ❦ RISTORANTE DELLA SALUTE // OLDA (TALEGGIO) €€
☎ 0345 4 70 06; www.albergodellasalute.com; Costa d'Olda 73; meals €25; ✆ Tue-Sun

This agreeable country hotel has a simple restaurant downstairs where a good number of the excellent home-cooked dishes feature the local speciality, Taleggio cheese. About halfway along the wild and woolly Taleggio valley, this place offers views of the surrounding greenery and dishes like *strozzapreti ai spinaci con crema di Taleggio* (a kind of spinach gnocchi bathed in a thick, creamy Taleggio cheese sauce).

## TRANSPORT

**BUS //** From Bergamo's **bus station** (www.berga
motrasporti.it, in Italian), **SAB** (☎ 800 139392, 035
28 90 00; www.sab-autoservizi.it, in Italian) operates
services to just about every village in the valleys, albeit
not with great frequency. Timetables are available at
the station.

**CAR //** Your own vehicle makes touring the valleys a
great deal easier. The SP470 road heads north from the
city along the Valle Brembana, while the SP671 takes
you northeast along the Valle Seriana.

# LAKE ISEO & AROUND

· · · · · ·

Less than 100km from both Bergamo
and Brescia, Lake Iseo (aka Sebino)
is one of the least known Lombard
lakes. Shut in by soaring mountains,
it is a magnificent sight. About halfway along the lake, another mountain
whose shape reminds vaguely of Rio
de Janeiro's Pao de Açúcar, soars
right out of the water.

With the exception of the south shore
and a series of tunnels at the northeast
end of the lake, the road closely hugs
the water on its circuit around Lake
Iseo and is especially dramatic south of
Lovere.

Various back roads lead high up behind Lovere for magnificent views. Of
the three main towns – Iseo, Sarnico and
Lovere – Sarnico is perhaps the prettiest,
sitting on the north bank of the Oglio
river.

To the lake's north stretches the Valle
Camonica, famed for its Stone Age rock
carvings. To the south stretches the rolling Franciacorta wine country and, to
the west, the picture-book-pretty Lake
Endine.

## ESSENTIAL INFORMATION

**TOURIST OFFICES //** **IAT Iseo** (☎ 030 98 02
09; www.agenzialagoiseofranciacorta.it; Lungolago Marconi 2, Iseo; ⊙ 10am-12.30pm & 3.30-6.30pm Easter-
Sep, 10am-12.30pm & 3-6pm Mon-Fri, 10am-12.30pm
Sat Oct-Easter); **Pro Loco Capo di Ponte**
(☎ 0364 4 20 80; www.proloco.capo-di-ponte
.bs.it; Via Briscioli 42, Capo di Ponte; ⊙ 9.30am-
12.30pm Sun, Mon & holidays, 9am-noon & 2.30-
4.30pm Tue-Sat); **Pro Loco Sarnico** (☎ 035 4
20 80; www.prolocosarnico.it; Via Lantieri 6, Sarnico;
⊙ 9.30am-12.30pm & 3-6.30pm Tue-Sat, 9.30am-
12.30pm Sun); **Tourist Office Lovere** (☎ 035
96 21 78; Piazza XIII Martiri 34, Lovere; ⊙ 9.30am-
12.30pm Mon-Thu, 9.30am-12.30pm & 2-5pm Fri,
9am-12.30pm & 2-5.30pm Sat & Sun).

## EXPLORING LAKE ISEO & AROUND

❤ **MONTE ISOLA // EXPLORE
EUROPE'S BIGGEST ISLAND-
IN-A-LAKE**
The towering island at the south end of
Lake Iseo is easily the lake's most striking feature and merits an effort to get
to know. Francesco Sforza granted the
people of **Monte Isola** (www.monteisola
.com, www.tuttomonteisola.it) special fishing
rights in the 15th century. Its people,
whose ancestors may have lived here in
Roman times, were also known for their
handmade fishing nets. Perched on Europe's biggest lake island (4.28 sq km),
they were also pretty self-sufficient in
basic land produce. A handful of villages
are scattered around the island. From
**Carzano**, in the northeast (where many
boats land), you can climb rough stairs
to scattered rural settlements and follow
a path to the top of the island (599m).
The town hall is in **Siviano**, on the
northwest shore. A 15km trail allows you
to walk or cycle right around the island.

**☙ ISEO // CANOE OR CYCLE IN ISEO**
At the lake's southeast edge, the sun sets directly in front of the lakefront promenade in **Iseo** (population 9060). The string of squares just behind the waterfront is great for hanging about in cafes and people-watching. About 500m west of the old centre, you can hire canoes and pedalos for about €6 an hour. At **Iseobike** ( ☎ 340 396 2095; Via Colombera 2; ☙ 9.30am-12.15pm & 2.30-7pm May-Aug, 9.30am-12.15pm & 2.30-7pm Fri-Sun Sep-Apr), Franco will put together tailor-made cycling tours around the lake and amid the vineyards of the Franciacorta wine area immediately to the south.

**☙ SARNICO // LIBERTY IN RIVERSIDE TOWN**
Approaching Lake Iseo from the southwest brings you to Sarnico (population 6230), prettily located on a corner of the lake and the Oglio river. It is characterised by several lovely *stile liberty* villas, many of them designed by Giuseppe Sommaruga. Among them, his lakeside **Villa Faccanoni** (Via Veneto) is the most outstanding. The heart of the old town,

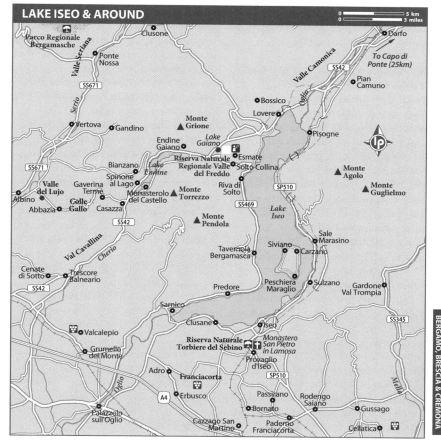

LAKE ISEO & AROUND

0 ___ 5 km
0 ___ 3 miles

BERGAMO, BRESCIA & CREMONA

known as La Contrada, straggles back from its pretty riverside location on the mouth of the Oglio river. It is perfect for a wander after a morning coffee along the riverside. Head up Via Lantieri, lined by shops and eateries, and along which you can make out vestiges from the past. Via Scaletta, which runs down to the lake, is where you'll find most evidence of Sarnico's medieval past, with the remnants of towers and stout surviving walls. The main sight is a small art gallery, the **Pinacoteca Gianni Bellini** ( ☎ 035 91 21 65; Via San Paolo 8; admission free; ☺ 9.30am-noon & 3-7pm Sat, 10am-noon & 3-7pm Sun), where some 130 paintings, mostly 16th-to-18th-century works from lesser-known artists across northern Italy, hang.

### ☙ LOVERE & BOSSICO // ADMIRE THE ART AND THE VIEWS

Perched on the lake's northwestern tip, the port town of **Lovere** (population 5410) is a gem, with a working harbour and a wealth of walking trails nearby. Its cobbled old town, punctuated by the occasional medieval tower, curves around the harbour, shadowed by a leafy lakefront promenade. Those in need of an art shot should consider the waterfront **Accademia Tadini** ( ☎ 035 96 27 80; www.accademiatadini.it; Via Tadini 40; adult/child & senior €5/3; ☺ 3-7pm Tue-Sat, 10am-noon & 3-7pm Sun & holidays), home to a considerable art collection with works by Jacopo Bellini, Il Parmigiano, Giambattista Tiepolo, Francesco Hayez, Antonio Canova and more.

Those with vehicles might want to drive 12km out of town and up into the hills behind Lovere to the hamlet of **Bossico** (900m). Several panoramic viewpoints offer great vistas over Lake Iseo from the village and nearby. Esmate, reached by Riva di Solto, 6km south

of Lovere, offers further great lookout points over the lake.

### ☙ FRANCIACORTA // TRUNDLE PAST ABBEYS AND WINE-COUNTRY CASTLES

South of Lake Iseo and stretching towards Brescia are the rolling fields, low hills and flourishing vineyards of the greatly applauded Franciacorta wine region. This is perfect cycling country, with no mountain rises to worry about and plenty of villages to explore. The Iseo tourist office (p158) can provide brochures with routes and wineries. The catch is that few wineries actually open their doors to passers-by. During the year, some open on certain weekends but tasting visits generally have to be booked.

**Provaglio d'Iseo**, 3.5km south of Iseo, is dominated by the Romanesque **Monastero San Pietro in Lamosa** (www .sanpietroinlamosa.org, in Italian). The 11th-century church was donated to the Cluniac order of monks, who later expanded the area into a monastery. You can see the outside but visits inside are by appointment only. The complex sits above a 2-sq-km protected wetland, the **Riserva Naturale Torbiere del Sebino** (www.torbiere.it), formed from 18th-century peat beds. In late spring the pools are smothered in water lilies. Getting in is hit-and-miss, although there is a walking path around it.

About 7km southeast of Provaglio, in **Rodengo Saiano**, is the more impressive **Abbazia di San Nicola**, set at the end of a short, cypress-lined avenue. The abbey in its present form dates largely from the 15th century and boasts a gracious Renaissance cloister. It is inhabited by Olivetan monks, and getting in just seems to be a matter of finding the doors open, or not.

BERGAMO, BRESCIA & CREMONA

Five kilometres south of Provaglio, in the hamlet of **Bornato**, stands a 13th-century **castle** (☎ 030 72 50 06; www.castellodi bornato.com; Via Castello 24; admission €6; ⏲ 10am-noon & 2.30-6pm Sun & holidays mid-Mar–mid-Nov), inside which was built a Renaissance villa. The castle's owners possess local vineyards around here and sell their wine here – a tasting is part of the visit.

### ❧ CASTELLO DEL GRUMELLO // TOUR THE WINE FACILITIES GLASS-IN-HAND

A 9km detour southwest of Sarnico brings you to **Grumello del Monte**, dominated by a partly overgrown **Castello del Grumello** (☎ 348 303 6243; www .castellodigrumello.it; admission €10; ⏲ book ahead), now part of a winery where you can book into guided tours with a glass of produce thrown in. Indeed, this is one of northern Italy's lesser-known wine areas, the **Valcalepio**.

### ❧ VAL CAVALLINA // STOP TO ADMIRE LORENZO LOTTO FRESCOS

The broad **Val Cavallina** (www.invalcaval lina.it) follows the Cherio river east of Bergamo toward Lake Endine. A brief stop in **Trescore Balneario** is justified for its pretty medieval core at Piazza Cavour and the frescos by Lorenzo Lotto depicting stories of St Barbara in the little **Chiesa di Santa Barbara** (☎ 035 94 47 77; Via Suardi; admission €6; ⏲ 3-4.30pm Sun or by appointment), which lurks in the luxuriant grounds of **Villa Suardi**, just off the SS42. Ask at the **tourist office** (☎ 035 94 47 77; www.prolocot rescore.it; Via Suardi 16) next door when you can join a guided tour. The tourist office also sells hiking maps for the surrounding area and nearby Lake Endine.

### ❧ LAKE ENDINE // STROLLING, CANOEING AND A MEDIEVAL PAGEANT

The Cherio river runs from the south into lovely, mirror-still Lake Endine, surrounded by woods and reed banks and where motorboats are banned. A minor road leads northeast off the main SS42 road to **Monasterolo del Castello**, a quiet medieval village on the south bank of the lake. The Monasterolo castle, turned into a country mansion in the 16th century, is just outside to the southwest. A lakeside path makes for pleasant strolls around Monasterolo. Or you can hire canoes (€5 an hour) at the Centro Nautico in **Spinone al Lago** on the opposite shore. The 4km road north off the SS42 to **Bianzano** offers panoramic views of the lake. Bianzano's **Castello Suardo** can occasionally be visited by guided tour. Better still, the whole hamlet becomes the scene of **Rievocazione Storica** (www.cortedeisuardo.com), a medieval feast, for a long weekend around the end of July, with parades, activities and some 300 locals going about their business in medieval dress.

### ❧ VALLE DEL FREDDO & ESMATE // AN EDELWEISS SURPRISE AND MAGIC LAKE VIEWS

About 2km northeast of the lake is the **Riserva Naturale Regionale Valle del Freddo** (☎ 035 22 48 02; www.italianostrabergamo .org; ⏲ 2-6pm Sat, 10am-1pm & 2-6pm Sun May-Jul), a short walk north of tiny **Lake Gaiano**. The Cold Valley has a unique microclimate, with a particularly cold subsoil (stick your hands into some of the holes in the ground) that allows 24 species of Alpine flowers (including edelweiss) and plants to flourish at an altitude of just 360m. From there, head on foot or by car to the hamlet of **Esmate**, from where you can enjoy splendid views of the northern end of Lake Iseo. The views are good from the churchyard but breathtaking if you follow Via Cerrete about 2.5km from the church (it changes names several times). Where it narrows amid thick woods, several brief trails (20m or so) lead out to magnificent, wild viewpoints high above the lake. You can also reach Esmate from the shores of Lake Iseo, following an 8km road northwest of Riva di Solto.

### ❧ VALLE CAMONICA // EXAMINE SOME OF THE WORLD'S MOST ANCIENT ART

Running northeast of Lake Iseo and marked by the course of the Oglio river, the Valle Camonica is best known locally for easy skiing at its northern extremity (beyond the reaches of this guidebook) but internationally as the sight of some quite extraordinary rock carvings, a collective World Heritage Site since 1979.

### Capo di Ponte's Ancient Rock Carvings

The rock carvings are concentrated in several sites around the small town of **Capo di Ponte** (www.capodiponte.eu), which sits on the Oglio river. The main site is the **Parco Nazionale delle Incisioni Rupestri** ( ☎ 0364 4 21 40; www.arterupestre.it; Località Naquane; adult/child/senior €4/2/free; ☾ 9am-7.30pm Tue-Sun May-Sep, 9am to 1hr before sunset Oct-Apr), on a rise just 1km out of the town centre on the east side of the river. It is a 30-hectare open-air museum containing a representative array of rock engravings going as far back as the Bronze Age. Colour-coded paths lead you past vast rock slabs that seem to have been created specifically for people to clamber around and chisel in their artistic talent. While engravings on some are barely distinguishable, on others you see a wealth of imagery, including animals, people in various poses and not a few inexplicable symbols. Especially rich is Rock No 1 (aka Roccia Grande).

Capo di Ponte is home to two other such parks, west of the river. One is closed for excavation but the **Parco Archeologico Comunale di Seraldina Bedolina** ( ☎ 334 657 56 28; adult/child/senior €2/1/free; ☾ 10am-5pm Fri-Wed) is also rich in engravings. To get here, head for the town cemetery in Cemmo (you can drive or walk up from the centre), from where it's a 10-minute walk.

### Pieve di San Siro

Also near the cemetery in Cemmo is one of the finest examples of Lombard Romanesque, the 11th-century **Pieve**

---

### TOP FIVE

#### CHURCHES

★ **Basilica di Santa Maria Maggiore** (Bergamo, p148) – a remarkable hotchpotch of Romanesque, Gothic and Renaissance in the heart of the Città Alta (Upper Town)

★ **Chiesa di San Tomè** (Almenno San Bartolomeo, p155) – a unique example of early Lombard Romanesque in a country setting

★ **Duomo** (Cremona, p169) – a towering brick cathedral in the Lombard Gothic style

★ **Tempio Civico dell'Incoronata** (Lodi, p174) – a gorgeous riot of colourful Renaissance artistry

★ **Santuario di Santa Maria della Croce** (Crema, p175) – a wedding-cake structure that is one of the finest examples of Renaissance building in Lombardy

di San Siro (⏰3-6pm Sat-Mon), or country church. Evidence suggests there may even have been a site of worship here in Roman times. Perched upon a rock ledge, the triple apse looks like it could easily topple into the Oglio river below. The geometric, animal and floral relief decoration on the entrance and inside is enchanting.

### Breno

The riverside town of **Breno** (www.proloco breno.it), 13km south of Capo di Ponte, is worth a stop for its extensive hilltop castle ruins. It is in fact a huddle of buildings built over centuries but consolidated as a defensive complex under Venetian rule from the 15th century on.

# GASTRONOMIC HIGHLIGHTS

### ❦ LA CONCA VERDE // TRESCORE BALNEARIO €€

☎035 94 02 90; Via Benedetto Croce 31; meals €35-40; ⏰lunch & dinner Wed-Sun, lunch Tue

Seasonal products determine to a large degree what you might find on the menu at this timeless family restaurant teetering on the western edge of town, just off the SS42. Cheese lovers will find the *casoncelli al Taleggio* a pasta treat, while that Lombard fave, polenta, serves as an accompaniment to such mains as *stufato d'asino* (donkey stew). In summer, the garden is the place to be.

### ❦ RISTORANTE GUALTIERO MARCHESI // ERBUSCO €€€

☎030 776 05 62; www.marchesi.it; Via Vittorio Emanuele 23; meals €150-200; ⏰lunch & dinner Tue-Sat, lunch Sun

Set in L'Albereta hotel (p299), this place is possibly one of the best-known names in contemporary Italian dining. Gualtie-ro Marchesi (once bemedalled with three Michelin stars, which he tossed overboard in a tiff with the French arbiters of taste at table) continues to experiment and create dishes that win the approval of most of the happy few that manage to dine here. You might try a *raviolo aperto* (open raviolo, where the stuffing is revealed) followed by seafood. The setting is as breathtaking as the grub. Erbusco lies 11.5km south of Sarnico on Lake Iseo.

### ❦ RISTORANTE MONTE ISOLA // CARZANO €€

☎030 982 52 84; www.ristorantemonteisola.it; Località Carzano 144; meals €30-35; ⏰lunch Tue, lunch & dinner Wed-Sun

It's worth jumping on a boat in Sale Marasino just to get across to Monte Isola and plonk yourself down in this restaurant. Those with their own boat can tie up at the restaurant's landing. The deal here is simple enough: nicely prepared meals dominated by lake fish, both in first and second courses. And when you're not chomping contentedly, you can just gaze outside over the water.

# TRANSPORT

**BOAT** // **Navigazione Lago d'Iseo** (☎035 97 14 83; www.navigazionelagoiseo.it) Ferries zigzag their way along the length of the lake, although the most frequent start in Iseo and at Tavernola Bergamasca after making several stops around Monte Isola. There are also fairly regular runs between Lovere and Pisogne in the north. Up to eight daily services (only two from September to April) run the whole way from Sarnico to Pisogne (a trip that can take two to three hours depending on stops, €5.75) and vice versa. Small boats make the quick crossing (10 minutes, every half-hour) from Sale Marasino and Sulzano, on the east shore, respectively to Carzano and Peschiera Maraglio on Monte Isola (€1.90/3.10 one way/return).

**CAR //** From Bergamo or Brescia you can take the A4 motorway then turn north to Sarnico. Otherwise, the SS42 road east out of Bergamo leads past Lake Endine to Lovere, while the SP510 from Brescia follows the eastern shore of the lake. They merge north of the lake as the SS42 and proceed up the Valle Camonica.

**BUS //** From Bergamo, SAB (☎ 800 139392, 035 28 90 00; www.sab-autoservizi.it, in Italian) operates services (Line E) to Sarnico (€2.80, 50 minutes) and Tavernola Bergamasca. Line D also goes to Sarnico, while Line C runs via Lake Endine to Lovere and on to Boario in the Valle Camonica. The same company also has a service along the Valle Camonica.

**TRAIN //** Trains run from Brescia to Iseo (€2.85, 30 minutes, hourly), up the east shore of the lake, and on up the Valle Camonica as far as Edolo, 56km north of the lake (up to 2½ hours).

# BRESCIA

· · · · · ·

**pop 189,700**

**Urban sprawl, a seedy bus and train station area, and the odd skyscraper don't hint at Brescia's fascinating old town. Its narrow streets are home to some of the most important Roman ruins in Lombardy, and an extraordinary circular Romanesque church.**

Brescia already had centuries of (now obscure) history behind it when the Romans conquered the Gallic town in 225 BC. In 89 BC, the inhabitants of Brixia, as the Romans called it, were granted Roman citizenship and the town began to grow in importance as a centre for the production of bronze implements. The Carolingians took over in the 9th century, and were followed by a millennium's worth of outside rulers including the Venetians.

The city rebelled against the decision to hand it over to Austria in 1797, and again in 1848, when it was dubbed the 'Lioness' for its 10-day uprising against the Austrians.

## ESSENTIAL INFORMATION

**EMERGENCIES //** Police station (☎ 030 3 74 41; Via Botticelli) Southeast of the centre; Spedali Civili (☎ 030 3 99 51; Piazzale Spedali Civili) Hospital north of the centre.

**TOURIST OFFICE //** Infopoint (☎ 030 240 03 57; www.provincia.brescia.it/turismo; Piazza della Loggia 6; ⊙ 9am-6.30pm Mon-Sat, 10am-6pm Sun & holidays)

## EXPLORING BRESCIA

❦ MUSEO DELLA CITTÀ //
UNCOVER BRESCIA'S HISTORY IN
CONVENT COMPLEX

The jumbled **Monastero di Santa Giulia & Basilica di San Salvatore** is Brescia's single most intriguing sight. Inside this rambling church and convent complex, the **Museo della Città** (City Museum; ☎ 030 297 78 34; Via dei Musei 81b; adult/student 14-18yr/child €8/6/free, temporary exhibitions extra; ⊙ 9am-7pm Tue-Thu & Sun, 9am-8pm Fri & Sat) houses collections that run the gamut from prehistory to the age of Venetian dominance.

Among the most striking collections on show is the Roman section. The building of the monastery, which started as early as the 8th century, absorbed two *domus* (Roman houses), which were left standing in what would become the monk's garden (Ortaglia) near the north cloister. The remains have thus come to be known as the Domus dell'Ortaglia and have been protected by the monastery walls from outside interference or bulldozers through the centuries. Raised walkways allow you to wander round the Domus di Dioniso (so called

# BRESCIA

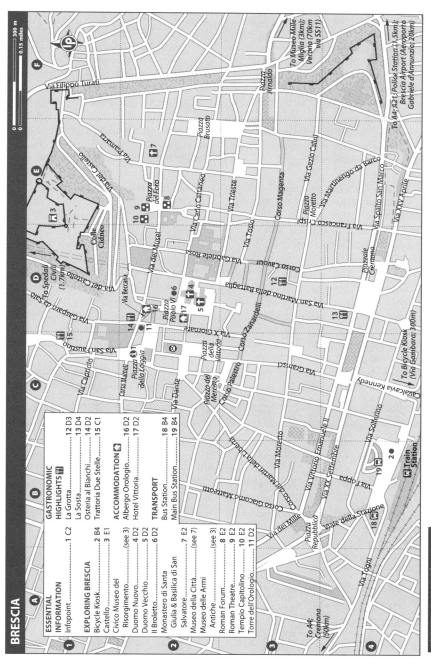

because of a mosaic of Dionysius, god of the grapevine) and the Domus delle Fontane (so called because of two marble fountains in it). The beautiful floor mosaics and colourful frescos in these two *domus* are the highlight of the monastery-museum.

The other star piece of the monastery collections is the 8th-century **Croce di Desiderio**, a Lombard cross encrusted with hundreds of jewels.

### ❦ ROMAN SITES // ADMIRE THE REMAINS OF ROMAN PRECISION BUILDING

The most impressive of Brescia's Roman relics are the remains of the **Tempio Capitolino** (Via dei Musei; admission free; 11am-4pm), a Roman temple built by the Emperor Vespasian in AD 73. Six Corinthian columns stand before a series of cells. About 50m east of the Tempio Capitolino along Via dei Musei, cobbled Vicolo del Fontanon leads to the well-preserved ruins of a **Roman theatre**. Limited remains of the ancient town's **forum** stand on Piazza del Foro.

### ❦ CATHEDRALS & CLOCK TOWERS // INDULGE IN A DOUBLE DUOMO DOSE

The most compelling of all Brescia's religious monuments is the 11th-century **Duomo Vecchio** (Old Cathedral; Piazza Paolo VI; 9am-noon & 3-7pm Tue-Sun Apr-Oct, 10am-noon & 3-6pm Tue-Sun Nov-Mar), a rare example of a circular-plan Romanesque basilica, built over a 6th-century church. The inside is surmounted by a dome borne by eight sturdy vaults resting on thick pillars. Interesting features include fragmentary floor mosaics (some think from a thermal bath that might have stood here in the 1st century BC) and the elaborate 14th-century sarcophagus of Bishop Berado Maggi. Next door, the **Duomo Nuovo** (New Cathedral; Piazza Paolo VI; 7.30am-noon & 4-7pm Mon-Sat, 8am-1pm & 4-7pm Sun), dating from 1604 (but not finished until well into the 19th century), dwarfs its ancient neighbour but is of less interest. Also on the square is **Il Broletto**, the medieval town hall with an 11th-century tower. On adjacent Piazza della Loggia, the **Torre dell'Orologio** (Clock Tower),

## ACCOMMODATION

With the exception of Bergamo, where booking ahead is not a bad idea (especially for the handful of lodgings in the Città Alta), the Lombard cities of the plains are not heavily touristed and generally pose no accommodation problems for those who simply turn up.

Lake Iseo can be busy in July and August, when booking ahead is prudent. In the mountain valleys, options can be scarcer, except at towns serving as ski bases in winter. Many of those hotels open again in summer for the hiking and cycling brigade but close in autumn and early spring. The Alpi Orobie mountains are peppered with mountain refuges.

The Accommodation chapter (p299) provides in-depth coverage, and here are some highlights of the region:

* ★ **B&B Alba** (Bergamo, p298) A rambling family house in the heart of the Città Alta
* ★ **Da Vittorio** (Brusaporto, p298) A gourmet country hideaway with gorgeous rooms
* ★ **Albergo Orologio** (Brescia, p299) Old-town charm in the heart of the action
* ★ **Hotel Astoria** (Cremona, p299) Quiet elegance down a narrow lane

with its exquisite astrological timepiece, is modelled on the one in Venice's Piazza San Marco.

### ❦ CASTELLO // CLIMB THE HILL TO THE CITY'S CASTLE

Brescia's historic centre is dominated by a hill, **Colle Cidneo**, crowned with the rambling **castle** (admission free; ☽ 8am-8pm) that for centuries was at the core of the city's defences. **Torre Mirabella**, the main round tower, was built by the Viscontis in the 13th century. The main reason to come up is to amble around the grounds, but the castle hosts two mildly diverting museums (admission to both €5), the **Museo delle Armi Antiche** ( ☎ 030 29 32 92; www.bresciamusei.it; ☽ 9.30am-1pm & 2.30-5pm Tue-Sun Oct-May, 10am-1pm & 2-6pm Tue-Sun Jun-Sep), with its extensive collection of vintage weaponry, and the **Civico Museo del Risorgimento** ( ☎ 030 4 41 76; ☽ 9.30am-1pm & 2.30-5pm Tue-Sun Oct-May, 10am-1pm & 2-6pm Tue-Sun Jun-Sep), dedicated to the history of Italian reunification (Risorgimento).

### ❦ MUSEO MILLE MIGLIA // CLASSIC CARS OF THE 1000-MILE RACE

The Mille Miglia is a classic Italian car race that ran over 1000 miles on no less than 24 occasions between 1927 and 1957. It started and ended in Brescia and took around 16 hours to complete. It was cancelled after 11 spectators died in an accident in 1957, although nowadays nostalgia races are still regularly held. The colourful **museum** ( ☎ 030 336 56 31; www.museomillemiglia.it; Viale della Rimembranza 3; adult/senior & child 13-18yr/child under 3yr €10/8/6; ☽ 10am-6pm Tue-Sun), loaded with some of the great cars to cross the finish line (Alfa Romeos and other local models tended to dominate), is housed outside central Brescia in the sprawling 11th-century Monastero di Sant'Eufemia della Fonte. The monastery was abandoned in the 15th century. As well as admiring the selection of racing cars, old-style petrol pumps and other paraphernalia, you can listen to audio material and watch race films.

### ❦ PIAZZA DELLA VITTORIA // SEE HOW MUSSOLINI LEFT HIS MARK

Perhaps not beautiful but nonetheless fascinating is a leftover of Il Duce's dreams of grandeur. One shudders to think what medieval jewels were swept away at the beginning of the 1930s to make way for **Piazza della Vittoria** (Victory Sq). Designed by Marcello Piacentini and opened in 1932, the square is lined with a compendium of Fascist architecture – imposing, Big Brotherish, some would say even boorish. At one end, the post office, with its soaring, right-angled columns, looks like some fear-inspiring ministry. Insurance companies with giant marble-faced porticoes line the square's sides. Perhaps most curious of all is the *arengario*, a rather small, rose-marble structure used to harangue the cheering crowds. Brescia, the Lioness of Italy, is inscribed on it.

## GASTRONOMIC HIGHLIGHTS

Risotto, beef dishes and *lumache alla Bresciana* (snails cooked with Parmesan cheese and fresh spinach) are common in Brescia. Via Beccaria is the small but fiercely pumping heart of central Brescia's evening action. By day, you'll find no shortage of cafes, pizzerias and the like, especially along Corso Cavour and Via Gabriele Rosa, as well as Piazza Paolo VI.

**BERGAMO, BRESCIA & CREMONA**

### ❤ LA GROTTA €€

☎ 030 4 40 68; www.osterialagrotta.it; Vicolo del Prezzemolo 10; meals €30; ⏰ Thu-Tue

Tucked down Parsley Lane off pleasant pedestrianised Corso Cavour, this is a hidden gem for good home cooking served at tables dressed in gingham. Frilly curtains coyly hide the vaults, cheerful frescos (food and wine-making scenes) and chattering diners from what few prying eyes might happen down the lane. A handful of tables are set up outside and in the tiny back courtyard. You can't go wrong with *casoncelli al burro e salvia* (typical local meat-filled pasta with butter and sage).

### ❤ LA SOSTA €€€

☎ 030 29 25 89; www.lasosta.it; Via San Martino della Battaglia 20; meals €50-60; ⏰ lunch & dinner Tue-Sat, lunch Sun, closed Aug

Set partly in the stables of a 1610 palace, flanked by columns, La Sosta excels at finely tuned gastronomic creations using the freshest regional produce. The *filetto di vitello alla scamorza affumicata* (veal filet cooked in smoked cheese) melts in the mouth and might be preceded by a *risotto al Franciacorta e zafferano* (Franciacorta red wine and saffron risotto).

### ❤ OSTERIA AL BIANCHI €

☎ 030 29 23 28; www.osteriaalbianchi.it; Via Gasparo da Salò 32; meals €20; ⏰ Thu-Mon

Crowd inside this classic old bar – in business since 1880 – and try for a seat at one of a handful of marble tables for a glass of wine and occasional snack. Or head out back and sit down at one of the timber tables for a meal. You might be tempted by the *pappardelle al Taleggio e zucca* (broad ribbon pasta with Taleggio cheese and pumpkin), followed by house specialities such as

*brasato d'asino* (braised donkey) or *pestöm* (minced pork meat served with polenta).

### ❤ TRATTORIA DUE STELLE €€

☎ 030 375 81 98; Via San Faustino 46; meals €30; ⏰ Wed-Mon

You won't regret stumbling across this classic little charmer. Beneath its vaults all is cosy. Timber-panelled walls, sturdy dark-wood dining tables (each with candle) and great grub invite locals and outsiders alike to sit down for a feast. It does some excellent risottos (try *agli scampi mantecato alla citronette* – a creamy risotto loaded with crayfish and touched with a citronette dressing). Most mains are meaty, from foal steaks to beef cuts.

## TRANSPORT

**AIR //** Brescia airport (Aeroporto Gabriele d'Annunzio; ☎ 030 204 15 99; www.aeroportobrescia .it) is 20km east of Brescia. Shuttle buses connect with Brescia's bus station (to/from airport €11/7.50, 25 minutes).

**TRAIN //** Regular trains run to and from Milan (€5.55 to €13.30, 45 minutes to 1½ hours) and Verona (€3.95, 40 minutes). Hourly trains connect with Cremona (€4.20, one hour). For Bergamo, there are trains every 30 to 60 minutes (€3.60, one to 1½ hours).

**CAR //** Brescia is on the A4 motorway between Milan and Verona. The A21 runs south to Cremona.

**PARKING //** Driving in the old centre is restricted and monitored by camera. People staying in hotels in the centre need to give the hotel reception their number-plate on arrival. You have 15 minutes to unload/load the vehicle before exiting again and parking elsewhere. There are car parks outside the old centre, where street parking is also possible.

**BICYCLE //** Usually, from June to September you can pick up a bicycle (€1/10 per two hours/day) from the bicycle kiosk ( ⏰ 7.30am-8.30pm) in front of the train station on Piazzale Stazione or from another bicycle station just off Via Gambara. **Bicimia** (www.bicimia .it) is a public bicycle service with pick-up and drop-off points around town. You must apply for an electronic card at the Infopoint tourist office.

**BUS //** From Brescia's **main bus station** ( ☎ 030 4 49 15; Via Solferino) buses operated by **SAIA Trasporti** ( ☎ 800 883999; www.saiatrasporti.it, in Italian) serve destinations all over Brescia province. Some leave from another station off Viale della Stazione.

# CREMONA

· · · · · ·

pop 72,000

**A wealthy, independent city-state for centuries, Cremona boasts some fine architecture. The city is best known around the world, however, for its violin-making traditions.**

Cremona was thought to have been founded by Celts, but the oldest archaeological finds date to the creation of a Roman outpost here around 218 BC. The city's glory days came as an independent *comune* (city-state) from the 11th century, until it was occupied by Milan in 1334. It would remain largely under the jurisdiction of the Duchy of Milan until the latter fell under the thumb of Spain in 1525.

The Piazza del Comune, the heart of the city, is where Cremona's historic beauty is concentrated. It's a wonderful example of how the religious and secular affairs of cities were divided neatly in two.

## ESSENTIAL INFORMATION

**TOURIST OFFICE //** **Tourist Office** ( ☎ 0372 2 32 33; www.turismo.comune.cremona.it, in Italian; Piazza del Comune 5; ⏱ 9am-12.30pm & 3-6pm daily Sep-Jun, 9am-12.30pm & 3-6pm Mon-Sat, 9am-12.30pm Sun Jul-Aug)

## EXPLORING CREMONA

❦ **PIAZZA DEL COMUNE // STEP BACK INTO THE MIDDLE AGES**
This beautiful, pedestrian-only square is considered one of the best-preserved medieval squares in all Italy. To maintain the difference between the secular and spiritual, buildings connected with the Church were erected on the eastern side of Piazza del Comune, and those concerned with secular affairs were constructed across the way. On Sundays, the piazza is filled with antique stalls. The business of city government was and still is carried out in the **Palazzo Comunale**. Begun in the 13th century, the arcaded walkways and courtyards of the *palazzo* were gradually extended and embellished through the centuries. On the central pillar of the main facade, a marble *arengario* (balcony from which decrees were made and speeches given) was added in 1507. South across a lane, the Loggia dei Militi was the headquarters of the long arm of the law. A delightful little Gothic gem built in 1292, it was where the captains of the citizen militia would meet.

❦ **DUOMO // INSPECT RENAISSANCE FRESCOS AND CLIMB THE BIG TOWER**
Across the square from the Palazzo del Comune, Cremona's **cathedral** (Piazza del Comune) started out as a Romanesque basilica. It was finished in 1107 but badly damaged by an earthquake in 1117 and rebuilt by 1190. In subsequent centuries, various embellishments left traces of Gothic, Renaissance and baroque taste. The facade reflects this mix. Romanesque sculptures from the prequake church adorn the facade, whose upper part is largely the result of Renaissance

renovation. Even the lower part, while retaining something of a Romanesque flavour, is the result of work in the early 16th century – notably replacing the timber frontage with marble. The brick north facade is a fine example of Lombard Gothic.

The interior is adorned with rich frescos and paintings. The central nave and apse, in particular, flaunt a series of scenes dedicated to the lives of the Virgin Mary and Christ. The local, Ferrara-born Renaissance master Boccaccio Boccaccino carried out many of them. Elegant

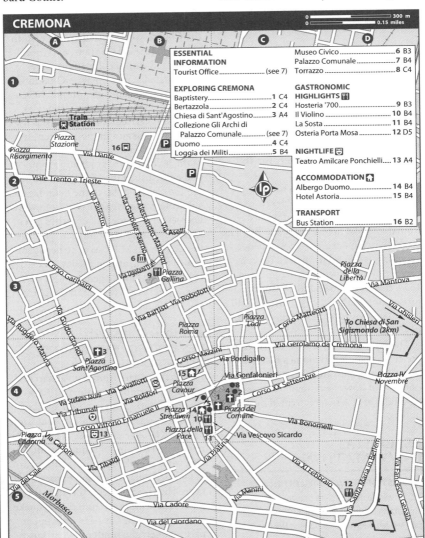

### CREMONA

**ESSENTIAL INFORMATION**
Tourist Office .......................... (see 7)

**EXPLORING CREMONA**
Baptistery ....................................1 C4
Bertazzola ....................................2 C4
Chiesa di Sant'Agostino ...........3 A4
Collezione Gli Archi di
    Palazzo Comunale ............. (see 7)
Duomo ..........................................4 C4
Loggia dei Militi .........................5 B4

Museo Civico ...............................6 B3
Palazzo Comunale ......................7 B4
Torrazzo ........................................8 C4

**GASTRONOMIC HIGHLIGHTS**
Hosteria '700 ..............................9 B3
Il Violino .....................................10 B4
La Sosta ......................................11 B4
Osteria Porta Mosa .................12 D5

**NIGHTLIFE**
Teatro Amilcare Ponchielli .....13 A4

**ACCOMMODATION**
Albergo Duomo ........................14 B4
Hotel Astoria ............................15 B4

**TRANSPORT**
Bus Station ................................16 B2

## CREMONA'S VIOLINS

It was in Cremona that Antonio Stradivari lovingly put together his first Stradivarius violins, helping establish a tradition that continues today. Other great violin-making dynasties that started here include the Amati and Guarneri families.

Some 100 violin-making workshops in the streets around Piazza del Comune can be visited. The tourist office has a list and at www.cremonaliuteria.it you will also find information on many of them.

Various events dedicated to violin-making take place each year, while the **Triennale Internazionale degli Strumenti ad Arco** (International Stringed Instrument Expo; www.ente triennale.com) is held in Cremona every third year in September/October; there is one in 2012.

The **Collezione Gli Archi di Palazzo Comunale** ( ☎ 0372 2 05 02; Piazza del Comune 8; adult/child €6/3.50, incl Museo Civico €10/5; ☺ 9am-6pm Tue-Sat, 10am-6pm Sun) features instruments from the Stradivari workshop.

The **Museo Civico** ( ☎ 0372 3 12 22; Via Ugolani Dati 4; adult/child €7/4, incl Collezione Gli Archi di Palazzo Comunale €10/5; ☺ 9am-6pm Tue-Sat, 10am-6pm Sun) holds drawings and tools, as well as instruments by Amati and Guarneri.

To hear Cremona's violins in action, the season at the 19th-century **Teatro Amilcare Ponchielli** ( ☎ 0372 02 20 01; www.teatroponchielli.it, in Italian; Corso Vittorio Emanuele II 52) runs from October to June.

though his compositions are, it is the *Storie di Cristo* (Stories of Christ) by Pordenone that stand out. His *Crocifissione* (Crucifixion) and *Deposizione* (Deposition) are especially powerful, filled with curvaceous movement and voluptuous colour. Other masters who contributed to the church's decoration include local boys Giulio Campi and Gian Francesco Bembo.

The cathedral's most prized possession is the Sacra Spina (Holy Thorn), allegedly from the Crown of Thorns worn by Jesus Christ, which was donated to the church by Cremona-born Pope Gregory XIV in 1591. It's kept behind bars in the Capella delle Reliquie, in the left transept. In the crypt, the robed and masked body of Cremona's 12th-century patron saint, San Omobono Tucenghi, is on show in a glass casket.

The adjoining 111m-tall **torrazzo** (bell tower; adult/child €4/3, incl baptistery €5/4; ☺ 10am-1pm Tue-Fri, 10am-1pm & 2.30-6pm Sat & Sun) is connected to the cathedral by a Renaissance loggia, the **Bertazzola**. It is fronted by a beautiful zodiacal clock, 8m wide and installed in 1583. It has been tinkered with considerably over the years (the last time in the 1970s) but remains an extraordinary example of European clockwork, designed not only to tell the time but to measure the phases of the moon and seasons as well as present astrological information.

A total of 487 steps wind up to the top of the tower. The effort is more than repaid with marvellous views across the city.

On the other side of the cathedral is the 12th-century **baptistery** (adult/child €2/1, incl torrazo €5/4; ☺ 10am-1pm & 2.30-6pm Tue-Sun), which houses some architectural fragments including a 12th-century figure of the Archangel Gabriel that once perched on the roof of the baptistery.

## ❦ SACRED ART // SEARCH OUT HIDDEN ART GEMS

Of the many other churches scattered about the city, two stand out for some impressive works of art inside. Inside the **Chiesa di Sant'Agostino** (Piazza Sant'Agostino), the Cappella Cavalcabò (third chapel on the right) is a stunning late-Gothic fresco cycle by Bonifacio Bembo and his assistants. One of the altars is graced with a 1494 painting by Pietro Perugino, *Madonna in trono e santi* (The Madonna Enthroned with Saints).

A couple of kilometres outside the old city, the **Chiesa di San Sigismondo** (Largo Visconti) was built between 1463 and 1492 to commemorate the wedding of Francesco Sforza to Bianca Maria Visconti in 1441. The fresco cycle was done from 1530 on and is a great example of Mannerist painting. All the big names of the Cremona art scene contributed, including all the Campi brothers and Camillo Boccaccino, son of Boccaccio. Camillo did the entire presbytery, with images including *Adultera* (Adultress) and *Risurrezione di Lazzaro* (Resurrection of Lazarus).

## FESTIVALS & EVENTS

**Festival di Cremona Claudio Monteverdi** (www.teatroponchielli.it, in Italian) A month-long series of concerts centred on Claudio Monteverdi and other baroque-era composers, held in the **Teatro Amilcare Ponchielli** ( ☎ 0372 02 20 01; www .teatroponchielli.it, in Italian; Corso Vittorio Emanuele II 52); early May to early June.

**Festa del Torrone** (www.festadeltorrone cremona.it) For a late-autumn weekend, the people of Cremona gather in the city centre for various exhibitions, performances and tastings all dedicated to that toffee-tough Christmas sweet and Cremona speciality, *torrone* (nougat); November.

# GASTRONOMIC HIGHLIGHTS

Plenty of charming eateries, some with a long history, offer a mix of local and more general Lombard dishes. Cremonese delicacies include *bollito* (boiled meats) and *cotechino* (boiled pork sausage) and *mostarda* (fruit in a sweet mustard sauce).

## ❦ HOSTERIA '700 €€

☎ 0372 3 61 75; Piazza Gallina 1; meals €25-30; ☺ lunch Mon, lunch & dinner Wed-Sun

Behind the dilapidated facade lurks a sparkling gem. A series of vaulted rooms, each with different colour scheme and some with ceiling frescos, winds off from the entrance and past the kitchen. There is something noble about the atmosphere, with the antique cupboards and dark timber tables and chairs. The hearty Lombard cooking comes in at a refreshingly competitive cost, so savouring *marubini al brodo o al burro fuso* (a Cremona speciality, meat-and-cheese stuffed discs of pasta in broth or melted butter), followed by a *coscia di maialino da latte al mirto* (leg of suckling pig cooked with myrtle) is all the more pleasurable.

## ❦ IL VIOLINO €€

☎ 0372 46 10 10; www.ilviolino.it; Via Vescovo Sicardo 3; meals €40-45; ☺ lunch Mon, lunch & dinner Wed-Sun

The name of the place is perhaps a trifle obvious in this town of violin-makers but Il Violino is Cremona's timeless class option. Smooth service and big tables are the key to this elegant (if somewhat dated) spot, where you might start with one of a number of risotto options or the *tortelli alle erbette al burro spumoso* (stuffed pasta in herbs and frothy hot butter), followed perhaps by a mouth-watering *San Pietro al vapore con salsa di limone e capperi* (John Dory in a lemon sauce with capers).

### ♥ LA SOSTA €€

☎ 0372 45 66 56; www.osterialasosta.it; Via Vescovo Sicardo 9; meals €30-35; ◷ lunch & dinner Tue-Sat, lunch Sun Sep-Jun

Surrounded by violin-makers' workshops, this is a beautiful place to feast on regional delicacies such as *bollito* or *cotechino* with polenta and *mostarda*. Pastas include melt-in-the-mouth *tortelli di zucca al pomodoro dolce* (pumpkin tortelli with sweet tomato). Snail lovers might be tempted by a round of them prepared in spinach and served with polenta. The entrance is plastered with so many approving restaurant-guide stickers that you can't see through the glass.

### ♥ OSTERIA PORTA MOSA €€

☎ 0372 41 18 03; Via Santa Maria in Betlem 11; meals €25-30; ◷ Mon-Sat

Don't be put off by the location in a drab street on the edge of old Cremona. Step inside and you feel instantly at home. Dark polished timber tables are offset by the aquamarine decor and art hanging on the walls. Expect home cooking that will take you far away from anything seeming like the tourist trail. The almost sugar-sweet *ravioli di zucca* (pumpkin ravioli) is especially good.

## TRANSPORT

**TRAIN //** The city can be reached by train from Milan (€5.55, 1¼ to 1¾ hours, several daily), Mantua (€4.60, 45 minutes to 1½ hours, about hourly) and Brescia (€4.20, one hour, hourly).

**CAR //** From Milan, take the A1 motorway and then the A21 to Cremona. The A21 proceeds north to Brescia. The SP415 heads northwest to Crema and on to Milan.

**PARKING //** Parking in the old centre, especially between Piazza Roma and Piazza del Comune, is difficult. Street parking becomes easier as you move away from the centre, and there is huge car-park space near the bus station.

**BUS //** Buses to surrounding towns leave from the bus station on Via Dante, near the train station.

# AROUND CREMONA

· · · · · ·

The plains around Cremona are dotted with interesting towns. Among the best are the following four. Pizzighettone boasts great defensive walls and Soncino a fine Sforza-era fortress. The more substantial towns of Crema and Lodi have interesting old centres, the former dominated by the pretty Piazza del Duomo and the latter by the Incoronata church. Lodi and Pizzighettone, both settled on the banks of the Adda river, are within the boundaries of the Parco Adda Sud (www.parcoaddasud.it) nature reserve. You can get some walking and cycling route ideas from the park's website. With your own transport, you could easily make a loop in a day from Cremona.

## EXPLORING AROUND CREMONA

### ♥ PIZZIGHETTONE // GET BEHIND THE FORTRESS WALLS

Just a 22km train ride west of Cremona, the walled town of **Pizzighettone** (population 6740) sits astride the Adda river. The bulk of the town, with its impressive defensive walls, rests on the east bank. The walls had been largely engulfed by vegetation until a volunteer organisation 'released' them from this green captivity in the 1990s, restoring them to their full majesty. Begun in the 12th century and constantly improved and expanded in the following centuries, especially under Visconti and Sforza rule, the **walls** ( ☎ 0372 73 03 33; www.gvmpizzighettone.it, in Italian; guided tours in Italian adult/student/child €2.50/1.50/free; ⏰ tours 9.30pm Sat, 4pm & 5.30pm Sun & holidays Jul-Aug, 3pm Sat, Sun & holidays Sep-Jun) are laced with passages and huge vaulted halls, some of which have been set aside as a small museum dedicated to the trades and traditions of local farmers. The most imposing part of the walls is known as the Rivellino, a series of casemates once used to house artillery and dating to the 15th century. You can wander much of the area any time. Across the river from the main part of town is the pretty hamlet of **La Gera**.

## ❦ LODI // BEHOLD THE RENAISSANCE GLORY OF THE INCORONATA

Capital of an essentially agricultural province (with dairy and bovine meat products leading the way), **Lodi** (population 43,110) was founded in the 12th century on the south bank of the Adda river after the original town (Lodi Vecchio, about 7km west) was destroyed by Milanese army. The old town centre, unknown to the majority of travellers, is well worth a half-day of your time. From the train station, head north about 300m to Piazza Castello. The castle alluded to is largely gone, excepting a tall round **tower** built on Francesco Sforza's orders. Corso Vittorio Emanuele II leads another 300m into the enormous, cobbled Piazza della Vittoria, fronted by the city's **Duomo** (Cathedral), **Palazzo Comunale** (Town Hall) and multicoloured houses atop sheltering porticoes. Work on the

cathedral began in 1160 and its towering brick facade betrays Romanesque, Gothic and Renaissance elements (the rose window being the clearest sign of the latter). Through an arch on its left flank you reach shady Piazza Mercato, tucked behind the cathedral's haughty triple apse. Attractive though the cathedral is, Lodi's real gem lies about 50m away on Via Incoronata. The **Tempio Civico dell'Incoronata** (Via Incoronata, btwn Nos 23 & 25; ⏰ 9-11.30am Mon, 9-11.30am & 3.30-6pm Tue-Sun) was built in the late 15th century at the prompting of the local citizenry, apparently after a sighting of the Virgin Mary with crown (hence the church's name 'Civic Temple of the Crowned One') on the spot, close to an infamous brothel. The church is a splendid, octagonal Renaissance affair, whose inside is a riot of gold leaf, frescos and paintings. Almost all the art, mostly depicting New Testament scenes, was done by Lodi's Piazza clan of artists (Callisto, Fulvio, Alberto and Scipione) over three decades in the first half of the 16th century.

## ❦ CREMA // HANG OUT IN PIAZZA DEL DUOMO

Huddled up against the Serio river and 15km northeast of Lodi, **Crema** (population 33,560) retains its huddled late-medieval and Renaissance core largely intact. Even parts of the Venetian-built defensive walls are still in place (the local tourist office organises guided tours of these remains; see www.prolococrema .it). Indeed, in 1449, Crema was one of the many Lombard cities to pass under Venetian suzerainty. The following centuries brought peace and prosperity, until Napoleon arrived to upset the apple cart in 1797.

At the heart of the city is enchanting, porticoed Piazza del Duomo, a Venetian renovation of the early 16th century dominated by the brick facade of the medieval **Duomo** (۞ 7am-noon & 4-7pm). Completed in 1341, the cathedral sports a giant *facciata a vento* (wind facade; see p251) and is of typically Lombard Gothic style, which uses Romanesque devices (especially the semicircular arch) but on a far grander scale. To the left of the cathedral rises the **Torre Pretoria**, a family watchtower dating to 1286 that bears a sculpture of the lion of St Mark. The porticoes across the way belong to the early 16th-century **Palazzo Comunale** – as ever, the secular arm of power looks the Church straight in the eye. The **Torrazzo** (Big Tower) had a defensive role but was reworked in baroque form in the 17th century and became purely decorative.

Crowning a Crema visit is one of the most striking Renaissance structures in Lombardy, the **Santuario di Santa Maria della Croce** (Piazza Papa Paolo Giovanni II; ۞ 7am-noon & 2.30-7pm Mon-Sat, 8am-7pm Sun), built between 1490 and 1500 and about 1.5km north of the old town along Viale di Santa Maria della Croce. The graceful circular central body of the church has wedding-cake layers of increasingly delicate arches, and four bronze-domed chapels push out from it below, forming a cross. The octagonal interior brims with frescos.

### ♥ SONCINO // CLAMBER ABOUT A SFORZA FORTRESS

With its four stout towers, crenellations, moat and drawbridge, you can almost see the **Rocca** ( ☎ 0374 84 88 83; www.proloco soncino.it; Largo Salvini 1; adult/senior & child €3/2.20; ۞ 10am-noon Tue-Fri, 10am-12.30pm & 3-7pm Sat, Sun & holidays Apr-Oct, closes earlier Nov-Mar) of **Soncino** (population 7590) under siege by some enemy of Milan's Sforza clan, which had it built on the site of a

more rudimentary fort in 1473. There's a modest history museum in rooms of two of the towers, while from the courtyard you can visit various underground rooms. Parts of the later Venetian city walls (Venice was in control for a brief decade from 1499) remain intact too. Another curiosity is the **Casa degli Stampatori** ( ☎ 0374 8 31 71; Via Lanfranco 6; admission & hours as for the Rocca). A Jewish family on the run from persecution in Germany wound up here in the mid-15th century, changed the family name to Sonsino and began a trade that, at the time, was entirely new – book printing. The Sonsino family soon established a Europe-wide reputation and printed the first Bible in Hebrew. On show in this charming, three-storey brick house are various printing machines from the 19th and early 20th centuries, a remake of a 15th-century model, and other tools of the trade.

## GASTRONOMIC HIGHLIGHTS

### ♥ ANTICA ROCCA // SONCINO €€
☎ 0374 8 56 72; Via Cesare Battisti 1; meals €30; ۞ lunch & dinner Tue-Sat, lunch Sun
Local products are the name of the game in this busy family-run eatery, barely a five-minute walk from the Rocca fortress, just over a canal from what is left of the old city walls. Inside, the muted tangerine decor, timber furniture and quality linen lend the place a peaceful quality in which to munch on a *risotto con asparagi e crema di formaggi* (risotto with asparagus and cream of cheeses). The best mains lean to meat, with items like a thick *filetto di manzo al pepe verde* (steak filet in green pepper) and a side of *zucchine trifolate* (zucchini cooked in oil, parsley and garlic).

### ♥ CASCINA VALENTINO // PIZZIGHETTONE €€

☎ 0372 74 49 91; Cascina Valentino 37; meals €25-30; ☺ dinner Sat & lunch Sun, otherwise by appointment

On a working farm where cows are raised and asparagus is grown, the owners also offer up fine local cooking with only the freshest in-season ingredients – this is a real rural eating experience. The menu changes often but you might be offered a strawberry risotto. Mains are mostly from the farm's own meat stocks. The dining area, with dark timber furniture, in the main farmhouse, is a treat in itself. Booking ahead is essential, even when it opens on the weekends. It's 2km away from central Pizzighettone. Cross the bridge east to La Gera and turn right along the river, then follow the signs along a dirt track past a dairy farm until you reach this second dairy farm.

### ♥ LA COLDANA // LODI €€

☎ 0371 43 17 42; Via del Costino; meals €35; ☺ Thu-Tue

A sprawling, yellow, 18th-century farmhouse, La Coldana seats its guests in four separate, bustling dining rooms or out in a quiet garden. The kitchen is a cauldron of ideas. For a first course, how about *il Carnaroli con fagioli borlotti mantecato alla crema di lardo e vongole veraci* (risotto with borlotti beans in a creamy bacon and clam sauce). You might follow with a rack of lamb or wild salmon. The two-course light lunch (€15) is excellent value. Head southeast along Corso Mazzini from Porta Cremona, in the southeast corner of the old centre. Turn left at Via Friuli and left again into Via del Costino. It's about a 1.5km wander.

### ♥ OSTERIA DEL RUMÍ // CREMA €€

☎ 0371 25 72 89; Piazza Trento e Trieste 12; meals €30-35; ☺ dinner Fri, lunch & dinner Sat-Wed

Just off Piazza del Duomo, this Tuscan-style eatery offers bags of boisterous atmosphere at timber tables beneath low-slung brick and stone vaults. You could start with a selection of bruschetta or choose from a range of first courses, from local risotto to southern Italian *orecchiette maritate con sugo di verdure* (ear-shaped pasta in a vegetable sauce), followed by *stufato d'anatra con polenta* (stewed duck in polenta).

## TRANSPORT

**CAR //** The SP415 main road northwest out of Cremona runs 38km to Crema, from where the SP236 road heads 18km northeast to Soncino. For Pizzighettone, take the minor SP234 road west out of Cremona. From there you can continue via Codogno until you hit the SS9 highway, which leads northwest to Lodi. Lodi is linked to Crema by the SP235 road.

**TRAIN //** Pizzighettone, Lodi and Crema are reached easily by train from Cremona. The former two are on the line from Milan to Cremona.

**BUS //** Buses run to Soncino from Bergamo, Cremona and Crema. There are also buses to Crema from Bergamo with SAB (☎ 800 139392, 035 28 90 00; www.sab-autoservizi.it, in Italian).

# THE BEST OF
# THE ITALIAN LAKES

It's hard to tire of seeking new views of the lakes from near and afar, or from another mesmerising mountain-top angle. Equally fascinating to witness are human contributions, from Milan's Duomo, to lush villa gardens, to local cooking, which spans fabulous rice and fish dishes, washed down with a stunning variety of wines.

**ABOVE** Lake Garda and Monte Baldo stretch before Malcesine

# THE BEST ARCHITECTURE

**1 DUOMO // MILAN**

With its ageless marble facade and count-less pinnacles and spires piercing the sky, Milan's splendid Gothic cathedral (p39) leaves visitors speechless. Building began in the 14th century, and it was still being tweaked in the 19th. Climb the 165 steps to the roof for a close-up of the spires.

**2 ROMAN ARENA // VERONA**

The cream and pink arches of Verona's amphitheatre (p215) are impressive by day and beautifully floodlit at night. The third largest Roman amphitheatre in existence was built in the 1st century, and originally seated 30,000 people. Today, it still hosts quite a few for the opera season (p220).

MARTIN MOOS

### 3 CASTLES // BELLINZONA

Bellinzona's three castles (p138) form a World Heritage trio, stacked one above the other in the Ticino canton's capital. Castelgrande, along whose walls you can wander, is the most impressive, and the views from Castello di Montebello and Castello Sasso Corbaro are worth the climb.

### 4 BASILICA DI SANTA MARIA MAGGIORE // BERGAMO

Already a noteworthy mix of Romanesque and Gothic, this basilica (p148) received a striking addition in 1472–76 – the Renaissance Cappella Colleoni. The mausoleum-cum-chapel contains frescos by Giambattista Tiepolo below the dome.

### 5 BASILICA DI SANT'ABBONDIO // COMO

Aside from being an unusually tall example of Lombard 11th-century Romanesque with beautiful external geometric decoration, the Basilica di Sant'Abbondio (p109) houses a remarkable fresco series inside the apse, charting scenes from the life of Christ.

3

**TOP** The roof of Milan's Duomo **BOTTOM LEFT** Frescos decorate the Basilica di Sant'Abbondio **BOTTOM RIGHT** The castles of Bellinzona

# THE BEST VILLA GARDENS

**1 VILLA TARANTO // VERBANIA**

In 1931 a Scottish captain bought the late-19th-century Villa Taranto (p80). He planted some 20,000 species and today it's one of Europe's finest botanic gardens. Revisit several times and witness how it transforms through the seasons – a June-to-October dahlia display is a highlight.

**2 ISOLA BELLA // STRESA**

Isola Bella (p86), a short ferry ride from Stresa, is a noble family's fantasy land. At its heart stands Palazzo Borromeo. Part of this sumptuous residence may be visited, after which you will emerge in its elaborate, baroque Italian garden, amid strutting white peacocks.

### 3 VILLA CARLOTTA // TREMEZZO

The botanic gardens of the 17th-century Villa Carlotta (p122) are filled with colour in spring, with orange trees knitted into pergolas, and some of Europe's finest rhododendrons, azaleas and camellias. The villa contains statues (some by Antonio Canova), tapestries and period furniture.

### 4 VILLA BALBIANELLO // LENNO

Occupying a steep and heavily wooded promontory just outside Lenno, Villa del Balbianello (p121) is one of northern Italy's most dramatic locations. The largely Italianate sculpted gardens, littered with statues and draped over the promontory, are the perfect place for hopeless romantics.

### 5 VILLA MELZI D'ERIL // BELLAGIO

Bellagio's lakeside neoclassical Villa Melzi d'Eril (p114), built in 1808 for one of Napoleon's associates, is at the heart of a beautiful stretch of gardens. This English-style park, the first of its kind on Lake Como, flashes to life with the flowering of azaleas and rhododendrons in spring.

TOP Villa Carlotta and its gardens **BOTTOM LEFT** The gardens of Palazzo Borromeo on Isola Bella **BOTTOM RIGHT** A detail in the English-style gardens of Villa Melzi d'Eril

# THE BEST VIEWPOINTS

## 1 MONTE MOTTARONE // LAKE MAGGIORE

Captivating views of Lake Maggiore unfold during a 20-minute journey on the Funivia Stresa-Mottarone, which ascends 1491m Monte Mottarone (p82). On a clear day you can see Lakes Maggiore and Orta, several smaller lakes, and Monte Rosa, on the Alpine border with Switzerland.

## 2 CIMA SIGHIGNOLA // LAKE LUGANO

For extraordinary views over Lake Lugano, and on to Monte Rosa and the Matterhorn, head for the high point known as the Balcone d'Italia (1320m; p120). Also look out for part of Lake Maggiore, Varese, the Alps and the Lombard plains.

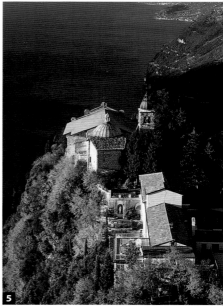

DAVIDE EBRETTA/ALCONERS IMAGES

### 3 CASTELLO DI VEZIO // LAKE COMO

A road leads 3km out of Varenna up to these castle ruins (p127). From the watchtower (which you can climb) there are great views across the three arms of Lake Como. You can also peer over the huddled rooftops of Varenna, far below.

### 4 MONTE BISBINO // LAKE COMO

Some 17km out of Cernobbio, a scenic road leads to Monte Bisbino (1325m; p119). At every turn on the way up, look back on the lake from different angles. At the top, the eye roams the Lombard plain and as far as the Jungfrau in the Alps.

### 5 SANTUARIO DI MONTECASTELLO // LAKE GARDA

Around 8km north of Gargnano, near the village of Tignale (500m) and clinging to a spur of rock above the hamlet of Gardola, is the 16th century Santuario di Montecastello (p202). Examine the 15th-century gilded wooden altar and Giotto school frescos before marvelling at the extraordinary views along all of Lake Garda.

3

**TOP** Stresa–Mottarone cable car **BOTTOM LEFT** Santuario di Montecastello **BOTTOM RIGHT** Lake Como through the turrets of Castello di Vezio

**TOP** Cracco Restaurant **RIGHT** Restel de Fer

# THE BEST RESTAURANTS

## 1 GATTO NERO // CERNOBBIO

Finding your way up from lakeside Cernobbio ain't easy but it's worth the effort. Book a front-row table in this locally renowned eatery for the unobstructed view of the lake far below (p124). It's the perfect setting for gourmet romantics, hushed and low-lit.

## 2 HOSTERIA '700 // CREMONA

A series of vaulted rooms, some with ceiling frescos, winds past the kitchen (p172), and antiques and dark timber furniture lend a noble air. It does hearty Lombard cooking and local specialities.

## 3 CRACCO // MILAN

Star chef Carlo Cracco (p51) keeps the Milanese in thrall with his inventiveness. Cherry-wood boiserie on the walls and creamy lighting are neutral enough to allow you to concentrate on your food, like the delicate *rognoni di vitello e ricci di mare* (veal kidney served with sea urchins).

## 4 RESTEL DE FER // RIVA DEL GARDA

This family-run *locanda* (inn; p206) is one to linger over. Expect worn leather armchairs, cooking pots and glinting blue glass. Seasonal delicacies include *tagliatelle alle erbe aromatiche con ragù di agnello da latte* (ribbon pasta with aromatic herbs and a suckling lamb sauce).

# LAKE GARDA, VERONA & MANTUA

# 3 PERFECT DAYS

### ❦ DAY 1 // A GOURMET'S LAKE

Lake Garda is ripe for culinary explorations. A fleet of ferries enables minivoyages of discovery in a landscape rich in food and wine. Torri del Benaco's museum (p209) is a charming introduction to the lake's olive oil and lemon-growing heritage, while just inland Bardolino's vineyard trail allows you to hunt out that perfect vintage – Guerrieri Rizzardi (p211) holds delightfully atmospheric tastings. Dinner is a gourmet treat; perhaps at nearby Il Giardino delle Esperidi (p213), which serves the best local delicacies and some 700 wines.

### ❦ DAY 2 // CULTURE-FIX VERONA

Exploring the sumptuous medieval and Renaissance art in the Castelvecchio (p215) could easily take all morning, while Verona's architecture-rich piazzas (p216) are perfect for a post-lunch stroll. Countless wine cellars offer a different slice of cultural life; Bottega del Vino (p219) is a great place to start. If you've booked for the opera in the Roman Arena (p215), it starts around 9pm – prepare for a spine-tingling time. The locals dine afterwards; the Tre Marchetti (p220) is just next door and, luckily, it's open until 4am.

### ❦ DAY 3 // MANTUA'S ART AND ARCHITECTURE

From fine art to frescos, in Mantua it's hard to know where to begin. Perhaps with the overwhelming painted giants in Palazzo Te (p223) or the sheer opulence of the Palazzo Ducale (p223), but the extraordinary Teatro Bibiena (p226) is another strong contender. You could wonder at the exquisite architecture of Mantua's interlocking central squares (p227) then dine out in one – at Masseria (p230) you can experience the culinary art that is *tortelli di zucca* and admire the views.

LAKE GARDA, VERONA & MANTUA

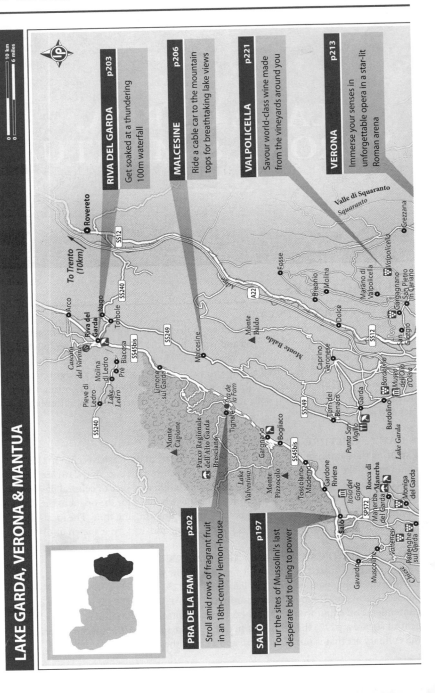

**RIVA DEL GARDA** p203

Get soaked at a thundering 100m waterfall

**MALCESINE** p206

Ride a cable car to the mountain tops for breathtaking lake views

**VALPOLICELLA** p221

Savour world-class wine made from the vineyards around you

**VERONA** p213

Immerse your senses in unforgettable opera in a star-lit Roman arena

**PRA DE LA FAM** p202

Stroll amid rows of fragrant fruit in an 18th-century lemon-house

**SALÒ** p197

Tour the sites of Mussolini's last desperate bid to cling to power

0    10 km
0    6 miles

To Trento (10km)

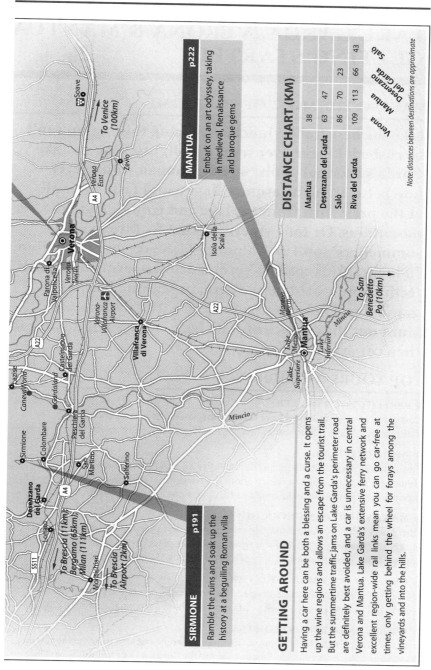

## MANTUA   p222

Embark on an art odyssey, taking in medieval, Renaissance and baroque gems

## SIRMIONE   p191

Ramble the ruins and soak up the history at a beguiling Roman villa

## DISTANCE CHART (KM)

|  | Verona | Mantua | Desenzano del Garda | Salò |
|---|---|---|---|---|
| Mantua | 38 |  |  |  |
| Desenzano del Garda | 63 | 47 |  |  |
| Salò | 86 | 70 | 23 |  |
| Riva del Garda | 109 | 113 | 66 | 43 |

Note: distances between destinations are approximate

## GETTING AROUND

Having a car here can be both a blessing and a curse. It opens up the wine regions and allows an escape from the tourist trail. But the summertime traffic jams on Lake Garda's perimeter road are definitely best avoided, and a car is unnecessary in central Verona and Mantua. Lake Garda's extensive ferry network and excellent region-wide rail links mean you can go car-free at times, only getting behind the wheel for forays among the vineyards and into the hills.

# LAKE GARDA, VERONA & MANTUA GETTING STARTED

## MAKING THE MOST OF YOUR TIME

Like the best Italian lunch, exploring this region can't be rushed. Linger over some highlights: soak in Lake Garda's thermal pools, wander Roman ruins, ferry-hop between picturesque villages, and taste olive oil at the press, fish from the lake and truffles from the mountains. Or tour vineyards that feature in many sommeliers' top 10s: Valpolicella, Soave and Bardolino. In incurably romantic Verona drink in exquisite architecture and world-class opera; in Mantua feast on grand ducal palaces overflowing with fabulous art. Hunt out the essence of Italy here – uncork it, savour it, then come back for more.

## TOP TOURS & COURSES

### ♥ PERFECT YOUR PALATE
Costaripa is one of countless Lake Garda wineries offering tours and tastings. See its vast vats and cellars full of bottles before sampling some chiaretto. All for €5. (p195)

### ♥ TASTE OLIVE OIL
Frantoio Montecroce has been producing olive oil amid Lake Garda's mild microclimate for four generations. Learn about the harvesting, crushing and blending process, then how to taste the final product like a pro. (p193)

### ♥ MAKE YOUR OWN GNOCCHI
Chef Luisa will have you rustling up risotto, pasta and polenta then eating your efforts alfresco with a glass of local wine. It all takes place just outside Verona; half-day courses from €160. (www.cooking-at-the-villa.com; Via Cadellora 15, Alpo di Villafranca)

### ♥ GET LOST ON A MARATHON ART TOUR
Of the 500 rooms in Mantua's Palazzo Ducale, 40 are open to the public, making it wonderfully easy to lose yourself among the dizzying, dazzling displays. (p223)

### ♥ CRUISE AMID LOTUS FLOWERS
Fleets of boats set sail from Mantua, opening up serene trips on the rivers that wind down to the Po. A highlight is floating among the flora on Lake Superiore. (p228)

# GETTING AWAY FROM IT ALL

Beautiful places inevitably draw the crowds and they may take the shine off your experience. If possible avoid the hot spots in July and August; otherwise hunt out these secret places.

★ **Trace a trail through a Renaissance labyrinth** If Verona's Romeo and Juliet circus gets too much, head for the lush, tranquil Giardino Giusti (p217)

★ **Wander mountain terraces** Just metres from Lake Garda's tourist honeypot Malcesine, discover a timeless rural landscape (p207)

★ **Head off the highway** Leave the traffic behind and explore Valpolicella's idyllic vineyards (p221)

★ **Sit quietly in Mantua's Teatro Bibiena** A hushed, hidden gem, graced by an extraordinarily ornate interior (p226)

# RESOURCES

★ **Garda Trentino** (www.gardatrentino.it) Covers the lake's far north bank

★ **Riviera dei Limoni** (www.rivieradeilimoni .it) Info on western Lake Garda

★ **Strada del Soave** (www.stradadelsoave.com) Outlines Soave's vineyard trails

★ **Strada del Valpolicella** (www.stradadel valpolicella.com) Advice on Valpolicella's wine routes

★ **Tourism Verona** (www.tourism.verona.it) Covers Verona and eastern Lake Garda

★ **Turismo Mantova** (www.turismomantova .it) Official site for Mantua

# ADVANCE PLANNING

Often this is a region for spontaneity, but in high season it's best to book accommodation and restaurants.

★ **Verona's summer opera festival** (p220) The world-class Roman Arena draws big names and huge crowds. Book seats and hotels well in advance.

★ **Camera degli Sposi, Palazzo Ducale, Mantua** (p223) Only 1500 people a day can see Mantegna's remarkable frescos. Booking ensures you're one of them.

★ **Lake Garda's ferries** (p191) These boats can be the quickest and most scenic way to travel. Some villages have scores of services a day, others only a handful. You can take pot luck or check the online schedule at www.navigazionelaghi.it.

# TOP EATING EXPERIENCES

🍴 **RESTEL DE FER**
Gourmet home cooking in a 600-year-old farmhouse (p206)

🍴 **AL POMPIERE**
Dine amid mountains of cheese at this bustling Verona institution (p219)

🍴 **VECCHIA MALCESINE**
Refined, elegant cuisine in a picture-postcard village (p208)

🍴 **TAVERNA SAN VIGILIO**
Lake Garda's most idyllic bar clings to a crab-claw harbour (p210)

🍴 **ZAPPAROLI**
Picnic supplies galore at this Mantuan deli of your dreams (p230)

LAKE GARDA, VERONA & MANTUA

# LAKE GARDA

· · · · · ·

**Poets and politicians, divas and dictators, they've all been drawn to captivating Lake Garda (Lago di Garda). The largest of the Italian lakes, this azure body of water pools between soaring northern mountains and softer southern hills. Vineyards, olive groves and lemon-houses range up on the slopes, while the lake laps the harbours of a string of picturesque villages where the atmosphere is pure holiday haven – places to unknot those muscles and unwind that mind.**

Pretty Sirmione offers a luxury thermal spa and impressive Roman ruins, while the Valtenesi provides swaths of vineyards for you to tour. Elegant Salò and Gardone Riviera are the gateways to an aristocratic island and extravagant palaces. Mountain-backed Riva del Garda delivers a waterfall, windsurfing and plenty of real-life charm. Punta San Vigilio bags the best beach and Torri del Benaco delights with its ancient harbour, while Malcesine adds a 1760m-high cable-car ride. There are endless things to do.

But Lake Garda also allows you to do very little: relax into a slower pace of life, hop on a ferry, wonder at the beauty and linger over the local wine. Here life seems simple and sweet, and you can sample it too.

## ORIENTATION

The southern part of Lake Garda is wider, more developed and backed by relatively low hills. North of the line between Salò and Garda the lake narrows sharply, the mountains climb dramati-

cally and settlements thin out, especially in the west.

The lake is governed by three different provinces. Brescia administers the west bank, including the popular resort towns of Sirmione and Desenzano del Garda, the Valtenesi, stately Salò and genteel Gardone Riviera and Gargnano. Trentino-Alto Adige governs a narrow north bank that includes the appealing town of Riva del Garda and the windsurfing resort of Torbole. The east bank falls under the province of Verona, and includes hugely popular Malcesine, the charming towns of Torri del Benaco and Lazise, idyllic Punta San Vigilio, Bardolino's wine routes, a clutch of amusement parks and the transport hub of Peschiera del Garda.

Our coverage of the lake starts in Sirmione and moves around in a clockwise direction. Locally, the 'del Garda' that features in some settlements' names tends to be dropped.

## TRANSPORT

### TO/FROM THE AIRPORT

Two airports are within easy striking distance of Lake Garda. **Verona-Villafranca** ( ☎ 045 809 56 66; www.aeroportoverona.it) is 20km from the lake. Regular buses link the airport with Verona train station (see p221); from there Peschiera del Garda is 15 minutes by train. **Brescia airport** (Aeroporto Gabriele d'Annunzio; ☎ 030 204 15 99; www.aeroportobrescia. it) is 12km from Lake Garda. Shuttle buses connect the airport with Brescia train station; from there Desenzano del Garda is 15 minutes by train.

### GETTING AROUND

**CAR //** Lake Garda sits just north of the A4 Milan–Venice autostrada, and just west of the A22 Modena–Trento route. Just one single-lane main road circles the lake shore and in summer traffic is very heavy. In the north the route is dotted with long tunnels and steep curving sections. Local tourist offices can advise about car hire.

## LAKE GARDA'S FERRIES

Fleets of ferries link many Lake Garda communities, providing a series of scenic, stress-free minicruises. They're run by **Navigazione sul Lago di Garda** (☎ 030 914 95 11, 800 551801; www.navigazionelaghi.it), which publishes English-language timetables online. Frequencies of the pedestrian ferries vary wildly; some villages have only a couple a day in each direction, others have 35 daily in peak season. Fares range from €2.20 (€4.40 return) for short hops (such as Salò to Gardone Riviera) to €11.30 (€22.60 return) for the four-hour Riva–Desenzano north–south run. A one-day, unlimited travel ticket costs €25.80/13.40 per adult/child, with cheaper options available for smaller zones. Some passenger ferries also take bicycles.

Car ferries yo-yo between west-bank Toscolano-Maderno and east-bank Torri del Benaco, and seasonally between Limone sul Garda in the west and Malcesine in the east. Transporting a small car on either route costs €8.10 one way. Ticketing booths and tourist offices have timetables.

**TRAIN //** The two train stations serving the lake, at Desenzano del Garda and Peschiera del Garda, are both on the Milan–Venice train line and have almost hourly trains in each direction. Excellent connections with Verona (p221) make the city an easy day trip.

**BOAT //** Lake Garda has an extensive, efficient ferry network (see above).

**BUS // APTV** (☎ 045 805 79 11; www.aptv.it) runs buses along the lake's banks, with services stopping at all the key towns and villages. In the west buses run between Desenzano del Garda train station and Riva del Garda (two hours, up to six daily). In the east an hourly service runs between Riva del Garda and Peschiera del Garda train station (1½ hours); it also goes on to Verona. **Società Italiana Autoservizi** (SIA; ☎ 030 377 42 37; www.sia-autoservizi.it) operates the Riva del Garda–Milan (3¾ hours, three daily) route and connects the western bank with Brescia. **Trentino Trasporti** (☎ 0461 82 10 00; www.ttesercizio.it, in Italian) runs hourly buses between Riva del Garda and Arco (20 minutes), Rovereto (45 minutes) and Trento (1¾ hours).

# WEST BANK

## SIRMIONE

**pop 7800**

Over the centuries impossibly pretty Sirmione has drawn the likes of Catullus and Maria Callas to its banks, and today thousands follow in the Roman poet and opera diva's footsteps. The village sits astride a slender peninsula, ensuring a wealth of wraparound lake views. Narrow streets, olive groves and a 13th-century castle that rises straight from the water add to its appeal. But the real reasons to visit are Sirmione's great range of lake-edge hotels, its extensive, ruined Roman villa and the serious pampering offered at its thermal spa.

### ESSENTIAL INFORMATION

**TOURIST INFORMATION // Tourist office** (☎ 030 91 61 14; iat.sirmione@tiscali.it; Viale Marconi 8; ☺ 9am-8pm Easter-Oct, 9am-12.30pm & 3-6pm Mon-Fri, 9am-12.30pm Sat Nov-Easter) At Sirmione's bus station.

### ORIENTATION

Sirmione's car park and bus station are at the neck of the peninsula, alongside the castle. The village's main streets lead north past the ferry jetty. The thermal pools are 600m further north, while the Grotte di Catullo is another 800m further.

LAKE GARDA, VERONA & MANTUA

## EXPLORING SIRMIONE

### ❦ GROTTE DI CATULLO // CLAMBER AMONG PHOTOGENIC ROMAN RUINS

Occupying a 2-hectare chunk of Sirmione's northern tip, this ruined **Roman villa** ( ☎ 030 91 61 57; adult/child €4/free; ⏱ 8.30am-7pm Tue-Sat, 8.30am-5pm Sun Mar-Sep, 8.30am-5pm Tue-Sun Oct-Feb) is a picturesque complex of teetering stone arches and tumbledown walls, some three storeys high. It's the largest domestic villa that's been uncovered in northern Italy and wandering the olive groves on its terraced hillsides opens up an appealing combination of trees, crumbling stone and suddenly revealed lake views.

The villa dates from the Augustan era (late 1st century BC) and was probably abandoned by the 4th century AD. Despite the name, there's no evidence Catullus lived here, although the poet did have a home in the village. Significantly, the living quarters were on the top floor – that they offered 360-degree views of the surrounding waters suggests the Romans too liked rooms with lake views.

On the way to the Grotte di Catullo, look out for the plaque marking **Maria Callas' villa**, just north of the Aquaria spa.

### ❦ AQUARIA // SOOTHE AWAY STRESS IN BUBBLING THERMAL POOLS

Sirmione is blessed with a series of offshore thermal springs that pump out water at a natural 37°C. They were discovered in the late 1800s and the town's been tapping into their healing properties ever since. At the **Aquaria** ( ☎ 030 91 60 44; www.termedisirmione.com; Piazza Don Angelo Piatti; pools weekdays/weekends €29/36, treatments from €25; ⏱ pools 2-10pm Mon, 10am-10pm Tue-Sun Mar-Dec, hours vary Jan & Feb) spa you can indulge in an array of treatments, from remineralising mud sessions (€50) to ayurvedic massages (€80) and reflexology (€70). Or just plump for five hours of wallowing in the two bubbling thermal pools – the outdoor one is set

---

## ∿ WORTH A TRIP ∿

A 19km drive south from Sirmione takes you to **Solferino**, a small village which played a huge part in Italian history – and helped spawn a global aid agency. On 24 June 1859, as part of the Risorgimento (Italian unification; p240), Solferino and nearby San Martino were the scene of two battles where the combined 135,000 Piedmontese and French forces took on and defeated 140,000 Austrians. Almost 980 cannons were on the battlefields, along with 19,000 horses. Casualties were horrendous: 9800 soldiers died; 20,000 were wounded; 11,400 went missing or were taken prisoner. A Swiss businessperson, Henry Dunant, witnessed the aftermath of the battle and was so appalled by the lack of care for the casualties that he set up the organisation that became the international Red Cross and Red Crescent movements.

After the happy holidays mood of Lake Garda, Solferino is a sobering place. The **Musei di Solferino** ( ☎ 0376 85 40 19; Via Ossario di Solferino; adult/child €2.50/1; ⏱ 9am-12.30pm & 2.30-7pm Tue-Sun Mar-Sep) displays small cannons, uniforms and gilt-framed paintings of the conflict, while the tower of the village's castle provides panoramic views of the battlefields. There is also a Red Cross monument, and a chilling ossuary in the church of San Pietro where the bones of more than 7000 soldiers are kept.

right beside the lake. Treatments have to be booked in advance but for the pools just turn up with your swimsuit (towels provided).

## GASTRONOMIC HIGHLIGHTS

### ☙ LA FIASCA €€

☎ 030 990 61 11; Via Santa Maria Maggiore; meals €31; ☾ Thu-Tue

Serving up the kind of sauces you can't help dunking your bread in, this authentic trattoria is tucked away in a back street just off the main square. The atmosphere is warm and bustling, and the dishes are packed with traditional Lake Garda produce. Prepare for some gutsy flavours: tagliatelle with perch and mushrooms; pappardelle with boar *ragù;* and duck with cognac and juniper.

### ☙ LA RUCOLA €€€

☎ 030 91 63 26; Vicolo Strentelle 7; meals €75; ☾ Fri-Wed

Sirmione's most elegant eatery is a re-fined affair. Modern art adds splashes of colour to the stone walls, while the chefs add a touch of class to a menu strong on sea and lake fish. Expect sea bass, prawns and the catch of the day to feature in numerous risotto, pasta and grilled guises, combined with flavour-enhancing confits, pâtés and marinades.

### ☙ LA SPERANZINA €€€€

☎ 030 990 62 92; Via Dante 16; meals €62; ☾ Tue-Sun

Although it's just a stone's throw from the castle, this trattoria is on the quieter side of the peninsula, well away from Sirmione's waterfront circus. Its lake-side terrace is shaded by olive trees and is a picturesque spot to dine on grilled *lavarello* (a white-fleshed fish), veal and salt cod, or pigeon with couscous and chestnuts.

## DESENZANO DEL GARDA

**pop 26,600**

An easygoing commuter town 9km southwest of Sirmione, Desenzano del Garda is known as the *porta del lago* (gateway to the lake) because of its key transport links. It's not as pretty as some of its counterparts, but its ancient harbour, broad promenades and vibrant Piazza Matteotti make for pleasant wanderings. Desenzano's best-known sights are its remarkably well preserved Roman mosaics, but the chance to sample olive oil at the press may also tempt you to town.

## ESSENTIAL INFORMATION

**TOURIST INFORMATION // Tourist office**
( ☎ 030 914 15 10; iat.desenzano@tiscali.it; Via Porto Vecchio 34; ☾ 10am-12.30pm & 3-6pm Mon-Fri, 10am-12.30pm Sat year-round, 3-6pm Sat Jun-Sep)

## EXPLORING DESENZANO DEL GARDA

### ☙ FRANTOIO MONTECROCE // SLURP (NOISILY) AWARD-WINNING OLIVE OIL

Set in the hills above Desenzano, this mill ( ☎ 030 991 15 04; www.frantoiomontecroce .it; Viale Ettore Andreis 84; admission free; ☾ 8am-noon & 3-7pm Mon-Sat) is the perfect place to be tutored in the subtleties of Lake Garda's olive oil. The same family has been harvesting the precious green and black fruit from the surrounding trees for four generations. The mill's granite wheels, gleaming machines and stainless-steel vats give a real insight into the modern production process, while family members provide tasting tips (see also the boxed text, p195). The four varieties of oil have won prestigious gold medals at international level – they'll probably go down quite well at your supper table, too.

DESENZANO DEL GARDA
0 300 m
0 0.2 miles
A
B
C
D
1
2
3
To Padenghe sul Garda (7km); Moniga del Garda (9km); Rocca di Manerba (12km); Salò (24km); Gargnano (57km)
Via Antonio Gramsci
Via Scavi Romani
Via Crocifisso
Via Roma
Lungolago Cesare Battisti
Lake Garda
Via Rimembranze
Via Vittorio Veneto
Piazza Duomo
Via Porto Vecchio
Via Mazzini
Via Annunciata
Piazza Malvezzi
Minitangenziale
Via Papa
Via Giuseppe Garibaldi
Piazza G Garibaldi
Via Castello
Castle
Piazza Matteotti
Piazza XXV Aprile
Viale Ettore Andreis
Viale Guglielmo Marconi
Via Monte Grappa
Via Sant'Angela Merici
Via Bagatta
Via Brescia
Via Milano
Via Irta
Viale Cavour
To Sirmione (9km); Peschiera del Garda (20km); Verona (45km)
To Brescia (30km)
Train Station
ESSENTIAL INFORMATION
Tourist Office ....1 C1
EXPLORING DESENZANO DEL GARDA
Frantoio Montecroce ....2 A2
Roman Villa ....3 C1
GASTRONOMIC HIGHLIGHTS
Al Fattore ....4 C1
TRANSPORT
Ferry Jetty ....5 D2

### ROMAN VILLA // DISCOVER THE ROMANS' PENCHANT FOR INTERIOR DESIGN

Some of the best mosaics in northern Italy are to be found in Desenzano's **Roman Villa** (☎ 030 914 35 47; Via Crocifisso 2; adult/child €2/free; 🕓 8.30am-7pm Mar–mid-Oct, 8.30am-4.30pm mid-Oct–Feb).

Built 2000 years ago, it was remodelled in the 2nd century, with most of the mosaics being added in the 4th century. They're still bright today – a colourful collage of black, red, olive and orange.

The images provide an evocative and very human insight into the tastes of the people who lived here. They clearly had a fondness for cherubs, which appear repeatedly, going fishing, riding chariots and gathering grapes. Wooden walkways lead directly over these vivid pieces of floor art, allowing you to stroll through the remains of a luxurious *triclinium* (dining room), past semicircular baths to a *cubiculum* (bedroom), before ending at a vestibule that opened towards the lake.

## GASTRONOMIC HIGHLIGHTS

### AL FATTORE €€

☎ 030 914 19 37; Via Roma 8; pizzas €6-9, meals €34; 🕓 daily, year-round

Robust dishes bursting with local flavours are the speciality of this popular little *ristorante*. Choose from trout with sautéed mussels, tagliatelle with duck *ragù* or baked pork saddle with sweet onions. Or if lunch was long and late, you can always opt for a pizza. Excellent, traditional food is guaranteed; comfortable in its origins and assured in its delivery.

# VALTENESI

The Valtenesi stretches languidly between Desenzano and Salò, its rolling hills etched with vine trellises and flecked with olive groves. The main lake road heads inshore, allowing for gentle explorations of an array of wineries, a scattering of coastal towns and a secluded nature reserve.

## ❦ TOURING THE VALTENESI // TAKING YOUR TIME AMONG RESTAURANTS, BEACHES AND VINES

The sunny slopes of the Valtenesi sit within the Garda Classico DOC wine region, and the scores of vineyards produce the light, rose-coloured chiaretto, the elegant groppello and the full-bodied Rosso Superiore. Olives also thrive here – try tasting the local oil at **Frantoio Montecroce** (p193) in Desenzano.

One of countless possible itineraries is to head just north of Desenzano to the small town of **Padenghe sul Garda**. It's home to **Zuliani** (☎ 030 990 70 26; www.vinizuliani.it; Via Tito Speri 28), a family-run vineyard that's been producing wine since 1589. The traditional farmhouse features dimly lit red-brick cellars and ranks of dusty bottles. Sampling chiaretto, olives and Parmigiano-Reggiano (Parmesan) in the atmospheric kitchen is a delight.

Meandering a few kilometres further north leads to the village of **Moniga del Garda**, with its pretty medieval castle and relatively quiet beachfront. The slick, ultramodern winery **Costaripa** (☎ 0365 50 20 10; www.costaripa.it; Via Costa 1; tours €5) is just off the main SP572 road. Tours here lead past 10,000L stainless-steel drums into rooms where each of the 12,000 upturned bottles is rotated a quarter turn every day to settle the sediment. Visits end in the chic, marble-lined lounge with a tasting session of one chiaretto, one rosso and one sparkling wine.

Nearby, the shaded terrace of **Ristorante Quintessenza** (☎ 036 550 21 16; Piazza San Martino 3, Moniga del Garda; 4/6 courses €45/60; ☽ lunch & dinner Fri-Wed year-round, dinner daily & lunch Thu-Tue Jul & Aug) is a great place to discover just how well excellent local

## LAKE GARDA'S OLIVE OIL

Lake Garda's microclimate resembles the Mediterranean's, ensuring ideal olive-growing conditions. The lake's banks produce a tiny 1% of Italy's olive oil, but the product is renowned for being light, soft and sweet. Some 15 varieties of olives are grown here; the local black fruit produces subtler tasting oil, while the green olives are spicier – the oil makers' skill lies in achieving the perfect blend. Lake Garda's lighter oils work well with fish, the medium blends are delicious drizzled over mozzarella, and the stronger, spicier varieties are superb with grilled meats and soup. Locals advise not to use the best oils for salads, arguing if you're adding vinegar it ruins the taste.

Sampling olive oil is an art in itself. It's normally tasted from tiny beakers or with bread (although purists argue this masks the delicate flavours). First drink in the smell, then take a sip and suck the oil, noisily, into the back and side of the mouth. The pros eat chunks of apple between each sample. Among the places you can taste Lake Garda olive oil are **Frantoio Montecroce** (p193) in Desenzano del Garda, the **Consorzio Olivicoltori di Malcesine** (p207) in Malcesine, and the **Museo dell'Olio d'Oliva** (p211) in Bardolino.

LAKE GARDA, VERONA & MANTUA

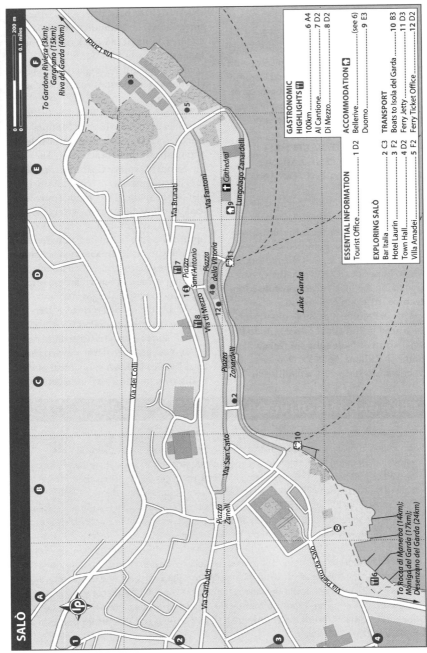

# SALÒ

Lake Garda

To Gardone Riviera (3km);
Gargagno (15km);
Riva del Garda (40km)

To Rocca di Manerba (14km);
Moniga del Garda (17km);
Desenzano del Garda (24km)

Via Landi
Via del Colli
Via Brunati
Via Fantoni
Via di Mezzo
Via Garibaldi
Via San Carlo
Via Pietro da Salò

Piazza Zanardelli
Piazza Sant'Antonio
Piazza della Vittoria
Piazza Zanelli

Cathedral
Lungolago Zanardelli

| ESSENTIAL INFORMATION | |
|---|---|
| Tourist Office | 1 D2 |

| EXPLORING SALÒ | |
|---|---|
| Bar Italia | 2 C3 |
| Hotel Laurin | 3 F2 |
| Town Hall | 4 D2 |
| Villa Amadei | 5 F2 |

| GASTRONOMIC HIGHLIGHTS 🍴 | |
|---|---|
| 100km | 6 A4 |
| Al Cantione | 7 D2 |
| Di Mezzo | 8 D2 |

| ACCOMMODATION 🏠 | |
|---|---|
| Bellerive | (see 6) |
| Duomo | 9 E3 |

| TRANSPORT | |
|---|---|
| Boats to Isola del Garda | 10 B3 |
| Ferry Jetty | 11 D3 |
| Ferry Ticket Office | 12 D2 |

0   200 m
0   0.1 miles

wines go with excellent local food. Here an antipasto of quail or pigs trotters could be followed by *coregone* (a white-fleshed fish) with artichokes and orange oil, or pike with capers, anchovies and roasted polenta.

A few kilometres north, the craggy promontory of **Rocca di Manerba** is home to the low rubble walls of a medieval castle and a restful nature reserve of evergreen woods and orchid meadows. The shores around here feature some of the best **beaches** on the lake. Strolling from Pieve Vecchia to Porto del Torchio via Punta del Rio reveals glorious views and idyllic spots for a dip or a paddle.

The **tourist office** ( ☎ 030 999 04 02; www .stradadeivini.it) in Desenzano (p193) can advise about the Valtenesi; it also stocks a *Strada dei Vini* map, which lists vineyards, olive oil producers and restaurants. Many wineries welcome visitors, but you should phone ahead to be sure of a tour.

## SALÒ

**pop 10,400**

Somehow wedged in between the lake and precipitous mountains, Salò exudes an air of courtly grandeur. Its long waterfront promenade is lined with ornate buildings and palm trees, while the graceful bell tower of its 15th-century cathedral overlooks atmospheric lanes studded with boutique shops. Add excellent restaurants and ferry connections and you have an appealing base for explorations which include an aristocrat's island and the scenes of Mussolini's desperate attempts to cling to power.

### ESSENTIAL INFORMATION
**TOURIST INFORMATION //** **Tourist office**
( ☎ 0365 2 14 23; www.rivieradeilimoni.it; Piazza Sant'Antonio 4; ⊙ 10am-12.30pm & 3-6pm Mon, Tue & Thu-Sat, 10am-12.30pm Sun)

### EXPLORING SALÒ
❦ **ISOLA DEL GARDA // TOUR A CONTESSA'S FAIRY-TALE ISLAND PALACE**
It's not often you get to explore a serene private island in the company of its aristocratic owners, so a trip to **Isola del Garda** ( ☎ 328 384 92 26; www.isoladelgarda.com; tours €21-27; ⊙ May-Oct) is a real treat. Sitting just off Salò, this tiny, comma-shaped speck of land is crowned with impressive battlements, luxuriant formal gardens and a sumptuous neo-Gothic Venetian villa. It's owned by Contessa Cavazza, and your visit is likely to be guided by a member of her family. The two-hour tour takes in a clutch of opulent rooms, some with a disarming real-life family feel, as well as the bewitching grounds. The end of the trip will see you ensconced beside the villa's elaborate tower, gazing over a vivid blue lake, sampling oil, wine and cheese from the family estates, and quite possibly rather wishing you lived here. Boats depart from Salò, Gardone Riviera, Garda and Sirmione, but they only leave each location one or two times a week, so plan ahead. Admission includes the boat fare; costs and tour times vary depending on the departure port.

❦ **THE REPUBLIC OF SALÒ // SEE WHERE MUSSOLINI TRIED TO CLING TO POWER**
Sedate and refined as Salò is today, its recent past has a darker side. In 1943 the town was named the capital of the Social Republic of Italy as part of Mussolini and Hitler's last-ditch attempts to organise Italian Fascism in the face of advancing American forces (see p241). This episode, often known as the Republic of Salò, saw more than 16 public and private buildings in the town

LAKE GARDA, VERONA & MANTUA

## MARKETS

Vibrant, eclectic and alive with banter, Lake Garda's weekly markets are the place to step off the tourist trail and see life as it's lived – this is shopping as social anthropology. Here are some of the best:

- ★ **Monday** Torri del Benaco
- ★ **Tuesday** Desenzano del Garda, Limone sul Garda (1st and 3rd of the month)
- ★ **Wednesday** Gargnano, Lazise, Riva del Garda (2nd and 4th of the month)
- ★ **Thursday** Bardolino
- ★ **Friday** Garda
- ★ **Saturday** Malcesine, Salò

commandeered and turned into Mussolini's ministries and offices. Today, strolling between the sites becomes a surreal tour of the dictator's doomed ministate, where the cheerful present sits alongside a grim, recent past.

To the east of town, the Foreign Ministry was based at the art-nouveau Villa Simonini (now **Hotel Laurin**); the nearby **Villa Amadei** was home to the Ministry of Popular Culture. In the centre, the Palazzo della Magnifica Patria (now the **Town Hall**) was the Interpreters' Office HQ, where foreign dispatches were translated. The Casa del Fascio, now **Bar Italia**, was commandeered to become home to Mussolini's guards, while what's now a local primary school became the base for Agenzia Stefani, the notorious news agency for Fascist propaganda. The tourist office has an English-language map and booklet featuring the Republic of Salò's significant locations. Look out too for the multilingual plaques around town.

## GASTRONOMIC HIGHLIGHTS

### ♥ 100KM €€

☎ 036 552 04 10; Hotel Bellerive, Via Pietro da Salò 11; 4 courses €45; ☾ daily year-round

What should a restaurant at the heart of a region of superb produce and excellent wine do? The folk at the place called 100km have the answer: only serve food from within the eponymous distance. The result? Dishes in tune with both surroundings and seasons. Look out for imaginative treatment of *trota* (trout), *coniglio* (rabbit) and *anatra* (duck), plus delicacies such as *polpo* (octopus) and *gambero* (crayfish).

### ♥ AL CANTIONE €

☎ 036 52 02 34; Piazza Sant'Antonio 19; meals €20; ☾ Fri-Wed

Heading just a few streets back from the waterfront leads one to this friendly neighbourhood *osteria* (wine bar), home to gingham tablecloths, fabulous cooking smells and a clutch of regulars playing cards in the corner. The ingredients used at Al Contione draw on Salò's lake-meets-mountains setting; try the *coregone,* simply grilled with lemon, or the mounds of intensely flavoured tagliatelle with mushrooms and truffle oil – a snip at €8.

### ♥ DI MEZZO €€

☎ 036 529 09 66; Via di Mezzo 10; meals €32; ☾ Wed-Mon

Another Salò eatery that leaves you in no doubt as to your location. At this intimate trattoria a constant stream of hearty meals heads into a dining room lined with antique mirrors and weathered stone. Pumpkin gnocchi, grilled perch, and rabbit with smoked ham and prunes are just some of the delights to choose from.

## GARDONE RIVIERA

**pop 2700**

Gardone's glory days were in the late 19th and early 20th centuries, and today the resort's opulent villas and ornate architecture lend it an air of faded elegance. But Gardone also offers the chance to tour the home of Italy's most controversial poet, and see some beautifully quirky contemporary art.

### EXPLORING GARDONE RIVIERA

**❧ IL VITTORIALE DEGLI ITALIANI // TOUR THE HOME OF ITALY'S ECCENTRIC, ULTRANATIONALIST POET**

Poet, soldier, hypochondriac and proto-Fascist – Gabriele d'Annunzio (1863–1938) defies easy definition, and so does his estate: **Il Vittoriale degli Italiani** ( ☎ 0365 29 65 11; www.vittoriale.it; Piazza Vittoriale; adult/child grounds €7/5, grounds & Prioria €12/8, grounds & Museo della Guerra €12/8, grounds, Prioria & Museo della Guerra €16/12; ☻ grounds 8.30am-8pm daily Apr-Sep, 9am-5pm daily Oct-Mar, Prioria 9.30am-7pm Tue-Sun Apr-Sep, 9am-1pm & 2-5pm Tue-Sun Oct-Mar, Museo della Guerra 9.30am-7pm Thu-Tue Apr-Sep, 9am-1pm & 2-5pm Thu-Tue Oct-Mar). Bombastic, extravagant and unsettling, it's home to every architectural and decorative excess imaginable and the decor helps shed light on the man.

By 1914 d'Annunzio was an established poet, but his fame was cemented by a series of daring military adventures in WWI. His most dramatic exploit was an unsanctioned occupation of Fiume, now Rijeka, on the Adriatic. Outraged that it was about to be handed over to Yugoslavia, not Italy, at the end of the war, he gathered a mini-army, invaded the port and proclaimed himself the ruler. Despite eventually surrendering he was hailed a national hero. In the 1920s d'Annunzio became a strong supporter of Fascism and Mussolini, while his affairs with rich and titled women were legendary.

In his main house, the **Prioria**, black velvet drapes line cluttered, gloomy rooms (he was allergic to sunlight) crammed with classical figurines, leopard skins, leather-bound books, gilded ornaments, lacquer boxes and masses of cushions and china. Highlights include the bronze tortoise that sits on the guests' dining table (it was cast from one that died from overeating); the bright blue bathroom suite; and his study with its very low lintel – designed so visitors would have to bow to d'Annunzio as they entered. Visits to the Prioria are by guided tour only (in Italian, 25 minutes, departures every 10 minutes). The estate's **Museo della Guerra** is full of mementoes, banners and medals of d'Annunzio's war-time exploits, while the **grounds** offer the chance to wander the deck of the full-sized battleship **Puglia**. Complete with machine guns, searchlights and anchor chains, her prow now sticks bizarrely out of the steeply sloping hillside, hundreds of metres above the lake.

**❧ GIARDINO BOTANICO FONDAZIONE ANDRÉ HELLER // CHILL OUT AMONG CACTI AND CONTEMPORARY ART**

A peaceful antidote to Lake Garda's crowds, and the Fascistic folly of Il Vittoriale (left), this compact flower-filled oasis is a delight for plant lovers and art fans alike. Multimedia artist André Heller has created a **garden** ( ☎ 336 41 08 77; Via Roma; adult/child €9/5; ☻ 9am-6pm Mar–mid-Oct) of pocket-sized climate zones where tiny paths wind from central American

LAKE GARDA, VERONA & MANTUA

plains to African savannah, via swaths of tulips and bamboo. Hidden among the greenery and vivid bursts of colour are 30 pieces of contemporary sculpture – look out for the jagged red figure by Keith Haring near the entrance, Rudolf Hirt's Gaudi-esque *Ioanes, God of Water,* and Roy Lichtenstein's polka-dot take on the pyramids. Countless playful touches include giant dominoes, a wooden chess set and a 'visitors' book', where messages are written then left dangling from a tree to swirl in the breeze.

### GASTRONOMIC HIGHLIGHTS
**AGLI ANGELI €€**
☎ 0365 2 08 32; Piazza Garibaldi 2; set menu €20, meals €37; Wed-Mon

A shaded terrace, rattan chairs and burgundy tablecloths set the scene beautifully for some classic Lake Garda cooking. Tempting choices include veal ravioli, sardines with potatoes and herbs, and fettucine with smoked eel. As Agli Angeli is tucked into the hillside on the way to Il Vittoriale, it makes an ideal post-sightseeing stop.

**LA STALLA €€€**
☎ 036 52 10 38; Via dei Colli 14; meals €39-79; Thu-Tue

There are touches of Gardone's heyday at La Stalla; risotto with oysters and champagne doesn't grace that many menus. It's not all extravagance though – octopus and clam soup, and pasta with prawns and mushrooms are other options, and the atmosphere is relaxed, especially on the patio edged by warm weathered stone.

## GARGNANO

**pop 3050**
There's a sense of Mediterranean meets mountains in Gargnano. Terraces of lemon and olive trees climb steep slopes, a restrained string of cafes and hotels loops along the shore, and narrow streets wind down to a tiny harbour. Normally the village is a relatively calm place to soak up some history and go for a swim, but in September it's all bustle as yachts gather for the Centomiglia – the lake's most prized sailing regatta, which starts just a few kilometers south at Bogliaco.

### EXPLORING GARGNANO
**CLOISTERS OF ST FRANCIS // EXPLORE 2000 YEARS OF GARGNANO'S PAST**
The 13th-century cloisters of the **Chiesa di San Francisco** may be small but they house a whole lot of history. The smooth

arched roof is supported by columns that feature a revealing array of carved designs: the lemons, citrons and melons speak of the area's unique industry and the monks' connection to it (see the boxed text, below), while the carvings of fish and friars reflect the lake's practical and spiritual past. The cloisters are also home to two local Roman-era altars: a 3rd-century one dedicated to Neptune and a 1st-century one dedicated to Re-vino, Gargnano's protector. Look out too for the 16th-century stone coat of arms featuring a she-wolf holding a rake and a fleur-de-lis – an image that forms part of the town's coat of arms today.

### ❦ PARCO LA FONTANELLA // SWIM OVERSHADOWED BY A MOUNTAIN PEAK

A 300m stroll north from Gargnano's ferry landing takes you to a **beach** (Via Rimembranze 18; ☺ 9am-9pm mid-Mar–mid-Sep, 10am-5.30pm mid-Sep–mid-Mar) where gleaming white pebbles fringe crystalline waters. The shore, bar and restaurant are backed by olive groves which look out directly onto a lake that's dwarfed by the craggy heights of Monte Baldo opposite.

If you're here in late spring, the mountain often still has snow clinging to its tip; enjoy the unusual sensation of swimming beneath a snowcapped peak.

## GASTRONOMIC HIGHLIGHTS

### ❦ AL VICOLO €€

☎ 036 57 14 64; Via dell'Angeloio; meals €26; ☺ Tue-Sun

Tables spill out onto the cobbled lane that gives this trattoria its name, making it a convivial spot to sample some upper Lake Garda cuisine. Lemons and olives from the surrounding mountains add zest and flavour to grilled local fish and meats, while the antipasti are a tempting array of carpaccio, rustic salami and local cheeses with mustard.

### ❦ CENTOMIGLIA €

☎ 036 57 26 56; Via Lungolago Zanardelli N 13; pizzas €5-9, meals €20; ☺ no closing day

For picturesque, flavoursome dining head to Centomiglia, fittingly set beside the yacht-filled harbour. Dishes are packed with local ingredients – enjoy them on the terrace or in a snug, vaulted interior full of warm stone, artistic flourishes and local families. An ideal

## LAKE GARDA'S LEMON INDUSTRY

It's thought monks from Genoa brought lemons to Gargnano when they arrived at the town's monastery of St Francis in the 13th century. Lake Garda's temperate climate provided good conditions for a fruit normally only grown commercially much further south, and by the18th century hundreds of *limonaie* (lemon-houses) were being built. These kept the frosts off the trees by laying sheets of glass over a wooden latticework supported by ranks of tall, thin stone pillars. Hundreds of thousands of lemons were exported annually to Germany and Russia, providing a crucial local income. But by the second half of the 19th century the industry fell into terminal decline due to disease and the discovery of artificial citric acid.

Today, terraces of weathered stone pillars are evidence of this lost industry. You can visit restored lemon-houses at **Pra de la Fam** (p202) in Tingale Porto and **Limonaia del Castèl** (p202) in Limone sul Garda on the west bank of the lake, and at Torri del Benaco's **Il Castello Scaligero** (p209) on the east bank.

bolt-hole when the wind whips up, lightning bounces off the so-close mountains and the rain pours down.

### ♥ LA TORTUGA €€€

☎ 036 57 12 51; Via XXIV Maggio 5; meals €53-65; ⊙ Wed-Mon

Lake Garda's classic produce gets an imaginative reworking at this elegant little *ristorante*. Appreciative diners at its handful of tables enjoy perch, pike and beef transformed by truffle butter, Gargnano extra virgin olive oil, Lake Garda wine sauces and grilled Bagoss (a local hard cheese).

## GARGNANO TO RIVA DEL GARDA

Although they loom on the horizon for much of the lake, it's around Gargnano that the mountains really kick in. They rear so steeply it's overwhelming – you don't just look at views like these, you step into them. The lakeshore between Gargnano and Riva del Garda is scattered with small communities crammed in between the water, the road and sheer cliffs. Scenery aside, this stretch also offers the chance to tour restored lemon-houses.

### ♥ UPPER LAKE ROAD TRIP // NAVIGATE SWITCHBACKS AND TUNNELS ON A WHITE-KNUCKLE DRIVE

Often on Lake Garda the ferry can be the most scenic way to travel, but to really get a feel for these mountains, take to the road. Heading north from Gargnano the SS45bis climbs steeply, its cliff-edge bends interspersed with long, dark tunnels and signs warning of rock falls; below sits an azure lake overlooked by the Monte Baldo chain. Around 8km north of Gargnano, a turn-off on the left leads via an ultra-steep detour to the atmospheric village of **Tignale** some 500m above the water. Somehow clinging to a spur of rock above the nearby hamlet of Gardola is the 16th-century **Santuario di Montecastello** ( ☎ 036 57 30 19; ⊙ 9am-7pm Easter-Oct), which has a 15th-century gilded wooden altar, frescos of the Giotto school and extraordinary views down the whole lake. Back on the main SS-45bis lake road, the route passes **Tignale Porto**, a popular windsurfers' hang-out that's home to a bar, a minuscule strip of shore and the restored lemon-house Pra de la Fam (below). A couple of kilometres further, the cliff-backed beaches at **Campione del Garda** provide views of fleets of windsurfers skimming the lake surface at exhilarating speeds.

The picture-postcard town of **Limone sul Garda** lies around 8km further north. Here stone houses tumble down steep slopes and cobbled lanes meander towards a waterfront lined with pastel-painted houses. Inevitably in the summer it's besieged by tourists and the trinket sellers and snack bars are there in force. The town is also home to **Limonaia del Castèl** (below), a restored lemon-house.

### ♥ PRA DE LA FAM & LIMONAIA DEL CASTÈL // TOUR THE SCENTED TERRACES OF RESTORED LEMON-HOUSES

Growing citrus was once a key industry on Lake Garda's banks (see the boxed text, p201), but now most of the lemon-houses are in ruins. At the carefully restored 18th-century **Pra de la Fam** ( ☎ 036 57 14 49; SS45bis, Tignale Porto; admission free; ⊙ 10am-noon Wed & Sun, 3-5pm Fri Apr-Oct) you can see how the area's unique greenhouse-style system worked: glass sheets sat over wooden grids supported by huge stone pillars. Fragrant terraces are scattered with windfalls and crowded with trees laden with fruit, while displays explore the cultivation process and show sepia photos of Pra de la Fam in the 1930s. It's a peaceful, low-key attraction that conjures a sense of this unique industry and its decline.

Pra de la Fam is beside the lakeshore SS45bis at Tignale Porto, around 10km north of Gargnano, and is only open a few days a week. A more accessible alternative is the **Limonaia del Castèl** ( ☎ 036 595 40 08; Via Capitelli; adult/child €1/free; ☺ 10am-6pm Apr-Oct), a restored 18th-century lemon-house in Limone sul Garda. It's bigger, it's more manicured and the trees are less established, but it still provides an interesting glimpse into this lost industry.

# NORTH BANK

## RIVA DEL GARDA & AROUND

**pop 15,600 / elev 73m**
Even in a lake blessed by dramatic scenery, Riva del Garda still comes out on top for sheer majesty of surroundings. Encircled by towering rock faces and a looping strip of beach, its appealing centre is a medley of grand architecture, mazelike streets and wide squares. Riva also boasts an awe-inspiring waterfall and some excellent hikes, while its museum sheds light on Lake Garda's martial past.

Riva lies across the border from Lombardy in the Alpine region of Trentino-Alto Adige. The village of Torbole, a magnet for windsurfers, is 3km to the east. Tiny Lake Ledro is high in the mountains 12km to the west.

### ESSENTIAL INFORMATION
**TOURIST INFORMATION // Tourist office**
( ☎ 0464 55 44 44; www.gardatrentino.it; Largo Medaglie d'Oro; ☺ 9am-7pm May-Sep, 9am-6pm Oct-Apr)

### EXPLORING RIVA DEL GARDA & AROUND
❦ **CASCATA DEL VARONE // GET SOAKED AT LAKE GARDA'S BIGGEST WATERFALL**
This 100m **waterfall** ( ☎ 046 452 14 21; Via Nuova; adult/child €5/4; ☺ 9am-7pm May-Aug, 9am-6pm Apr & Sep, 9am-5pm Mar & Oct, 10am-5pm Sun only Nov-Feb) thunders down sheer limestone cliffs to an immense, dripping cavelike gorge. Walkways snake 50m into the mountain beside this crashing torrent, and strolling along them is like walking in a perpetual thunderstorm – thrilling and slightly frightening, it will leave you more than a little wet. The waterfall has been a tourist attraction since 1874 and has drawn the likes of Prince Umberto II, Emperor Franz Joseph, Franz Kafka and Thomas Mann, as well as the ultranationalist soldier-poet Gabriele d'Annunzio (p199); the waterfall's gatehouse was designed by the same architect behind d'Annunzio's villa, Il Vittoriale (p199). The waterfall is 3km northwest of Riva's centre.

❦ **MUSEO RIVA DEL GARDA // CHART RIVA'S TURBULENT HISTORY**
For centuries Lake Garda has been a key transport route between the Alps and the Mediterranean, and Riva's position at the north of the lake has lent it a vital strategic role. In the Middle Ages the town was fought over by the Prince-Bishops of Trento, the republic of Venice and Milan's Visconti and Verona's Della Scala families. Trentino-Alto Adige, which as the Südtirol (South Tyrol) remained part of Austria until 1919, saw fierce fighting in the Italian wars of independence and WWI, and was home to anti-Nazi resistance groups in WWII.

LAKE GARDA, VERONA & MANTUA

# RIVA DEL GARDA

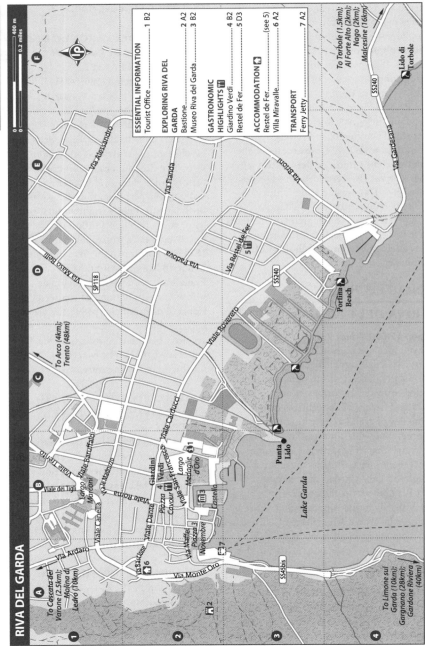

| ESSENTIAL INFORMATION | |
|---|---|
| Tourist Office | 1 B2 |

| EXPLORING RIVA DEL GARDA | |
|---|---|
| Bastione | 2 A2 |
| Museo Riva del Garda | 3 B2 |

| GASTRONOMIC HIGHLIGHTS | |
|---|---|
| Giardino Verdi | 4 B2 |
| Restel de Fer | 5 D3 |

| ACCOMMODATION | |
|---|---|
| Restel de Fer | (see 5) |
| Villa Miravalle | 6 A2 |

| TRANSPORT | |
|---|---|
| Ferry Jetty | 7 A2 |

To Torbole (1.5km);
Al Forte Alto (2km);
Nago (2km);
Malcesine (16km)

Lido di Torbole

SS240

Via Gardesana

Via Brioni

Via Restel de Fer

Via Padova

SP118

Via Fianda

Via Alessandro

Via Maso Belli

SS240

Porfina Beach

Viale Rovereto

To Arco (4km);
Trento (48km)

Viale Carducci

Punta Lido

Lake Garda

Viale Trento

Viale dei Tigli

Viale Baruffaldi

Via Canella

Viale Martiri

Via Roma

Viale Roma

Largo Marconi

Piazza Cavour

Viale San Francesco

Giardini Verdi

Largo Medaglie d'Oro

Castello

Viale Dante

Via Maffei

Piazza 3 Novembre

Via Bastione

Via Ardaro

Via Monte Oro

To Cascatta del Varone (2.5km);
Molina di Ledrò (10km)

SS45bis

To Limone sul Garda (10km);
Gargnano (28km);
Gardone Riviera (40km)

0   400 m
0   0.2 miles

Riva's **museum** ( ☎ 0464 57 38 69; Piazza Cesare Battisti 3; adult/child €2/free; ☼ 10am-12.30pm & 1.30-6pm Tue-Sun) reflects this past – both in terms of the displays and the building they're set in. The museum itself occupies a 12th-century **castle** that was built by a Trento Prince-Bishop and later enlarged by the Della Scalas. Displays include coats of arms and an evocative 18th-century oil painting of Riva crawling with red-coated soldiers about to set sail. Perhaps the most revealing exhibits are the antique maps dating from 1579 and 1667 and a 1774 *Atlas Tyrolensis,* which evocatively convey the area's shifting boundaries. Other highlights include 14th-century stone carvings, Roman-era archaeological finds and evocative displays on the area's Bronze Age stilt dwellings.

### ♥ LAKE LEDRO // EXPLORE ANCIENT AND MODERN LAKE AND MOUNTAIN LIFE

From Riva first the SP37 then the SS240 wind their way west up the mountains, in and out of tunnels, past olive groves and vine-lined terraces. The road signs here speak volumes, warning of low cloud, rockfalls and ice. It's an ear-popping drive past rural villages lent an Alpine feel by the firewood stacked outside and the balconies overlooking the valleys; detouring off the main road into villages such as **Biacesa** and **Pré** provides an insight into mountain life. Around 11km from Riva the road flattens and **Lake Ledro** comes into view. Only 2.5km long and 2km wide, this diminutive lake sits at an altitude of 650m, set in a bowl of tree-covered mountains. **Molina di Ledro** is at the lake's eastern end, where tiny thatched huts line up beside a string of beaches and boat-hire pontoons.

The shores around Lake Ledro have produced some of the region's most important evidence of Bronze Age life. Archaeological finds reveal a thriving community which lived in *palafittes* (stilt dwellings) and produced high-quality tools, goods and jewellery. Molina's **Museo delle Palafitte** ( ☎ 0464 50 81 82; Via Lungolago 1; adult/child €2.50/1.50; ☼ 10am-6pm Jul & Aug, 9am-5pm Tue-Sun Mar-Jun & Sep-Nov) explores this past with a wealth of daggers, bronze pins, bellows and intricate headdresses. It also features *il nuovo villaggio* – a recreation of the stilt houses themselves. A few kilometres further west, the lake's main settlement **Pieve di Ledro** has more beaches and a cluster of hotels, *osterie* and shops selling cheeses and other local foods.

Lake Ledro is the springboard for **outdoor activities** ranging from hiking to sailing and canyoning to paragliding. It also has 200km of mountain-bike trails. Riva del Garda's tourist office (p203) can provide more information.

### ♥ BASTIONE // CLIMB TO A VENETIAN FORTRESS FOR STUNNING VIEWS

From the centre of Riva, the **Bastione** (admission free; open access) is the chalk-white castle clinging to sheer cliffs high above the west edge of town. The 3.5km hike to this picturesque ruin is as steep as it looks and leads up hairpin bends past oleanders, cypresses and wayside shrines. The castle was built by the Venetians in a desperate, and doomed, bid to hold onto power. A series of steps allows you to clamber over its three floors. Needless to say the views of a now tiny town, a big lake and even bigger mountains are superb. Pick up the (signed) path to the Bastione where Via Bastione joins Via Monte Oro.

## WATER SPORTS

Lake Garda has an unusual meteorological quirk – the winds that blow over its surface are almost as regular as clockwork. The Pelèr gusts from the north, lasts 12 hours and is normally done by 10am, while the Ora blows from the south between noon and sunset. Their predictability has ensured Riva, Torbole and Malcesine are magnets for windsurfers and sailors.

Fleets of operators provide tuition. **Surfsegnana** ( ☎ 0464 50 59 63; www.surfsegnana.it) operates from Lido di Torbole in Torbole and Porfina Beach in Riva del Garda. It runs sessions in windsurfing (one/three/seven three-hour lessons €68/180/330) and sailing (one/three/six two-hour lessons €70/185/305), and hires out equipment. So slip on a wetsuit then get to grips with winds like the less common Bali, which occasionally whips down from Monte Baldo, and the even trickier Ponale.

### GASTRONOMIC HIGHLIGHTS
### ♥ AL FORTE ALTO €€
☎ 0464 50 55 66; Via Castel Pedede 16, Nago; 5 courses €30; ☽ dinner daily, lunch Sat & Sun

This 19th-century Austro-Hungarian fort clinging to the cliffs above Torbole is a study in beautiful presentation, from the cream chairs dotting the barrel-vaulted dining room to the imaginative takes on Trentino cuisine. Look out for venison *ragù* with ricotta gnocchi, and a platter of six minidesserts that looks, almost, too good to eat.

### ♥ GIARDINO VERDI €€
☎ 0464 55 25 16; Piazza Giardino Verdi 4, Riva del Garda; meals €38; ☽ daily, year-round

More local flavours grace the menu of this little *ristorante* set on a shaded deck beside one of Riva's green squares. It's a place to sample gnocchi with white truffles, Parma ham with pears and Parmigiano Reggiano, and pork in white wine with spinach.

### ♥ RESTEL DE FER €€
☎ 0464 55 34 81; Via Restel de Fer 10, Riva del Garda; 4/6 courses €35/50; ☽ lunch & dinner daily Jul & Aug, lunch & dinner Thu-Tue Sep-Oct & Dec-Jun

Don't make any other plans for the evening – the restaurant at this family-run *locanda* (inn) is one to linger at. It feels like dropping by a friend's rustic-meets-swish house: expect worn leather armchairs, cooking pots, sleek chair covers and glinting blue glass. The menu might feature seasonal, local delicacies such as rabbit wrapped in smoked mountain ham, char with crayfish, and veal with Monte Baldo truffles – followed by the best Trentino cheese. Team each course with wine for only €10 more. Accommodation is also available (see p301), allowing you to really settle in for the night.

## EAST BANK

### MALCESINE

**pop 3640**

With the lake lapping right up to the tables of its harbourside restaurants and the vast ridge of Monte Baldo looming behind, Malcesine is quintessential Lake Garda.

Steep, narrow, cobbled streets fan from its ancient centre to complete the scene. As ever, pretty equals popular but you can dodge Malcesine crowds to explore its olive oil heritage and soar up a mountain for spectacular views.

## ESSENTIAL INFORMATION

**TOURIST INFORMATION //** Tourist office
( ☎ 045 740 00 44; www.malcesinepiu.it; Via Capitanato
6; 🕙 9.30am-12.30pm & 3-6pm Mon-Sat, 9.30am-
12.30pm Sun)

## EXPLORING MALCESINE

### ☙ MONTE BALDO // SWOOP UP A MOUNTAIN, STROLL AMONG OLIVE GROVES

The **Funivia Malcesine-Monte Baldo**
( ☎ 045 740 02 06; Via Navene Vecchia; adult/child
under 1.4m return €18/15; 🕙 8am-6.30pm) whisks
you 1760m above sea level in a noise-
less, dizzying glide. For the first 400m
the slopes are covered in oleanders and
olive and citrus trees – after that, oak and
chestnut take over.

Monte Baldo is actually a 40km-long
chain of mountains rather than a single
peak, and the ridges are the starting
point for **mountain-bike tours** and
**paragliding**, as well as **skiing** in the
winter. The tourist office can provide
more information. The views from the
top are remarkable – the entire lake and
surrounding mountains spread out like a
brightly coloured, textured map.

Getting off the cable car at the intermediate station of **San Michele** (Malcesine to San Michele one-way/return €5/9)
opens up some excellent hikes; pick up
a map from the tourist office before you
set out. The hour-long walk back to Malcesine along quiet roads and steep, rocky
mountain paths reveals a rural world of
hillside houses and working farms. Trails
wind beside olive groves where people
do what they have for centuries: prune,
burn lopped off branches and gather the
harvest.

It's a peaceful, authentic insight into
everyday Monte Baldo life, just metres
above hordes of holidaymakers. You
can taste the local olive oil back in town

at Consorzio Olivicoltori di Malcesine
(below).

### ☙ MALCESINE'S STREETS // GETTING LOST (AND FOUND) IN WINDING LANES

Malcesine's streets are cobbled with
thousands of lake pebbles, worn smooth
by countless feet. Although often
crowded – a startling 90% of the town's
income comes from tourism – the lanes
still contain hidden gems. From the ferry
landing beside the harbour, Via Capitanato heads north to **Palazzo dei Capitani**
(Via Capitanato; admission free; 🕙 10am-5pm).
This was home to Malcesine's governor
when it was ruled by the Republic of
Venice, largely between 1405 and 1797.
A single, large hall leads onto a secluded
waterfront terrace through an archway
that frames a beautiful lake view. The
entrance is a few doors up from the tourist office.

From Via Capitanato winding lanes
lead to the chalky-white **Castello Scaligero** ( ☎ 045 740 08 39; Via Castello; adult/child
€5/2; 🕙 9am-7pm). This late-6th-century
fortress was built by the Franks and
consolidated by the Della Scala family, who ruled Malcesine between 1277
and 1387. The poet Goethe thought the
castle so beautiful he sketched it, was
mistaken for a spy and was temporarily thrown into its cells – you can see
his drawings in the old gunpowder
magazine.

At the nearby **Consorzio Olivicoltori
di Malcesine** ( ☎ 045 740 12 86; Via Navene;
🕙 9am-1pm & 4.30-7pm) a local consortium
runs mini **olive oil tastings**. The 550
members all come from Malcesine's hills
and produce 400,000kg of olives and
75,000L of oil annually – only half of that
goes on sale. The oil is renowned for a
light, sweet, fruity taste with traces of

almonds. Prices of the cold-pressed extra virgin DOP oil range from €11 for 0.5L to €52 for 5L.

These explorations are likely to leave you gently lost, but as the streets all wind down to the water eventually, it's easy to find your way again soon.

## GASTRONOMIC HIGHLIGHTS

### 🍴 RE LEAR €€
☎ 045 740 06 16; Piazza Cavour; set meals €25, meals €36; ☷ Thu-Tue
Settle into Re Lear's red stone dining room and choose from antipasti of

grilled cheese with truffles or foie gras with wine jelly. Lobster tagliatelle and guinea fowl ravioli feature in the *primi*, while the *secondo* will have you considering duck breast, stewed escargot or mussels in saffron.

### 🍴 VECCHIA MALCESINE €€€
☎ 045 740 04 69; Via Pisort 6; meals €45-100; ☷ Thu-Tue

A short walk up a steep, cobbled street leads to a renowned *ristorante* with an elegant terrace and delightful lake views. Imaginative treatments of local ingredi-

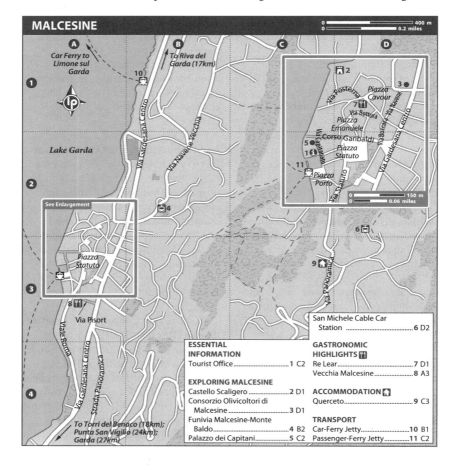

MALCESINE

Lake Garda

To Riva del Garda (17km)

Car Ferry to Limone sul Garda

See Enlargement

Piazza Statuto

Via Pisort

Viale Roma

Strada Panoramica

Via Gardesana Centro

Via Navene Vecchia

To Torri del Benaco (18km); Punta San Vigilio (24km); Garda (27km)

Piazza Cavour

Via Posterna

Via Bottura

Piazza Emanuele

Corso Garibaldi

Piazza Statuto

Piazza Porto

Via Statuto

Via Prealto

Via Gardesana Centro

| ESSENTIAL INFORMATION | |
|---|---|
| Tourist Office | 1 C2 |

| EXPLORING MALCESINE | |
|---|---|
| Castello Scaligero | 2 D1 |
| Consorzio Olivicoltori di Malcesine | 3 D1 |
| Funivia Malcesine-Monte Baldo | 4 B2 |
| Palazzo dei Capitani | 5 C2 |

| GASTRONOMIC HIGHLIGHTS | |
|---|---|
| Re Lear | 7 D1 |
| Vecchia Malcesine | 8 A3 |

| ACCOMMODATION | |
|---|---|
| Querceto | 9 C3 |

| TRANSPORT | |
|---|---|
| Car-Ferry Jetty | 10 B1 |
| Passenger-Ferry Jetty | 11 C2 |

San Michele Cable Car Station .................... 6 D2

ents ensure sardines come with caviar, langoustines with green peas and mint, and rabbit ravioli with onion fondue. Prices range from €45 for three courses (€60 with two wines) to €75 for seven courses (€100 with three wines).

## TORRI DEL BENACO

**pop 2850**
Picturesque Torri del Benaco is one of the most appealing stops on the eastern bank. A 14th-century castle overlooks a pint-sized harbour, while a handful of yacht masts sway in front of ivy-draped, 16th-century houses. The town also boasts one of the best hotels on the lake (see p301) and an evocative museum.

### ☙ IL CASTELLO SCALIGERO // CLAMBER UP TOWERS AND EXPLORE LAKE GARDA'S PAST

This atmospheric **museum** ( ☎ 045 629 61 11; Viale Frateli Lavanda 2; adult/child €3/1; ☙ 9.30am-12.30pm & 2.30-6pm Apr–mid-Jun & mid-Sep–Oct, 9.30am-1pm & 4.30-7.30pm mid-Jun–mid-Sep) packs a wealth of history into the rough stone walls of a 14th-century castle. The fortification was built in 1338 as part of the Della Scala family's attempts to fend off the Venetian Republic. Exhibits scattered around the castle's rooms explore the lake's traditional industries: fishing, olive oil production and lemon growing. Displays include boatbuilding tools, antique nets and a traditional flat-bottomed fishing gondola, as well as huge olive oil presses and the donkey-drawn sledges that were used to haul olive harvests down steep hill paths like those still found on Monte Baldo today (p207).

You can also stroll through a restored **lemon-house** (see the boxed text, p201), which dates from 1760 – it's crowded

with fragrant citrus trees and windfalls litter the floor. Finally, climbing the castle's main towers reveals Lake Garda's key income source today: those captivating lake views.

### ☙ RESTAURANT GARDESANA // DINE WATCHING THE SUN SET OVER THE LAKE

The artfully lit arches of Hotel Gardesana's **restaurant** ( ☎ 045 722 54 11; Piazza Calderini 20; pizzas €5-7, meals €35) make a romantic spot for dinner as the sun sinks over a pink-tinged lake and the distant mountains beyond. The food is understated but excellent – try the pappardelle with butter and sage, carpaccio with Parmigiano Reggiano, or perch in white wine with brioche croutons – although you may be distracted by the views.

## GARDA & PUNTA SAN VIGILIO

**pop 3800**
The bustling town of Garda stretches out beside a long lakefront promenade lined with restaurants and cafes, its cluster of lanes squeezing between the water and the main road. It lacks the obvious charm of some of its sister towns, but can boast Punta San Vigilio just to the north, which is home to a great beach, one of Lake Garda's best hotels and an utterly idyllic spot for a drink.

### EXPLORING GARDA & PUNTA SAN VIGILIO

### ☙ PUNTA SAN VIGILIO // SWIM OFF SOME OF LAKE GARDA'S BEST BEACHES

The leafy headland of Punta San Vigilio curls out into a crystal-blue lake 3km north of Garda. An avenue of cypress trees leads from the car park towards a

…rescent of bay backed by olive … The privately owned **Parco Baia** … Sirene ( ☎ 045 725 58 84; Punta San Vigilio; ⏲ 10am–7pm Apr–mid-May, 10am-8pm mid-May–early Jun, 9.30am-8pm early Jun–early Sep) has a beach with sun loungers, deckchairs and picnic tables arranged beneath the trees; there's also volleyball, table tennis and a children's play area. Prices are seasonal, and range from €5 to €11 per adult (€2 to €5 per child) per day.

Alternatively, from the parking place walk north a short distance and head off down the paths to a couple of smaller, quieter **public coves**. The tiny headland is also home to the plush Locanda San Vigilio (p301). Its excellent restaurant and bar (see right) are at the foot of a steep, roughly cobbled lane which winds to the lake from the end of the cypress avenue.

### ☘ MARKET DAY // BUY INTO AN AUTHENTIC SLICE OF LAKE LIFE

It's worth timing a visit to Garda to coincide with its exuberant **Friday market**, one of the biggest on the lake's eastern bank. Vans, awnings and stalls stretch south from the central Piazza Catullo in an apparently endless stream, providing the usual joyful medley of the exotic and the pragmatic. You can buy everything from saucepans to sunglasses, handbags to high heels and espresso cups to underwear. Look out too for fragrant Lake Garda lemons and jars of golden local honey. Arrive early and bag a pavement cafe table to watch the bustle at its best. For a list of Lake Garda's market days, see p198.

### GASTRONOMIC HIGHLIGHTS
#### ☘ SAN VIGILIO €€€
☎ 045 725 66 88; Punta San Vigilio; meals €80; ⏲ daily, year-round

In the restaurant of the Locanda San Vigilio the setting almost upstages the food. Dark beams, rustic tables, elegant tableware and crisp fabrics combine to bewitching effect. The sophisticated menu includes rabbit with wild fennel, lake-fish risotto, and quail with polenta and caramelised onion. For a special touch ask for a table in the open-sided loggia – a chance to dine suspended directly over the lake.

#### ☘ TAVERNA SAN VIGILIO €€
☎ 045 725 51 90; Punta San Vigilio; mains €14-25; ⏲ 10am-5.30pm

With tables strung out along Punta San Vigilio's tiny crab-claw harbour and vine-shaded chairs scattered all around, this is one of the most atmospheric bars on the lake. Taverna San Vigilio's salad-based menu includes lobster, veal with tuna sauce, and prosciutto with mozzarella. The candle-lit buffets (Friday and Saturday from mid-June, booking required, €45) are truly memorable, featuring a gourmet spread accompanied by superb wines, live music and stunning sunsets.

## BARDOLINO

### pop 6500

Prosperous Bardolino is a town in love with the grape. The scores of wineries that stack up in the hills behind it have made it rich, while its narrow streets are peppered with wine bars, first-rate eateries and shops selling local vintages by the bottle or the crate. It's a place to linger over a glass in an *osteria* before setting off into the hinterland to find your own favourite. Wine aside, Bardolino is also the springboard for the ancient walled village of Lazise and a museum focusing on olive oil.

## ESSENTIAL INFORMATION

**TOURIST INFORMATION // Tourist office**
( ☎ 045 721 00 78; www.tourism.verona.it; Piazzale
Aldo Moro; ⊙ 9am-6pm Apr-late Jun & Sep-Oct, 9am-
7pm late Jun-Aug, 10am-4pm Mon-Sat Nov-Mar)

## EXPLORING BARDOLINO

### ❦ STRADA DEL VINO // EXPLORE BARDOLINO'S RICH HISTORY OF WINE

More than 70 vineyards and wine cellars grace the gentle hills that roll east
from Bardolino's shores, many within
DOC and the even stricter DOCG quality boundaries (see p270). They produce
an impressive array of pink chiaretto,
ruby Classico, dry Superiore and young
Novello. One of the most atmospheric
ways to savour their flavours is a tutored
tasting at **Guerrieri Rizzardi** ( ☎ 045 621
04 09; www.guerrieri-rizzardi.com; Piazza Guerrieri 1;
⊙ shop 10am-1pm daily & 3-7pm Mon-Sat Apr-Oct,
9am-12.30pm Mon-Sat & 2.30-6pm Mon-Fri Nov-Mar)
in the centre of Bardolino. After a tour of
wine cellars full of cobweb-laced bottles,
relaxed tastings take place in the ancient
walled kitchen garden, with tables laid
out beside salad crops, an orangery and
a vineyard labyrinth. You get to sample
local olive oil, cheeses and ham, too.
Booking is required for these **tastings**
(€15; ⊙ 5pm Wed May-Oct); you can also sample some products in the shop.

The **Museo del Vino** ( ☎ 045 622 83 31;
www.zeni.it; Via Costabella 9; admission free; ⊙ 9am-
1pm & 2-7pm Mon-Fri, 9am-1pm & 2-6pm Sat & Sun
mid-Mar–Oct) is set inside the Zeni winery
on the outskirts of Bardolino. Rarely has
a museum smelt so good; rich aromas
accompany displays of wicker grape
baskets, cooper's tools, drying racks and
immense old wooden presses. Check to
see if the bottling plant is running – this
series of whirring, rotating, trundling
machines processes 3000 bottles an hour.

The museum visit includes free tastings
of Zeni's red, white and rosé wines or you
can pay to sample the more expensive
vintages, including barrel-aged Amarone.

To experience some authentic Bardolino atmosphere head for **La Bottega
del Vino** ( ☎ 348 604 18 00; Piazza Matteotti 46;
snacks €5, glass of wine from €2; ⊙ Tue-Sun), a no-
nonsense bar in the centre of town. Head
past the pavement tables and duck inside
for walls lined with bottles four deep and
a stream of lively banter between locals
and staff; a place to watch the world go
by while bottle after bottle is opened.

Bardolino is at its most Bacchic during
the **Festa dell'Uva e del Vino** in early
October, when the town's waterfront
fills with food and wine stands, as well as
musicians and dancers. The tourist office
stocks a Bardolino *Strada del Vino* map
of local producers.

### ❦ MUSEO DELL'OLIO D'OLIVA // SOAK UP LAKE GARDA'S OLIVE OIL HERITAGE

In this slick **museum** ( ☎ 045 622 90 47; www
.museum.it; Via Peschiera 54, Cisano; admission free;
⊙ 9am-12.30pm & 2.30-7pm Mon-Sat year-round,
9am-12.30pm Sun Mar-Dec) audiovisual displays
chart the history of olive oil production
in Lake Garda (see p195) and explain
how the crop is harvested today. Highlights include the huge mule-driven
presses, complete with immense wooden
corkscrew threads and large granite
millstones. Look out too for the circular sacks the oil paste was put in to be
crushed, and the early-20th-century olive
oil tins. Destined for Italian emigrants in
America, they feature evocative images
of their homeland – this is olive oil not
just as industrial heritage, but as a form
of cultural identity too. The museum is
2km south of Bardolino, beside the main
SS249 lake road.

LAKE GARDA, VERONA & MANTUA

## LAKE GARDA'S AMUSEMENT PARKS

The lake's lower eastern bank is home to larger-than-life dinosaurs, pirate ships, roller coasters and a dolphinarium at the kid-oriented **Gardaland** (☎ 045 644 97 77; www.gardaland.it; adult/child €35/29; ⏰ 10am-6pm Apr–mid-Jun & last 2 weeks of Sep, 9am-11pm mid-Jun–mid-Sep, 10am-6pm Sat & Sun Oct & Dec–1st week Jan).

To its north, **CanevaWorld** (☎ 045 696 99 00; www.canevaworld.it; Via Fossalta 1; adult/child aqua park & Movieland €31/25) features an **aqua park** (adult/child €23/18; ⏰ 10am-6pm mid-May–Jun & Sep, 10am-7pm Jul & Aug) and **medieval shows** (adult/child dinner & show €28/20; ⏰ 1-2 shows daily Apr–Sep) complete with medieval banquet. Within the same sprawling park is CanevaWorld's **Movieland Studios** (adult/child €23/18; ⏰ 10am-6pm Easter–Jun & Sep, 10am-7pm Jul & Aug, 10am-6pm Sat & Sun Oct), featuring stunt-packed action shows. Opening times vary slightly throughout the year, so check the website for details.

Both parks are just off the main lake road. Gardaland is 2km from Peschiera del Garda; CanevaWorld is a similar distance from Lazise. Free buses shuttle visitors to both parks from Peschiera del Garda train station.

### ♣ LAZISE // CIRCUMNAVIGATE AN ENTIRE 14TH-CENTURY WALLED TOWN

The picturesque town of Lazise, some 5km south of Bardolino, is relatively rare in that its encircling walls are almost intact; they're also full of interesting features. On the harbour's south side (opposite the ferry jetty) the cream stone Romanesque **San Nicolo** sits beside Via Castello. This heads right, towards the five towers of the **Rocca Scaligera** – look out for the huge hole in the north wall of its main tower, made by a canon during the 15th-century wars between Venice and Milan. The town's south gate is alongside. Known as the **Porta del Lion**, it features a bas-relief carving of the eponymous big cat, the symbol of the Venetian rulers who seized power in Lazise in 1405.

Via Rocca continues east beside the weathered town walls leading away from the main tourist drag and towards the town's **eastern gate**, which is dedicated to San Zeno; his images feature in a **mosaic** on the outer side. At the neighbouring neoclassical **Chiesa San Martino** leave the walls temporarily, head a few

steps down Via Chiesa, then right into Via Francesco Feliciano Scolari, through a couple of small squares and into Corso Cangrande, which again hugs the walls.

Lazise's final gate is **Porta Nuova**, 'new' in that it was built by the ruling Della Scala family in the 14th century. Look out for the mosaic of San Martino, complete with the castles of Lazise in the background. A few metres more leads back to the harbour. You could do the whole circumnavigation in 10 minutes flat, but picturesque alleyways, squares and shops provide plenty of appealing detours.

### GASTRONOMIC HIGHLIGHTS
#### ♣ CORTE SAN GIOVANNI €€
☎ 045 621 11 06; Piazza San Giovanni 8; pizzas €8; meals €32; ⏰ daily year-round

This is the kind of fabulous, friendly *ristorante* you'd love to fold right up, pack in a suitcase and smuggle back home. Legions of staff swirl past with plates of golden pasta scattered with truffle shavings, grilled *lavarello* made tangy with lemon, and cheese platters piled with Parmigiano Reggiano and Gorgonzola.

❤ **COSTADORO €€**

☎ 045 721 08 06; Via Costadoro; meals €27; ♥ Tue-Sun

The garden of this rustic trattoria in Bardolino's wine country is framed by rows of vines and the menu is laced with local flavours: linger over lake fish and polenta, macaroni with rabbit *ragù* or beef with Amarone sauce. It's best washed down with Bardolino wine – with the grapes growing this close, it's rude not to. Around 2km from the centre of Bardolino.

❤ **IL GIARDINO DELLE ESPERIDI €€**

☎ 045 621 04 77; Via Goffredo Mameli 1; meals €32; ♥ Wed-Mon

Bardolino's gourmets head for this intimate little *osteria* where sourcing local delicacies is a labour of love for its sommelier-owner. The intensely flavoured baked truffles with Parmigiano Reggiano are legendary, and the highly seasonal menu may also feature rarities like goose salami or guinea fowl salad. With 700 wines to choose from, 30 of those by the glass (€2.50 to €12), the stage is set for a meal to remember.

# VERONA

· · · · · ·

**pop 264,200**

**Verona is a city well versed in romance. Shakespeare was drawn to set *Romeo and Juliet* here and 400 years later its appeal is still strong. Narrow, secretive streets dart between buildings whose architecture alternates between medieval terraces, baroque facades and Renaissance palaces, their colours a palate of faded terracotta, yellow ochre and burnt sienna.**

**Verona has latched onto its Shakespearean legacy, but thankfully this is not just a city for the lovestruck. Its attraction also lies in a superbly preserved Roman arena, a sumptuous collection of art and a serene Renaissance garden. Whether revelling in the artistry of its world-class opera festival, the creativity of some inspired chefs or sipping a local Valpolicella in a snug *osteria*, Verona's charms are hard to resist.**

Verona is known as *piccola Roma* (little Rome) for its importance in imperial days, but its truly golden era came as a city state during the 13th and 14th centuries under the Della Scala family (also known as the Scaligeri) – a period noted for the savage family feuding that Shakespeare wrote about in his play. Between 1405 and 1797 Verona was ruled by Venice, before a spell under Austrian control, prior to the Unification of Italy in 1866.

## ESSENTIAL INFORMATION

**EMERGENCIES //** **Guardia Medica** (☎ 045 807 56 27; ♥ 8pm-8am) Medical services; the staff usually come to you. **Ospedale Civile Maggiore** (☎ 045 812 11 11; Piazza Aristide Stefani) Hospital northwest of Ponte Vittoria.

**TOURIST INFORMATION //** **Tourist office** (www.tourism.verona.it) Main tourist office (☎ 045 806 86 80; Via degli Alpini 9, Piazza Brà; ♥ 9am-7pm Mon-Sat, 9am-5pm Sun); Verona-Villafranca airport (☎ 045 861 91 63; ♥ 10am-4pm Mon & Tue, 10am-5pm Wed-Sat); Train station (☎ 045 800 08 61; ♥ 9am-7pm Mon-Sat)

## ORIENTATION

Verona is a 30km drive or 20-minute train trip from southern Lake Garda (see p221). Mantua lies 45km south. Buses leave for the centre from the main train

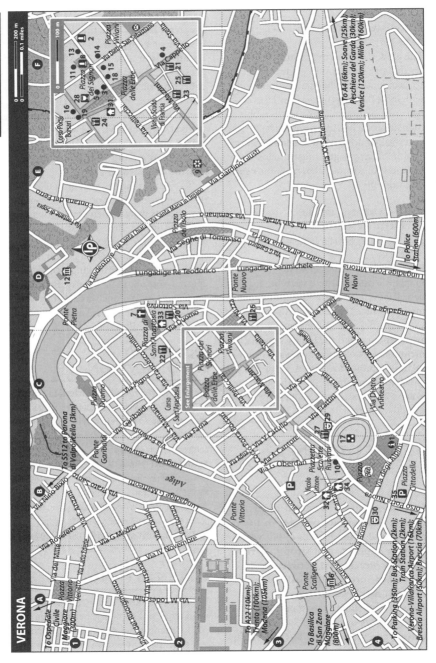

VERONA

station, Verona Porta Nuova, south of town (see p221). Alternatively walk north, past the bus station, and along Corso Porta Nuova to Piazza Brà, 2km away. Much of Verona's old city lies between Piazza Brà and a sharp bend of the river Adige.

# EXPLORING VERONA

Many sights are closed, or only open for a half-day, on Mondays. The excellent-value **Verona Card** (VC; 1/3 days €10/15) covers free entry into the main attractions and churches. It's available at sights and tobacconists and includes free use of the town's buses.

### ♥ ROMAN ARENA // WALK IN THE FOOTSTEPS OF GLADIATORS

The immense cream and pink arches of Verona's Roman **amphitheatre** ( ☎ 045 800 32 04; www.arena.it; Piazza Brà; free with VC, adult/student/child €6/4.50/1; ☉ 8.30am-7.30pm Tue-Sun, 1.30-7.30pm Mon Oct-Jun, 8am-3.30pm opera season mid-Jun–Aug) sweep across a large chunk of Piazza Brà, hugely impressive by day and beautifully floodlit at night. Built in the 1st century AD, this is the third-largest Roman amphitheatre in existence and originally seated 30,000 people. Over the centuries gladiatorial combat and public executions have taken place here; now it's the atmospheric setting for Ve-

rona's celebrated opera festival (p220). The arena is remarkably well preserved, despite a 12th-century earthquake. Cavernous honeycombed passages dripping with water lead out onto a dusty arena floor which is dwarfed by ranks of marble steps. A steep clamber to the top tier emphasises just how big this structure is and brings you out amongst the rooftops for expansive city views.

### ♥ CASTELVECCHIO // MARVEL AT THE PICK OF VERONA'S ART HERITAGE

This 14th-century **fortress** ( ☎ 045 806 26 11; Corso Castelvecchio 2; free with VC, adult/student/child €6/4.50/1; ☉ 9am-5pm Mon-Thu, 9am-1.30pm Sat, 2-7pm Sun), packed with statues, frescos, paintings, jewellery and armour dating from the medieval to the Renaissance periods, is an absolute treat for art lovers.

The first two rooms feature delicate medieval statuary, while room 7 has a vivid 14th-century painted panel of San Bartolomeo, partly picked out in gold leaf. Room 8 provides a fascinating insight into the fresco painting process; look out for the *sinopie* (underdrawing), in which the artist sketched out the design of the 14th-century *Cerchia di altichiero* (Coronation of the Virgin) before adding the final plaster layer. In these red and yellow ochre drawings you can spot the bearded men and cherubs that appear in the finished fresco, displayed alongside.

The heavily frescoed room 10 has a vibrant *Madonna of the Quail* by Pisanello dating from 1420, while room 12's sombre Flemish paintings include *Portrait of a Woman* by Rubens. In room 17, look out for the clearly recognisable Verona landmarks of the Piazza di Signori and the Della Scala palaces in the painted *predella* (altarpiece) depicting the *Storie di Santa Barbara* (Trials of St Barbara). All the exhibits are beautifully and simply displayed, and part of the appeal is exploring the fortress itself with its warren of passageways, courtyards and battlements – the views down onto the river Adige and the Ponte Scaligero, rebuilt after being destroyed in WWII, are superb.

## ♥ VERONA'S PIAZZAS // EMBARK ON AN ARCHITECTURAL ODYSSEY
### Piazza delle Erbe

Walking into Verona's main square is like walking into an opera set: sumptuous buildings tower on all sides, while the dramas of everyday life are played out in its pavement cafes and market stalls. The baroque carvings of the **Palazzo Maffei** frame the northwest end, topped by statues of Roman gods and book-ended by the 14th-century redbrick **Torre del Gardello**. To the right (east) weathered frescos line the **Casa Mazzanti**, a former Della Scala family residence. Separating Piazza delle Erbe from Piazza dei Signori is the **Arco della Costa**, beneath which a whale's rib is suspended. Legend says it will fall on

## 48 HOURS IN VERONA

### WALKING
Strolling around Verona's compact old city is a great way to begin feeling at home. A walk of a few hundred metres spans thousands of years, from the **Roman Arena** (p215) in Piazza Brà to the medieval palaces in **Piazza dei Signori** (opposite). Wandering the manicured Renaissance **Giardino Giusti** (opposite) reveals another era again, while joining the ritual **passeggiata** (p218) connects you with modern city life.

### THE ARTS
Top of the list are the exquisite paintings and sculptures at the **Castelvecchio** (p215), where treasures range from the medieval to the Renaissance. For sacred art in situ head to **Basilica di San Zeno Maggiore** (opposite) to admire Andrea Mantegna's delicate *Maestà della Vergine*. In the evening dodge the crowds aiming to recreate Juliet's balcony scene at **Casa di Giulietta** (p218), and instead join 14,000 others at the Roman Arena for a night of high drama and truly unforgettable open-air **opera** (p220).

### CULINARY EXPLORATIONS
Verona is packed with places to linger over lunch after a morning's sightseeing. The convivial **Al Pompiere** (p219) is popular with locals – trying to match them course for course is an experience in itself. Or try the atmospheric **Bottega del Vino** (p219), but be warned: a wine list this long makes it hard to leave. For dinner, **Il Desco** (p219) is stylish; **Al Carro Armato** (p219) is rustic; and, after you've enjoyed a pre-opera **picnic** (p219), the **Tre Marchetti** (p220) will feed you in style after the show.

the first 'just' person to walk beneath it. It's never fallen, not even on the various popes who have paraded beneath it.

### Piazza dei Signori

The entrance to the **Torre dei Lamberti** ( ☎ 045 927 30 27; free with VC, adult/child €6/1; ⏱ 9.30am-8.30pm Mon-Thu, 8.30am-10pm Fri-Sun, till midnight Jun–mid-Sep) is immediately after the Arco della Costa. This soaring, red and white tower was begun in the 12th century but only completed in 1463. A combination of lift and steps leads to massive bells and panoramic views down onto the city. The **Palazzo degli Scaligeri**, another Della Scala residence, sits opposite the Arco della Costa. To the left is the pale yellow **Loggia del Consiglio**, an arched, elegant Renaissance structure built in the 15th century as the city council chambers. In the middle of the piazza is a statue of **Dante**, who was given refuge in Verona when he was exiled from Florence in 1302.

The piazza's southeast side has arches leading into the brick and tufa stone **Palazzo della Ragione**, which dates from the Della Scala era. Next door the **Palazzo del Capitano** is fronted by a cobbled square with two huge round windows in the ground, which reveal the excavated Roman and medieval basements beneath. To the northeast loom the **Arche Scaligere**, the ornate, Gothic creamy-white funerary monuments of the Della Scala family.

### ❦ GIARDINO GIUSTI // LOSE YOUR WAY IN A RENAISSANCE LABYRINTH

Offering the perfect escape from Verona's tourist crowds, these tranquil **gardens** ( ☎ 045 803 40 29; Via Giardino Giusti 2; admission €6; ⏱ 9am-8pm Apr-Sep, 9am-sunset Oct-Mar) are tucked away on the east side of the river Adige. The lush greenery is alive with birdsong, soaring cypresses tower over clipped symmetrical hedges, classical statues peep from behind citrus trees, and stone seats are hidden among ivy-framed gazebos.

From the formal lower gardens, steps lead up a tower onto a compact wooded terrace with grandstand views over Verona's terracotta rooftops. The gardens were set out in 1570 by a knight of the Venetian Republic, Agostino Giusti, and past visitors have included Goethe, Emperor Franz Joseph and Mozart. Hunt out the massive stone face that was designed to have flames shooting out of it, and the charming, and surprisingly difficult, Renaissance labyrinth in the lower garden – a delightful place to become just a little lost. The gardens are a signed, 400m walk from Ponte Nuovo.

### ❦ SACRED ART // TOUR TWO OF VERONA'S BEST CHURCHES FOR FRESCOS

#### Basilica di San Zeno Maggiore

A masterpiece of Romanesque architecture, this **basilica** ( ☎ 045 59 28 13; Piazza San Zeno; free with VC, adult/child €2.50/free ⏱ 9am-6pm Mon-Sat, 1-6pm Sun Mar-Oct, 10am-1pm & 1.30-4pm Tue-Sat, 1-5pm Sun Nov-Feb) dates in part from the 12th century. Marble and red-brick stripes line a vast, echoing interior which features a magnificent rose window depicting the Wheel of Fortune. The highlight is Andrea Mantegna's exquisite *Maestà della Vergine* (The Majesty of the Virgin Mary), the triptych above the high altar. Evocative frescos dating from the 12th to the 15th century grace the walls. Look out for a delicate white Madonna of the Giotto school; a towering 12th-century St Christopher; and a Last Supper near the entrance, complete with scorpions on the tablecloth symbolising

Judas' betrayal. The basilica is dedicated to Verona's patron saint, San Zeno – you'll see his eerily lit tomb at the end of a forest of columns in the crypt. The basilica is 1.2km west of Piazza Brà; you can walk there along the riverfront from the Castelvecchio.

### Chiesa di Sant'Anastasia

The Gothic **Sant'Anastasia** (☎ 045 59 28 13; Piazza di Sant'Anastasia; free with VC, adult/child €2.50/free; ⏰ 9am-6pm Mon-Sat, 1-6pm Sun Mar-Oct, 10am-1pm & 1.30-4pm Tue-Sat, 1-5pm Sun Nov-Feb) stands near the centre of Verona. Started in 1290, it wasn't completed until the late 15th century. The pick of its numerous artworks is in the sacristy – a beautiful fresco by Pisanello of *San Giorgio che parte per liberare la donzella dal drago* (St George and the Dragon)

### PASSEGGIATA // JOIN THE LOCALS IN THEIR RITUAL EVENING STROLL

Verona's beauty makes Italy's traditional nightly promenade all the more appealing. A popular route starts amid the dramatic architecture of the beguiling **Piazza delle Erbe**, perhaps with an *aperitivo* at **Caffè Filippini** (p220). From there crowds surge up the narrow **Via Mazzini**, a street of pink marble pavements and boutique **shops**; a spot of retail therapy in Gucci, Mont Blanc, Armani or Ralph Lauren might be in order. Via Mazzini spills out onto **Piazza Brà**, where a string of pavement cafes overlooks the wide square and the rose stone arches of a **Roman arena** that glows in the evening sun. If you want to linger, **Le Cantine del'Arena** (☎ 045 802 63 73; Piazza Scalette Rubiani 1; meals €25, pizza €8) provides a good vantage point of the parading crowds and serves flavoursome, competitively priced food. On opera nights the *passeggiata* follows a slightly different timetable: it's traditional to promenade after the performance and before eating, so be prepared to join a mass pre-dinner stroll around 1am.

### MUSEO ARCHEOLOGICO // TAKE IN ROMAN RELICS AND PANORAMIC VIEWS

The trek to the top of this former convent is worth it for the views alone; from the terrace beside its frescoed chapel the whole city is laid out below. The convent is now home to Verona's archaeological **museum** (☎ 045 800 03 60; Regaste Redentore 2; free with VC, adult/child €4.60/1; ⏰ 8.30am-7.30pm Tue-Sun, 1.30-7.30pm Mon) and an engaging collection of Roman-era bronzes, beauti-

## ROMEO & JULIET IN VERONA

Shakespeare had no idea what he'd start when he set his (heavily derivative) tale of star-crossed lovers in Verona, but the city has seized the commercial possibilities with both hands – everything from *osterie* (wine bars) and hotels to embroidered kitchen aprons get the R&J branding. While the play's depiction of feuding families has genuine provenance, the lead characters themselves are fictional. Undaunted, in the 1930s the authorities settled on a house in Via Cappello (think Capulet) as Juliet's and added a 14th-century-style balcony and a bronze statue of our heroine. You can squeeze through the crowds at this **Casa di Giulietta** (☎ 045 803 43 03; Via Cappello 23; free with VC, adult/child €6/1; ⏰ 1.30-7.30pm Mon, 8.30am-7.30pm Tue-Sun) onto the balcony itself, or see the circus from the square below, a spot framed by a slew of scribbled love graffiti that doesn't compare well to the bard's sonnets.

fully carved friezes and brightly coloured mosaics. On the way in you also pass the crumbling ruins of Verona's 1st-century **Roman Theatre**.

# GASTRONOMIC HIGHLIGHTS

Central Verona teems with inviting little *osterie* and trattorias serving hearty Veronese cooking, with its emphasis on meats and thick sauces.

### ☙ AL CARRO ARMATO €€
☎ 045 803 01 75; Vicolo Gatto 2a; meals €25-30; ☺ Tue-Sun

The perfect example of a down-home Veronese *osteria*: rough timber benches, high ceilings and hearty local dishes like *tagliatelle con ragù* (a take on the so-called 'bolognaise sauce') and *tagliata di manzo* (a thin-sliced beef dish served with rocket).

### ☙ AL POMPIERE €€
☎ 045 803 05 37; Vicolo Regina d'Ungheria 5; meals €27-64; ☺ Tue-Sat & dinner Mon

The hams hanging from beams, the bottles lining the walls and an enormous array of local cheeses have made this trattoria a local institution – look out too for the *pompiere* (firefighter's) hat also on display. The menu bursts with local ingredients: try a plate of *bigoli con le sarde* (chunky spaghetti with sardines); some gutsy *pastissada de caval* (a horsemeat dish typical of Verona); oven-cooked pork with polenta or the *grande degustazione di formaggi* – a plate of six local cheeses that costs €40.

### ☙ BOTTEGA DEL VINO €€€
☎ 045 800 45 35; Vicolo Scudo di Francia 5; meals €44-55; ☺ Wed-Mon

At this age-old *osteria* your choice from an apparently endless wine list is served

with all the ceremony of an upmarket tasting session. Excellent food keeps those vintages company: try sea bass with balsamic vinegar and rosemary, fettucine with chicken liver, or polenta with gorgonzola and wafer-thin slices of lard.

### ☙ DIY €
For supplies for a **picnic** or pre-opera snack in the Roman Arena (see p220), pick up fresh fruit and veg from market stalls full of tomatoes, strawberries and melons in **Piazza delle Erbe**. The nearby **De Rossi** (☎ 045 800 24 89; Corso Porta Borsari 3) sells fresh bread, tempting pastries, marinated artichokes and plump olives, as well as mounds of homemade gnocchi and pasta. For meats, cheese and a rich waft of deli, stroll 50m northeast to **Albertini** (☎ 045 803 10 74; Corso Sant'Anastasia 41). Select your cuts and a bottle of local Soave or Valpolicella, and wonder why similar ingredients never taste quite this good at home.

### ☙ GREPPIA €€
☎ 045 800 45 77; Vicolo Samaritana 3; meals €36; ☺ Tue-Sun

Heading down an uninspiring dog-leg alley leads to one of Verona's hidden gems. Choose to eat in an intimate courtyard or cool, classy dining room, then enjoy mounds of buttery pasta followed by perfectly cooked meats and fish – try the veal with mushrooms and polenta or the *bresaola* (aged air-dried beef) with lemon and oil.

### ☙ IL DESCO €€€
☎ 045 59 53 58; Via Dietro San Sebastiano 7; meals €82-150; ☺ Mon-Sat Jul-Aug & Dec, Tue-Sat Jan–mid-June & Sep-Nov

What lies behind the green door? One of the best restaurants in Italy and an elegant option for meticulously prepared local cuisine. Dishes are refined takes on northern cooking, so expect pasta soup with oysters, braised beef with goose liver, and liquorice ice cream with caramel sauce.

### ♥ MAFFEI €€

☎ 045 801 00 15; Piazza delle Erbe 38; meals €45; ☺ daily

The tempting menu at this stylish *ristorante* includes Monte Veronese filo pastry parcels, saffron and asparagus risotto, braised beef in Valpolicella sauce, and sweet pumpkin strudel with white chocolate and cardamom. Dine inside where it's all polished oak and stained glass, or eat in the cobbled courtyard, surrounded by the baroque pillars of the Palazzo Maffei.

### ♥ TRE MARCHETTI €€

☎ 045 803 04 63; Vicolo Tre Marchetti 19; meals €37; ☺ Mon-Sat

Just yards from the Roman Arena, the Tre Marchetti is ideal for a post-opera meal – its sky-blue dining room, Itali-

anate murals and gold-leaf vine leaves lend it the air of a stage set. It's been a restaurant since the 1400s and traditional dishes include pumpkin risotto with Amarone, and pasta with hare *ragù*, but the king prawns flambéed in Armagnac are tempting too.

## NIGHTLIFE

### ♥ CAFFÈ FILIPPINI

☎ 045 800 45 49; Piazza delle Erbe 26; ☺ 8am-2am Thu-Tue

Where else to be on a warm evening but at an outdoor table at this classic Verona bar sipping the house speciality, a Filippini (mix of vermouth, gin, lemon and ice)? On Friday and Saturday night this and adjacent bars fill to bursting with folks quaffing wine and cocktails.

### ♥ TEATRO FILARMONICO

☎ 045 800 51 51; www.arena.it; Via dei Mutilati 4

This 18th-century theatre just southwest of Piazza Brà is run by the Arena

---

## VERONA'S OPERA FESTIVAL

Even those normally immune to arias will be swept up in the occasion. On balmy summer nights, when 14,000 music lovers fill the Roman Arena and light their candles at sunset, expect goosebumps even before the performance starts. The **festival** ( ☎ 045 800 51 51; www .arena.it; Via Dietro Anfiteatro 6), which runs from mid-June to the end of August, was started in 1913 and is now the biggest open-air lyrical music event in the world. It draws performers such as Placido Domingo, and the staging is legendary – highlights have included Franco Zeffirelli's lavish productions of *Carmen* and *Aida*.

Prices rise at weekends and range from €18 to €21 on unreserved stone steps and €183 to €198 on the central gold seats. Seats in the stalls start at €116, while numbered seats on the stone steps cost €59 to €104, becoming more expensive closer to the stage. Some regular opera goers argue that gold seats aside, the views and the acoustics can be as good from the cheaper stone steps as they are from some of the stalls. Performances start around 9pm with locals booking their dinner table for after the show. Tucking into a pre-show picnic on the unreserved stone steps is fine, so decant that wine into a plastic bottle (glass and knives aren't allowed), arrive early, rent a cushion and prepare for an utterly unforgettable evening.

di Verona. Ballet, classical music and opera dominate the program, but you might just as easily come across a jazz night.

# TRANSPORT

## TO/FROM THE AIRPORT

**Verona-Villafranca** ( ☎ 045 809 56 66; www .aeroportoverona.it) is 16km outside the city and is linked to Verona Porta Nuova train station by APTV bus (€4.50, 20 minutes, every 20 minutes from 6am to 11pm). Verona-Villafranca has direct links with airports all over Italy and some European cities, including Amsterdam, Barcelona, London and Vienna. Ryanair flies in from several cities to **Brescia airport** (Aeroporto Gabriele d'Annunzio; ☎ 030 965 65 99; www.aeroportobrescia.it) 50km west of Verona. **Buses** (www.cgabrescia.it) connect Verona Porta Nuova train station with Brescia airport (€11, 45 minutes).

## GETTING AROUND

**CAR //** Verona is at the intersection of the A4 auto-strada between Milan and Venice (exit at Verona East) and the A22 between Modena and Trento (exit at Verona North). Southern Lake Garda is 30km away.

**PARKING //** The centre of Verona is restricted to traffic. Useful park and rides fringe the city, some as cheap as €5 a day. The nearest car park to the city centre is 400m south of Piazza Brà at Piazza Cittadella (per hour/day €2/14).

**TRAIN //** Verona's rail links include those with Milan, Mantua, Modena, Florence and Rome. Regular services also connect with Austria, Switzerland and Germany. Lake Garda is only a short hop away, with hourly links to Desenzano del Garda (€9, 20 minutes).

**BUS //** Verona's bus and main train station are both at Porta Nuova. **AMT** (www.amt.it) bus numbers 11, 12, 13 and 51 (numbers 90, 92, 93 and 98 on Sunday) shuttle between the train station and Piazza Brà (hourly tickets €1). Buy tickets from newsagents and tobacconists before you board.

# AROUND VERONA

Verona's hinterland is like a dictionary of wine. Exploring to the north leads to the vineyards of the Valpolicella, to the east lie the white-wine makers of Soave, while to the west are Lake Garda's delicious Bardolino reds (see p210).

## ♥ STRADA DEL VINO // MEANDERINGS IN WINE TERRITORY
### Valpolicella

Wine has been made in these hills since Roman times and today Valpolicella produces some of Italy's most renowned reds. A key grape is corvina, which adds a distinctive cherry note and rich colour.

The best way to explore is to get behind the wheel and follow the SS12 highway northwest out of town. At the turning for **Parona di Valpolicella** a warren of narrow country lanes straggle north. About 10km northwest, **San Pietro in Cariano** has a Pro Loco **tourist office** ( ☎ 045 770 19 20; www.valpolicellaweb.it; Via Ingelheim 7; ☙ 9.30am-1pm & 1.30-5.30pm Mon-Fri, 9am-1pm Sat), which can advise on vineyards to visit and has leaflets on local wineries and accommodation, as does the tourist office in Verona.

Vineyards dominate a countryside sprinkled with villages and the occasional 16th-century villa and Romanesque church. From San Pietro heading northeast leads past a vineyard-carpeted valley to **Marano di Valpolicella**. As you continue north towards **Fosse**, the road rises towards the Monti Lessini mountains. From Fosse you could bend back south through sleepy **Breonio** and on to **Molina** and the cool waterfalls of the **Parco delle Cascate** ( ☎ 045 772 01 85;

www.cascatemolina.it; adult/child €5/3; ☒ 9am-7.30pm Apr-Sep, 10am-6pm Sun Mar & Oct).

Back down in the south of the valley, a few kilometres northwest of San Pietro, **Gargagnano** is especially known for that smoothest of Valpolicella wines, Amarone. From here a 2km uphill detour to **San Giorgio** is a must. At the pretty hill village's heart is the early Romanesque **Pieve di San Giorgio** (☎ 045 770 15 30; ☒ 8am-5pm), with frescos dating from the 11th century and a wonderfully crooked cloister. The nearby **Trattoria Dalla Rosa Alda** (☎ 045 680 04 11; meals €35-40; ☒ Mon-Sat, closed dinner Mon) serves fine local fare laced with truffles, mushrooms and wild asparagus, but the speciality, fittingly, is beef braised in Amarone wine.

### Soave

From the reds of Valpolicella and on to the whites of Soave, a village and wine district some 30km east. The Della Scala family expanded Soave's medieval **Castello** (☎ 045 68 00 36; adult/child €4.50/3; ☒ 9am-noon Tue-Sun year-round, 3-6.30pm Tue-Sun Apr–mid-Oct, 3-5pm Tue-Sun mid-Oct–Mar), a magnificent, soaring storybook ramble of crenellated walls, courtyards and a central tower. It's a short, signed walk from the village centre through gardens and vineyards.

To savour some Soave over a plate of excellent pasta, settle down in the medieval vaults of **Enoteca Il Drago** (☎ 045 768 06 70; Piazza Antenna 1; meals €28-39; ☒ Tue-Sun). The *bigoli con pomodorini, lardo di Colonnata ed erba cipollina* (fat spaghetti with cherry tomatoes, bacon and spring onion) is fabulous.

For more information on Soave's vineyards contact **Consorzio Tutela Vini Soave** (☎ 045 7681578; www.ilsoave.com) or check out www.stradadelsoave.com.

# MANTUA
······

**pop 47,650**
**As serene as the three lakes it sits beside, Mantua (Mantova) is home to sumptuous ducal palaces and a string of atmospheric, cobbled squares. The city allows you to trace a timeline of the best in Italian art, from austere medieval frescos and soaring Gothic facades to rich Renaissance paintings and ornate baroque interiors. But Mantua is also a city in which to experience an ideal slice of modern Italian life. Relaxed, cultured and charming, its vibrant streets are home to restaurants serving up distinctive local delicacies, while its lakes and waterfront promenades offer the chance to explore by boat and by bike.**

Mantua was settled by the Etruscans in the 10th century BC and prospered under Roman rule. The poet Virgil was born just outside the modern town in 70 BC. The city fell to the Gonzaga dynasty in 1328, under whose rule it flourished, attracting the likes of Petrarch and Rubens. The golden days of 'La Gloriosa' ceased when Austria took control in 1708 and ruled (aside from the Napoleonic interlude in the late 1700s) until 1866, when Mantua joined Italy.

## ESSENTIAL INFORMATION

**EMERGENCIES //** Hospital (☎ 0376 20 11; Via Albertoni 1)
**TOURIST INFORMATION //** Tourist office (☎ 0376 43 24 32; www.turismo.mantova.it; Piazza Mantegna 6; ☒ 9am-6pm Apr-Sep, 9am-5pm Oct-Mar)

# ORIENTATION

Mantua sits on an open plain 45km south of Verona and 55km south of Lake Garda. The compact old city is framed by Lake Superiore, Lake Mezzo and Lake Inferiore, which are effectively glorified widenings of the river Mincio. The centre is 800m east of the train station, up Via Solferino e San Martino and Via Fratelli Bandiera.

# EXPLORING MANTUA

## ❦ PALAZZO DUCALE // LOSE YOURSELF AMID AN EXTRAORDINARY ARRAY OF ART

The 32,000-sq-metre **Palazzo Ducale** ( ☎ 0376 22 48 32; www.mantovaducale.it; Piazza Sordello 40; adult/child €6.50/3.25; ⏰ 8.30am-7pm, last entry 6.20pm Tue-Sun) was the seat of the ruling Gonzaga family from the 14th to the 18th centuries. Its 500 rooms, three squares and 15 courtyards occupy a huge section of the city's northeastern corner. In an orgy of self-aggrandisement, the Gonzagas commissioned the cream of the artists of each era to produce pieces – the result is some 40 display rooms featuring a feast of works by Pisanello, Giulio Romano, Andrea Mantegna and Rubens. You have to **book** ( ☎ 041 241 18 97) to see the biggest draw – the wonderful mid-15th-century frescos by Mantegna in the **Camera degli Sposi** (Bridal Chamber). His playful trompe l'œil oculus features cherubs apparently just managing to hang onto a painted balcony, clouds that scud across the sky and a tub of greenery which looks as if it's about to fall on the viewer below. For conservation reasons visitor numbers are limited to 1500 a day.

The palace's first room features a painting depicting a key moment in the Gonzaga's fortunes: the defeat in 1328 of their rivals, the Bonacolsi family. A few rooms further on the **Sala del Pisanello** has fragments of Pisanello frescos dating from 1430, recounting tales of Arthurian knights. Some scenes are half finished, revealing fascinating preliminary sketches in red and black. Other highlights include the cream and gold **Galleria degli Specchi** (Gallery of Mirrors), an early-17th-century confection of reflective glass, gilt and vibrant frescos, and the golden mazelike ceiling in the **Stanza del Labirinto**. Look out too for the charming, gilt-heavy **Corridoio dei Mori** (Corridor of the Moors); the **Camera dello Zodiaco**, with its magnificent deep-blue ceiling and constellations picked out in gold; and the 18th-century **Sala dei Fiumi** (Room of Rivers), a Habsburg-era folly with artificial grottoes covered in shells and mosaic.

## ❦ PALAZZO TE // WALK AMONG GIANTS; DECODE RENAISSANCE LOVE MESSAGES

Playful motifs, encoded symbols and stunning frescos fill the rooms of this opulent 16th-century **palace** ( ☎ 0376 32 32 66; Viale Te; adult/child €8/2.50; ⏰ 1-6pm Mon, 9am-6pm Tue-Sun). It was built by Giulio Romano on the orders of Federico II Gonzaga as a suburban villa where the duke could meet his mistress, Isabella Boschetti, and a playboy theme crops up repeatedly.

The second room, the **Camera delle Imprese** (Room of the Devices) features a number of 'devices'. During the Renaissance symbolic devices, usually a picture, often featured a motto (or 'soul'), and were used to encode the ideals, virtues or actions of the commissioner. Look out for Federico's device, a salamander, accompanied by the soul:

LAKE GARDA, VERONA & MANTUA

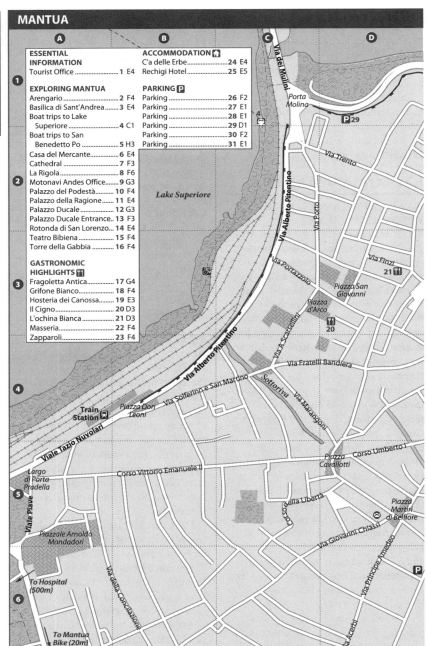

# MANTUA

**ESSENTIAL INFORMATION**
Tourist Office ........................ **1** E4

**EXPLORING MANTUA**
Arengario ............................... **2** F4
Basilica di Sant'Andrea ....... **3** E4
Boat trips to Lake
 Superiore ........................ **4** C1
Boat trips to San
 Benedetto Po ................. **5** H3
Casa del Mercante ................ **6** E4
Cathedral ............................... **7** F3
La Rigola ............................... **8** F6
Motonavi Andes Office ....... **9** G3
Palazzo del Podestà .......... **10** F4
Palazzo della Ragione ....... **11** E4
Palazzo Ducale ................... **12** G3
Palazzo Ducale Entrance ... **13** F3
Rotonda di San Lorenzo .... **14** E4
Teatro Bibiena .................... **15** F4
Torre della Gabbia ............. **16** F4

**GASTRONOMIC HIGHLIGHTS**
Fragoletta Antica ............... **17** G4
Grifone Bianco ................... **18** F4
Hosteria dei Canossa ......... **19** E3
Il Cigno ............................... **20** D3
L'ochina Bianca .................. **21** D3
Masseria ............................. **22** F4
Zapparoli ............................. **23** F4

**ACCOMMODATION**
C'a delle Erbe ..................... **24** E4
Rechigi Hotel ...................... **25** E5

**PARKING**
Parking ............................... **26** F2
Parking ............................... **27** E1
Parking ............................... **28** E1
Parking ............................... **29** D1
Parking ............................... **30** F2
Parking ............................... **31** E1

*Lake Superiore*

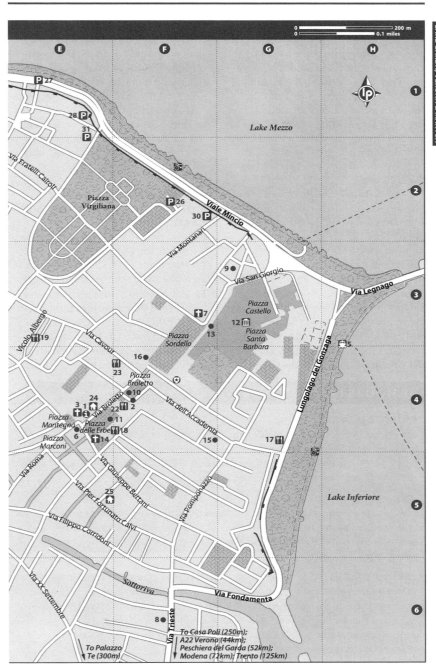

'*quod hic deest, me torquet*' (what you lack, torments me). This plays on Federico's notoriously passionate nature when compared to the cold-blooded salamander. There's also a nod to the surname of Federico's mistress, with a play on the word for wood (*bosco*) in a device depicting love holding a green tree and a dry tree barring the way to a wood. Here Federico's life (the green tree) or death (the dry one) depends on access to the wood (Boschetti).

In the **Sala dei Cavalli** (Room of the Horses), six life-sized stallions gaze from frescoed walls, representing Federico's hobby of breeding racehorses. Some of the best frescos lie in the **Camera di Amore e Psiche** (Chamber of Cupid and Psyche), where the palace's amorous theme is far from subtle – here erotic images of frolicking Gods, nymphs and satyrs fill the walls and ceiling. The most impressive room though is the overwhelming **Camera dei Giganti** (Chamber of the Giants).

Here towering painted figures represent rebel giants being punished for an assault on Mount Olympus. Every conceivable space is covered by collapsing pillars and immense struggling, dying giants, while ranks of gods and goddesses look on from the clouds. Look out too for the ancient graffiti on one wall – some dates from the 16th century – which has been retained for its historical value.

☙ **TEATRO BIBIENA // RELIVE MOZART'S GLORY DAYS AT THIS BAROQUE GEM**
If ever a theatre was set to upstage the actors, it's the 18th-century **Teatro Bibiena** ( ☎ 0376 32 76 53; Via dell'Accademia 47; adult/child €2/1.20; ☉ 9.30am-12.30pm & 3-6pm Tue-Sun). Its design is highly unusual: a bell-shaped four storeys of intimate, gilded balconies interspersed with tiny candelabra-lined curving walls. The theatre's shape was specifically intended to allow its patrons to be seen – balco-

## 48 HOURS IN MANTUA

### PASSEGGIATA
You can get the measure of Mantua by strolling its four central, cobbled squares, drinking in the **architecture** (opposite) along the way. Feel at home by watching the *passeggiata* from one of the many pavement cafes in **Piazza delle Erbe** (opposite) or join local families strolling the **promenades** (p229) beside Lake Inferiore.

### ART
You could spend two whole days in the **Palazzo Ducale** (p223) and still not be able to take in all its art. In **Palazzo Te** (p223) the coded love messages in the Camera delle Imprese are worth lingering over, while the extraordinary Camera dei Giganti delivers art that overwhelms.

### TAKING TIME OUT
**Teatro Bibiena** (above) is a spot to sit and wonder at an opulent theatrical gem. Its antithesis is a short walk away; the pared-down interior of **Rotonda di San Lorenzo** (opposite) is an intimate, hushed sacred space. Or settle back and let the sights come to you – on the **boat trip** (p228) to San Benedetto Po, reed beds, ancient floodgates and sleepy towns float by.

LAKE GARDA, VERONA & MANTUA

nies even fill the wall behind the stage. The whole confection is only dimly lit and when combined with the hushed atmosphere the effect is magical. Just a few weeks after it opened in 1769, the theatre hosted a concert by the 14-year-old Wolfgang Amadeus Mozart. It's undoubtedly one of Mantua's hidden gems, and today you can wander the stage, peek into a box, settle back into one of the plush velvet chairs and imagine past concerts.

### ❦ ARCHITECTURAL PASSEGGIATA // STROLL PAST BUILDING STYLES SPANNING SIX CENTURIES

The centre of Mantua is like a giant alfresco museum of architecture. The old city is made up of four interlocking squares, from north to south: Piazza Sordello, Piazza Broletto, Piazza delle Erbe and Piazza Mantegna. All four fill with market stalls on a Thursday morning. **Piazza Sordello** is the oldest and was probably the location of the Etruscan town. The existing layout is down to the Gonzagas whose immense living quarters, fronted by the Palazzo Ducale (p223), frame the east side. Sideways onto the palace, the towering, creamy **cathedral** sports three styles: a late-baroque facade (c 1750), a Gothic left side and a Romanesque belfry. At the square's southwest corner the flat-fronted, red-brick **Torre della Gabbia** dates from the 13th century. Look out for the *gabbia* (cage) dangling from one side – people who'd offended the authorities were incarcerated in it, legend has it sometimes for months.

Heading through the archway leads to **Piazza Broletto** and the **Palazzo del Podestà**, complete with its tower and coat of arms. Once home to the city's highest official, it also features a white

stone shrine to **Virgil**, depicting the poet sitting at his desk. The brick arch to the left, the **Arengario**, bears evidence of more medieval Mantuan punishments. Prisoners were suspended from the iron rings in the ceiling and the ropes pulled taught; a torture known as *squassi di corda*.

The next square, **Piazza delle Erbe**, is south again; its arcaded **Palazzo della Ragione** was built in 1250 as the town court. The 15th-century tower at the south end features a clock which signals phases of the moon and signs of the zodiac. Mantua's oldest church, the 11th-century **Rotonda di San Lorenzo** ( ☎ 0376 32 22 97; Piazza delle Erbe; admission free; ◷ 10am-1pm & 3-6pm Mon-Fri, 10am-6pm Sat & Sun), sits just below street level alongside. In this tiny, dimly lit sanctuary everything, including the balcony, arches and floor, is made of a weathered red brick, while the walls are studded with fresco fragments. Outside, a sharp right leads past the 15th-century **Casa del Mercante**. Look out for the stone carvings depicting the things it used to sell: wool, buckles and buttons. Next door is the diminutive **Piazza Mantegna**, dominated by the classical facade of **Basilica di Sant'Andrea** (below).

### ❦ BASILICA DI SANT'ANDREA // SEE THE SITE OF MANTUA'S HOLIEST RELIC

This towering **basilica** ( ☎ 0376 32 85 04; Piazza Andrea Mantegna; admission free; ◷ 8am-noon & 3-7pm Mon-Fri, 10.30am-noon & 3-6pm Sat, 11.45am-12.15pm & 3-6pm Sun) safeguards the golden vessels said to hold earth soaked by the blood of Christ. Longinus, the Roman soldier who speared Christ on the cross, is said to have scooped up the earth and buried it in Mantua after leaving Palestine. Today, these containers

LAKE GARDA, VERONA & MANTUA

## ACCOMMODATION

From ducal palaces and elegant lakeside villas to snug *alberghi* (hotels), this region's got the lot. Booking is essential in July and August, when prices also rise – especially for Verona's opera festival. In Lake Garda rooms with lake views cost more; specify if you want one. There's in-depth coverage in the Accommodation chapter (p299), but here are some highlights of the region:

★ **Agli Angel** (p299) History meets high design at this *locanda* (inn) in an elegant Lake Garda town.

★ **Gardesana** (p301) A gorgeous, great-priced lakeside hotel beloved by statesmen, actors and kings.

★ **San Vigilio** (p301) Effortlessly elegant sumptuousness hidden away on a lake-framed headland.

★ **Colomba d'Oro** (p302) Sink into opulent, affordable luxury in this central Verona hotel.

★ **Casa Poli** (p302) A warm welcome and ultracool rooms combine at Mantua's oasis of boutique chic.

rest beneath a marble octagon in front of the altar and are paraded around Mantua in a grand procession on Good Friday. Ludovico II Gonzaga commissioned Leon Battista Alberti to design the basilica in 1472. Its vast, arched interior is free from pillars and has just one sweeping central aisle, which is dotted with frescos, gilded ceiling bosses and columns cleverly painted to look like carved stone.

The first chapel on the left as you go in contains the tomb of the celebrated fresco artist Andrea Mantegna, the man responsible for the splendours in the Palazzo Ducale's Camera degli Sposi (p223). The chapel is beautifully lit and also contains a painting of the Holy Family and John the Baptist, attributed to Mantegna and his school.

### ❧ BOAT TOURS // CRUISE ON A LAKE SMOTHERED IN LOTUS FLOWERS

Bordered on three sides by water, Mantua offers plenty of opportunities for boat trips. Tours offered by **Motonavi Andes** ( ☎ 0376 32 28 75; www.motonaviandes .it; Via San Giorgio 2) include a summertime cruise on **Lake Superiore** (Monday to Saturday €9, Sunday €10; 1½ hours) which skirts lotus flowers, reed beds and heron roosts, and provides great city views. The 1½-hour cruise departs from alongside Porta Molina.

The trip to **San Benedetto Po** (one-way/return Monday to Saturday €13/18, Sunday €15/20; 2½ hours one-way) floats past floodgates and the Mincio natural park. This sleepy town is home to a Benedictine **abbey** ( ☎ 0376 62 00 25; Piazza Matteotti; church free, museum €2; ☉ church 7.30am-12.30pm & 3-7pm, cloisters 8am-7pm) that was founded in 1007. Little remains of the original buildings, although the Chiesa di Santa Maria still sports a 12th-century mosaic. Don't miss the Correggio fresco, which was discovered in the refectory in 1984. The last boat back from San Benedetto is usually around 4pm. The trip leaves Mantua from the jetty on Lungolago dei Gonzaga.

## ☙ LAKEFRONT PROMENADES // STROLL, CYCLE OR PICNIC BESIDE TRANQUIL WATERWAYS

On a sunny day the people of Mantua head for the waterfront, where grassy banks are thronged with wildfowl, people fishing and picnicking families. Each of the city's three lakes has a distinct style. The compact shore of **Lake Mezzo**, complete with the child-friendly gadgets of the **Parco dell Scienza** (outdoor science park), is the most crowded; the quieter path beside **Lake Superiore** meanders amid reed beds and wading birds before petering out; while the shore of **Lake Inferiore** brings broad views and a sense of space. At all three you'll encounter waterside snack bars in which to enjoy a cool drink and watch the world and the water drift by.

You can rent **bikes** from **La Rigola** ( ☎ 0376 36 66 77; Via Trieste 7; per day from €10), near the cycle path; otherwise try **Mantua Bike** ( ☎ 0376 22 09 09; Viale Piave 22; per day €8), 400m south of the train station. The tourist office stocks booklets in English detailing cycling itineraries along the Po river, in the **Parco del Mincio** ( ☎ 0376 36 26 57) and around the lakes.

# GASTRONOMIC HIGHLIGHTS

Mantua's most famous dish is *tortelli di zucca* (sweet, melt-in-your-mouth pumpkin-stuffed cushions of pasta). Pork also features on many menus; look out for *salumi* (salt pork), pancetta (salt-cured bacon), *prosciutto crudo* (salt-cured ham) and *risotto alla pilota* (risotto with minced pork). Sweet specialities include *torta di tagliatelle* (an unusual blend of crunchy tagliatelle, sugar and almonds) and *torta sbrisolona* (a hard biscuit with almonds).

Open-air cafes abound on Piazzas Sordello, Broletto and delle Erbe.

## ☙ FRAGOLETTA ANTICA €€

☎ 0376 32 33 00; Piazza Arche 5; meals €35; ⏰ Tue-Sun

Set just back from the waterfront, this rustic place serves tasty dishes such as *risotto alla pilota,* and gnocchi with ricotta, burnt butter and Parmigiano-Reggiano. The dining room is warm, cosy and filled with heavy wood and lined with bottles of wine.

## ☙ GRIFONE BIANCO €€

☎ 0376 36 54 23; Piazza delle Erbe 6; meals €47; ⏰ Thu-Mon

Several stellar restaurants congregate on Piazza delle Erbe, but Grifone is particularly elegant. Damask tablecloths, heavy silverware and sparkling glasses sit beneath the Palazzo della Ragione's ancient red-brick colonnades. Its dishes also make it stand out, including slithers of spicy local salami, creamy risotto with asparagus and tomatoes, and a tasty pike with salsa and polenta.

## ☙ HOSTERIA DEI CANOSSA €€

☎ 0376 22 17 50; Vicolo Albergo 3; meals €34; ⏰ Wed-Mon

A tiny, pebbled terrace fronts this local gem, and its snug dining room is framed by red-brick walls. Dishes packed with flavour feature on the menu – try the risotto with mushrooms and truffles; fillet of beef with balsamic vinegar; or Mantuan specialities including *asino* (donkey) with polenta. Team the lot with hard-to-find Lombard wines.

## ☙ IL CIGNO €€€

☎ 0376 32 71 01; Piazza d'Arco 1; meals €52; ⏰ Wed-Sun

The building is as beautiful as the food: a lemon-yellow facade dotted with faded olive-green shutters, and a terracotta *cigno* (swan) above the door. Inside Mantua's gourmets tuck into pumpkin risotto, poached cod with polenta or veal in white wine, perhaps followed by pungent goats' cheese with tomatoes. The extensive wine list includes fine Bardolino vintages.

### ❦ L'OCHINA BIANCA €€

☎ 0376 32 37 00; Via Finzi 2; meals €36; ☺ Tue-Sun
Stone floors, rustic rugs and a door framed by painted vines give this respected *osteria* a homely feel. Quality, seasonal ingredients help create dishes full of regional flavours; try the *pappardelle con frutti di mare* (seafood pasta) or tuna with peppers, tomatoes and roast potatoes. Save room though for the rich chocolate tart, laced with orange sauce.

### ❦ MASSERIA €€

☎ 0376 36 53 03; Piazza Broletto 7; meals €36; ☺ lunch Fri-Tue, dinner Thu-Tue)
Masseria's supremely sweet *tortelli di zucca* is among the best in town; other house specialities include Mantuan beef stew with Lambrusco and polenta, and platters piled with local cheeses and dollops of mustard. Choose to eat in the cobbled square or in a 13th-century dining room overlooked by a 15th-century fresco that is the oldest depiction of the city in existence.

### ❦ ZAPPAROLI €

☎ 0376 32 33 45; Via Cavor 49
A one-stop-shop for all your picnic needs. The counters of this deli are crammed with delights, from the mounds of marinated olives, oil-soaked artichokes and local cheese to salamis, roast chickens and hanging hams. Regional wines line the shelves and there are speciality breads and local pastries

too. Stock up, then join the locals beside the grassy lakeshores for an alfresco meal with a view (see p229).

## TRANSPORT

**CAR //** Mantua is just west of the A22 Modena–Verona–Trento autostrada; the best exit is Mantua North. The city is 45km south of Verona and around 50km south of Lake Garda.

**PARKING //** Much of old Mantua is a traffic-restricted zone. There is free parking along the city's northern lake road (Viale Mincio) and to the south of the city along Viale Isonzo, near Palazzo Te.

**TRAIN //** Direct trains link Mantua with Verona (€3, one hour, hourly) and Milan (€13, two hours, every two hours). The trip to Lake Garda's Peschiera del Garda train station (€5, 1½ hours, hourly) involves a change at Verona.

**BIKE //** For bike hire, see p229.

**BUS // APAM** ( ☎ 0376 23 01; www.apam.it, in Italian) operates city-wide buses.

# BACKGROUND

**HISTORY**
People have been holidaying on the Italian lakes since Roman times but powerhouse Milan and nearby cities have attracted as much trouble as prosperity. (p232)

**FINE ARTS**
Florence is far away but Renaissance ripples washed across Milan and the lakes region. (p244)

**FROM ROMANESQUE TO RENAISSANCE**
Like the Renaissance did later on, the 11th-century Romanesque building revival took inspiration from classical models. (p250)

**VILLAS & GARDENS**
Throughout the centuries, the great and good have lavished wealth on lakeside pleasure domes. (p255)

**OUTDOOR PURSUITS**
Break out your hiking boots or get on your bike, boat or (water)skis for some physical effort. (p260)

**SMOOTH AS SILK**
Como is Europe's last bastion of quality silk production. (p265)

**WINE**
Wine lovers will celebrate drops from Valpolicella to Valtellina. (p270)

**FOOD**
From *pizzoccheri* (buckwheat pasta) to polenta and lake perch, Lombard and lake cooking (p274) has a flavour all its own. We've included a food glossary (p283) with everything you need to know to eat like a local.

# HISTORY

· · · · · · ·

## AN ANCIENT PRESENCE

The Po plains that make up the southern half of Lombardy were, hundreds of thousands of years ago, awash with the Mediterranean. As the waters ebbed, leaving behind highly fertile land that today produces oodles of rice, prehistoric clans began to move into the area.

Evidence of a human presence reaches back about 10,000 to 12,000 years. As Alpine glaciers of the last ice age retreated north, late Early Stone Age families began to settle mountain valleys and caves along the shores of the main lakes. The most remarkable testament to Stone Age cultures is to be found in the Valle Camonica in the north of Brescia province (see p162). Here, more than 150,000 rock-art petroglyphs testify to the lively imagination of people living in or around this valley as long ago as 8000 BC. More engravings are being discovered all the time and the entire collection was recognised as a World Heritage treasure in 1979. The ancient engravings depict figures hunting, farming, making magic and indulging in wild sexual antics. The art is a record of the passing millennia, with items dating to various eras including Roman times and the Middle Ages.

## GAULS & ROMANS

Archaeological evidence and the accounts of Roman historian Titus Livius point to the invasion of the Lombard plains and Po valley by Celtic tribes from southern France as early as the 10th century BC. The Celts mixed with other tribes in the area, such as the Liguri, an ancient people (going back as far as 25,000 BC) who had emerged in Liguria and spread across parts of Italy and Western Europe.

Further Celtic invasions are hinted at around the 7th century BC. It appears that the Etruscans, moving north from Etruria (present-day Tuscany), also established settlements in the Po valley. Some historians claim that the Etruscans founded Mantua.

Among the Celtic tribes were the Insubres (or Insubri), who, it appears, occupied an area between the Ticino and Adda rivers and either conquered or founded the town of Mediolanum ('Middle of the Plain', later changed to 'Milan'). Just when this happened is unclear.

| » 11,000 BC | » C 600 BC | » 388 BC |
| --- | --- | --- |
| Small groups of Mesolithic tribes settle in caves around the shores of Lake Como, Lake Maggiore and Lake Garda. | The Insubres (or Insubri), a migrating Celtic tribe, settle in the Po plain between the Ticino and Adda rivers and, it is thought, found what will one day be Milan. | A coalition of Gallic tribes swarms into northern Italy and spreads Celtic-Gallic control of the Po valley to the Adriatic coast. A year later a band of them sacks Rome. |

In 388 BC another Celtic invasion began. These tribes (possibly coming from Eastern Europe and eventually settling in France) crossed the Alps at the Brenner Pass. In alliance with tribes such as the Insubres, they swept along the Po valley, occupying the area from Lake Maggiore to the Adriatic coast and crushing the Etruscans along the way. The entire area between the Alps and Apennine range came to be known as Cisalpine Gaul (meaning 'Gaul on the near side of the Alps') and its many tribes came under the umbrella term of Gauls.

A band of these tall, reckless, blue-eyed plunderers, fierce warriors, raided south of the Po and sacked Rome in 387 BC. Rome recovered and went on to unite the peninsula south of the Po under its rule. Rome and the Gauls rubbed along tolerably well until several Gallic tribes united to invade Roman territory in 225 BC. But Roman forces under Consul Lucius Aemilius Papus and Consul Ganes Cornelius Scipio Calvus defeated the invaders at the Battle of Telamon and pursued the campaign into the Po valley. By 221 BC, Gnaeus had taken Mediolanum. The Romans established the towns of Placentia (Piacenza) and Cremona (formerly a Celtic settlement).

'The most remarkable testament to Stone Age cultures is to be found in the Valle Camonica'

When Carthage's general Hannibal crossed the Alps into the Lombard plains in 218 BC, at the start of the Second Punic War (218–201 BC), 50,000 Gauls joined his force of 26,000 infantry and cavalry. After several defeats at Hannibal's hands, Rome emerged the total victor and undisputed master of the western Mediterranean.

The province of Cisalpine Gaul played a key role in the rise to absolute power of Julius Caesar (100–44 BC). Consul Caesar was made governor of the province in 59 BC (he held the post until 50 BC) and found it a fruitful recruitment ground. He took his legions into neighbouring Gaul (modern France) on a campaign of conquests that would last until 51 BC and provide him with a strong enough power base to embark on the Italian civil war (49–46 BC) that would lead to him being declared dictator of all Rome. None of this would have been possible without the loyalty of Cisalpine Gaul.

One reason for that loyalty was that Caesar had long advocated granting Roman citizenship to the people of Mediolanum and other Cisalpine cities. This right to declare *civis romanus sum* (I am a Roman citizen) was finally granted in 49 BC, the year Caesar marched on Rome.

Mediolanum was by then a prosperous city astride key routes linking the south over the Apennines, the coast west into Gaul and north over the Alps. Wool, hides and

| » 225–221 BC | » 49 BC | » AD 292 |
|---|---|---|
| Roman troops defeat the Insubres and other invading Gallic tribes at the Battle of Telamon in Tuscany. Consul Gnaeus Cornelius Scipio Calvus takes Mediolanum (Milan) in 221 BC. | After long years of forced alliance with Rome, the people of Milan and other Po towns are granted full Roman citizenship. | Emperor Diocletian makes Milan capital of the western half of the Roman Empire (with Byzantium, later renamed Constantinople, capital of the eastern half). |

metalwork were its main products, and the city boasted a theatre, university, forum, temples and a mint.

The lakes became a favoured holiday destination for the Roman elite; it was to a villa in Sirmione that the poet Catullus retreated when 1st-century-BC it-girl Clodia Metelli broke his heart. Caesar founded Como as a fort on Lake Como – in the 1st century AD, Pliny the Elder and his nephew Pliny the Younger (famous for his account of the eruption of Mt Vesuvius that destroyed the city of Pompeii) were born here.

Confirmation of Mediolanum's importance came in AD 292, when Emperor Diocletian (co-emperor with Maximian) declared it capital of the western half of the empire. Maximian took up residence there and embarked on a massive building program. Unfortunately, little of what he built remains visible.

## CHRISTIANITY & UNCERTAINTY

It was in Mediolanum that Emperor Constantine made his momentous edict granting Christians freedom of worship in AD 313. Later that century St Ambrose (Sant'Ambrogio) came to embody the extent to which Constantine's decision would change the Roman world.

Born into a Roman family in modern-day Belgium in 339, St Ambrose arrived in Mediolanum as governor of northern Italy. A skilful mediator between Christians and the Arian sect (which claimed Jesus was not divine but rather had been a messenger from God), he was acclaimed bishop of Mediolanum by the people in 374. Although Christian, he had not been baptised, so once this was taken care of he was given a one-week crash course as a priest and declared bishop on 7 December 374 (now a public holiday). He became a powerful figure who, in 390, obliged Emperor Theodosius to apologise for a massacre carried out in Greece. St Ambrose became the patron saint of the city (and also of domestic animals, bee-keepers, candle-makers, chandlers and learning).

Five years after the saint's death (in 397), an army of Visigoths appeared at the walls of Mediolanum, and the imperial court removed to Ravenna. A month later the barbarian army moved off towards Asti and was later defeated. Mediolanum insisted the court return but it was not to be.

The appearance of the Visigoths was a sign of things to come. In 452, Attila the Hun rampaged through northern Italy and Mediolanum was among the cities sacked and pillaged. The Roman Empire was crumbling and its western half collapsed 24 years

BACKGROUND

| » 313 | » 568 | » 774 |
|-------|-------|-------|
| Roman Emperor Constantine issues the Edict of Milan, declaring Christianity the official state religion. St Ambrose (Sant'Ambrogio) becomes Bishop of Milan 61 years later. | Germanic tribes known as Lombards (or Longobards) occupy northern Italy, making their capital at Pavia and giving the Po valley region under their control its present name. | The Frankish king Charlemagne leads Frankish troops into Italy, defeats his erstwhile Lombard allies and seizes Milan. Twenty-six years later he is crowned Holy Roman Emperor in Rome. |

## THE TALL TALE OF ST BARNABAS

Most Christian cities have their own legend linking them to the lives of the martyrs.

The story goes that, on 13 March 52 AD the Christian preacher Barnabas turned up at the gates of Mediolanum (present-day Milan). He plunged his walking stick into a mass of rock and started preaching. Some days later he entered the city proper and, by a miracle, all the statues to pagan deities collapsed in deference to the new faith as he walked past them. Suitably impressed, the town authorities left Barnabas in peace. His work done in Mediolanum, he went on to Bergamo, Brescia and beyond, finally winding his way back to his native Cyprus, where he was martyred around 63 AD.

The idea of claiming St Barnabas (San Barnaba) as Milan's founding Christian came from none other than St Ambrose. Apart from being a nice story for the faithful, the idea was to underline Mediolanum's importance in the uncertain world of the late Roman Empire.

later. Mediolanum, a shadow of its former self, was attacked several times by invading Goths before the Germanic Lombards (Longobards) arrived in 568. They quickly occupied Verona and then concentrated on modern Lombardy in the following four years – Milan (its name changed from Mediolanum), Bergamo and Brescia fell in 569, Pavia in 572. The Lombards initially established their capital at Pavia but later moved it to Milan. Cremona and Mantua resisted until 603 and, in the end, Lombard rule extended to Friuli.

Queen Theodolinda (b?–627), wife of two Lombard kings and from 616 regent for her young son, was instrumental in converting the Lombards to Christianity. She elected Monza (see p62) as her favourite residence.

In the complex cut and thrust of Dark Ages politics, the Lombards had forged an alliance with an increasingly strong ally in France, the Franks. All being fair in love and war, however, the Frankish king Charlemagne turned on his allies in 774 and invaded Lombardy, claiming Milan for his own. In a deal with the pope, Charlemagne was crowned Holy Roman Emperor (in exchange for backing papal control over the Papal States in central Italy). Charlemagne's successors would for centuries thereafter consider Italy a fiefdom, though they quickly lost much control of the area. Indeed, in the Lombard cities it was the bishops who had real power.

| » 1098 | » 1127 | » 1176 |
|---|---|---|
| Milan becomes a commune, an increasingly independent city state. Bergamo, Brescia, Como, Cremona, Mantua and Verona follow suit in the ensuing 30 years. | After nine years of warring between the two communes, Milan crushes Como's forces and razes the town. | The Lombard League of city states, including Bergamo, Brescia, Cremona, Lodi, Mantua, Milan and Verona, defeats Holy Roman Emperor Barbarossa in the Battle of Legnano. |

# RISE OF THE CITY STATES

In reaction to the ecclesiastical stranglehold on power and the ever-present claims to domination of all Italy by the Holy Roman Empire (which passed from Carolingian to German control in 887), the cities of northern Italy began to clamour for greater control of their own affairs. An emerging, rich business and trading class furnished powerful figures able to face down both bishops and feudal lords (the power of the latter lay mostly in their countryside estates). By the early 12th century most northern cities had some form of communal government, in which leaders were elected on a rotating basis (often not lasting more than a year). With time these semidemocratic regimes would give way, in most cases, to hereditary ducal arrangements.

The first big showdown came when an alliance of these cities (including Bergamo, Brescia, Cremona, Lodi, Mantua, Milan and Verona), along with such heavyweights as Venice, defeated Holy Roman Emperor Frederick Barbarossa in the Battle of Legman in 1176.

This weakening of the imperial hold over Italy fuelled the independence of the city states. Among the strongest dynasties to emerge were the Visconti in Milan (from 1278), the Dalla Scala (or Scaliger) in Verona (from 1262) and the Gonzaga in Mantua (from 1328). The rulers of Milan came to lord it over much of Lombardy, with the notable exception of Mantua, which remained independent until the Austrian Habsburg Empire acquired it in 1708.

Under Azzone Visconti (who ruled from 1330 to 1337), Milan took control of Bergamo, Brescia, Como, Cremona, Lodi, Novara, Piacenza and Sondrio. Milan thus held a considerable chunk of territory, from Ticino (at least as far as Bellinzona) and the Alps north of the Valtellina to the Po river in the south.

*'Venice...now butted up directly against the Duchy of Lombardy, with the dividing line at Lake Garda'*

Gian Galeazzo Visconti became Duke of Milan in 1395 and, two years later, Duke of Lombardy. By then he had grabbed Verona and Vicenza in the east (with only Padua separating him from the maritime power of Venice) and Bologna, Siena and Perugia in the south.

With around 150,000 people, Milan was now one of the biggest and most prosperous cities in Europe. It flourished on the back of textile and arms manufacturing as well as its fertile and well-managed farmlands to the south, much of them given over to rice production. The Visconti also attracted Italy's best artisans. Work began on the Duomo in 1386, the

| » 1329 | » 1428 | » 1450 |
|---|---|---|
| Azzone Visconti becomes the first strongman of Milan. In his 10 years as Lord of Milan he annexes Bergamo, Como, Crema, Cremona, Lecco, Lodi and Vercelli among other territories. | After defeat at the hands of Venice in the Battle of Maclodio, Milan cedes control of Bergamo and Brescia to the Serenissima, which holds them until the arrival of Napoleon in 1797. | Swashbuckling Francesco Sforza enters Milan and becomes duke, founding a new, if short-lived, ruling dynasty. |

marble transported from Candoglia to Milan via newly built canals. Unfortunately, plague-infested rats came along for the ride and more than 30,000 Milanese died.

By 1400, Gian Galeazzo was possibly the most powerful sovereign in Europe. He had control over a territory that covered all of Lombardy, much of Ticino, as well as considerable slices of the Veneto, Emilia-Romagna and Umbria.

But, as they say, easy come, easy go. Just five years after his proclamation as Duke of Lombardy and amid preparations for a hammer blow against Florence, Gian Galeazzo was struck down by fever and died in 1402. Within three years his successors lost Siena, Bologna and all Milan's possessions in the Veneto. Venice, which had effortlessly benefited from the windfall and incorporated Padua, Vicenza and Verona into its growing mainland empire, now butted up directly against the Duchy of Lombardy, with the dividing line at Lake Garda.

Worse was to come. Filippo Maria Visconti, proclaimed duke in 1412, had barely a moment of peace, dealing with internal squabbles and almost constant battles to retain or recover possessions in and beyond Lombardy. By now the three main power centres in the northern half of Italy were Milan, Florence and Venice. A league of the latter two against Milan in 1425 lead to yet another war, in which the latter was crushed at the Battle of Maclodio (1427). The following year, under the peace treaty of Ferrara, Brescia and Bergamo were permanently ceded to Venice.

## SFORZA'S FOLLY & SPANISH RULE

After Filippo Maria Visconti's death, in 1447, a shaky republic sprang up but lasted only three years. Soldier of fortune Francesco Sforza, married to Filippo Maria's daughter, grabbed power in 1450. He forged a friendship with Florence and aimed to maintain a balance of power within Italy while keeping France

**BACKGROUND**

### DON'T MISS...

#### HISTORY ON SHOW

★ **Parco Nazionale delle Incisioni Rupestri, Valle Camonica** // Rock drawings going back to the Bronze Age (p162)

★ **Musei di Solferino, Solferino** // Mementos and photos of one of the bloody battles fought to eject the Austrians from northern Italy in 1859 (p192)

★ **Bellinzona Castles** // Three castles that marked the fortunes of the Lombards and Swiss through the centuries (p137)

★ **Duomo, Monza** // Holds the Corona Ferrea (Iron Crown), used to crown everyone from Charlemagne to Napoleon (p62)

| » 1510 | » 1515 | » 1535 |
|---|---|---|
| Pietro Boldoni establishes the first spinning mills for silk along Lake Como but the industry does not take off until the mid-18th century, under Habsburg Austrian rule. | Milanese and Swiss forces are defeated by François I at Marignano (modern-day Melegnano); the present-day border between Lombardy and Ticino is established. | The death without heir of Francesco II Sforza leaves the Duchy of Milan and its Lombard territories in the hands of Spain until 1713. |

BACKGROUND

## DON'T MISS...

### THE GOOD, THE GREAT & THEIR LEGACIES

★ **The Scaliger Clan //** Verona's long-time rulers built that city's Castelvecchio (p215) and Arche Scaligeri (p217)

★ **The Gonzaga Dynasty //** The Gonzaga took on the likes of Andrea Mantegna to contribute to the Palazzo Ducale (p223)

★ **Gian Galeazzo Visconti //** The figure behind the building of the Certosa di Pavia (p59)

★ **Ludovico Sforza (Il Moro) //** Largely responsible for the Renaissance creation of Vigevano's Piazza Ducale (p61)

★ **Bartolomeo Colleoni //** Venice's mercenary commander had the Cappella Colleoni (p148) built in Bergamo in his own memory

★ **Empress Maria Theresa //** The empress ordered the building of La Scala (p48) in Milan

★ **Benito Mussolini //** Responsible for the grandiose architecture of Milan's Stazione Centrale and Arengario (p42), and Brescia's Piazza della Vittoria (p167)

out. After his death, in 1466, the duchy knew relative calm until the arrival of Ludovico Sforza, also known as Il Moro (The Moor) because of his dark complexion. He was married to the brilliant Beatrice d'Este, widely credited with luring the Renaissance geniuses Leonardo da Vinci and Donato Bramante to Milan.

Ludovico embarked on a foolhardy policy of provoking the Holy Roman Emperor Maximilian I and France's Charles VIII into clashing in Italy. He hoped to reap rewards whichever side won. Instead, abandoned by his Swiss mercenary forces, he lost to the new French king, Louis XII, in 1500. Ludovico was imprisoned in France and the Duchy of Milan passed into French hands.

The Swiss, meanwhile, had entered the dangerous playing fields of northern Italian politics and warfare. A confederation of Swiss-German cantons won independence from Austrian Habsburg control after defeating Maximilian I at battle in 1499. Four years afterwards they profited from the Sforzas' ill fortune by taking fortified Bellinzona, thus securing the confederation's vulnerable underbelly. In the following years, the Swiss continued south, even taking control of parts of Lombardy.

In 1512 the Swiss helped Ludovico's son Massimiliano return to the ducal throne of Milan but a Franco-Venetian alliance soon reversed that situation. Beaten by the forces of François I at the Battle of Marignano (modern day Melegnano) in 1515, the

| » C 1550 | » 1630–31 | » 1714 |
|---|---|---|
| Lombard farmers take up corn production. Corn becomes a standard staple in the form of polenta, popular to this day. | A devastating bout of plague ravages Lombardy and leaves Milan with more than half its population dead, according to most estimates. | The end of the War of the Spanish Succession leads to the withdrawal of Spanish forces from Lombardy, which comes under Austrian control. |

Swiss retreated (over what is still today the Swiss–Italian border between Lombardy and Ticino). Thus bitten, the Swiss judged it prudent not to embark on foreign wars ever again.

The Duchy of Milan was back in French hands but Paris' joy was short lived. Habsburg Emperor Charles V (who as emperor and king of Spain, with its American colonies, was easily the most powerful ruler in Europe) and François clashed in 1525 at the Battle of Pavia. The latter came off second best and Lombardy passed to Spanish control. The Spaniards later named a favourite dish of fried strips of cod *soldados de Pavía* (Pavia soldiers) – apparently they reminded someone of the uniforms of the Pavia regiment (the mind boggles).

After Charles' abdication in 1556, Lombardy and the Habsburg Emperor's other Italian possessions went to his son, Spain's King Philip II. Largely neglected by its Spanish governors, Milan and its Lombard territories sank into provincial decay. The most notable event of this period was the devastating wave of plague that swept across the region in 1630–31, described by Milan's (and Italy's) great 19th-century novelist Alessandro Manzoni in his classic *I promessi sposi* (The Betrothed).

## FROM DEJECTED SUBJECTS TO INDEPENDENCE

The War of the Spanish Succession (1702–13) was a personal victory for the Bourbon ascendant to the Spanish throne, Philip V, but a disaster for the Spanish nation, which lost many of its territories under the Treaty of Utrecht. The bulk of the Duchy of Milan fell to the Austrians, who promptly moved in and, most Milanese and Lombards had to admit, improved things markedly. Milan blossomed again under stylish Empress Maria Theresa.

The Austrians imposed a centralised bureaucracy across Lombardy (now including Mantua) but reformed the tax system to encourage an increase in farming output. Comparatively liberal legislation was accompanied by increased efficiency in the running of public affairs. In this context the Marquis Cesare Beccaria wrote a treatise in the 1760s urging the abolition of torture and the death penalty. As Milan picked itself up, a growing intellectual class also flourished and the ideas of French Enlightenment philosophers made inroads in Milan's cafe culture. In the arts, too, things picked up: Venice artist Giambattista Tiepolo spent time in Milan and Bergamo around 1740; and Maria Theresa had La Scala opera house built in 1778.

This period of comparatively enlightened, if not overly popular, rule was interrupted by the arrival of the revolutionary general Napoleon in 1796. He created a

| » 1799 | » 1805 | » 1814–15 |
|---|---|---|
| Como's most famous son, Alessandro Volta (1745–1827), invents the electric battery. Professor at the University of Pavia, he is made a count by Napoleon in 1810. | Having made himself emperor of France, Napoleon is proclaimed king of the newly constituted Kingdom of Italy, comprising most of the northern half of the country. | The Congress of Vienna, held after the fall of Napoleon, re-establishes the balance of power in Europe. The result for much of northern Italy is the return of Austrian rule. |

BACKGROUND

Cisalpine Republic that, by 1805, had been transformed into the so-called Kingdom of Italy, with Milan as capital. Much art was confiscated, especially from monasteries, convents and churches across northern Italy. Some wound up in Milan's Brera art gallery, opened in 1809.

A building fever gripped Milan and other cities across northern Italy – many villas and palaces in places such as Como and other spots around the lakes date from around this time. Napoleon was also at work in neighbouring Switzerland. In 1803 Ticino entered the new Swiss Confederation concocted by Napoleon as a free and equal canton for the first time in its history.

The Austrians returned after Napoleon's demise in 1814, joining Lombardy and the Veneto in a single 'kingdom', with co-capitals in Milan and Venice. This time, the mood had changed. The Austrians seemed set on squeezing their prize economically and imposed an unfavourable customs regime (in favour of their port at Trieste).

Opposition grew and, following the example of many cities across Europe, Milan rose in its Cinque Giornate (Five Days) revolt, in March 1848. By the third day of the rising, central Milan was in rebel hands and Austrian forces had retreated to the city outskirts. Two days later, the rebellion was snuffed out.

The revolts (in Milan and, more importantly, in Venice, where the rebels held out until well into 1849) failed on the ground but doubt provided propaganda material for those clamouring for Italian unification or Risorgimento (revival). The diplomatic offensive to this end came from the Duchy of Savoy, whose capital was in Turin (awarded to the French Alpine duchy in the 16th century). Ably led by the wily prime minister, Count Camillo Benso Cavour, the House of Savoy struck a deal with France's Napoleon III under which the latter would help oust the Austrians from Italy. In return, the King of Sardinia, as the Savoy duke was also known, would cede Savoy to France and head a new Italian kingdom.

Savoy's Vittorio Emanuele II and Napoleon III defeated the Austrians at the battles of Magenta (4 June) and Solferino (24 June) in mid-1859. Within a year all of Lombardy had joined the nascent Italian kingdom. Venice would not do so until 1866 and unification was completed in 1870 with the taking of Rome.

With unification, the political capital moved from Turin to Florence and, ultimately, to Rome. There was never any suggestion that Milan might be a candidate. Probably the Milanese were indifferent, concentrating on business and industrialisation. From the 1870s to the outbreak of WWI, the city became the country's railway hub and leading industrial centre, while Milan's banks dominated the country's financial

| » 1848 | » 1861 | » 1915 |
|---|---|---|
| Revolts across Europe spark rebellion in Italy. King Carlo Alberto of Piedmont joins the fray against Austria, but within a year the latter recovers Lombardy and the Veneto. | By the end of the 1859–61 Franco-Austrian War, Vittorio Emanuele II has much of central Italy under his control and is proclaimed king of a newly united Italy. | Italy enters WWI on the side of the Allies to win Italian territories still in Austrian hands. Austria had offered to cede some of these territories but Italy insists the offer is insufficient. |

markets. In 1883 one of Europe's first electric power stations, a modest affair near the Duomo, was opened in Milan.

It was not all success stories. The working classes frequently came off second best. In Milan they staged some of Europe's first mass strikes in 1872. Ten years later, as recession hit, Italy's first socialist party was founded in Milan, and in May 1898 more than 100 people died when four days of demonstrations over inflation were crushed with cannons and gunfire.

## THE CARNAGE OF WAR & MUSSOLINI'S MADNESS

When the great powers plunged headlong into the nightmare that would be WWI in summer 1914, Italy was technically allied with the Central Powers of Habsburg Austria and Germany. Italy, however, had territorial bones to pick with Austria. The country's politicians divided largely along antiwar and pro-intervention lines – *against* their Austrian allies.

Fervently in favour of entering the war, the pamphleteer Benito Mussolini (1883–1945) was expelled from the Socialist Party in 1914 and led big pro-war demonstrations in Milan in 1915. In May that year, Italy declared war and opened a front in the north of the country. There ensued three-and-a-half years of carnage that cost the lives of some 600,000 young Italians. That toll was doubled by the flu pandemic that raged across Italy and the rest of Europe even before the war ended in 1918.

*'Mussolini returned wounded to Milan from the battlefields in 1917'*

Mussolini returned wounded to Milan from the battlefields in 1917. The experience of war and the frustration shared with many at the disappointing outcome at the Treaty of Versailles in 1919 led him to form a right-wing militant political group that, by 1921, had become the Fascist Party, with its black-shirted street brawlers and Roman salute. These were to become symbols of violent oppression and aggressive nationalism for the next 23 years.

After his march on Rome in 1922 and victory in the 1924 elections, Mussolini (who called himself the Duce, or Leader) had taken full control of the country by 1926, banning other political parties, trade unions not affiliated to the party, and the free press.

He threw in his lot with Nazi Germany, entering WWII in 1940. In September 1943, with Allied troops marching up the Italian peninsula, Italy surrendered and Mussolini was arrested. Two weeks later the Germans occupied most of the country and freed

| » MARCH 1919 | » 1922 | » 1943 |
|---|---|---|
| Two years after returning wounded from WWI, former socialist journalist Benito Mussolini forms a right-wing Fasci Italiani di Combattimento (Italian Combat Fasces). | Mussolini stages a march on Rome in October. King Vittorio Emanuele III, fearful of the movement's growing popular power, entrusts Mussolini with the formation of a government. | As Italy surrenders to the Allies, German forces free imprisoned Mussolini and occupy most of the country. Mussolini is later installed as puppet leader of the so-called Republic of Salò. |

BACKGROUND

Mussolini, who declared a new Fascist republic in the Lake Garda village of Salò. Backed by the Germans, who had no intention of giving up Italy without a fight, Mussolini's puppet regime meant another bitter 20 months of suffering for the people of northern Italy.

Allied air raids, which began in earnest in August 1943, destroyed more than a quarter of Milan. In April 1945, partisans nabbed Mussolini on the shore of Lake Como, just short of the dictator's objective, the Swiss border. Switzerland had remained neutral throughout the war and the canton of Ticino alone hosted some 150 camps for refugees. Starting with Jews fleeing Italy's race laws, they were soon augmented by a broad variety of civilians and military personnel of various nationalities seeking haven. Some of these camps were still open as late as 1948.

## THE CARROCCIO

Lombard soldiers-at-arms first trundled out the *carroccio,* a lumbering, ox-drawn war cart, in the 11th century. The *carroccio* was highly symbolic to troops: it carried the standards of the Duchy of Milan, was used as a rallying point and its loss in battle usually meant defeat. It was used by the Lombard League in its victorious campaign over Barbarossa in the 12th century. In the 1980s a different Lombard League, Umberto Bossi's Lega Lombarda, couldn't resist appropriating the symbol of the *carroccio* for its right-wing secessionist movement. Later allied with similar movements elsewhere across northern Italy to create the Lega Nord (Northern League), Bossi's party came to be commonly known as the Carroccio.

## COMEBACKS & KICKBACKS

Lombardy was at the forefront of Italy's 'economic miracle' in the latter half of the 1950s and 1960s. With low salaries and booming export businesses, Milan and its surrounding area attracted vast waves of internal migrants from the poor south – more than 80,000 settled in Milan in 1961 alone. The city's population peaked in 1971 at 1,723,000.

One north–south cliché suggested that corruption and organised crime were the monopoly of a supposedly backward southern Italy. So it came as something of a shock when, in 1992, a group of Milanese judges opened the floodgates on investigations and trials implicating thousands of northern politicians and high-flyers in a panoply of white-collar crimes (together known as Tangentopoli, or 'kickback city') ranging from embezzlement and fraud to kickbacks. Led by judge Antonio di Pietro, the series of trials came to be known as Mani Pulite (Clean Hands) and rocked the political and business establishment in and beyond Milan.

| » APRIL 1945 | » 1946 | » 1982 |
|---|---|---|
| Partisans capture and execute Mussolini and his companion Clara Petacci on the shores of Lake Como. Their bodies are later strung up in Milan's Piazzale Loreto. | Italians vote to abolish the monarchy and create a republic. King Umberto II, who had succeeded to the throne in May, leaves Italy and refuses to recognise the result. | Umberto Bossi founds the right-wing, separatist Lega Lombarda movement, which in 1991 becomes Lega Nord and later an ally of prime minister Silvio Berlusconi. |

Many spoke of the coming of a new republic, as traditional parties such as the centre-right conservative Catholic Democrazia Cristiana and centre-left Partito Socialista Italiano (PSI) crumbled. PSI chief and former prime minister Bettino Craxi chose exile in Tunisia rather than face the music. An old pal of his, the Milan business magnate Silvio Berlusconi, saw his chance to enter politics, created the Forza Italia (Go Italy) party and was elected prime minister in 1994 with the support of an equally colourful character from near Varese – Umberto Bossi.

Bossi's Lega Nord (Northern League), founded in the 1980s on a narrow anti-immigration, anti-Rome and pro-secession (now watered down to devolution) platform, quickly pulled the rug from under Berlusconi's feet by withdrawing from the coalition, but stood with him again in his election victories of 2001 and 2008.

Since 1997 Milan has been run by mayors close to Berlusconi and the regional government of Lombardy has also been in the hands of a close Berlusconi ally, Roberto Formigoni, since 1995. Although the Lega Nord often wins as much as 20% of the vote in northern Italy, most northern cities (apart from Milan) have tended to vote centre-left. Recent exceptions to that rule have been Verona and Brescia, and in municipal and provincial elections in 2009 the Lega saw its vote increase some 10%.

Berlusconi's Cheshire cat grin broadened in March 2009, when he orchestrated the fusion of his party with his once Fascist Alleanza Nazionale (National Alliance) allies, creating a single centre-right party, Il Popolo della Libertà (The Free People), of which he is undisputed master. His wife's announcement that she would seek divorce and claims that Berlusconi was consorting with teenage girls may have dented his electoral sheen in mid-2009, but he remains firmly in control.

Milan's judges have repeatedly brought Berlusconi to trial on a number of corruption charges but failed to make anything stick. Berlusconi, who controls much of the private TV sector and is Italy's third richest man, has long maintained that the judiciary is run by crypto-Communists on a vendetta mission. In 2008 he had an immunity law passed that protects him from prosecution while in office.

By mid-2009 the economic woes besetting the world were making themselves felt in Lombardy. From the silk business in Como, already hurt by competition from Asia, to tourism on the lakes and elsewhere, the crisis was beginning to bite. Industrial output was down more than 6% in the last quarter of 2008 compared with the previous year, and a March 2009 study showed that 60% of business owners were stumping up money from personal funds to keep their businesses afloat. It was estimated that throughout Lombardy the contraction in business and falling orders had cost companies some €12 billion in the first three months of 2009.

| » 2006 | » 2007 | » 2008 |
|---|---|---|
| AC Milan is one of the five top Serie A football teams to lose competition points and receive hefty fines in a match-rigging scandal. | Former heir to the throne Vittorio Emanuele di Savoia is cleared of charges in connection with alleged illicit dealings involving the casino in Campione d'Italia, among others. | Milanese media mogul and Italy's third richest man, Silvio Berlusconi, sweeps to power for his third mandate as prime minister. |

# FINE ARTS

· · · · · · ·

Lombardy and the surrounding lakes area have rarely been in the artistic driver's seat. In Roman times, as in the Renaissance, the centres of glory lay elsewhere. Some of their light was reflected on the cities of the north, though, and a wealth of local talent emerged.

## ANCIENT TALENT

Italians didn't need the Renaissance to discover their artistic bent. As early as the Bronze Age, modest village folk in settlements along the Valle Camonica, north of Lake Iseo, started etching their impressions of the world around them into rocky walls in caves near Capo di Ponte. These ancient rock carvings (see p162 and p232) are among the earliest signs of artistic pursuits across northern Italy.

By the time of Hannibal's defeat in the Second Punic War in 201 BC, Rome had full control of northern Italy and its lakes. Surprisingly few Roman remains have been left in the area between Milan and Verona but a little gem in Brescia gives the modern world our single best opportunity of admiring what the Romans were capable of when they turned their attention to decoration. The ruins of two Roman country houses, preserved within the walls of an ancient medieval monastery that today serves as the Museo della Città (p164), are filled with beautiful wall frescos and pavement mosaics.

> 'richly painted panels by Gothic artists can be seen in various museums across the region'

The Romans' successors in northern Italy, the Lombards, also left behind precious few reminders of their presence. A handful of items show that, in their own fashion, they too had an eye for beauty. In the same museum in Brescia, a fine example of their work is the 8th-century Croce di Desiderio, a Lombard cross encrusted with hundreds of jewels. Monza's Museo Serpero (p62) also houses some spectacular pieces from those early medieval years.

## THE RENAISSANCE COMES NORTH

Carried through from Roman traditions, the fresco survived as a typical form of painting in the early Middle Ages and down through the Gothic period. Much of this work, done above all in churches, has faded away, but some remarkable examples survive (as in the Basilica di Sant'Abbondio, in Como, p109). More survives from Gothic times, and richly painted panels by Gothic artists can be seen in various museums across the region.

Meanwhile, in Florence, an extraordinary revolution was taking place. Injecting a hitherto unthinkable element of humanity into their commissions and making use of perspective to create a sense of three-dimensional reality, a bevy of artists working mostly in Florence turned the European art world on its head. As their fame spread, the powerful ruling families of Milan and other northern Italian cities began to commission these artists to embellish their own fiefdoms.

Alone in the north, Venice would take the baton from Florence and embark on its own magnificent golden era of painting, which would reach into the baroque and rococo periods. It was only natural that some greats of Veneto art, as the Tuscans before them, should look west for commissions. For a roll-call of the some of the big invitees that worked in various locations from Mantua to Milan over the centuries, see the table, p248.

The masters trained disciples, and plenty of local talents emerged across the towns and cities near the lakes, although few gained the notoriety of the Tuscan, Venetian and Roman masters. The single best place to come to know this 'second tier' of Lombard and Veneto masters is the Pinacoteca di Brera (p47).

## DON'T MISS...

### ART MUSEUMS & GALLERIES

* **Pinacoteca di Brera, Milan** // Italian masters and an assortment of foreign painters (p47)

* **Castello Sforzesco, Milan** // This castle contains a series of museums and galleries (p43)

* **Accademia Carrara, Bergamo** // An exceptional repository of Italian Old Masters (p149)

* **Museo Poldi-Pezzoli, Milan** // Botticelli leads the way in this private collection (p49)

* **Museo Serpero, Monza** // One of the greatest treasures of religious art in Europe (p62)

BACKGROUND

An admirer of Leonardo da Vinci during the latter's long stint in Milan was Bernardino Luini (1485–1532). He left works as far away from the ducal capital as Lugano, in the Chiesa di Santa Maria degli Angioli (p133) and the Certosa di Pavia (p59). The great Tuscan art historian Vasari described Luini's style as 'delicatissimo'. Also at work in the Certosa was Il Bergognone (who died c 1522), about whom little is known. Cited as a registered artist in Milan in 1481, Bergognone reached one of his crowning moments with paintings for the Incoronata church in Lodi (p174).

The city of Cremona produced a raft of fine artists, especially in the 16th century, starting with the Campi brothers: Giulio (1507–73), Antonio (1523–87) and Vincenzo (c 1530–91). Although largely identifiable with the latter days of the Renaissance, their works sometimes entered the territory of Mannerism, a kind of timid transitional stage from the classical lines of the Renaissance to the unfettered voluptuousness of the baroque.

Giulio left frescos inside Cremona's Duomo (p169), alongside works by other key local masters like Ferrara-born Boccaccio Boccaccino (c 1467 to c 1525) and Gian Francesco Bembo (b?–1543). Boccaccino studied in Rome and Venice – in the latter he was associated closely with the Bellini clan of painters. Little is known about Bembo.

Boccaccino's son Camillo Boccaccino (c 1504–46) followed in his father's footsteps, studied in Venice and was influenced by the likes of Pordenone and Titian. You can judge the results of his lagoon-city apprenticeship best in Cremona's Chiesa di San Sigismondo (p172).

In Brescia, meanwhile, the leading light at the outset of the Renaissance, and heavily influenced by Mantegna and Venice's Jacopo Bellino, was Vincenzo Foppa (1427–1515). He worked across Lombardy and elsewhere in northern Italy and some of his works hang in museums in Brescia, Milan (Castello Sforzesco, p43) and Bergamo (Accademia Carrara, p149). Many works carried out for churches in Milan have been lost but, by all accounts, Foppa was the leading light in Lombard art until Leonardo da Vinci turned up in Milan. Perhaps the latter's arrival explains why Foppa eventually returned to Brescia. There, he trained two successors, Il Moretto (Alessandro Bonvicino, 1498–1554) and Giovan Gerolamo Savoldo (c 1480 to c 1548). The former worked mostly in Brescia, while the latter wound up in Venice and Treviso.

> 'Foppa was the leading light in Lombard art until Leonardo da Vinci turned up in Milan'

## TO THE 20TH CENTURY

The fall of the Duchy of Milan into Spanish hands from 1535 to 1713, and the anchoring of cities like Verona, Brescia and Bergamo as provincial expressions of a gradually waning Venetian power, especially in the 18th century, no doubt did little to foster artistic greatness. Indeed, the stultifying atmosphere of occupied Milan may have pushed Caravaggio (Michelangelo Merisi, 1571–1610) born in the town whose name became his pseudonym, to move to Rome in 1592. It was in Rome that he blossomed as an artist.

Eight years after Caravaggio's death, Cardinal Federico Borromeo founded a fine arts academy in Milan, with orders to produce religious art according to lines established at the Council of Trent in 1545–63. More important, however, would be the creation of the Accademia di Belle Arti di Brera, under the patronage of Austria's Maria Theresa, in 1776.

Venice-born Francesco Hayez (1791–1882) was the towering figure of the art world in 19th-century Milan, where he moved in 1820. By then, however, the epicentre of European art had long shifted away from Italy – to Paris. Hayez kicked off a romantic stint in his career in the 1820s, and was clearly respected, being made director of the Brera academy in 1850, by which time he had become more interested in portraying historical events. He also churned out numerous portraits.

The latter half of the century in Milan was marked by *verismo* (naturalism) and realist painting. Angelo Morbelli (1853–1919), Giovanni Segantini (1858–99) and Giuseppe Pellizza da Volpedo (1868–1907), all students of the Brera academy, all sought, to varying degrees, to infuse their art with a realism that frequently carried social-political messages. They were then swept up by the *divisionismo* movement at the end of the 19th century. Inspired by the *pointillisme* of French artists like Paul Signac, they aimed to distort light and colour in their pen strokes to lend either greater strength to the realism of some paintings or increase the allegorical sense of others. A handful of their works can be seen in the gallery of the academy where they studied.

Milan made its last big artistic noise in 1910. There, led by incendiary writer Filippo Marinetti, five Italian artists signed the futurist manifesto. Of them, Umberto Boccioni (1882–1916) and Giacomo Balla (1871–1958) would become futurism's key exponents. Their line of thought was roughly 'out with the old and in with the new', and the futurist painters certainly brought drama, passion and not a little confusion to their works. Any momentary scandal their work and 'ideology' might have caused in high Milanese society was soon drowned out by the guns and horrors of WWI that engulfed northern Italy from 1915 to 1918.

BACKGROUND

# GREAT GUEST ARTISTS

## ❦ GIOTTO DI BONDONE // (C 1266–1337)

**ONE OF THE KEY** precursors of the Florentine Renaissance, Giotto marks a transformation in the two-dimensional, deadpan painting of the Gothic period by injecting humanity, movement and subtleties of light that were decades ahead of his time. Known for master- pieces in Florence and Padua, he was sent for by Milan's Azzone Visconti in 1335. Giotto worked for two years in Milan but none of his work there has survived. His teaching, however, acquainted local artists with the avant-garde of Italian painting.

## ❦ MASOLINO DA PANICALE // (C 1383–1440)

**MUCH INFLUENCED** by younger fellow Tuscan painter Masaccio, with whom he created extraordinary works in Florence and Rome, Masolino wound up in Castiglione Olona (p93), near Varese, in 1435. He had been commissioned to carry out frescos above all in the Collegiata, Castiglione's main church. Masolino had at first remained faithful to classic Gothic precepts but, exposed to the whirlwind genius of Masaccio, quickly changed his tune to become one of the early exponents of perspective and the Florentine Renaissance.

## ❦ PISANELLO // (C 1380–1455)

**IT IS THOUGHT** that Antonio Pisano il Pisanello, who was born in Pisa but long lived and worked in Verona and Mantua, met Masolino and other Renaissance painters. Knowing on which side his bread was buttered (the bulk of his commissions came from powerful Church figures as yet unimpressed by the new-fangled Renaissance), Pisanello remained faithful to his late-Gothic leanings. Some of his greatest works are frescos left behind in the San Fermo Maggiore and Sant'Anastasia churches in Verona (p217).

## ❦ ANDREA MANTEGNA // (1431–1506)

**PADUA-BORN MANTEGNA** had the fortune to meet such visiting stars of the Florentine Renaissance firmament as Paolo Uccello, Filippo Lippi and Donatello. Mantegna absorbed their lessons on perspective and became a key figure in the launching of Venice's artistic glory days. He left behind major works in Verona's Basilica di San Zeno Maggiore (p217) but is known principally for his work in Mantua (above all, the Palazzo Ducale's Camera degli Sposi, see p223), where he remained from 1460 until his death.

## ☙ LEONARDO DA VINCI // (1452–1519)

**MORE THAN A CENTURY** after Giotto, the ruling Sforza clan managed to lure Leonardo from his native Tuscany. He must have liked it (perhaps the pay was good too), for he stayed from 1482 to 1499, working as architect (Piazza Ducale in Vigevano, p61), engineer (defensive works and canals) and painter. He left behind one of Milan's most cherished works of art, *Il cenacolo Vinciano* (The Last Supper, p42). Leonardo returned to Milan, then under French control, in 1506–13.

## ☙ LORENZO LOTTO // (1480–1556)

**EVEN AS LEONARDO'S** influence on Lombard painters waned, new artistic winds blew from the east. By the mid-15th century Venice had extended its control as far west into Lombardy as Bergamo and Crema. A product of the Venetian Renaissance, Lorenzo Lotto was a wild and sensitive soul. He was studying in Rome in 1513 when he was summoned to Bergamo, where he remained for 12 years, leaving behind plenty of works (p152) that combine Venetian, Roman and Lombard influences.

## ☙ IL PORDENONE // (1484–1539)

**BORN IN THE TOWN** of Pordenone in Venetian-controlled Friuli, Il Pordenone ranged across northern Italy. Trained in Venice, he was a direct competitor of Titian, against whom he often came off second best despite the quality of his work. Later influenced by Raphael, Il Pordenone's painting took on a wildness of colour and movement that is never more evident than in one of his most exacting commissions, the *Storie del Cristo* (Stories of Christ) frescos (1520–22), in the cathedral of Cremona (p171).

## ☙ GIAMBATTISTA TIEPOLO // (1696–1770)

**LORD OF VENICE'S** art scene in the 18th century and a master of rococo caprice, Giambattista Tiepolo towered above all those around him. He spent most of his life in Venice, although his last years were spent with the Spanish court in Madrid. Before Spain he embarked on several other foreign jaunts, in 1731–33 hitting the road for Milan and Bergamo. In the latter, he added frescos in the Cappella Colleoni (p148) that have survived to this day.

# FROM ROMANESQUE TO RENAISSANCE

· · · · · · ·

## THE BIRTH OF THE BASILICA

It all started in Rome. Often accused of having copied half their culture from the Greeks (from their arts to their religion), few would argue with the engineering and architectural prowess of the Romans. With the exception of the magnificent Roman Arena in Verona, along with that city's amphitheatre, surprisingly little testimony of Rome's imperium has remained in northern Italy. Other sites include the ruins in Brescia (p166), and Sirmione, on Lake Garda (p192).

As early as the 2nd century BC, the Romans were building basilicas, often for dealing with business and legal matters, but also at times as religious places. The basic structure was held up by semicircular arches and, inside, often one or two colonnades dividing the space into two or three aisles. At one end (and sometimes at both) was a semicircular apse. After Emperor Constantine made Christianity the official religion of the empire, basilicas were also used as Christian houses of worship. Possibly the grandest basilica built by the Romans was that of Maxentius, in Rome.

The impression that after the fall of the western Roman Empire, in AD 476, all of Italy and Europe plunged into a hopelessly dark period of chaos seems to be supported by the apparent lack of any substantial building activity for several centuries thereafter. In Milan, however, this is not quite true. A good half dozen churches that still stand were raised in this turbulent time – the Basilica di San Lorenzo is a good example (p50). The Lombards also built forts and churches and, although little evidence remains, in Castelseprio you can see vestiges of both (p93).

## RENEWAL IN LOMBARDY

By about the 11th century, Lombard builders were raising churches in ever greater numbers and building them to last. While some early Christian churches had tended to be circular or octagonal (often built around a baptismal font), these new churches represented the rediscovery of the Roman basilica. Indeed, in most cases, they followed the Roman model to a tee. The term Romanesque was not coined to describe this state of affairs until 1818, when French archaeologist Charles de Gerville used it to distinguish the style from later Gothic creations.

The word basilica is thus an architectural term that also came to have an ecclesiastical meaning. It is usually applied to larger, more important churches (the term is not the equivalent of 'cathedral', which refers to a church that contains the seat – *cathedra* – of a bishop).

Romanesque churches in the Lombard plains were mostly built as grand brick affairs with semicircular arches above doorways and windows, much like their Roman basilica predecessors. The semicircle was also the main structural element in vaults and arches, and in the apse. Semicircular arches separated the columns that marked the two aisles from the central nave. In more elaborate churches, a transept (forming a cross-shaped ground plan, in memory of the cross on which Christ died) was added across the nave before the apse, and with increasing frequency a dome would be placed above the spot where nave and transept crossed.

Around the lakes, especially Lake Como, dozens of small village and country churches and chapels were built of stone. Some boast apses on three sides, and almost all are accompanied by tall, slender bell towers. The bulk have slate roofs. Many were built by master builders from Como (the Maestri Comacini). The more you explore villages around Lake Como and, to a lesser extent, Lake Maggiore and beyond, the more of these gems you'll turn up.

The style spread from Lombardy across much of Italy and western Europe. Over the four or so centuries that it held sway, a broad palette of variations emerged. More daring builders went to town with embellishment: adding more and more layers of arches in decorative fashion to doorways and windows; expanding the apse into triple and even quintuple apses; and adorning exteriors and interiors with fanciful sculptural detail, from simple floral and geometrical shapes inherited from the Lombards and other Germanic tribes to mythical animals and, later, human images. Cloisters, peaceful quadrangular galleries built around a garden, were added.

In some cases, availability of materials had an enormous impact – Tuscan Romanesque churches are clad in marble, a material in abundant supply there. In Lombardy and beyond (Verona, for example), red brick and, sometimes, stone were preferred. Typically, Lombard churches sport a *facciata a capanna* (hut facade), so-called because it looks like a simple hut or warehouse, with the roof sloping off to two sides. A variation on that theme, the *facciata a vento* (wind facade), is like a great flat sail that extends well above the naves behind it. One wholly original departure from Roman basilica models was the addition of a separate, usually square-based bell tower.

Across the area covered in this book, examples of the Romanesque style abound. One of the most spectacular is Verona's Basilica di San Zeno Maggiore (p217). Milan's Basilica di Sant'Ambrogio (p50), actually a renovation of an earlier church, is also beautiful. From charming countryside churches like the Chiesa di San Tomè, in Almenno San Bartolomeo (p155), San Pietro al Monte, in Civate (p117), and the Pieve di San Siro, in Capo di Ponte (p162), to the imposing Basilica di San Michele, in Pavia (p59) and Como's Basilica di Sant'Abbondio (p109), there is no shortage of fine examples across this territory.

## DON'T MISS...

### ROMANESQUE CHURCHES

- ★ **Basilica di Sant'Abbondio, Como //** Colourful frescos contrast with grey stone sobriety (p109)

- ★ **Basilica di San Zeno Maggiore, Verona //** A spectacular construction filled with frescos (p217)

- ★ **Basilica di Sant'Ambrogio //** A link to early-Christian days (p50)

- ★ **Chiesa di San Tomè, Almenno San Bartolomeo //** Where the circle signifies perfection (p155)

- ★ **San Pietro al Monte, Civate //** Beauty at the end of a high hill trek (p117)

# TRANSITION & GOTHIC

The Gothic style (the term coined during the Renaissance and long used in derogatory fashion by aesthetes) was born in and around Paris in the 12th century, largely out of architectural ambition. The desire to build larger, higher places of worship led to the use of a variety of engineering tricks such as buttresses, flying buttresses, larger windows to reduce structural weight, new methods of vaulting and so on. The penchant of the Gothic style for soaring pinnacles and towers, elongated, tapering windows and a clear Latin cross floor plan with generous transept, makes a clear break from the stout, rounded look of the Romanesque and its Roman basilica prototypes. It is as though medieval Christian Europe finally cast off its Roman heritage to assert its own force and identity.

Italian Gothic churches tend to be sober affairs, not overly rich in spires and pinnacles and generally eschewing such details as flying buttresses (designed to help hold up tall walls from without). The style spread slowly in Italy and did not have the universal appeal that it won elsewhere in Europe. Northern Italy's Gothic seems more an adaptation of Romanesque rather than a wholesale replacement – in countless cases Gothic building methods and style were incorporated into buildings already underway. Considering that the completion of a cathedral could often take a century or more, this is hardly surprising.

Clear examples of this transition abound. In Verona, the Duomo and the Basilica di San Fermo Maggiore combine the two styles. Bergamo's Basilica di Santa Maria Maggiore (p148) is decidedly Romanesque around the apse, becomes Gothic towards the front and has a Renaissance overlay thrown in for good measure.

Examples of the north European style of Gothic are rare in Italy – Milan's Duomo (p39) is an exception, and then only up to a point. But what an effort to get it finished. Begun in 1387 under French architects (which probably explains its somewhat un-Italian northern look), this spiked and spired marble colossus was still having bits and pieces added in the 1960s. With five aisles and the highest nave (45m) of any completed Gothic church, it is a unique masterwork.

That such an undertaking could even be considered was, in no small part, a reflection of the times. Gian Galeazzo Visconti was in charge of a prosperous Milan and he had the political weight and financial clout to help get the ball rolling. A further expression of his power and that of his successors was the extensive castle-building and renovation program across the territories under Visconti control. Galeazzo II had started with his stout Castello Visconteo (1360; p58) and the Visconti also took over and largely renovated the like-named fort in Locarno (p70). Even many of the castles (such as in Milan and Vigevano) today named after Visconti successors, the Sforza clan, started off as Gothic-era forts established or significantly rebuilt by the Visconti.

Over in Verona, the Scaligeri rulers also built Castelvecchio (p215), a fine example of a secular Gothic building. At about the same time, most cities raised powerful secular buildings (generally called *broletto* or *palazzo della ragione* – 'palace of reason') to house their town halls. Fine examples stand today in Bergamo, Brescia and Cremona.

Another Gothic masterpiece is the Certosa di Pavia (p59), one of several Gothic monastery complexes to dot the Lombard countryside. This one is especially interesting as it bears a heavy Renaissance overlay. From the early 15th century a new creative wind began to blow, this time coming from the south, more specifically from Florence.

Lombard Gothic churches are scattered across the region. More often than not they display some Romanesque influences, such as the semicircular arch and the region's characteristic reddish brick.

## ROME'S REVENGE & THE RENAISSANCE

The flurry of learning in all fields of the arts and sciences that began in the enlightened Florence of the Medici in the late 14th century would lead to an artistic revolution in the 15th century. Artists and architects travelled with growing frequency to Rome to rummage around in that city's classical ruins. All that fossicking around the Colosseum, in the forums and basilicas, wrought an extraordinary about-face in the minds of medieval artisans. The classical lines of ancient Roman buildings and art came back into vogue. Allied with the techniques refined in the centuries of Gothic construction, this new fashion would lead to the creation of prodigious new buildings. In one sense, architecture had turned full circle, back to Rome. In another, the heady alloy of classical and Gothic would lead to a new aesthetic.

Much as with painters and sculptors, genius architects waving the new Renaissance banner soon began to range across Italy. Under Ludovico Sforza, Leonardo da Vinci

**BACKGROUND**

## DELVING INTO WORLD HERITAGE

Unesco has been pretty busy in and around the northern Italian lakes down the years. From Bellinzona, in Swiss Ticino, to Mantua, in southeast Lombardy, a surprisingly varied array of locations have been selected as World Heritage sites.

With 43 sites at last count, Italy has more World Heritage listings than any other country in the world. Switzerland has a more modest 10. Among what one might call the 'senior' sites in the lakes region are the old city of Verona (p213); the combined site of Mantua and Sabbioneta; *Il cenacolo Vinciano* (Leonardo da Vinci's *The Last Supper*; p42) in Milan; and the three fortified castles, walls and ramparts of Bellinzona (p137).

Less obvious sites include the late-19th-century workers' village of Crespi d'Adda (p154), the ancient rock drawings of Valle Camonica (p162) and the geological site of Monte San Giorgio (p137).

Finally come the Sacri Monti (Sacred Mounts) of Piedmont and Lombardy. Nine of these hilltop church sanctuaries (usually arrived at by a chapel-studded walk of penance) are included in a single listing and some of them fall within the area covered by this book: the Sacro Monte del Rosario di Varese (p93); Sacro Monte della Beata Vergine del Soccorso, Ossuccio (Lake Como); and the Sacro Monte della Santissima Trinità, Ghiffa (p80). Another in Orta San Giulio (p98) did not make it on to the Unesco listing.

and Donato Bramante were called to serve the Duchy of Milan. The latter worked on Milan's Castello Sforzesco, the castle in nearby Vigevano, Pavia's Duomo and more. Leonardo, in his usual style, worked on everything from fortifications and engineering works on Milan's Navigli (canals) to creating the superb Piazza Ducale in Vigevano (p61).

In Mantua, meanwhile, Leon Battista Alberti, the great Florentine theoretician of Renaissance building, arrived to start work on various churches and advise the Gonzaga family on giving their city a new architectural lease on life. Alberti had a decisive influence on Giulio Romano, who was commissioned with the design of Palazzo Te (p223). And the stormy Florentine genius Brunelleschi had, according to some, a direct hand in the design of the Chiesa di Villa in Castiglione Olona (p93).

'As the Renaissance gave way to mannerism and the baroque, the sun set on Milan's greatness'

The appearance of Renaissance design could be a matter of considered town planning, as in Bergamo's Piazza Vecchia (p146), or the result of the spendthrift whim of a powerful individual, as in the Cappella Colleoni (p148), just off that same square.

As the Renaissance gave way to mannerism and the baroque, the sun set on Milan's greatness in the early 16th century. Cities like Bergamo, Brescia and Verona continued to prosper quietly under the Lion of St Mark (Venice) but somehow seemed to stand still in time. Then, decadence and stagnation overtook even Venice. Building on a grand scale, especially of churches, continued, but somehow the creative verve of earlier centuries seemed to decline. Great architects were still at work in the likes of Venice and Rome but the rest of northern Italy slipped gradually into a gentle torpor.

# VILLAS & GARDENS

. . . . . . .

The country residence as (to say it with Coleridge) 'pleasure dome' has always been an expression of wealth and taste (the latter, of course, is open to interpretation). In Italy, the Romans started the trend. Emperors, senators and wealthy merchants all had a hankering for a seaside palace, rustic estate or lakeside villa to escape to. From the 16th century on, wealth and power led to a similar result, but it was mostly nobles and cardinals behind the lakeside building boom. In the late 19th century, with Italy unified and confident prior to the nightmare of WWI, the wealthy business class and social climbers with money built their own villas, many in the new and eclectic art nouveau style (or its Italian expression, *stile liberty*), around the southern end of the main lakes. Permits to build more modern affairs are harder to come by these days but an exploration of the lake shores reveals that much of the prime real estate is lined with pleasure domes big and small, whether built in recent decades or with the cache of a century or three of history. The underlying factor remains unchanged: fine secondary residences in privileged positions were, and remain, a sign of prosperity.

## ROMAN HOLIDAYS

For prestige and display of financial ease, in Roman times as now, there was nothing like a spread, surrounded by soothing and often lavish gardens, by the sea or one of northern Italy's lakes. Remnants of a couple of Roman *domus* (country houses) with some fine mosaics survive in Brescia, in what is now the Museo della Città (p164).

Pliny the Elder (AD 23–79) had several villas along Lake Como. His nephew Pliny the Younger (AD 62–115) was brought up in his uncle's residences and later built two of his own, one at what is today Bellagio. Many of the Plinys' writings have survived, but none of their properties. Catullus (c 84 to c 54 BC), another man of Roman letters, supposedly lived in the villa whose ruins stand in Sirmione. Known popularly as the Grotte del Catullo (p192), it is the largest villa uncovered in northern Italy, dates to the late 1st century BC and was probably abandoned by the 4th century AD.

> '*Remnants of a couple of Roman* domus *(country houses) with some fine mosaics survive in Brescia*'

## RENAISSANCE REVIVAL

It was not until the Renaissance washed over Italy from Florence that the idea of the bucolic villa and garden as getaway was reborn.

The Renaissance was fuelled by an admiration for the classical world and its various expressions, in art, architecture and planning. Where medieval houses and palaces tended to look into internal courtyards and gardens, those with serious chunks of property now began to build their residences with a greater outward ostentation and a surrounding garden. While the original impulses to create splendid gardens came with the Renaissance, their creation around villas and palaces only took off in the 16th century. A

BACKGROUND

good example of the urban villa and garden is Verona's Giardino Giusti (p217). These Renaissance gardens were set out in 1570, with cypresses, clipped symmetrical hedges, ivy-framed gazebos, a labyrinth and classical statues scattered about.

In the latter half of the 16th century, the first great lakeside villas were built or bought and subjected to a metamorphosis, becoming holiday pleasure domes for the wealthy. The Marquis Stanga acquired Villa Serbelloni, in Bellagio (p114), and set about creating its gardens. Until then, here and in a handful of other older villas, the grounds had served as orchards and herb gardens, grown amid chestnut forests and freely running streams. All this was gradually cleared to make way for cypresses, symmetrically laid out lawns and topiary, pergolas and terraces. Water was channelled into fountains and artificial ponds. In 1565 work on what is now Villa d'Este (p118) began, and around 1600 the Sfondrati family came into possession of what would be transformed into Villa Monastero (p126).

The powerful Milanese Borromeo clan turned the barely inhabited Isola Bella (p86) into a luxurious family getaway in the course of the 17th century. The palace – four floors of endlessly interlocking rooms and halls – leaves one gasping. The visual overload continues outside. Isola Bella's gardens are perhaps the greatest baroque riot of any Italian garden. Its statue-laden terraces, a sort of Italianate vision of the Hanging Gardens of Babylon, can be fairly safely described as OTT. Another view might be that they are the ultimate expression of the Italianate garden. A new century would bring more sober tastes from the north.

---

**DON'T MISS...**

**VILLAS & GARDENS**

★ **Isola Bella, Lake Maggiore //** The most luxurious of the Borromeo creations, an enormous mansion with a delirious baroque garden (p86)

★ **Villa Balbianello, Lenno //** Possibly the most striking of the lake villas, combining a personal museum with staggering promontory grounds (p121)

★ **Villa Taranto, Verbania //** A botanist's dream, with some 20,000 species on show (p80)

★ **Villa Serbelloni, Bellagio //** An Italianate garden dream on which work began in the 16th century (p114)

★ **Villa Monastero, Varenna //** A warm family villa set amid a densely florid garden with a centuries-old magnolia (p126)

★ **Villa Carlotta, Tremezzo //** Canova's statues inside are outdone by the combination of Italian and English gardens and vivid flowers outside (p122)

---

## THE ENGLISH GARDEN

In the course of the 18th century, a growing number of well-off northern Europeans would embark on a jaunt of several months, which came to be known as the Grand Tour, to round off their education by visiting great cities and sights, above all those of France and Italy. Most passed by the lakes and few failed to be enchanted by the mildness of the climate and richness of the flora (both in and outside villa gardens).

Many were English, and it is probably through them that a new fad took hold among the well-to-do Italian lakeside villa owners – English-style gardens supposedly emulating nature. This trend had emerged in the first half of the 18th century; a fine example in England is Blenheim Palace, in Oxfordshire, with its rolling countryside, thickets and clearings, all apparently random but, in fact, meticulously planned.

Possibly the most visually striking of the lakes' villas, Villa Balbianello (p121) was built at the end of the 18th century on a ridgeback promontory jutting into Lake Como. The villa buildings have a neoclassical flavour with some lightly baroque elements and the gardens are a mix of Italian and English, with little of the layout left to hazard.

To get a clear idea of the difference between the Italianate and English style gardens, visit Villa Olmo, in Como (p110). Work on the villa began in the early 18th century and it was completed in low-slung neoclassical fashion. Fronting the lake is a highly ordered garden, labelled Italianate but more soberly French than anything else. Behind the villa is a tree-filled park – apparently natural but all planned. Indeed, the word 'park' would seem a more accurate label than 'garden' for English-style gardens.

Although the fad for English-style gardens was powerful, it never completely overran the Italians' continental tastes. The gardens of early-19th-century Villa Melzi d'Eril (p114), in Bellagio, are often cited as the first English-style gardens to be laid out at a lakes villa. There are clear English elements, such as the irregularly shaped pond surrounded by seemingly random thickets of trees at the north end, but there remain elements more at home in an Italian garden, such as the symmetrically laid out flower beds and lily pond around the villa itself.

One of the best examples of the English villa garden is Lake Como's Villa Carlotta (p122). It was built in the 17th century and given as a present to a Prussian princess in 1847. Around the villa itself, the ordered layout suggests the Italianate approach, though as you explore this changes radically. At one part of the northern end of the garden is the cool and magical Valle delle Felci (Fern Valley), a dense forest full of ferns and all sorts of other trees, such as towering sequoias. This 'wilderness' is perhaps the best example of the English ideal on the lakes.

## A BOTANICAL BENT

Another fine example of the English garden is the Borromeos' Isola Madre (p87). This is not so much because of the layout, although that element is certainly present, with forests of all kinds of trees bordering an irregularly shaped lawn clearing, but because of its botanical vocation. The gardens are full of exotics imported from around the world and were designed to not only be pleasing to the eye, but with a decidedly didactic purpose.

This focus on showcasing exotic species is also shared by the above-mentioned Villa Carlotta, though nowhere is it more consciously the case than at Villa Taranto, in Verbania on Lake Maggiore (p80). Villa Taranto was purchased in 1931 by a Scottish officer who devoted his life to the development of its extensive grounds. Today they hold some 20,000 species and constitute one of Europe's finest botanic gardens.

BACKGROUND

Budding botanists will find plenty more opportunities to indulge their passion. Not far up the road from Villa Taranto, across the Swiss border, a notable excursion takes you to Ticino's botanic gardens on the Isole di Brissago (p74).

## THE 19TH CENTURY & A NEW ART

From the latter end of the 19th century, there was a boom in villa construction on the lakes, a symbol of self-worth among moneyed families at a time of confidence following Italian unification. The villas became the focus of a high-class dolce vita, and their gardens, perfect for long *passeggiate* (promenades), were seen as a kind of open-air salon, an extension of the villas themselves. The villas and their well-off owners attracted a coterie of socialites and artists, the latter inspired by the beautiful countryside.

It was the belle époque, and for some decades a fresh new wave in art and architecture, taking its cue from applied arts and strong Japanese influences, had been spreading across Europe. Known as art nouveau in France, it came to be called *stile liberty* (liberty style) in Italy. Indeed, there was a great deal of liberty in what architects designed in this joyously experimental moment, and the wealthy had money to spend on new residences and the new style (or styles). Key points for identifying such buildings are the proud and visible use of materials previously considered 'ignoble', such as wrought iron, ceramics, stained glass, brick and, in some cases, cement. In addition, liberty and art nouveau designers and architects favoured curves and natural motifs (flowers, vines etc) over straight lines, particularly in decorative elements (from door handles to windows, sculptural reliefs to door frames). In the liberty period these elements were applied to buildings from the conventional to turreted castles.

It is hardly surprising that many buildings in this style should have popped up on the lakes. They did so mainly in more popular, accessible locations. Since the opening of the Sempione (Simplon) Pass from Switzerland and the arrival of rail connections, Stresa on Lake Maggiore had become a key holiday spot. It is dotted with liberty villas, all very different from one another, precisely because their architects were looking for new expressions. One of the great Italian liberty architects was Giuseppe Sommaruga, who left several villas in Sarnico (p159; the most noteworthy is Villa Faccanoni), on Lake Iseo. On Lake Como, only the Villa Bernasconi (p119) is a clear liberty example, though it's one of the best.

## WHEN TO SEE THE FLOWERS

One of the greatest treats for the senses along the Lombard lakes, especially Lake Como and Lake Maggiore, are the gorgeous flowers in the many villa gardens. The mild climate allows a surprising variety of flora to flourish. The best time to experience these flowers in full glory is spring but you'll find something most months of the year. In January and February you can spot certain camellias and a handful of other winter flowers. In March camellias and magnolias start to flower, joined in April by azaleas and rhododendrons. In May come late magnolias, cornus and peonies. By June the last of the azaleas, rhododendrons and cornus flower. From June to early October a magnificent parade of dahlias is on show in Villa Taranto (p80). Autumn flowers include some types of camellia and citrus.

Houses, villas and hotels either in the liberty style or with some liberty elements (such as the use of floral motifs or materials such as wrought iron or ceramics) were built all over Lombardy, from Milan to San Pellegrino Terme (p156), where the seven-storey Grand Hotel (1904) and exuberant Casinò Municipale (1907) form a treasure chest of the liberty style.

Sometimes the architects got a little carried away, as with the somewhat outlandish neo-Gothic and liberty mix of Villa Feltrinelli, in Gargnano (p200) on Lake Garda – a suitable location, perhaps, for Mussolini's final residence towards the end of WWII. Lake Garda certainly attracted some eccentrics, such as poet, soldier, aviator and nationalist Gabriele d'Annunzio, who created the Vittoriale degli Italiani (p199), his residence-cum-monument, which can hardly be fitted into any category, in Gardone Riviera. It too has gorgeous gardens.

BACKGROUND

# OUTDOOR PURSUITS

· · · · · · ·

Touring the lakes can be as active as you want to make it. With endless, breathtaking scenery, the temptation to give your motorised steed a rest and get about on your own two pins will doubtless overcome you on more than a few occasions. Cycling is also an excellent way to get around the lakes, although some roads can be more busy than one would like.

In summer, lovers of water sports can take up a position on various key points of the lakes to enjoy sailing, windsurfing, kitesurfing, wakeboarding or just a swim and sunbathe. Winter sports abound for those who venture here in the 'wrong' season. Northern Italy abounds with excellent skiing, and Switzerland needs no introduction. The best of the Alpine fun lies beyond the confines of this book but the area around the lakes and especially in the province of Bergamo is littered with minor ski stations, ideal for locals heading up for a day or for families with beginners in tow.

## WALKING

At first glance, one might think there is little in the line of walking to be done around Italy's northern lakes except for the occasional shoreline promenade. Nothing could be further from the truth.

The best news is that there really is something for everyone, from short, pleasant walks suitable for any level of fitness, through to some serious mountain hikes and even mountaineering options.

### EASY WALKING

Of course, in many towns along all the lakes, you can simply head for a short stroll along the shoreline. For instance, the road leading north out of Orta San Giulio (p97) to Villa Motta is a pleasant stroll. Other pleasant waterfront promenades, some of which can extend for a few kilometres if you wish, include Lugano (in either direction) on Lake Lugano, Ascona (p74) on Lake Maggiore, Sarnico or Iseo (p159) on Lake Iseo, Gardone Riviera and Riva del Garda (p203) on Lake Garda.

> *'the road leading north out of Orta San Giulio to Villa Motta is a pleasant stroll'*

On Lake Como, one suggested strolling route of 10km between Cadennabia and Colonno is the **Greenway del Lago di Como** (www.greenwaydellago.it). The walking is easy and it takes you through Tremezzo (with Villa Carlotta), Lenno (Villa Balbianello), Ossuccio (look out for the bizarre bell tower) and Sala Comacina (from where you can get a boat to Isola Comacina). Back on Lake Orta, it is possible to walk right around the lake in three fairly relaxed days (p99).

Options multiply away from the banks of the lakes. In some cases, no more than a couple of hours of walking can bring you to lovely sights and viewpoints. On Lake Garda, a 3km walk north out of Riva del Garda leads to the Cascata del Varone (p203),

BACKGROUND

## HIGHLAND HIKES IN THE ALPI OROBIE

The Alpi Orobie rise east of the north end of Lake Como and stretch east to the region of Trentino-Alto Adige. Separated from a first phalanx of the Swiss-Italian Alps to the north by the Valtellina and marked by a series of valleys that lead towards Bergamo and Lake Iseo to the south, this mountain range is full of beauty, with peaks rising to altitudes of between 2000m and 3000m. Most of their area is covered by two parks, the Parco delle Orobie Valtellinesi and Parco delle Orobie Bergamasche (for more on these, see www .parks.it). The mountains are rich in forest and upland pastures but the first of the two parks is easily the most spectacular. The Orobie Alps are dotted with *rifugi* (mountain huts), where you can stay overnight and get meals in summer.

A good place to start looking at the hiking options in this mountain range, most of which has natural park status, is **Sentiero delle Orobie** (www.sentierodelleorobie.it, in Italian).

the biggest waterfall around the lake. On the west bank of Lake Como, a somewhat more demanding two-hour hike from near Menaggio brings you to a mountain refuge with breathtaking lake views (p122).

### HEADING FOR THE HILLS

More seasoned walkers have unlimited choices. The lakes are surrounded by hills and mountains, some of which exceed 2000m in altitude.

On Lake Garda for instance, you could take the cable car from Malcesine to Monte Baldo and alight at the intermediate station of San Michele (p207), from where numerous hiking options open up. The walk back down to Malcesine takes about an hour. Similarly, you can walk up and/or down Monte Mottarone (p82), outside Stresa.

In Lake Como's Triangolo Lariano, there are more challenging walking options that require some fitness and preparation. They include the two-day Dorsale hike (p116), which takes you across the mountainous centre from Brunate, outside Como, to beautiful Bellagio. There's a mule-trail option or you can follow the mountain crests.

Club Alpino Italiano (CAI) trails are staked out in a web across northern Italy. You could search out little known Romanesque churches like the Abbazia di San Pietro al Monte (p117), at the southeast end of Lake Como, or perhaps drive up to Monte Bisbino (p119) and embark on some high-level walks from there. One of the best walks in this area, requiring no particular skills but quite a bit of time, is the Via dei Monti Lariani, a 130km trail from Cernobbio in the south to Sorico in the north (p122).

In and around the valleys north of Bergamo, endless possibilities unfold. The tourist office in Bergamo (p146) can provide some basic maps to get you orientated.

More serious mountain hikes can be undertaken in the Parco delle Grigne (p128). This can be challenging stuff, with *vie ferrate* (climbing trails with permanent steel cords) and mountaineering skills required on some trails. There's more of this in the Alpi Orobie mountains north of Bergamo (above).

# CYCLING

Italians (some of them anyway) are cycling fanatics. And no more so than in northern Italy. On weekends you can see whole gangs on shiny new racing bikes, scooting up hill and down dale with sometimes frightening alacrity. This being Italy, many riders go the whole hog with the accoutrements too. Why buy a pair of boring cycling pants and a helmet when you can kit yourself out like a pro, complete with corporate sponsor advertising on your *maillot* (jersey)?

As bicycle hire is not always that common, keen cyclists may want to bring their own. Some local outlets also provide guides, such as Lake Como Cycling (p106) or Iseobike (p159).

The main problem with cycling along the lakes is traffic. Depending on the route you choose, this can be less of a problem midweek (eg on the Como–Bellagio road). The second issue is the terrain. Although much of the cycling lakeside is comparatively easy on the legs, as soon as you move inland you can be confronted by considerable climbs. More relaxed cycling is possible on the Lombard plains. Perhaps the most fun is the Franciacorta wine territory (p160), mostly flat or gently rolling countryside dotted with villages, castles and wineries. Tourist offices in Como, Lecco and Varese can supply a map with suggested cycle routes between Lake Maggiore and the east bank of Lake Como.

Mountain-bike riders have plenty of scope too. Some walking trails (such as the Dorsale between Brunate and Bellagio on Lake Como) are also suitable for mountain bikes. The Lecco tourist office includes this route on a general map and booklet with mountain-bike itineraries, mostly inland from the east bank of Lake Como.

## DON'T MISS...

### HIKES, BIKES & WATER SPORTS

* **Monte Mottarone hikes** // A popular mountain with amazing views and cable-car access (p82)

* **Waterskiing in Alto Lario** // Get some water thrills at the north end of Lake Como (p124)

* **Windsurfing off Torbole** // Pick up the best winds on the lakes (p206)

* **Follow the Giro d'Italia** // Cycle to Bellagio and then follow the steep Giro d'Italia stage to the Santuario della Madonna del Ghisallo (p116)

* **Rifugio Menaggio** // Hike to the refuge for Lake Como views (p122)

# WATER SPORTS

Italy's lakes are probably not the first place that spring to mind when considering a summer beach holiday. But, in fact, there is plenty of water fun to be had.

All the main lakes have beaches, albeit often tiny, pebble affairs. But with a sun lounge, some of these beaches can be beautiful settings for a dip and sunbake. On Lake Como the only serious sand beach is a very pleasant artificial arrangement that is part of a summer chill-out bar at Lenno. The towns of Como and Lugano have similar lidos (bathing beaches). Lake Garda's best beach is at Punta San Vigilio.

Some of these beaches and other key lakeside spots offer summer hire of pedalos and kayaks. The lakes area has produced several rowing champions down the years but you needn't be so extreme. A lovely spot for a row is Lake Endine (p161), where motorised boats are forbidden.

More exciting for some are wind-and-water pursuits. Wind- and kitesurfing both have a keen following, especially around Torbole, Riva and Malcesine on Lake Garda and at the north end of Lake Como around Gera Lario and Colico. This is largely because of the predictability and constancy of summer south winds during the day. You'll find hire outlets and schools at these locations.

For those after more motorised movement, waterskiing and wakeboarding are popular activities on Lakes Maggiore, Como and Garda.

Various boat hire outlets on the main lakes will also rent out zodiacs and other small boats for a run-around.

# HORSE RIDING

A smattering of *maneggio* (horse-riding centres) are scattered about the lakes area, usually a fair way inland. A few *agriturismi* (farm-stay accommodation) also have horse-riding facilities though some will only take people who already know how to ride. You won't find too many groups trotting around the lakes themselves – excursions tend to be inland. Ask at tourist offices for nearby locations.

## BREAK OUT YOUR SKIS!

The lakes are surrounded by hills and mountains that are home to a plethora of little family-oriented ski stations that make for an original winter visit. From many vantage points around the lakes, the Italian Alps are visible, and some more challenging ski resorts are not all that far off.

The most varied and interesting ski options within the boundaries of this book are in the valleys that stretch north of Bergamo into the Alpi Orobie mountains. The most popular of these ski centres is **Foppolo** (p156) with six runs and, generally, no shortage of snow.

Between Lakes Orta and Maggiore, the popular Monte Mottarone (p82) turns into a modest ski resort in winter. With 21km over seven runs, **Mottarone** (www.mottaroneski .it) is a popular family ski location and easily accessible by the cable car from Stresa. On a crisp, clear winter's day, the views are fabulous.

Locarno locals sometimes head up to **Cimetta** (p70) to slide around a little on a day off.

The main ski option around Lake Garda is at **Monte Baldo** (p207). Take the cable car from Malcesine to get to a small selection of shortish runs, including a black one and a couple of reds that are OK for middle-level skiers. It's a handy spot near Verona if you just want a half-day's snow fun.

On Lake Como there is some modest cross-country skiing in **Valsassina** (Piani di Bobbio; p128), northeast of Lecco, and at **Pian del Tivano** (p116).

For reference, more serious skiing not far from the lakes area happens at Bormio (www.bormio.it), at the northeast end of the Valtellina, and around Monte Rosa (especially Macugnaga, www.macugnaga.it), west of Lake Maggiore in Piedmont.

# ADVENTURE SPORTS

Canyoning, white-water rafting and the like are possible not too far from Lake Maggiore (in Valsesia) but just beyond the scope of this book. Ask at tourist offices on the west (Piedmont) side of the lake.

You can also get hang-gliding and paragliding thrills above Lake Maggiore, by taking the Sasso del Ferro cable car from Laveno (p89), on the lower east bank of the lake. Bring your own kit or get some lessons at the local school. Another launch point for those who want to fly is Monte Baldo (p207).

# SMOOTH AS SILK

· · · · · · ·

When you buy a Calvin Klein silk tie, a feather-light foulard by Chanel, or Prada's latest silk dress, you will never know who actually produced your new acquisition. The bulk of the big fashion names in Italy and many of those beyond rely on a network of specialist silk producers in Como for their wares. The brands may supply the designs or work with the silk-makers on new designs but the labels of the silk companies never appear.

For centuries Como and its surrounding lake region has been one of the great centres of European silk production. Originally better known for its wool (an industry that died over the course of the 16th and 17th centuries), Como had two main European rivals in silk production: Lyon (France) and Krefeld (Germany). Of these three, only Como has remained as a major silk centre, with as much as 70% of its economy coming from this luxury textile.

While it's extremely important for Como, a few numbers can set the silk business in perspective. According to Moritz Mantero, president of one of Como's leading silk manufacturers, silk makes up just 0.2% of textiles (natural and artificial) produced around the world. Some 85% of Italian silk production takes place in Como, which is the only serious centre of production left in Europe (providing 80% of that continent's output). But in terms of total world production of silk (raw and finished), the big players are China (54%), India (14%) and Japan (11%). What sets Como apart is quality, but heat from the competition is uncomfortably intense.

## THE BEGINNING

A jealously guarded secret for millennia in China, the art of silk-making began to spread beyond the Middle Kingdom around 200 BC, although it is said to have only reached Europe when two travelling monks arrived in Constantinople in AD 550 with silkworm eggs hidden in hollow canes. The Byzantine authorities were enchanted though equally protective of their new secret. Chinese and Byzantine silk commanded high prices around Europe.

The art did not reach Italy until the 13th century. It appears silk manufacture in Italy began on a small scale in various parts of the country (with centres as far apart as Sicily and Lucca, depending on the sources one reads). Merchant cities such as Venice and Florence soon traded profitably in silk, selling Italian products elsewhere in Europe.

In the 14th century a handful of silk-weavers established themselves on the shores of Lake Como, and the Duchy of Milan promoted the planting of mulberry trees to feed silkworms, mainly along the Po valley and in the Brianza region immediately south of Como. The first news of manual spinning machines to make silk in the area goes back to 1510, when a certain Pietro Boldoni (a street in central Como is named after him) set up shop.

The industry was seasonal and involved the use of farm labour. Women and children would look after the silkworms day and night, feeding them mulberry leaves, from

## RAISING SILKWORMS

Caring for silkworms (*baco da seta;* actually larvae hatched from 300 to 500 eggs by the *Bombix mori* moth) is a painstaking business. Just 1mm at birth, a silkworm reaches 9cm to 10cm after 25 days of nonstop gulping (no chewing is involved) down mulberry leaves. In about 30 days, its weight multiplies some 10,000 times. It sheds its skin four times, after which it looks for a suitable place (like a thin branch) upon which to spin its cocoon.

Como farming families raised silkworms and produced raw silk for delivery to mills until the 1920s. Along the Po valley and around Lake Como, men (mostly from poor farming families) would collect mulberry leaves and cut them into minuscule strips that the worms could eat, while women would watch over their gorging charges spread out in stacks of wooden trays over the feeding frenzy period. Then the women would move the worms to separate compartments with straw stems, to which the silkworms would attach themselves and create cocoons with their own spittle.

After three days, the cocoons would be placed in an oven to kill the silkworms. The cocoons were then placed in hot water to tease out the raw silk strands. This was just the beginning of a long process of spinning, dyeing and weaving to create material and garments. At Como's Museo della Seta (p110) the process of raising silkworms is described in some detail and the various tools of the trade are displayed.

April to October. The spread of mulberry plantations was good news for landowners who benefited from the silk and wine businesses (vineyards were increasing at the same time, for unrelated reasons), but less so for the farmers employed as labour. Territory used for staple crops was reduced and chestnut forests destroyed, meaning that often not enough food was produced to meet local needs.

## MARIA THERESA COMES TO COMO'S RESCUE

When Pietro Boldoni set up the first silk-spinning mills in the early 1500s, Como already had a name for itself as a centre of wool. Spinning mills for any fibre need water, and Lake Como and the Adda river were lined with them. Then, in the 16th century, the powerful Milanese Borromeo family used its influence to induce merchants to trade and travel on and around Lake Maggiore, a Borromeo fiefdom. This fuelled a boom on Lake Maggiore but cut Lake Como out of the picture, spelling doom for the latter's wool manufacturers, now too far from preferential trade routes. New mills prospered on Lake Maggiore while the people of Como sank into misery.

An initial response was to attempt conversion: the wool-spinning mills tried their hand at spinning silk, initially without much success. Silk quality was poor, buyers therefore few, and the Lake Como district remained stuck in a rut of poverty and frequent social unrest. Lombardy's Spanish overlords in Milan took little interest in the situation and even aggravated it with extortionate taxes.

In the meantime, France's King François I (r 1515–47) invited a handful of Italian artisans to establish a silk manufacture centre at Lyon. That city later rose to be Europe's leading producer of quality silk garments until WWII.

Como would have to wait for the arrival of more benevolent and far-sighted masters. Things began to look up when the Habsburg Austrian Empire took over Lombardy in 1713. Empress Maria Theresa (who ruled from 1740 to 1780), while carrying out numerous reforms across the empire, took notice of the plight of Como and, in 1751, declared all textiles produced on and around the lake to be duty-free.

All went well until Napoleon marched into northern Italy in 1796. Chaos ensued and the Como silk industry only recovered with the return of the Austrians after 1815.

By the mid-19th century, the silk industry had become central to the Como economy, providing work for thousands of people in hundreds of spinning mills around the lower half of the lake and along the Adda river. Much of the work in these mills was done by children (mostly girls, and some under 12 years), who worked 14-hour days in far-from-ideal conditions.

> 'Much of the work in these mills was done by children, who worked 14-hour days'

The Industrial Revolution in the UK and Germany left Italy technologically behind but, although the advanced countries could produce greater quantities of material at lower prices, their quality was often inferior. This would be a key to Como's survival. Newfangled machines did begin to appear in Como but part of the work was still done by hand, giving the product a qualitative edge over rivals from Europe (except Lyon) and Asia. Even today some design work is done manually before being digitalised. Como's exports continued to be strong along the so-called 'Silk Road' (up Lake Como and over the Swiss Alps) and 80% of the province's workforce was employed in the silk business.

## DECLINE & COMEBACK

In 1856 a disease called *pebrina* struck. Passed on by mulberry leaves, the disease prevents silkworms from producing spittle and, hence, the cocoons that are the basis of silk. This disaster virtually wiped out the Italian moth species and over the next decades, moth eggs were largely imported (mostly from Japan). In the early 1900s, incubators were introduced, revolutionising the raising of silkworms.

In the first two decades of the 20th century, silkworm-raising declined. This has been partly attributed to fewer people wanting to work in this labour-intensive industry. Many families, with all that practice making trays and other instruments for silkworms, had turned instead to carpentry. It is no coincidence that the town of Cantù, southeast of Como, is today one of Italy's furniture-making capitals. Whatever the reasons, the raising of silkworms ended by the time the Great Depression struck and, ever since, almost all of Italy's raw-silk needs have been met by imports from China. Today, raw and rough finished silks are imported, the latter often needing refinement before proceeding to design and printing.

The outbreak of WWII in 1939, the development of synthetic materials in the 1940s and Italy's pitiful state in the postwar years shook Como's silk industry to the core.

BACKGROUND

The interwar years had already been rough, but the second world conflict all but put paid to Como silk and definitively killed off its competitors in Krefeld and Lyon.

With Italy in a pitiable state, Como's skint silk barons looked abroad for customers, with the USA and France principal hunting grounds. In the early 1950s, as the pace of world recovery quickened, Como's became the silk of choice for the international set and a growing coterie of fashion designers. The selling points were simple enough – high quality and low prices. From then until the early 1990s, Como's silk families did very nicely thank you, selling their product to all the big names in Italian and international fashion.

Then came increased trade liberalisation and the arrival of China on world markets. Always an enormous exporter of raw silk, China embarked on massive exportation of medium- to low-quality finished products. In Como, smaller silk companies began to fold, leaving four big names (see below) and a leaner, perhaps meaner, workforce.

> ## DON'T MISS...
>
> ### SILK SPECIALISTS
>
> ★ **Museo della Seta** // Explore Como's silk history and the craft of silk-making in this museum (p110)
>
> ★ **La Tessitura** // Silk shopping on a grand scale, along with more on the history and production of silk (p111)

## COMO'S FUTURE

Even in these times of tough competition, the silk industry accounts for about 70% of the economy of Como city. But sales have dropped. In 2003 alone, for instance, women's silk fashion products contracted by 13%.

Seteria Ratti (www.ratti.it), founded in 1945, is the biggest silk company in Como but has seen its workforce shrink from about 3000 in the early 1990s to 500 in 2008, most of them working part time as orders have shrunk. More venerable competitors, Mantero Seta (www.mantero.com), founded in 1902, have a similar number of employees. The other main players are Canepa (www.canepa.it) and Clerici Tessuto (www.clericitessuto.it). The latter and Mantero surprised everyone in 2009 by fusing, a process that, when complete, will make the combined firm bigger than Ratti.

The fusion is just one response to a situation of growing competition, and is aimed both at reducing fixed costs and creating a synergy of the two companies' strengths. All four houses share the view that survival means producing the very best quality products to top-level customers (read: mostly fashion labels). Some, like Ratti, have moved printing and other factory work to countries like Romania. Mantero maintains all its design, printing and final manufacture in Como. All of them hope that one advantage they offer will be proximity. For Italian fashion houses, for instance, it will always be easier to deal with Como designers (and consult their massive historical archives for inspiration) than to head further afield.

Some 2100 firms in the silk business are scattered around Como province, employing 27,000 people (a third of Como's workforce, though this number is down from

40,000 in the early 1990s). Nowhere else in the world is there such a concentration of textile design studios (albeit some of them one-person shows). Italy's only technical textile institute, Como's Istituto Tecnico Industriale di Setificio, was founded in 1869 and still turns out designers, printers and chemical dyeing experts.

Mantero president Moritz Mantero is guardedly optimistic about the future: 'The more companies are capable of redesigning themselves, processes and structures to be the first to meet changes in the market, the better they will do.' It wouldn't be the first time the Como silk industry has pulled through a crisis.

BACKGROUND

# WINE

· · · · · · ·

The Bible tells us that, after the flood, 'Noah, a tiller of the soil, was the first to plant the vine. He drank some of the wine, and while he was drunk…' (Genesis 9, 20–21). So the fruit of the vine has been giving pleasure for some time. And according to the Bible, 'Noah's life lasted nine hundred and fifty years; then he died.' The wine evidently did no harm. By the time the Romans were conquering Italy, it was a long-established part of Mediterranean culture. It appears the Romans began storing the drink in wooden casks and glass bottles (the Greeks had only used terracotta amphorae) and even classing good and not-so-good years.

The region around the northern Italian lakes has been producing wine at least since Roman times and today contributes some fine labels to Italian wine cellars. The principal wine-making areas range from the Oltrepò Pavese area of Pavia province, south of Milan, across the Valcalepio and Franciacorta zones between Bergamo and Brescia. The latter produces some of the country's best sparkling wine. To the north, some excellent reds come from the Valtellina valley and, over the border, Ticino fairly bristles with fine merlots. Further east, fizzy wines are made around Mantua, and several decent drops come from around Lake Garda. More big names come from the Valpolicella region, just east of Lake Garda and northwest of Verona, and just to the east of Verona, Soave produces excellent whites.

Italy boasts a complex grading system for its wines that gives an indication of where the quality is, but is by no means definitive. Wines that come from areas classed as DOC *(denominazione di origine controllata)* meet a certain set of quality criteria in terms of grape variety, methodology etc. There are more than 300 such areas (which can range from one vintner to an extended zone) in Italy, with 16 in Lombardy (and 47 in neighbouring Piedmont, 21 in the Veneto and 17 in Trentino-Alto Adige, all regions touched by this guide). One step further, DOCG *(denominazione di origine controllata e garantita)* wines should generally be top-notch – only wines that have had DOC status for at least five years can be awarded this title. There are just over 42 such wines or wine areas in Italy. Additional terms indicating quality are *riserva, speciale* and *superiore,* which can denote special ageing conditions or other factors that make the wine stand out.

Many fine wines are given another classification, IGT *(indicazione geografica*

## DON'T MISS…

### TOP TIPPLES

★ **Amarone della Valpolicella DOC //** A velvety red from one of northern Italy's best-known wine regions

★ **Bardolino Superiore DOCG //** An excellent, dry red

★ **Franciacorta DOCG //** Top-notch sparkling whites and rosés

★ **Oltrepò Pavese Sangue di Giuda DOC //** An unusual sweet red known as Judas' Blood

★ **Soave Superiore DOCG //** Among Italy's best white wines

★ **Valtellina DOCG //** It was good enough for Leonardo da Vinci and remains a fine red today

*tipica*), which covers wines from specific areas or grape varieties not covered by the DOC system and for which the rules are more relaxed.

Many other fine wines are simply classed as *vini da tavola* (table wines) because their producers don't adhere to the strict rules imposed by the classification system. This might be through the use of nontraditional grape varieties or production methods.

If a local warmly recommends a wine that bears no official classification, don't scoff – s/he is probably in the know and revealing a lovely local 'secret'.

All of that said, the classification system provides an initial guide to wines in the area. Here follows a tippler's summary of the wine areas and some specific drops to look out for:

> *'If a local warmly recommends a wine that bears no official classification, don't scoff'*

**BACKGROUND**

**Bardolino** (www.winebardolino.it) On the southeastern banks of Lake Garda, one of the Veneto region's best-known reds is cultivated. Of the several fine reds produced in the area, made of four local grape varieties, the Bardolino Superiore DOCG leads the way. It's a delicate, dry drop that goes very nicely with strong meat and game dishes. For information on local outlets and producers, as well as plenty of local tourist information, try Strada del Bardolino (www.stradadelbardolino.com).

**Botticino DOC** A small town 9.5km east of Brescia, Botticino is at the heart of a diminutive DOC wine area. Better known for its marble, Botticino produces a limited quantity of reds (standard and *riserva,* both classified DOC) using a majority of barbera grape, along with the plummy Trentino grape, marzemino.

**Capriano del Colle** A small village 17km south of Brescia, Capriano del Colle is at the heart of another small wine-producing area that manages to turn out four DOC wines. The one to keep an eye out for is the Capriano del Colle Riserva, an intense red made mainly with Tuscan sangiovese and marzemino grapes and aged up to five years.

**Cellatica DOC** Just 8km northwest of Brescia and touching on Franciacorta territory, this village and its surrounding rocky hills produce a medium red wine whose main grape varieties are marzemino and barbera. They are great with any meat dish but produced in pretty small quantities.

**Franciacorta** Leading the way in this area stretching between Brescia and the south end of Lake Iseo, are the spumante (sparkling) whites and rosés rated as DOCG. Look out also for Satèn, a *blanc de blanc* almost exclusively made of chardonnay grapes. The area produces many other fine drops too. The Curtefranca DOC covers a series of whites and reds (the latter dominated by cabernet franc and the local carmenere grape varieties). For more on the wines from this area, have a look at the website of Franciacorta DOCG (www.franciacorta.net).

**Garda Colli Mantovani DOC** On the low ranks of hills south of Lake Garda and en route to Mantua, various red and white grape varieties flourish, leading to the production of some relatively little known but pleasant wines. Look out in particular for the merlot and cabernet reserves (aged for two years).

**Lambrusco Mantovano DOC** Rules were made to be broken, and this light-hearted and slightly fizzy (yes, fizzy) red has been a Milanese favourite for more than a millennium.

**Lugana DOC** (www.consorziolugana.eu) Fine seafood demands something extra, and this underappreciated charmer from Lombardy's border with the Veneto shows crisp flair. The trebbiano Lugana grape type leads the way in the clusters of wineries gathered around the southern end of Lake Garda.

**Oltrepò Pavese** Riots broke out in the Middle Ages when Milan was cut off from Oltrepò, Lombardy's most renowned wine region. No fewer than 20 wines are classified as DOC in this area, and the Oltrepó Pavese spumante is a DOCG. Keep an eye out for reds like the Oltrepò Pavese Barbera and the Bonarda, among the stars of the area's DOC wines. The leading grape variety is the local croatina but a wide range is used and there are plenty of others to choose from, including a long list of whites (anything from chardonnay to sweet muscat) and a handful of rosés. A curious sweet dessert red is the curiously named Sangue di Giuda (Judas' Blood). For more information, look up the Consorzio Vino Oltrepò Pavese website (www.vinoltrepo.it, in Italian and German).

**Riviera del Garda Bresciano** The hills on the Brescia side of Lake Garda produce some good reds and claret-style wines, along with a few riesling-style whites. Look for Garda DOC or Garda Classico DOC. The reds predominantly use the local gropello grape (those wines indicated as gropello must have at least 85% gropello to qualify as a DOC drop). Vineyards straggle along the west shore of Lake Garda, across to Lake Idro and down into the Valtenesi area. Barely known outside the region, they can hold their own quite nicely with the more renowned Bardolino and Valpolicella reds on the east side of the lake. Check out www.gardaclassico.it.

**San Colombano al Lambro** A little island of territory belonging administratively to Milan province but actually separated from it by 22km, the municipality of San Colombano al Lambro (15km south of Lodi) has the honour of being able to say it has the only wine produced in the province of Milan. Documents attest that wine was grown on the hill next to the town as long ago as the 14th century. Today, various wines in small quantities are produced by mostly family-run wineries. The San Colombano al Lambro DOC is a red whose dominant grape variety is the croatina. Some whites and spumante are also produced.

**Soave** West of Verona, the pretty town of Soave rests next to a castle-topped hill whose slopes are dense with vineyards. Some of Italy's finest white wines come from here. The local garganega grape dominates the area's two white DOCGs, Recioto di Soave and Soave Superiore. For more details look up the website of the Consorzio Tutela Vini Soave e Recioto Soave (www.ilsoave.com).

**Ticino** Wine is also a big part of the Ticino experience. The bulk of production is merlot (imported into the region in the early 20th century). The better quality ones tend to come with the Ticino DOC or Ticinese DOC label (a classification system similar to that used in Italy operates in Switzerland). To learn more about Ticino merlot mania, see www .ticinowine.ch.

**Tocai di San Martino della Battaglia DOC** Two tasty little tipples are produced around a village whose name evokes a fierce battle fought in 1859 during the Franco-Piedmontese offensive to drive the Austrians out of Italy. The Tocai di San Martino della Battaglia DOC is a pleasant, light, dry white made with the tocai grape from Friuli, in northeast Italy. The same grape is used to produce the Liquoroso DOC version, a full-bodied, sweetish dessert white.

**Valcalepio** (www.valcalepio.org, in Italian) Previously little known about beyond Bergamo, the Valcalepio wine region between Bergamo and Lake Iseo is beginning to make a name for itself. It is something of a local success story, as wine-making had been in steep decline until the 1970s. Since then, small local holdings have been continually refining their two main DOC products: a red that blends merlot and cabernet sauvignon (and which also comes in an aged *riserva* version) and whites that combine pinot bianco and pinot grigio varieties. You will also come across a sweet dessert *passito* using moscato grapes, which is perfect as an accompaniment for pastries and dessert. The Valcalepio wine-makers spread in an arc just south of Bergamo from Lake Iseo in the east to the Adda river in the west.

**Valpolicella** (www.valpolicella.it, in Italian) Hemingway swigged it and thought it grand and Valpolicella reds have long graced north Italian dining tables. Led by the outstanding, velvety Amarone della Valpolicella DOC (using dried corvina, rondinella and molinara grapes), this region, which stretches north-northwest up the valleys parallel to Lake Garda from Verona, is one of the best-known names in northern Italian wine. While many Valpolicella reds are fairly light and pleasant table wines, the flagship Amarone (literally 'big sour one', because it is quite a dry drop) is accompanied by another signature red, also made with dried grapes, the somewhat sweeter Recioto. In days gone by, the Amarone was considered a mistake, when the grapes had been allowed to dry too much and lose too much sugar. Tastes have changed and the Amarone is now considered superior.

**Valtellina** Like a well-behaved Milanese dinner companion, this red is dry, distinctive and rich without being too forward – Leonardo da Vinci loved the stuff. The area boasts two DOCG classifications, a general one (Valtellina Superiore DOCG) and one applied to a particular style of wine, the Sforzato (or Sfursat) di Valtellina DOCG. The nebbiolo grape (locally known as chiavennasca) is by far the most important and this is one of the few regions in which it thrives. A standard Valtellina wine contains about 70% nebbiolo, and a Sforzato DOCG must contain at least 90% nebbiolo, while the Superiore (with four subdenominations) reaches 95%. The Sassella subdenomination is considered by some to be the best. For more information, take a look at www.consorziovinivaltellina.com (in Italian) or www.valtellina vini.com.

# FOOD

. . . . . . .

The stretch of northern Italy marked by its glittering lakes takes in a broad cultural and culinary sweep. From Piedmont across Lombardy and on to the Veneto and the southwestern tip of Trentino, the palette of options for the palate is tasty and varied. Add the canton of Ticino in Switzerland, and what visiting Germans so colourfully refer to as *Gaumenfreude* (joy of the gums!) is assured.

Lombardy and its capital may well have said good riddance to the Austrians in 1860, but they owe some of their dining tastes and even signature dishes to the creaky old central European empire of yore. Take the *scaloppina alla Milanese* (which has a smaller, more prosaic form in the *cotoletta* – cutlet). Sounds about as Italian as it gets, right? Actually it is nothing more than a pan-fried, breaded veal escalope. Very good, mind you, but better known to us as...*Wiener Schnitzel*. That Lombard penchant for heavy meat dishes and stews, such as osso bucco (veal shank stew scattered with *gremolata* – parsley, garlic and lemon rind) and *bollito misto* (mixed boiled meats, especially beloved in Cremona and normally including beef, calf's head, chicken and cow's tongue), might also have something to do with the long years of Austrian presence.

You'd be a silly sausage not to try some of the many *insaccati* (literally 'bagged things') here. *Cotecchino* is a popular pork sausage made across the region. A chubbier version is the *cotecotto* from the Valtellina valley in the north of Lombardy. In Pavia they make goose-meat sausages and the tangy *salame di Varzi*. Another Valtellina fave is *mortadella di fegato*, which is about 15% pig liver. The dark-red dried and cured horse-meat sausages from the Val Chiavenna are laced with local herbs.

Before you get the impression that northern Italian cooking is little more than a Germanic kitchen copy, a brief scan of a menu soon proves that the above selection is just the tip of the iceberg. Centuries of rice-growing in the Lombard (and Piedmontese) plains have turned risotto, in all its many variants, into a dish as redolent of this part of Italy as that other renowned rice creation, *paella*, is of Valencia. The area is also rich in cheese production (see p276) and produces many fine wines (p270).

**BACKGROUND**

## DON'T MISS...

### SIGNATURE DISHES

★ **Casonsèi** // Big egg-based ravioli (aka *casoncelli*) from Bergamo, stuffed with meat, cheese or spinach

★ **Gnocchi di patate** // Verona is the home to these pastalike potato-based balls usually served dripping in a meat or tomato sauce

★ **Marubini** // Meat and cheese stuffed disks of pasta served in a broth, a speciality from Cremona

★ **Pastissada de caval** // Horse-meat stew, a favourite in Verona

★ **Pizzoccheri** // Hearty buckwheat tagliatelle served with melted cheese, potatoes and cabbage

★ **Risotto** // A dish with limitless variations, using premium local rice, from Milan's saffron *(alla milanese)* to Pavia's frog *(alla certosina)* version

★ **Scaloppina alla milanese** // A classic, breaded veal escalope

Within this rich culinary universe, Milan is something of a world apart. Immigration from other parts of Italy since the 1950s has long made it a showcase for regional cuisines from around the country. Genovese and Piedmontese dishes often share menu space with the local lads: *trofie* (pasta twists) with pesto, onion-strewn focaccia, and *fonduta* (fondue) make regular appearances. Restaurants serving the staples of Lazio, Campania, Tuscany and Puglia are easier to find than those selling local Lombard fare.

Milan's increasingly diverse global population is also reflected in the city's eating habits. Unusually for Italy, Japanese and Chinese restaurants are commonplace, and the cuisines of India, Latin America, the Middle East and both North and sub-Saharan Africa are all well represented. Beyond Milan tastes have remained far more anchored in local tradition – something that the average gourmand is unlikely to have a problem with.

> *'The nuances are mind-boggling, as are the passions they frequently excite'*

The region, but especially Milan, is home to a clutch of Michelin-starred chefs, who cook some of Italy's most innovative and sophisticated food. Some deconstruct regional standards, others imbue them with new-world twists; while the culinary antics are hotly debated, the produce is always sublime and the results often stunning. In lesser hands, however, the experimental verve can be downright silly and the PR hype as tired as the fusion on the plate.

But the fundamental rules don't change. Even the zaniest of chefs chooses each ingredient for its scent, texture, ripeness and ability to play well with others. This means getting to the right market early and remaining open to seasonal inspiration. It's a matter of proportions and balance too, which sometimes leads to a tendency to conservatism. Italians, not just Lombards, are always ready to explain why only such-and-such a sauce can go with a particular kind of spaghetti. The nuances are mind-boggling, as are the passions they frequently excite.

Restaurant guides to look for include *Gambero Rosso* (www.gamberorosso.it) and *Guida Critica Golosa – Lombardia, Liguria & Valle d'Aosta*. The latter has a wealth of information and suggestions for eating in the farthest flung corners of Lombardy (the lion's share of the region covered in this guide).

## COLAZIONE (BREAKFAST)

Breakfast in Italy is, if not the most lavish meal of your day, a perfectly good excuse to get out of bed. Think Continental (coffee, pastry and optional fruit juice), not eggs, pancakes, ham, sausage and toast. Those menu offerings are only likely to appear at weekend *'brrrunch'* (pronounced with the rolled Italian r), an American import now ensconced in trendy urban eateries from Milan to Lugano. Expect to pay upwards of €20 to graze a buffet of hot dishes, cold cuts, pastries and fresh fruit, usually including your choice of coffee, juice or cocktail.

On more workaday occasions, the ideal accompaniment to your coffee is a pastry, usually without adornments such as butter and jam. Diabetics are best off sticking to bread, since most Italian pastries are faintly sweet.

## SAY CHEESE!

One of the wonders of wandering around any northern Italian town centre is stumbling across *alimentari* (general food stores) or specialist shops overflowing with all sorts of cheeses. They seem to come in every possible size, form, colour and texture. While some are imports from other regions or even abroad, a good deal come from Lombardy or adjacent regions. The majority of cheeses from this part of the world are made from cow's milk.

One of the most widespread and best known Lombard cheeses is *stracchino*. The name is derived from *stracca*, meaning tiredness. It is said that the milk of tired cows (during the seasonal move to and from Alpine pastures) is richer in fats and acids, giving this cheese its tang. It is usually eaten as a dessert cheese.

Once known as green stracchino, Gorgonzola is also made of autumn cow's milk (collected after the return from the Alps) and is one of several cheeses made with blue mould. One legend says its production was first recorded in the village of Gorgonzola in AD 879. Laced with blue veins, the so-called 'two-curd' version has an intense, piquant flavour, well ensconced in the category of what some refer to as 'smelly cheese'. Processing of the 'one-curd' version is different and results in a milder cheese that lacks the blue mould.

Another popular Lombard-name autumn product is Taleggio, a soft cheese set in square forms and originally made in the like-named valley north of Bergamo. It is a fairly mild cheese matured in six to 10 weeks and regularly washed to prevent mould or a thick rind forming. Unfortunately, most Taleggio you find today is factory produced.

Originating from the Lodi area is the soft cream cheese known as mascarpone, a versatile product obtained from milk cream and used to make desserts (among other things). Other cheeses from Lodi include *pannerone*, a soft, fatty cheese made without any salt, and Grana Lodigiano. The latter is similar to the better-known Parmigiano-Reggiano (Parmesan) and Grana Padano, and is made a little further south across the Po river, but very hard to find now. Unlike its two more famous cousins, it 'weeps' a drop of whey when flakes of it are cut away. Indeed, this cheese, matured over anything from 20 months to four years, cannot be grated like Parmesan.

From the province of Brescia comes *bagoss*, a well-matured, straw-coloured cheese traditionally made in cowherds' huts in the summer mountain pastures. Robiola is a soft pasteurised cow's milk cheese made in Lombardy and Ticino. It comes in small discs. A cool, fresh alternative in Ticino is *robiolino*, tubes of pasteurised cow's milk cheese often seasoned with herbs or pepper.

Various types of *formaggella*, a semihard cheese with a greyish crust, are produced throughout the region.

Several goat's cheeses, such as *cadolet di capra* (from the Valle Camonica north of Lake Iseo) and *fatulì*, are made in spring and summer and lightly smoked. *Caprino Lombardo*, a generic name, covers a range of such cheeses and indeed is also applied, inappropriately, to several industrially produced cow's milk cheeses. True goat's milk cheese ranges from the fresh, soft white variety to those matured over several months in oil and laurel leaves.

For everything you ever wanted to know about Italian cheeses, head for www.formaggio.it (in Italian only).

The most common item is the *brioche,* or *cornetto,* Italy's version of the croissant. It is usually smaller, lighter, less buttery and slightly sweet, with an orange-rind glaze brushed on top. Another great option for those with a sweetish tooth is the *crostata,* a tart with a dense, buttery crust and filled with your choice of fruit jam, such as *amarena* (sour cherry), *albicocca* (apricot) or *frutti di bosco* (wild berries). You can usually buy by the slice. The *ciambella,* a classic fried-dough treat rolled in granulated sugar, is sometimes filled with jam or custard. You will also come across *strudel di mele,* an Italian adaptation of the traditional Viennese *Apfelstrudel* without the rum and nuts.

## PRANZO (LUNCH)

Many shops and businesses still close for *la pausa,* a two- to three-hour midday break to return home, enjoy lunch, rest up and come back to work wired on espresso and ready for action. In the cities, few people have time to go home for lunch, so bars and restaurants fill up.

In frenetic Milan especially, many folks settle for something quick, like a *pizza al taglio* (pizza by the slice). Quick bites found at bakeries and bars include *panini* (crusty sandwiches featuring Italian cold cuts) and *tramezzini* (triangular, stacked sandwiches made with squishy white bread). You can often get delicatessens to make up a *panino* of whatever you like. A *rosticceria* (rotisserie) or *tavola calda* (literally 'hot table') also serve hot items on the go, which you can eat in or take away. The *tavola calda* usually displays all its wares at the counter, so you can point and then scoff the dish down.

Plenty of people make time for a full sit-down meal and many restaurants offer various set lunch menus and other fiscally attractive formulas. This can be a good way of sampling the wares of more expensive restaurants without making the financial outlay that dinner would entail.

What's on the menu?

### ANTIPASTI (APPETISERS)

Bread is deposited on the table as part of your €1 to €3 *pane e coperto* (bread and 'cover', or table service), along with oil and vinegar for dipping. You might also score some olives or *sott'aceti* (vegetables such as artichokes or red peppers, in olive oil and vinegar), *grissini* (breadsticks), or even a basket of salami or other cured meats.

Tantalising offerings on the antipasti menu may include the house *bruschetta* (grilled bread with a variety of toppings, from chopped tomato and garlic to black truffle spread) and seasonal treats such as *insalata caprese* (fresh mozzarella with ripe tomatoes and basil leaves) or *prosciutto e melone* (cured ham and cantaloupe). Many people skip the antipasto and go straight for a primo (or vice versa).

### PRIMO (FIRST COURSE)

The highlights of this course are pasta, risotto and gnocchi. You may be surprised how generous the portions are – a *mezza porzione* (half-portion) might do the trick for kids.

*Primi* menus usually include ostensibly vegetarian or vegan options, such as pasta *al pesto* (basil with Parmigiano cheese and pine nuts) or *alla norma* (with eggplant and tomato), or the extravagant *risotto al Barolo* (risotto with high-end Barolo wine). But even if a dish sounds vegetarian in theory, before you order you may want to ask about the stock used or the ingredients in that suspiciously rich tomato sauce – there may be beef, ham or ground anchovies involved.

For centuries the Lombard plains have been given over to the cultivation of rice, so it comes as no surprise that rice dishes, such as the many takes on risotto, should play a capital role in local cooking. Historically, rice was long a more important local staple than pasta, and some 50 varieties are grown in the area. Among the best known is *carnaroli*, a medium-grain rice mostly grown in neighbouring Piedmont but also in parts of Pavia province, south of Milan. Others, such as arborio (a short grain rice) and *vialone nano* (a thicker grain), are equally prized. Pavia is considered the capital of Italian rice production.

How should we count the ways of preparing risotto? The Milan standard is with saffron and some kind of meat sauce. In Pavia a speciality is *risotto con le rane* (with crispy fried frogs). *Risotto ai porcini* (risotto with pungent, earthy porcini mushrooms) is a universal favourite, and risottos done with wines as a basis (as in the above-mentioned Barolo version) are legion. In Mantua, *risotto alla pilota* (made with minced pork) is the signature dish. Seafood variations include *risotto al nero* (risotto cooked with the black ink of octopus or squid) and a meat fave is *ossobuco con risotto alla milanese* (veal shank and marrow melting into saffron risotto).

> 'Historically, rice was long a more important local staple than pasta'

Pasta lovers need not be concerned. While rice has the upper hand by tradition, pasta has long since taken its place alongside the grains. Meat eaters especially will rejoice in such legendary dishes as *pasta all'amatriciana* (pasta with a spicy sauce of tomato, Pecorino cheese and *guanciale* – pigs' cheeks) and *pappardelle al cinghiale* (ribbon pasta with wild boar sauce), while *spaghetti con le vongole* (spaghetti with clam sauce) and other seafood pasta options are ubiquitous.

A very Lombard choice are *pizzoccheri* – a buckwheat tagliatelle served in a bowl with, say, melted cheese, potatoes and cabbage to make a hearty winter dish. *Ravioli di brasato* (ravioli stuffed with braised beef) are typical of Pavia.

Verona is the birthplace of *gnocchi di patate* (little potato-based pasta balls) that can be served with all sorts of accompaniments. The most traditional options include melted butter with Parmesan, tomato sauce, or *pastissada de caval*, a horse-meat stew that is also a Verona speciality. It is also perfect with *pappardelle* (broad ribbon pasta) and often appears as a main course.

## SECONDO (SECOND COURSE)

Light lunchers may call it a day after the *primo*, but foodies pace themselves for a meat or fish main in the second course. These options may range from the outrageous *bistecca alla fiorentina*, a thick T-bone steak served on the bone in a puddle of juice, to the already mentioned *scaloppina alla Milanese*.

Many dishes, especially in winter, come with polenta, a maize-based staple that comes as a thick yellow wedge or in a more liquid, porridgelike form. There is nothing better than a chunk of the yellow stuff served with, say, a generous portion of game meat.

If you want vegetables, you frequently have to order a *contorno* (side dish) of them separately.

On the lakes, check out the local fish options. Fish and seafood transported from the Mediterranean and beyond will often appear on menus and there's nothing wrong with them. But locally caught *persico* (perch), *coregone* or *lavarello* (whitefish) and *salmerino* (a cross between salmon and trout, only smaller) have a freshness that is hard to beat. Regrettably, as on the high seas, overfishing is a problem and even these babies can be imported or from fish farms. A Lake Como classic are *missoltini,* small sun-dried fish.

Other freshwater fish you will probably come across are *carpa* (carp), *trota* (trout), *tinca* (tench), *luccio* (pike) and maybe even lake sardines, traditionally hung out to dry on big arches.

## DOLCI (SWEETS, DESSERT)

Some might say the best comes last. Go for whatever homemade dessert options are on offer. A classic is *panna cotta* (literally 'cooked cream'), a creamy, slightly wobbly set dessert bathed in, say, a sauce of wild berries. Of Piedmontese origin, it is commonly served throughout northern Italy. Other popular options include *zabaglione* (egg and marsala custard, often served with some kind of sweetish biscuit, like *savoiardi* – ladies' fingers), cream-stuffed profiteroles, or Sicilian *cannoli* (a crunchy pastry tube with a sweet, creamy ricotta cheese filling). An excellent Mantua dessert is *torta sbrisolana,* a kind of crumble made with yellow flower, almonds and lard.

Some restaurants will offer the alternative of a cheese selection for those with less of an inclination to tooth decay.

## TALL STORIES & STICKY TOWERS

According to legend, the typical, sticky, tooth-wrenching Christmas sweet *torrone* (nougat) was invented in Cremona. Local pastry-makers prepared this special new culinary invention to celebrate the 1441 marriage of Bianca Maria Visconti, daughter of the Duke of Milan, Filippo Maria Visconti, to the dazzling captain and later duke, Francesco Sforza. The wedding took place in Cremona and the sweet (made of eggs, vanilla, honey, almonds and toasted hazelnuts) was presented in a form reminiscent of that city's great tower, the Torrazzo. And so they called it *torrone* (another name for 'big tower').

Nice story but probably rubbish, as the sweet is attributed to Arab origins. Either way, Cremona became known as a centre of *torrone* production. The city celebrates this agreeable dental disaster with the annual Festa del Torrone in November (see p172).

# DRINKS

Beer is fine with pizza but for other dishes you may get a funny look from your waiter if you order anything but wine. Asking for *acqua dal rubinetto* (tap water) will also provoke arched eyebrows. There's nothing wrong with it, of course, so if you have moral objections to forking out for *acqua minerale* (mineral water), whether *ferma* (still) or *gasata* (sparkling), go right ahead! To finish off, coffee is the most common request (either *caffè* or *macchiato*), although many places will offer tea. For something stronger, a *digestivo* (digestive drink, useful for burning through the masses of food you've just enjoyed) is the way to go. This could be anything from a *grappa* through to an *amaro* (a somewhat tart herbal concoction – there is an infinity of types).

# APERITIVO (HAPPY HOUR)

To head out for an *aperitivo* (aperitif) is rather more than a simple early evening glass of bubbly. It could easily wind up being a meal in itself.

A whole bar-snack culture is built around this after-work tradition. Some would go so far as to say that this Italian 'happy hour' is dinner disguised as a casual drink, as the latter is accompanied by a buffet of antipasti, pasta salads, cold cuts and some hot dishes. You can methodically pillage the buffet from about 5pm to 8pm for the price of a single drink, which crafty diners nurse for the duration. Although a very Milan phenomenon, you can find places doing this in most other cities too.

Drink prices range from €6 to €12, but be prepared to fork out up to €15 at some of the more luxury locations. Usually, the higher the drink price, the more lavish the

## COFFEE SPEAK

The mainstay of Italian breakfast is scalding espresso, cappuccino (espresso with a goodly dollop of foamed milk) or *caffè latte* (the hot, milky espresso beverage Starbucks mistakenly calls a *latte,* which will get you a glass of milk in Italy). Don't believe the hype about espresso: one diminutive cup packs less of a caffeine wallop than a large cup of French-pressed or American-brewed coffee, and will leave you less jittery. An alternative beverage is *orzo,* a slightly nutty, noncaffeinated roasted-barley beverage that looks like cocoa.

**Americano** A long black; as the name implies, a foreign concept.

**Un caffè** Single, strong shot of coffee; an espresso.

**Caffè corretto** An espresso 'corrected' with a shot of grappa or other heart-starting liquor.

**Caffè doppio** Two shots of *un caffè.*

**Caffè latte** A hot, milky espresso.

**Caffè lungo** A shot with a dash of hot water.

**Cappuccino** (aka cappuccio) Similar to caffè latte, only with frothy milk and usually a dash of cocoa on top. Locals usually only order it for breakfast.

**Decaffeinato** Decaf, to be applied to your choice of coffee.

**Macchiato** An espresso 'stained' with a dash of frothy milk, either *caldo* (hot) or *freddo* (cold).

**Marocchino** Uniquely Milanese, a small, cocoa-topped cappuccino ('Moroccan').

## WHAT'S COOKING IN TICINO?

Not a few Italians have chosen to live in the Swiss canton of Ticino but locals like to make it clear that they do not consider themselves simply a detached region of Italy. And while you will often come across the same or similar dishes that can be found south of the border, there are some notable peculiarities about Ticino kitchens.

The quintessential Ticino experience is the grotto. Dining or lunching in one of these rustic, out-of-the-way eateries, where in the warmer months you can sit outside at granite tables, has its own convivial vibe. Fare is generally far from elaborate; rather it's of the heart-warming, tried-and-true variety. The best of these places are found in or near small towns and villages in the valleys of Ticino. Fan(atic)s might want to track down the trilingual *Guida a Grotti e Osterie.*

Perhaps even more than in northern Italy, polenta is a standard. You might find it with *brasato* (braised beef) or *capretto in umido alla Mesolcinese,* a tangy kid-meat stew with a touch of cinnamon, cooked in red wine. Polenta is good served with any *cacciagione* (game meat) in autumn.

*Cazzöla* is a dish with a savoury selection of pork or sausage and perhaps some other meats teaming up on a plate and served with cabbage and potatoes. More delicate dishes include *cicitt* (small sausages) and *mazza casalinga* (a selection of delicatessen cuts).

Portions tend to be generous in Ticino, so the Italian habit of eating a *primo* (first course, generally of pasta) followed by a *secondo* (main) is by no means obligatory. Prices often make such gluttony onerous anyway. Another common option is to have a *mezza porzione* (half-serving) of a first course and then a full serve of a second course.

buffet, although sometimes you're paying for a bar's fashion cred rather than wild salmon *crudo* (raw). At the more sumptuous joints you may see a lot of raw fish, oysters, prosciutto, salami and roast beef, barley and trout salads, chickpeas and couscous, cauliflower and cardoon fritters, baked ricotta, *caprese* (mozzarella, tomato and basil) salad on a stick, and a few platters of hot pasta. Simpler spreads make the most of pizza, *crostini* and bruschetta, with cured meats, cheese, grilled eggplant and smoked salmon being the favoured toppings, and *frittata, arancini,* potato croquettes, au gratin peppers and olives often making an appearance too.

## CENA (DINNER)

Dinner is usually less demanding than a sit-down lunch, unless you've been invited to someone's home – in which case all bets are off, and elastic-waist pants seem a wise investment.

As a rule, there is little to distinguish the business of lunching from dining. Traditionally the former was the bigger meal of the day, and plenty of people still find time for a full meal in the middle of the day (no doubt more healthy than stuffing yourself at night but hardly conducive to a hard-working afternoon in the office). The modern economy and urban realities have changed things for many people, though, especially in frenetic Milan, where finding adequate time for lunch cannot be taken for granted.

The courses are the same at lunch and dinner. Again, there is no obligation to order a *primo* and *secondo,* and antipasti and dessert are entirely optional. Partly for health and partly for budgetary reasons, most Italians themselves skip one or two of the courses.

Money-saving set meals are the exception in the evening. More likely in swishy restaurants are *menù di degustazione* (tasting menus), which allow you to range over a variety of the house specialities without having to make any difficult choices (the chef takes care of that). You may find it hard to resist occasionally pushing the boat out at one of the region's top restaurants, such as Cracco (p51), Da Vittorio (p151) or Ristorante Gualtiero Marchesi (p163).

In summer especially, many locals skip restaurant sweets and head out into the night in search of a soothing dollop of gelato. In busy nightlife areas of Milan and in the centre of most towns, you'll usually find an obliging gelateria or two open late enough to cater for such whims.

# FOOD & DRINK GLOSSARY
· · · · · · ·

## THE BASICS

**alla griglia** *a*·la *gree*·lya grilled (broiled)
**arrosto/a** (m/f) *a*·*ro*·sto/a roasted
**bollito/a** (m/f) bo·*lee*·to/a boiled
**cameriere/a** (m/f) ka·mer·*ye*·re/a waiter
**cena** *che*·na dinner
**coltello** kol·*te*·lo knife
**cotto/a** (m/f) *ko*·to/a cooked
**crudo/a** (m/f) *kroo*·do/a raw
**cucchiaio** koo·*kya*·yo spoon
**enoteca** e·no·*te*·ka wine bar
**forchetta** for·*ke*·ta fork
**fritto/a** (m/f) *free*·to/a fried
**(non) fumatori** (non) foo·ma·*to*·ree (non)smoker
**pranzo** *pran*·zo lunch
**prima collazione** *pree*·ma ko·la·*zyo*·ne breakfast
**riso** *ree*·zo rice; the Carnaroli variety grown in much of the Lombard plains is popular
**ristorante** ri·sto·*ran*·te restaurant
**spuntino** spoon·*tee*·no snack
**trattoria** tra·to·*ree*·a informal, family-style restaurant

## STAPLES

**aceto** a·*che*·to vinegar
**aglio** *a*·lyo garlic
**burro** *boo*·ro butter
**formaggio** for·*ma*·jo cheese
**olio** *o*·lyo oil
**oliva** o·*lee*·va olive
**pane** *pa*·ne bread
**panna** *pa*·na cream
**pepe** *pe*·pe pepper
**polenta** po·*len*·ta maize-based meal
**sale** *sa*·le salt
**uovo/uova** *wo*·vo/*wo*·va egg/eggs
**zucchero** *tsoo*·ke·ro sugar

## FRUTTA E VERDURA (FRUIT & VEGETABLES)

**arancia** a·*ran*·cha orange
**asparago/i** as·*pa*·ra·jo/ee asparagus
**carciofo** kar·*cho*·fo artichoke
**carota** ka·*ro*·ta carrot
**cavolo** *ka*·vo·lo cabbage
**ciliegia** chee·lee·*e*·ja cherry
**fagiolino** fa·jo·*lee*·no green beans
**finocchio** fee·*no*·kyo fennel
**fragola** *fra*·go·la strawberry
**fungo/hi** *foon*·go/ee mushroom/s
**limone** lee·*mo*·ne lemon
**mela** *me*·la apple
**melanzane** me·lan·*dza*·ne aubergines
**melone** me·*lo*·ne cantaloupe; musk melon; rockmelon
**patata** pa·*ta*·ta potato
**peperoncino** pe·pe·ron·*chee*·no chilli
**peperone** pe·pe·*ro*·ne capsicum; pepper
**pera** *pe*·ra pear
**pesca** *pe*·ska peach
**piselli** pee·*ze*·lee peas
**pomodoro** po·mo·*do*·ro tomato
**rucola** *roo*·ko·la rocket
**spinaci** spee·*na*·chee spinach
**tartufo** tar·*too*·fo truffle
**uva** *oo*·va grapes
**zucca** *tsoo*·ka pumpkin

## CARNE (MEAT)

**agnello** a·*nye*·lo lamb
**bistecca** bees·*te*·ka steak
**capretto** ka·*pre*·to kid (goat)
**coniglio** ko·*nee*·lyo rabbit
**fegato** *fe*·ga·to liver
**manzo** *man*·zo beef
**pollo** *po*·lo chicken

BACKGROUND

**prosciutto cotto** pro-*shoo*-to *ko*-to
cooked ham
**prosciutto crudo** pro-*shoo*-to *kroo*-do
cured ham
**salsiccia** sal-*see*-cha sausage
**trippa** *tree*-pa tripe
**vitello** vee-*te*-lo veal

## PESCE & FRUTTI DI MARE (FISH & SEAFOOD)

**acciuga** a-*choo*-ga anchovy
**aragosta** a-ra-*go*-sta lobster
**branzino** bran-*zee*-no sea bass
**calamari** ka-la-*ma*-ree squid
**carpa** *car*-pa carp
**coregone** ko-re-*go*-ne whitefish
**cozza** *ko*-tsa mussel
**gambero** *gam*-be-ro prawn
**gamberone** gam-be-*ro*-ne big prawn
**granchio** *gran*-kyo crab
**merluzzo** mer-*loo*-tso cod
**ostrica/he** *os*-tree-ka/e oyster/s
**persico** *per*-si-ko perch
**pesce spada** *pe*-she *spa*-da swordfish
**polpo** *pol*-po octopus
**sardina** sar-*dee*-na sardine; pilchard
**seppia** *se*-pya cuttlefish
**sgombro** *sgom*-bro mackerel
**tinca** *tin*-ka tench
**tonno** *to*-no tuna
**triglia** *tree*-lya  mullet
**trota** *tro*-ta trout
**vongola** *von*-go-la clam

## COLAZIONE (BREAKFAST)

**brioche** bree-*osh* the Italian version of the
croissant
**ciambella** cham-*be*-la kind of doughnut
**cornetto** kor-*ne*-to another word for
croissant
**crostata** kro-*sta*-ta breakfast tart with a dense,
buttery crust and jam
**zeppola** *dze*-poo-la chewy doughnut enriched
with ricotta or pumpkin

## ANTIPASTI (APPETISERS) & PRIMI (FIRST COURSES)

**câsonséi** (aka **casoncelli**) ka-zon-*say*
(ka-zon-*che*-lee) large egg-based ravioli stuffed with
meat, cheese or spinach, a Bergamese speciality
**crespelle** kres-*pe*-le a kind of cross between pasta and
crêpes
**insalata** in-sa-*la*-ta salad
**marubini al brodo** ma-roo-*bee*-nee al *bro*-do disks
of pasta stuffed with meat and cheese and served in a
broth (*o ai tre brodi*, a mix of three meat-stock broths), a
Cremonese speciality
**minestra** mee-*ne*-stra soup
**minestrone** mee-ne-*stro*-ne literally 'big soup'; usually
a hearty broth full of vegetables and other ingredients
**orecchiette** o-re-*kye*-te Puglian ear-shaped pasta
**pappardelle** pa-par-*de*-le broad ribbon pasta, often
served with meat sauces
**pizzoccheri** pee-*tso*-ke-ree buckwheat *tagliatelle*, typical of the mountainous and country areas of Lombardy
**riso mantecato con pere e Taleggio** *ree*-zo
man-te-*ka*-to kon *pe*-re e ta-*le*-jo creamed rice with
pears and Taleggio cheese
**risotto** ree-*zo*-to typical first course which comes in
endless varieties (the traditional Milanese version is done
with saffron) throughout northern Italy, but especially
Lombardy
**schisöl** schee-*zeul* polenta cooked with cheese and
mushrooms, a Bergamese speciality
**spaghetti alla carbonara** spa-*ge*-tee *a*-la
kar-bo-*na*-ra classic pasta dish with cheese (Pecorino or
Parmesan) and bacon
**strozzapreti** stro-*tsa*-*pre*-tee literally 'strangle the
priest'; long strips of pasta; in some regions it's also the
name of dumplings made with spinach, chard and ricotta
**tagliatelle** ta-lya-*te*-le narrow ribbon pasta
**zuppa** *tsoo*-pa soup

## SECONDI (SECOND COURSES)

**brasato d'asino** bra-*za*-to *da*-zee-no braised donkey
**cazzoeula** ka-*zew*-la stew of pork rib chops, skin and
sausage
**cotechino** ko-te-*kee*-no boiled pork sausage
**filetto ai ferri** fee-*le*-to ai *fe*-ree grilled beef fillet

BACKGROUND

**fritto misto** *free*·to *mees*·to mixed fried fish

**lumache alla bresciana** loo·*ma*·ke *a*·la bre·*cha*·na snails cooked with Parmesan and fresh spinach, a Brescia speciality

**maialino da latte** ma·ya·*lee*·no da *la*·te suckling pig

**ossobuco con piselli** o·so·*boo*·ko kon pee·*ze*·lee sliced shin of veal with peas

**pestöm** *pes*·teum minced pork meat served with polenta

**San Pietro al vapore con salsa di limone e capperi** san *pye*·tro al va·*po*·re kon *sal*·sa dee lee·*mo*·ne e ka·*pe*·ree John Dory in a lemon sauce with capers

**stinco di maiale** *steen*·ko dee ma·*ya*·le pork shank

**tagliata di scottona lombarda** ta·*lya*·ta dee sko·*to*·na lom·*bar*·da a cut of Lombard beef best eaten rare

**vitello tonnato** vee·*te*·lo to·*na*·to veal in a tuna sauce

## DESSERTS & SWEETS

**miele** *mye*·le honey

**mostarda (di frutta)** mos·*tar*·da (dee *froo*·ta) fruit in a sweet mustard sauce, a Cremonese speciality

**pandoro** pan·*do*·ro literally 'golden bread', a sweet, eggy yeast bread once made only for the nobility

**panettone** pa·ne·*to*·ne the Milanese version of *pandoro*

**panna cotta** *pa*·na *ko*·ta wobbly set dessert usually bathed in a fruit sauce

**polenta e osei** po·*len*·ta e o·*zay* pudding-shaped cakes filled with jam and cream, and topped with sugared polenta icing and chocolate birds – a Bergamese speciality

**torta sbrisolana** *tor*·ta sbree·zo·*la*·na kind of crumble made with yellow flower, almonds and lard, a Mantua speciality

## DRINKS

**acqua** *a*·kwa water

**birra** *bee*·ra beer

**caffè** ka·*fe* coffee

**latte** *la*·te milk

**tè** te tea

**vino (rosso/bianco)** *vee*·no (*ro*·so/*byan*·ko) wine (red/white)

# ACCOMMODATION

## FINDING ACCOMMODATION

Accommodation in the Lombardy and lakes area in northern Italy ranges from the simple *rifugio* (mountain hut), through grand lakeside villas, to fashion-conscious, avant-garde digs at the hip and high end of the scale in Milan.

*Alberghi* (hotels) and *pensioni* (guest houses) make up the bulk of the offerings, covering a rainbow of options from cheap dives near train stations to grand hotels oozing luxury. There is often little difference between a *pensione* and an *albergo* but a *pensione* will generally be of one- to three-star quality and tradition-ally has been a family-run operation, while an *albergo* can be awarded up to five stars.

The star system gives limited clues to quality. One-star hotels/*pensioni* tend to be basic and without private bathrooms. Two-star places are similar but each room will generally have a private bathroom. At three-star joints you can assume reasonable standards. Four- and five-star hotels offer facilities such as room service, laundry and dry-cleaning.

*Locande* (inns) long fell into much the same category as *pensioni,* but the term has become trendy and reveals little about the quality of a place – not infrequently it will be attached to a nice bijou spot. *Affittacamere* are rooms for rent in private houses and are generally simple. B&Bs have become a popular alternative to hotels since the 1990s, partly due to relaxed regulations that have allowed their proliferation.

For those looking for a base for a week or two, an apartment, house or villa is tempting. There is enormous variety, from studio flats in towns like Como

## BOOK YOUR STAY ONLINE

For more accommodation reviews and recommendations by Lonely Planet authors, check out the online booking service at www.lonelyplanet.com/hotels. You'll find the true, insider low-down on the best places to stay. Reviews are thorough and independent. Best of all, you can book online.

## ONLINE RESOURCES

The following is a non-exhaustive list of websites where you can begin your search for lodgings in and around the lakes area of northern Italy.

**Agriturismo in Lombardia** (www.lombardia.campagnamica.it, in Italian) One of the most exhaustive sites on farm-stays and farm restaurants in Lombardy, which takes in most of the lakes district.

**Agriturismo.com** (www.agriturismo.com) Search system by region and province.

**Agriturist** (www.agriturist.com, in Italian) Limited selection of farm-stays.

**Alberghi in Italia** (www.alberghi-in-italia.it) Search by region and province with direct links to hotel websites.

**All Hotels in Italy** (www.hotelsitalyonline.com) US-based hotel booking agency.

**Bed & Breakfast Italia** (www.bbitalia.it) With about 30 options in Milan, a dozen in Verona and a sprinkling across the rest of the region.

**Club Alpino Italiano** (CAI; www.cai.it, in Italian) Owns and runs many of the *rifugi* (mountain huts).

**Cottages & Castles** (www.cottagesandcastles.com.au) An Australian-based specialist in villa-style accommodation, with 20 addresses in the lakes area.

**Cuendet** (www5.cuendet.com) Has some attractive properties (mostly holiday houses sleeping up to 10 people) on Lakes Como and Garda.

**Guest in Italy** (www.guestinitaly.com) Click on Lakes and then search for hotels by town.

**Holiday Lettings** (www.holidaylettings.co.uk) Has several hundred apartments to let in the lakes area, especially Lake Como.

**In Italia** (www.initalia.it) Detailed site with hotel descriptions, photos and occasional comments from guests.

**Interhome** (www.interhome.co.uk) Click on Lakes & Mountains and search on Italy and Switzerland for apartments.

**Monastery Stays** (www.monasterystays.com) A good starting point for searching out accommodation in convents or run by religious orders.

**Parker Villas** (www.parkervillas.co.uk) Has a limited selection of houses and villas, mostly on Lakes Como, Maggiore and Garda.

ACCOMMODATION

through to more spacious flats scattered about lakeside villages, or independent houses and villas (more often than not equipped with swimming pools). In some cases, historic buildings have been completely refurbished and divided into holiday apartments. Holiday apartment blocks (containing anything from four to 100 apartments) known as *residenze* are another option for stays packaged in weeks.

Tourist offices can usually supply you with exhaustive lists of all these options.

*Agriturismi* (farm-stays) are also an option. Some are working farms, others converted farmhouses (often with a pool). Provinces especially blessed with such options include Brescia, Mantua and Verona but you'll find a handful scattered across the whole lakes area – there is no shortage of websites.

The network of *rifugi* in the Alps and Lombard pre-Alps are usually only open from July to September. Accommodation is generally basic and in dormitories but some of the larger refuges have doubles. The price per person (which usually includes breakfast) ranges from €17 to €26 in a dorm depending on the quality of the refuge. A hearty postwalk single-dish dinner will set you back another €11.50. Many huts belong to the Club Alpino Italiano (CAI). Book in advance where possible.

With one or two notable exceptions, we don't list youth hostels or camping grounds in this guide. For leads on the former, check out www.hihostels .com and www.hostelworld.com. Lists of camping grounds are available from local tourist offices or can be looked up on various sites including www.campeggi .com, www.camping.it and www.ital camping.it. The Touring Club Italiano (TCI) publishes the annual *Campeggi in Italia* (Camping in Italy), listing all camping grounds across the country.

## PRICES & BOOKINGS

In this book a range of prices are quoted (reflecting low to high season rates) and are intended as a guide only. Half board equals breakfast and either lunch or dinner; full board includes breakfast, lunch and dinner.

Prices can fluctuate considerably depending on the season, with Easter, summer and the Christmas/New Year period being the typical peak tourist times. Indeed, around the lakes, many hotels only open from Easter to October and much of the lakes area goes into hibernation in winter, though hill and country areas with ski centres tend to perk up again in the cold months.

Milan is a case of its own, with price variations linked more to the trade-fair and events calendar – the bigger the fair, the higher the price and the greater degree of difficulty in locating a room. Summer (especially August) is something of a low season. With the exception of Verona and, to a degree, Bergamo, other cities away from the lakes (Brescia, Cremona, Mantua and Pavia) are largely immune to major seasonal swings.

Some hotels barely alter their prices throughout the year. This is especially true of the lower-end places, although in low season there is no harm in trying to bargain for a discount. You may find hoteliers especially receptive if you intend to stay for several days.

To make a reservation, hotels usually require confirmation by fax or, more commonly, a credit card number. In the latter case, if you don't show up you will be docked a night's accommodation. On average, you are looking at about €450 to €550 a week for an apartment sleeping four people on the lakes, although much depends on the quality and position of the digs (right on the lake will cost you more). Houses and villas sleeping eight to 10 people can be found for €1000 to €1500 a week. Some climb to €3000 a week in July and August. B&B tariffs per person cover a wide range from around €25 to €75.

## MILAN

The tourist office distributes *Milano Hotels,* a free annual listings guide to Milan's more than 350 hotels. Great value is difficult to come by in most budget ranges, and downright impossible during the Salone del Mobile, the fashion shows or other larger fairs. That said, booking ahead and comparison-shopping online for 'special rates' can result in excellent deals, especially out of ultrapeak times.

## PRICE GUIDE

The following is a guide to the pricing system used in this chapter. Unless otherwise stated, prices are for a low-season double room with private bathroom.

|  | Italy | Switzerland |
|---|---|---|
| € | up to €80 | up to Sfr120 |
| €€ | €80 to €200 | Sfr120 to Sfr300 |
| €€€ | €200 plus | Sfr300 plus |

Don't forget to factor in location. The city's sprawl means that what constitutes 'the centre' can be highly subjective.

### ☙ 3ROOMS €€€

Map pp40-1; ☎ 02 62 61 63; www.3rooms-10Corso como.com; Corso Como 10; d €270-310; Ⓜ Porta Garibaldi; Ⓟ ⊠ 🖳 🛜

Can't drag yourself and your shopping bags away from concept shop Corso Como? You don't have to – the villa's three guest rooms let you sleep amid Eames bedspreads, Arne Jacobsen chairs and Saarinen leather. Thrown in are some vintage items and a few items of artwork, just to keep you on your toes.

### ☙ ALLE MERAVIGLIE €€

Map pp44-5; ☎ 02 805 10 23; www.allemeraviglie.it; Via San Tomaso 8; d €180-247; Ⓜ Cairoli; Ⓟ ⊠ 🛜

There are just six soothing rooms at this boutique hotel in a pretty side street in the city centre. Each is uniquely decorated with beautiful fabrics and fresh flowers and there are no TVs. Indeed, there is a pleasingly hushed atmosphere about this retreat from the daily hustle outside.

### ☙ ANTICA LOCANDA LEONARDO €€

Map pp44-5; ☎ 02 4801 4197; www.anticalocanda leonardo.com; Corso Magenta 78; s €120, d €165-245; Ⓜ Conciliazione; ⊠ 🛜

Rooms ooze homey comfort, from the timber beds and parquet floors in some, to the antique furniture and plush drapes in others. All are quite different. Breakfast in the scented, internal garden of this atmospheric 19th-century residence.

### ☙ ANTICA LOCANDA SOLFERINO €€

Map pp44-5; ☎ 02 657 01 29; www.anticalocanda solferino.it; Via Castelfidardo 2; s €140-270, d €180-400; Ⓜ Moscova; ⊠ 🛜

A genuinely charming hideaway with 11 rooms, decorated in a bygone style with some nice paintings and prints. This understated Brera boutique beauty attracts artists, writers and other layabouts so booking is essential. The hotel is located at a pretty cobblestone intersection with nearby shops, cafes and restaurants (the hotel has its own restaurant too). It has a quite decent-sized single.

### ☙ ART HOTEL NAVIGLI €€

Map pp40-1; ☎ 02 8941 0530; www.arthotelnavigli .com; Via Angelo Fumagalli 4; incl breakfast s €148-320, d €168-385; Ⓜ Porta Genova; Ⓟ ⊠ 🖳

Behind its nondescript facade, which has the look of off-colour orange ceramics, and just off the canal, this four-star hotel hides 99 minimalist-sleek rooms, with glossy timber and flat-screen TVs. Parking is free.

### ☙ FORESTERIA MONFORTE €€

Map pp40-1; ☎ 02 7631 8516; www.foresteria monforte.it; Piazza del Tricolore 2; d €150-190; Ⓜ San Babila

With Philippe Starck chairs, flat-screen TVs and a communal kitchen, the three classy rooms in this upmarket B&B are just a short walk from the Duomo. Ceilings are high, rooms are filled with natural light and bathrooms are dizzyingly contemporary. Take breakfast in your room.

### ☙ HOTEL ARISTON €€

Map pp44-5; ☎ 02 7200 0556; www.aristonhotel .com; Largo Carrobbio 2; s €110-200, d €160-290; Ⓜ Missori; Ⓟ ⊠ 🖳 🛜

This ecofriendly hotel offers such touches as herbal tea made with purified water, organic breakfast, natural fibre-filled mattresses, soaps and shampoos with all-natural ingredients, and a free

ACCOMMODATION

bicycle at the door. Sunny colours and warm parquet floors give rooms a welcoming feel.

### ❦ HOTEL DEL SOLE €€

Map pp40-1; ☎ 02 2951 2971; www.delsolehotel
.com; Via Gaspare Spontini 6; s/d €50/95; Ⓜ Lima; ✕

One of the best options for those wanting to be near Stazione Centrale, this cheerful hotel has unadorned but welcoming rooms, some with terracotta and others with parquet floors. A few have little balconies. If you're a light sleeper, ask for a room overlooking the courtyard. Rooms with shared bathroom go cheaper.

### ❦ HOTEL ETRUSCO €€

Map pp40-1; ☎ 02 236 38 52; www.hoteletrusco.it;
Via Porpora 56; s/d €60/80; Ⓜ Piola; Ⓟ ▯

This elegant little three-star place features a lovely garden and pleasant rooms, and is certainly the pick of the bunch around Piazza Aspromonte. Rooms are furnished in a clean, unfussy style and some are nonsmoking. Six rooms with terraces overlook the garden area.

### ❦ STRAF €€€

Map pp44-5; ☎ 02 80 50 81; www.straf.it; Via San
Raffaele 3; s/d from €295/320; Ⓜ Duomo; ✕ ▯

Too cool for anything much, let alone school, this ultradesigner address is a shout from the Duomo. Some rooms have massage chairs and aromatherapy and all share some extreme decor ideas. Cement, black stone and scratched glass are common features. The bar downstairs hosts art installations and there's a gym for guests.

### ❦ VIETNAMONAMOUR €€

Map pp40-1; ☎ 02 7063 4614; www.vietnamon
amour.com; Via Alessandro Pestalozza 7; s/d from
€80/120; ✕ 🛜

## SMALL & STYLISH

- ★ **3 Rooms** (p289)
- ★ **Antica Locando Leonardo** (p289)
- ★ **Antica Locanda Solferino** (p289)
- ★ **Foresteria Monforte** (p289)
- ★ **Vietnamonamour** (left)

Beautiful bamboo parquet floors and Vietnamese furnishings set the tone in this 1903 residence-turned-B&B with four romantic rooms. Tropical tones inform the decor, with Vietnamese textiles throughout. Downstairs, the Paris-born Vietnamese owner offers an equally welcoming Vietnamese restaurant. You'd never know you were in Italy!

## PAVIA

### ❦ HOTEL MODERNO €€

Map p59; ☎ 0382 30 34 01; www.hotel
moderno.it; Viale Vittorio Emanuele II 41; s/d
€125/160; Ⓟ ✕

Housed in a 19th-century family *palazzo*, this swish hotel's rooms blend antique style with contemporary comforts. A fitness centre and free bikes are available. This is the city's top lodgings, and the hotel restaurant, Bistrot Bartolini, is one of the city's finer dining options too.

### ❦ LOCANDA DELLA STAZIONE €

Map p59; ☎ 0382 2 93 21; www.locandadella
stazione.it; Viale Vittorio Emanuele II 14; d €60, s/d
without bathroom €30/40; ✕

With parquet and mosaic floors, stucco ceiling ornaments and early-20th-century decor, this is something of a history time-warp as well as pleasant, well-priced digs. It's easily missed, though, so look out for the name on the buzzers by the front door.

# LAKE MAGGIORE & LAKE ORTA

## LOCARNO & AROUND

During the film festival in August, room prices soar by 50% to 100%.

### ♥ ALBERGO RISTORANTE CITTADELLA // LOCARNO €€

Map p71; ☎ 091 751 58 85; www.cittadella.ch; Via Cittadella 18; s/d Sfr100/170

The handful (10 in total) of pretty rooms are individually decorated with chessboard tile floors, and the ones in the attic, with sloping timber ceilings, are especially snug. A few items of wooden furniture and bed linen that seems like it might have been handmade all add to the cosiness factor. It has a popular fish restaurant downstairs (p75).

### ♥ CASTELLO SEESCHLOSS // ASCONA €€€

☎ 091 791 01 61; www.castello-seeschloss.ch; Piazza Motta; s/d from Sfr184/348; ℗ ⊠ 🖵 .

A 13th-century castle/palace that never saw military action but has undergone numerous overhauls, this spot is now a romantic waterfront hotel in the southeast corner of the old town centre. Standard rooms are in the main building and the most extraordinary rooms, some full of frescos, are in the ivy-covered tower.

### ♥ SCHLOSS HOTEL – ALBERGO CASTELLO // LOCARNO €€

Map p71; ☎ 091 751 23 61; www.schlosshotel locarno.ch; Via Bartolomeo Rusca 9; s/d Sfr145/224; 🖵 🖳

Tucked in behind the Visconti clan castle through which Milan once lorded it over Locarno (see p70), this hotel has something of the bearing of a castle itself, with its five storeys, fine arches and Mediterranean feel. Inside, grand fireplaces, heavy rugs and the 16th-century restaurant all chime in to add atmosphere, and the pool adds to the Med mood.

### ♥ VECCHIA LOCARNO // LOCARNO €

Map p71; ☎ 091 751 65 02; www.hotel-vecchia -locarno.ch; Via della Motta 10; s/d Sfr55/100

Rooms are gathered around a sunny internal courtyard, evoking a Mediterranean mood, and some have views over the old town centre and hills. The digs are simple enough, but comfortable (heaters are provided in the colder months), and at these prices it's hard to complain. Bathrooms are in the corridor.

## TICINO'S WESTERN VALLEYS

### ♥ ANTICA OSTERIA DAZIO // FUSIO €€

☎ 091 755 11 62; www.hats.ch; dm/s/d Sfr19/135/152, ste Sfr198-260; ☙ Mar-Nov; ℗

The 'Old Customs Inn' is a beautifully renovated place to sleep, with loads of Alpine charm. Some rooms are timber panelled, with terracotta floors, heavy wood bedheads and even the odd rocking chair. Others have a more neutral look with parquet floors and light-coloured decor. Try not to bump your head if you take one of the 15 dorm spots up in the roof.

### ♥ OSTERIA VITTORIA // LAVERTEZZO €€

☎ 091 746 15 81; www.osteriavittoria.ch; s Sfr70-100, d Sfr120-140

A bustling, riverside family lodge with its own restaurant and garden, the three-storey, rose-tinted Osteria Vittoria is a welcoming place to use as a base for exploring the Val Verzasca. Most rooms, which are pleasant, white-washed jobs with terracotta floors, have balconies with views over the Verzasca stream. You can relax out on the terrace, which offers views to the old core of Lavertezzo.

## LAKE MAGGIORE WEST BANK

### ♨ ALBERGO VILLA MON TOC // STRESA €€
Map p81; ☎ 0323 3 02 82; www.hotelmontoc.com; Viale Duchessa di Genova 67-69; s/d €55/85; Ⓟ ⊠
A cheerful, three-storey, orange residence, this is a very comfortable spot just back from the railway and nicely priced. Rooms have a pleasingly old-fashioned air, with dark wooden furniture, big beds and throw rugs on the tile floors. A big plus is the lovely garden out the back.

### ♨ CASA KINKA // STRESA €€
off Map p81; ☎ 0323 3 00 47; www.casakinka.it; Strada Comunale Lombartino 21, Magognino; s/d €80/100; Ⓟ ▭
This lovely B&B is set on a rise high above Stresa, about 6km out of town. The friendly owners have two comfortable rooms. You can sit back on a sun lounger on the garden lawn and gaze down over the lake. To get here from Stresa, follow the road for Mottarone and turn off towards Vedasco.

### ♨ GRAND HOTEL MAJESTIC // VERBANIA PALLANZA €€€
☎ 0323 50 97 11; www.grandhotelmajestic.it; Via Vittorio Veneto 32; d from €210; Ⓟ ⊠ ▭ ⛫ ▨
With its private boat landing, private little beach, wellness centre, bars and restaurants, you may never feel inclined to penetrate the outside world. Even some of the smaller, cheaper rooms have lake glimpses, while many of the more generously appointed rooms and suites, draped in fine textiles and equipped with marble faced bathrooms,

have balconies looking straight over the lake.

### ♨ HOTEL ELENA // STRESA €€
Map p81; ☎ 0323 3 10 43; www.hotelelena.com; Piazza Cadorna 15; s/d €55/80; Ⓟ
Adjoining a cafe, the old-fashioned Elena is slap-bang on Stresa's central pedestrian square. Wheelchair access is possible, and all of Elena's comfortable rooms, with parquet floors, have a balcony, many overlooking the square.

### ♨ HOTEL PIRONI // CANNOBIO €€
☎ 0323 7 06 24; www.pironihotel.it; Via Marconi 35; s €120, d €130-170
In a 15th-century mini-monastery (later home of the noble Pironi family) amid Cannobio's cobbled maze, Hotel Pironi is number one of several charming hotels in this town. Behind its thickset stone walls lurks a beautifully restored excursion into the past, with antiques sprinkled about, frescoed vaults, exposed timber beams, stairs climbing off in odd directions, a frescoed breakfast room and an assortment of tastefully decorated rooms, some with lake views.

### ♨ LA STELLINA // STRESA €€
Map p81; ☎ 0323 3 24 43; www.lastellina.com; Via Molinari 10; s/d €70/80
A couple of blocks' stroll from the main square is an early-19th-century building that makes a beautiful backdrop for this charming little B&B. One of its three floral-themed rooms, the 'rose room', has a wooden spiral staircase leading to an attic sitting room.

## BORROMEAN ISLANDS

### ♨ ALBERGO RISTORANTE BELVEDERE // ISOLA SUPERIORE €€
☎ 0323 3 22 92; www.belvedere-isolapescatori.it; s/d €110/170; ⊠

Perfectly located at the serene northeast end of the island, this cheerful little hotel-restaurant has eight modern, comfortable rooms, most with balcony or terrace offering lake and mountain views. The hotel restaurant has two pleasant garden areas where you can flop about.

### ☙ ALBERGO VERBANO // ISOLA SUPERIORE €€

☎ 0323 3 04 08; www.hotelverbano.it; s/d €120/185; ☺ Mar-Dec

You'll be tempted to stay in this three-storey Bordeaux-tinted charmer. The hotel, in business since the late 19th century, has a dozen rooms with wrought-iron bedsteads, and half-and full-board options. Each room is named after a flower and given its own decorative style and lake views are the norm. The hotel will send its own boat out free for guests once the ferries have stopped running (but no later than 11.30pm).

## LAKE MAGGIORE EAST BANK

### ☙ LIDO ANGERA // ANGERA €€

☎ 0331 93 02 32; www.hotellido.it; Viale Libertà 11; s/d €78/110; Ⓟ ☒

In a stout orange building set amid greenery and just back from a modest sandy beach just outside central Angera, this hotel is an excellent deal. Rooms are generally spacious, mostly decorated in creams and whites and, in some cases, with windows or balconies opening up right over the lake.

## VARESE & AROUND

### ☙ AL BORDUCAN // SACRO MONTE DEL ROSARIO €€

☎ 0332 22 29 16; www.borducan.com; d/ste €130/230; ☒ ▱

This building, home to a local herbs-and-orange based elixir, has been standing high in the medieval hamlet of the Sacro Monte del Rosario since 1924. Inside are nine enchanting rooms with art-nouveau furniture. Room styles vary – the smallest is a little tightly packed, while the suites, with their hardwood floors and high ceilings, will warm the heart. Downstairs is a fine restaurant.

## LAKE ORTA

### ☙ HOTEL LEON D'ORO // ORTA SAN GIULIO €€

Map p97; ☎ 0322 91 19 91; www.albergoleondoro.it; Piazza Mario Motta 42; s €100, d €110-180; ☺ Feb-Dec; ☒

Any closer to the lake and you'd be in it. A centuries-old building on Piazza Motta, this hotel is ideally located and irresistibly romantic, with its more expensive doubles looking directly across to Isola San Giulio. Sunny yellows and deep blues dominate the decor, with heavy window curtains, timber furniture, tiled floors and, in some rooms, jacuzzi-style baths. It also has some smallish suites.

### ☙ LA CONTRADA DEI MONTI // ORTA SAN GIULIO €€

Map p97; ☎ 0322 90 51 14; www.orta.net/la contradadeimonti; Via dei Monti 10; s/d €90/110; ☺ Feb-Dec; ☒

You never know what might lurk behind the walls of an 18th-century building on a medieval cobbled lane. Here, a noble house has been brought back to life to host a boutique hotel. Rooms are all very different, some with bare, stone walls and timber ceilings, others with a more classical look and high ceilings. In summer, breakfast is served in the peaceful rear courtyard.

### ❦ PICCOLO HOTEL OLINA // ORTA SAN GIULIO €€

Map p97; ☎ 0322 90 56 56; www.orta.net/olina; Via Olina 40; s/d €75/100; ⊠

Artistically decorated with contemporary prints, bright colours and light-wood furniture, this ecofriendly hotel with a touch of modern design right in Orta San Giulio's medieval heart is a gem. It also has a fine, somewhat avant-garde restaurant downstairs (p100).

### ❦ VILLA CRESPI // ORTA SAN GIULIO €€€

Map p97; ☎ 0322 91 19 02; www.slh.com/crespi; Via Giuseppe Fava 18; s/d from €220/280; ⊗ Apr-Dec; Ⓟ ⊠ ▣ ▨

Staying at this Moorish extravaganza, which is topped with an aqua-coloured onion-dome spire, is to enter the madcap design dream of the family (a rich textile clan) that built this caprice. The opulent interiors and sprawling gardens, designed for cotton trader Benigno Crespi in 1879, are one-of-a-kind.

# LAKE COMO & LAKE LUGANO

## COMO

### ❦ ALBERGO DEL DUCA €€

Map pp108-9; ☎ 031 26 48 59; www.albergodel duca.it; Piazza Mazzini 12; s/d €75/120; Ⓟ ⊠ ▣

Set on a peaceful square in central Como, the hotel occupies a renovated 17th-century building with a pleasant internal courtyard. Rooms, which exude the warmth that comes from hardwood floors, look either on to the square or the courtyard.

### ❦ IN RIVA AL LAGO €

Map pp108-9; ☎ 031 30 23 33; www.inrivaallago .com; Piazza Matteotti 4; s/d €45/63, without bathroom €38/47, 2-person apt from €70; Ⓟ

Don't be deceived by the unassuming exterior of this hotel, situated right behind the bus station. The simple but pleasing rooms with tile floors are tastefully furnished, some with original wood beams, and there are a handful of apartments for up to five people.

### ❦ LE STANZE DEL LAGO €

Map pp108-9; ☎ 339 544 65 15; www.lestanzedellago .com; Via Rodari; apt for 2/4 people from €70/90; ⊠

Five cosy apartments, nicely decked out in modern but understated fashion, make for a good deal in the heart of Como. For stays of five days or longer you can use the kitchen too. All apartments feature double bed, sofa bed, timber ceiling and tiled floor.

## TRIANGOLO LARIANO

### ❦ AGRITURISMO MUNT DE VOLT // PIAN DEL TIVANO €

☎ 031 91 88 98; Via Monti di Là 3; r per person €20

It would be difficult to feel more deeply ensconced in the rural world. Off the Pian del Tivano, a high country plain some 7km from lakeside Nesso, this farm in dairy country offers four simple rooms. To the front of the house are views over thickly forested valleys, while behind, spring flowers carpet the slopes (where there are some swings for kids). It lies 1km off the main road (look for Via Battista Longoni, opposite the helipad and sign to Albergo Dosso, 1.5km east of Zelbio). It serves meals too (€20 per person).

### ❦ ALBERGO BELVEDERE // TORNO €

☎ 031 41 91 00; Piazza Casartelli 3; d €55; ⊗ Mar-Dec

Next to the lake and Torno's pretty lakeside square (with its minuscule port), the Belvedere is a simple option with straightforward rooms. Some overlook the lake and others the square, and that alone is worth the booking.

### ✿ ALBERGO GIARDINETTO // BELLAGIO €

Map p115; ☎ 031 95 01 68; www.bellagiolakecomo .com; Via Roncati 12; s/d €45/65; ☼ Apr–Nov

Tucked up in a narrow shady lane at the high end of the village, the Garden Hotel is what it says: set around a pergola and garden. Simple, pleasant rooms are gathered around the pergola area and some have views westward over the town and lake from the balconies.

### ✿ ALBERGO SILVIO // BELLAGIO €€

off Map p115; ☎ 031 95 03 22; www.bellagiosilvio .com; Via Carcano 12; s/d from €65/85; ☼ Mar–mid-Nov & Christmas week; Ⓟ ⚒ ☐ 🛜

The high position over the western arm of Lake Como is enough to recommend this spot, 1km short of the centre of Bellagio. The prettily furnished rooms are a mix: some have balconies and side views, others are mansard rooms with sloping ceiling and frontal lake views. It is worth shelling out the €15 extra for a lake view.

### ✿ HOTEL AURORA // LEZZENO €€

☎ 031 91 46 45; www.hotelauroralezzeno.com; Via Sossana 2; s €45, d €85-110; ☼ Apr-Oct; Ⓟ ☐ 🛜

In the heart of Lezzeno (the longest village on Lake Como), 11km southwest of Bellagio, this is a comfy family hotel in a village off the mainstream tourist radar. Singles look inland but the best doubl... have balconies with lake views. Ac... the road, take breakfast with a la... breeze in the hotel restaurant... the restaurant, the hotel ha... along a wooden boardwa... a whole range of water... aqua trampoline fo... skiing and wakeb... Racing Club (w...

### ✿ HOTEL LA PERGOLA // PESCALLO (BELLAGIO) €€

off Map p115; ☎ 031 95 02 63; www.lapergolabel lagio.it; Piazza del Porto 4; s/d €70/120

A 15-minute (1km) walk from Bellagio along cobbled lanes leads to sheltered Pescallo, a tiny port. Pescallo's quiet hotel is right on the water (and the pergola referred to shades a fine restaurant jutting out over it). The 16th-century one-time convent has pleasant rooms, some of which look directly over the lake.

### ✿ RESIDENCE LA LIMONERA // BELLAGIO €

Map p115; ☎ 031 95 21 24; www.residencelalimon era.com; Via Bellosio 2; 2-person apt €70-100; ☐

This elegant villa is perched high up... in the town in an old lemon grove... has been divided into 11 spacio... thoughtfully furnished self-c... apartments for two to fou...

## LAKE COMO W...

### ✿ ALBERGHET... MARIANNA ...

☎ 0344 4 30 95;... Cadenabbia di... About ... in Ca... th...

a red-brick cellar, and a tavern serving pizzas baked in a wood-fired oven. The early-20th-century building has 22 rooms with parquet floors, muted pastel colours and high ceilings.

### ❧ HOTEL REGINA // GRAVEDONA €€

☎ 0344 8 94 46; www.reginahotels.it; Via Regina Levante 18; s €65-100, d €100-140; P X ⊜
The hotel fronts the beach and has a full range of facilities including a gym, and mountain bikes to explore the surrounding mountains. It has a sunbathing area __ __y shower for those leaving

## LAKE COMO EAST BANK

### ❧ ALBERGO CONCA AZZURRA // ABBAZIA DI PIONA €

☎ 0341 93 19 84; www.concazzurra.com; Via per l'Abbazia di Piona 19; s €44-65, d €70-85; P X ⊇ ⊜
One kilometre short of the Cistercian abbey, on a verdant promontory jutting into the lake, this bucolic, three-storey hotel is a peaceful hideaway, with gardens and wooden shutters, in a lovely location. It offers a variety of rooms, many with balconies and lake views, and has its own restaurant-bar. The cobblestone path stroll to the abbey is marvellously restorative.

### ❧ ALBERGO MILANO // VARENNA €€

☎ 0341 83 02 98; www.varenna.net; Via XX Settembre 35; d €130-160; ⊙ Mar-Nov; X ⊇ ⊜
__ __ middle of the village on the pe__ __ street (well, lane), Albergo __ the slope and opens __ __gnificent lake __ approach by __ have some __ and are __ __nted colours, offer lake views__

ACCOMMOD__

__us and __ering People.

__EST BANK

__TO DELLA CADENABB__

www.la-marianna.c__
Griante; s/d €65/95; __
__00m north of th__
denabbia, this r__
lakeside road o__
__place, with dark__
charmingly cb__
all like the g__
the ro__

__R__ LAGI

☎ 031__ __
⊙ Mar-Oct__
Via Vecchie__
Want to s__
near Georg__
charming vi__
Laglio, 200m__
__ Regina m__
can approach__
has a private landi__
be greeted by pleasa__
rooms, decorated tast__

__ss __e

Just below __ sun loungers __k and access to __ activities, from an __ the kids to water-__oarding with the Jolly __w.jrcwakeboard.com).

Regii__
Situat__
Cernob__
shuttere__

__les

__ou __r- __al

__ience __The

minimum stay is three days and includes use of the pool, jacuzzi and gym. Possibilities for mountain hikes of varying degrees of difficulty abound.

## LAKE LUGANO

### ❤ ALBERGO ROSA // LUGANO €€

Map p132; ☎ 091 922 92 86; www.albergorosa.ch; Via Landriani 2-4; s/d Sfr125/175, without bathroom Sfr72/124; P

A cheerful little four-storey retreat in a nice spot near the Parco Civico, this family-run hotel is gathered around a courtyard and offers clean rooms (shame about the carpet in some rooms). Singles are small. Prices drop about a quarter in slow periods.

### ❤ HOTEL & HOSTEL MONTARINA // LUGANO €€

Map p132; ☎ 091 966 72 72; www.montarina.ch; Via Montarina 1; s/d Sfr85/125; P 🖾

Behind the train station is this charming hotel, whose most attractive rooms are airy, with timber floors and antiques. Some have private kitchen. They are a little cheaper than the more modern rooms, which are equipped with full bathroom. The pool is set in pleasant gardens with views.

### ❤ HOTEL INTERNATIONAL AU LAC // LUGANO €€

Map p132; ☎ 091 922 75 41; www.hotel-international.ch; Via Nassa 88; s Sfr125-185, d Sfr220-310; 🕙 Apr-Oct; P 🖾 🖾

From the balconies of the front rooms of this 1906 grand hotel you look straight out over Lake Lugano. These rooms are by far the best, but other cheaper rooms are scattered about the hotel. Rooms are comfortable, with a smattering of antique furniture, although the standard singles are rather small.

### ❤ LOCANDA DEL GIGLIO // ROVEREDO, CAPRIASCA €€

☎ 091 930 09 33; www.locandadelgiglio.ch; dm/s/d Sfr40/95/150

In the village of Roveredo, Capriasca, 12km north of Lugano, this is a lovely place to spend a night or two. It is a warm timber building powered on solar energy. Rooms have balconies offering mountain views and even lake glimpses. Take a bus from Lugano to Tesserete (30 minutes) and change there for another to Roveredo (about 10 minutes).

# BERGAMO, BRESCIA & CREMONA

## BERGAMO

The most charming accommodation is on Bergamo's hilltop.

### ❤ AGRITURISMO CASA CLELIA // SOTTO IL MONTE GIOVANNI XXIII €€

☎ 035 79 91 33; www.casaclelia.com; Via Corna 1/3; s/d from €55/95

Barely a 10-minute stroll from the centre of Sotto il Monte Giovanni XXIII, on the initial rise to the mount that backs the town, this working farm offers 10 spacious, beautiful rooms in the carefully restored 16th-century main farmhouse, set amid gardens and outhouses. Exposed stone and brick, timber beams and dark wood furniture characterise the rooms.

### ❤ ALBERGO IL SOLE // BERGAMO €€

Map p150; ☎ 035 21 82 38; www.ilsolebergamo.com; Via Bartolomeo Colleoni 1; s/d €65/85

The picture windows and colourful bedspreads at Il Sole lend its otherwise fairly straightforward but immaculately maintained rooms a countrified air. This is perhaps odd, given that it is jammed deep inside the medieval rabbit warren of the Città Alta.

### ❦ B&B ALBA // BERGAMO €€
Map p150; ☎ 349 575 25 96; www.bbalbachiara .info, in Italian; Via Salvecchio 2; d/tr €100/120
Three spacious rooms are available in this rambling old town house. Mosaic and terracotta floors, high frescoed ceilings, the odd item of antique furniture and loads of atmosphere make this B&B a quiet option with a family feel.

### ❦ DA VITTORIO // BRUSAPORTO €€€
☎ 035 68 10 24; www.davittorio.com; Via Cantalupa 17; s/d €200/280; ⊗ closed most of Aug
Not only is Da Vittorio a noteworthy gourmet hideout (see p151), it also offers 10 quality suites in its low-slung country estate. Each of the generous rooms enjoys its own sumptuous decor, with beautifully woven fabrics and marble bathroom. Indulge in a tasting menu breakfast, with a series of miniportions of various sweet and savoury options. The place looks over a park and vineyard.

### ❦ HOTEL PIAZZA VECCHIA // BERGAMO €€
Map p150; ☎ 035 428 42 11; www.hotelpiazza vecchia.it; Via Bartolomeo Colleoni 3; s €135-170, d €150-190; ⊠ 🖵
Carved out of a 13th-century building a few steps off Piazza Vecchia, this hotel's 13 rooms are all quite different. All have parquet floors and bath set in stone, but decor varies. Some have exposed beams, some a balcony, some a king-size bed.

### ❦ NUOVO OSTELLO DI BERGAMO // MONTEROSSO €
Off Map p147; ☎ 035 36 17 24; www.ostellodiber gamo.it; Via Galileo Ferraris 1; dm/s/d €18/35/50; ⊗24hr; 🅿 🖵

Bergamo's state-of-the-art HI hostel is about 4km north of the train station. Its 27 rooms offer views over Bergamo's Città Alta old centre. Take bus 6 from Largo Porta Nuova near the train station (get off at Leonardo da Vinci stop) or bus 3 for Ostello from the Città Alta.

## LAKE ISEO & AROUND

### ❦ B&B BORGO DEI LANTIERI // SARNICO €
☎ 035 91 40 76; www.borgodeilantieri.it; Via Lantieri 31; s/d €35/65
A handful of rooms, all rather different (one with bunk beds for four people), are gathered in a modernised house in the old centre of Sarnico, a couple of minutes' stroll from the river. You can sit in the lovely internal plant-filled courtyard or head for the rooftop terrace to catch some rays.

### ❦ B&B IN COLLINA // ESMATE €
☎ 347 256 13 21; www.comeacasatua.com; Via Cerrete 6; s/d €35/50; 🅿
About 1km out of the hamlet of Esmate, high above Lake Iseo, this family house is hidden in a dale of dazzling green. The friendly couple here offer two rooms and will happily show you around their herb garden. The location is the definition of tranquillity but you need your own wheels – and Lake Iseo and Lake Endine are about 10 minutes' drive away.

### ❦ HOTEL MILANO // ISEO €€
☎ 030 98 04 49; www.hotelmilano.info; Lungolargo Marconi 4; s/d €50/90; ⊠ 🖵 🛜
One of only two hotels in the centre of Iseo, the lakefront Milano is an excellent deal. Prices quoted are for pleasant rooms with lake views (one-week minimum stay mid-July to mid-August) – so you have a front row seat for sunset behind the mountains over the lake.

### ❦ L'ALBERETA // ERBUSCO €€€
☎ 030 776 05 50; www.albereta.it; Via Vittorio
Emanuele 23; s/d from €220/315; Ⓟ 💥 🖳 🛜 🛋
This country estate, sheathed in creep-
ing ivy, has been converted into luxury
Relais & Châteaux digs. Set on a rise
overlooking the surrounding Franciacorta wine country and with state-of-the-art
spa (with Henri Chenot products) and
gym, it's perfect for a pamper. The rooms
are spacious and tastefully decorated and
the grounds and public spaces impeccable. You can round off the experience
by dining at Marchesi (p163).

## BRESCIA

### ❦ ALBERGO OROLOGIO €€
Map p165; ☎ 030 375 54 11; www.albergoorologio
.it; Via Beccaria 17; s/d €115/130; 💥 🖳
Right by its namesake clock tower in the
pedestrianised old town, fine art and artefacts, and soft gold, brown and olive furnishings and terracotta floors make this
boutique hotel a gem. It has just 16 varied
rooms carved out of a medieval building
that combine warmth in the decor with
contemporary design in the bathrooms.

### ❦ HOTEL VITTORIA €€€
Map p165; ☎ 030 28 00 61; www.hotelvittoria.com;
Via X Giornate 20; s/d €166/274; 💥 🖳
Given this grand 1938 hotel's chandeliers,
sweeping ballrooms and luxurious guest
rooms, resting your head here represents
unexpectedly good value. After sweeping
through the grand hall and public spaces,
which drip with marble and walnut, you'll
see the rooms have a restrained elegance
and mostly enjoy wads of natural light.

## CREMONA

### ❦ ALBERGO DUOMO €
Map p170; ☎ 0372 3 52 96, 0372 3 52 42; fax 0372
45 83 92; Via Gonfalonieri 13; s/d €45/65; Ⓟ 💥

Just a few steps from Cremona's cathedral and ablaze with wrought-iron flower
boxes in spring, Albergo Duomo offers
decent rooms with basic furniture and
all-white decor. Given its privileged position, it is hard to beat on price.

### ❦ HOTEL ASTORIA €€
Map p170; ☎ 0372 46 16 16; www.astoriahotel
-cremona.it; Via Bordigallo 19; s/d €60/90; 💥
Down a quiet, narrow lane near Piazza
Cavour is this charming spot, with
French-washed corridors and immaculate rooms (including some with separate
bedrooms that are handy if you're travelling with kids). Its quiet position, muted
pastel colours and generous buffet breakfast make it a good option.

## AROUND CREMONA

### ❦ LA CASA DI OLIVER // LODI €
☎ 0371 41 17 77; www.lacasadioliver.it; Via Defend-
ente 60; s/d €40/75; Ⓟ 💥
Set in a two-storey early 1900s *stile
liberty* (Italian art nouveau) building
about a five-minute walk from the
centre of Lodi, this charmer has three
spacious rooms overlooking an extensive garden. Parquet floors and soft
decor make the nicely renovated rooms
welcoming. Hang out in the reading
room, wander the gardens…or even
explore the town.

# LAKE GARDA, VERONA & MANTUA

## LAKE GARDA WEST BANK

### ❦ AGLI ANGELI // GARDONE RIVIERA €€
☎ 036 52 08 32; www.agliangeli.com; Piazza
Garibaldi 2; d €105-160; Ⓟ 💥 🛋
A delightful renovation has produced
an 18th-century *locanda* of old polished

ACCOMMODATION

wood, gauzy fabrics and bursts of lime, orange and aquamarine. The terrace has a compact pool and views across rooftops to the lake beyond. The owners offer similar but simpler rooms (singles/doubles €55/95) next door.

### ☙ BELLERIVE // SALÒ €€€
Map p196; ☎ 036 552 04 10; www.hotelbellerive .it; Via Pietro da Salò 11; s/d/ste €180/245/350; Ⓟ Ⓧ ⬚ 🖭
The chic lobby of this elegant hotel features sculpted lights, modern art and tiny candles, while delicate colours, candy stripes and clean lines define bedrooms with views over a marina of bobbing yachts.

### ☙ DUOMO // SALÒ €€
Map p196; ☎ 036 52 10 26; www.hotelduomosalo .it; Lungolago Zanardelli 63; s €80-140, d €130-195; Ⓧ ⬚ 🖭
Hotel Duomo exudes old-style comfort, with its plump leather armchairs, marble-lined lobby and bedrooms rich in blue and gold satin. Both your balcony and the hot tub on the terrace have grandstand views of the lush green Gulf of Salò.

### ☙ GARGNANO // GARGNANO €
☎ 036 57 13 12; Piazza Feltrinelli 29; s/d €45/60
DH Lawrence slept at this no-frills, well-worn, harbourfront *albergo* while writing *Twilight in Italy*. Roughly plastered walls and faded shutters add to its appeal. The balcony room has five-star views at one-star prices.

### ☙ GRAND HOTEL GARDONE // GARDONE RIVIERA €€
☎ 036 52 02 61; www.grangardone.it; Via Zanardelli 84; d €190-254; Ⓟ Ⓧ ⬚ 🖯
Built in 1884, this palatial hotel speaks eloquently of Gardone's belle époque.

Chandeliers illuminate wood-panelled reception rooms, while the floral-themed bedrooms are upstaged by panoramic lake views.

### ☙ GRAND HOTEL TERME // SIRMIONE €€€
☎ 030 91 62 61; www.termedisirmione.com; Viale Marconi 7; d €304-470, ste €474-660; Ⓟ Ⓧ ⬚ 🖭
From the secluded waterfront deck of this idyllic retreat the only sound is the occasional hum of a motorboat. In the best bedrooms it's all plush furnishings, monogrammed slippers, luxury oils and lotions and views of open water.

### ☙ GRIFONE // SIRMIONE €
☎ 030 91 60 14; grifonesirmione@gmail.com; Via Bocchio 4; s/d €40/67
The rustic rooms of this two-star *albergo* look directly onto the lake and Sirmione's waterfront castle. The only other place with views this good is the five-star Grand Hotel Terme opposite.

### ☙ MARCONI // SIRMIONE €€
☎ 030 91 60 07; www.hotelmarconi.net; Via Vittorio Emanuele II 51; s/d €65/115; Ⓟ Ⓧ
Blue and white striped umbrellas line the lakeside deck at this stylish, family-run hotel. The restrained rooms are all subtle shades and crisp fabrics, and the breakfasts and homemade pastries are a treat.

### ☙ VILLA GIULIA // GARGNANO €€€
☎ 036 57 10 22; www.villagiulia.it; Viale Rimembranze 20; d €220-335; Ⓟ Ⓧ ⬚ 🖰 🖭
Lakefront gardens dotted with palm and olive trees make this 18th-century villa feel like a Mediterranean hideaway. Bedrooms are either snazzy and modern, or rich in antiques, thick rugs and soft gold fabric. Service is faultless (they stop hoovering when you walk past) and your biggest dilemma will be whether to swim

in the pool or the lake after that spell in the sauna.

## LAKE GARDA NORTH BANK

### ❤ RESTEL DE FER // RIVA DEL GARDA €€

Map p204; ☎ 0464 55 34 81; www.resteldefer.com; Via Restel de Fer 10; s/d €68/90; Ⓟ

The Meneghelli family's been running this charming *locanda* since 1400 and its rustic rooms are chock-full of old oak dressers, hand-woven rugs and brass bedsteads. Dinner in their restaurant downstairs is truly memorable; see p206.

### ❤ VILLA MIRAVALLE // RIVA DEL GARDA €€

Map p204; ☎ 0464 55 23 35; www.hotelvilla miravalle.com; Via Monte Oro 9; s €70-90, d €120-140; Ⓟ ⚅ ⚏

The raspberry-red lobby is dotted with blue armchairs and artfully twisted bamboo, bedrooms feature sleek furniture, restful tones and splashes of colour, and the palm-fringed balconies overlook a gorgeous pool. It's a beautiful, boutique hideaway.

## LAKE GARDA EAST BANK

### ❤ COSTADORO // BARDOLINO €€

☎ 045 621 04 93; www.agriturismocostadoro.com; Via Costabella 29; s €60-85, d €80-90; Ⓟ ⚏

Offering a real flavour of Bardolino's wine country, the fresh rooms of this spick and span little *agriturismo* are done out in peach and distressed pine. You can see Lake Garda from the swimming pool, while a winery and great restaurant (p213) are right next door.

### ❤ GARDESANA // TORRI DEL BENACO €€

☎ 045 722 54 11; www.hotel-gardesana.com; Piazza Calderini 20; s €78-103, d €126-176; Ⓟ ⚅ ⚎

The guest list at this gorgeous 15th-century hotel has featured actors, writers, statespeople and kings. Painted wood and antiques fill the bedrooms, while the vine-fringed breakfast terrace has delightful harbour views. Ask for Room 123 with its wraparound balcony – Winston Churchill and King Juan Carlos of Spain no doubt enjoyed their stay in it too.

### ❤ LOCANDA SAN VIGILIO // PUNTA SAN VIGILIO €€€

☎ 045 725 66 88; www.punta-sanvigilio.it; d €270-375, ste €440-890; Ⓟ ⚅ ⚏ ⚎

Hidden away on a headland, this 16th-century *locanda* is one to remember for a very, very long time. It feels like a stately English home: discreet, understated and effortlessly elegant. Dark woods, stone floors and plush furnishings ensure an old-world-meets-new-luxury feel. It's prestigious, perfect and hard to leave.

### ❤ QUERCETO // MALCESINE €€

Map p208; ☎ 045 740 03 44; www.parkhotelquer ceto.com; Via Panoramica 113; s €115-145, d €170-210; Ⓟ ⚅ ⚎ ⚏

This Swiss chalet–style Monte Baldo hotel is an ideal bolt-hole. Views onto the lake far below are stunning, bedrooms are made cosy by oak furniture and bright rugs, and a dip in its cliff-edge infinity pool is a swim to remember.

### ❤ VITTORIA // GARDA €€

☎ 045 627 04 73; www.lavittoria.eu; Lungolago Regina Adelaide 57; d €98-160; Ⓟ ⚅

This chic little three-star spot sits right on Garda's waterfront promenade. Spacious lake-view rooms are done out in delicate cream and gold, while free mini-antipasti and afternoon tea – best sampled on the palm-dotted terrace – add to the appeal.

ACCOMMODATION

## VERONA

### ♥ AURORA €€

Map p214; ☎ 045 59 47 17; www.hotelaurora.biz;
Piazza delle Erbe; d €100-150; ⊠ ⊚

Some of this hotel's bright, simple rooms
overlook the bustling Piazza delle Erbe,
as does its 2nd-floor terrace – a perfect
spot for breakfast or a lazy afternoon of
people-watching.

### ♥ COLOMBA D'ORO €€

Map p214; ☎ 045 59 53 00; www.colombahotel
.com; Via Carlo Cattaneo 10; s €140-170, d €144-237,
ste €192-284; Ⓟ ⊠ ⊚

In this plush hotel, polished floors, painted wood and rococo mirrors are offset by
candy-striped fabrics, gauzy drapes and
the odd Italianate painting. Bathrooms
are luxurious, and the breakfast buffet
immense.

### ♥ DUE TORRI HOTEL BAGLIONI €€€

Map p214; ☎ 045 59 50 44; www.baglionihotels
.com; Piazza di Sant'Anastasia 4; s/d €390/620, ste
€930-1000 Ⓟ ⊠ ⊡ ⊚

Refined and exquisite, this former Della
Scala palace exudes wealth, from the vel-
vet-clad sofas in the cavernous lobby to
the tapestries on the walls. Suites feature
burnished antiques, embossed leather
books and monogrammed towels, and
even the guest list is impressive, featuring Mozart, Goethe and Garibaldi.

### ♥ TORCOLO €

Map p214; ☎ 045 800 75 12; www.hoteltorcolo.it;
Vicolo Listone 3; s €55-110, d €70-155; Ⓟ ⊠

Cosy Torcolo is perfectly placed just behind Piazza Brà. Polished wooden chairs
dot high-ceilinged rooms done out in
light terracotta and cool blue. The owner
is superhelpful too.

## MANTUA

### ♥ C'A DELLE ERBE €

Map pp224-5; ☎ 0376 22 61 61; www.cadelleerbe.it;
Via Broletto 24; r €60-120; ⊠

With an unbeatable location in the heart
of old Mantua, this exquisite 16th-
century townhouse teams exposed brick
walls with lavish bathrooms and modern
art. Ask for the room with the balcony
overlooking Piazza delle Erbe.

### ♥ CASA POLI €€€

Off Map pp224-5; ☎ 0376 28 81 70; www.hotelcasa
poli.it; Corso Garibaldi 32; d €240; ⊠ ⊡ ⊚

Expect a warm welcome, ultracool decor
and boutique rooms full of soft greys,
crisp lines and occasional splashes of
orange. Imaginative touches are everywhere, from tucked-away TVs to room
numbers projected onto the floor. Breakfasts feature classic Mantuan pastries.

### ♥ RECHIGI HOTEL €€

Map pp224-5; ☎ 0376 32 07 81; www.rechigi.com;
Via Pier Fortunato Calvi 30; s €98-145, d €150-200,
ste €170-215; Ⓟ ⊠ ⊡

This chic hotel has more modern art on
display in its stark lobby than most galleries. Here Rothko-esque blocks of colour meet Le Corbusier designer chairs.
Opt for a chocolate-brown deluxe room
or suite, with pared-down furniture, pale
stripes and hydromassage showers.

# DIRECTORY

## BUSINESS HOURS

### ITALY

Generally shops open from 9am to 1pm and then from 3.30pm to 7.30pm (or 4pm to 8pm) Monday to Saturday. Many close on Saturday afternoon and some close on a Monday morning or afternoon, and sometimes again on a Wednesday or Thursday afternoon. In major towns, most department stores and supermarkets have continuous opening hours from 10am to 7.30pm Monday to Saturday. Some even open from 9am to 1pm on Sunday. In Milan, many shops (especially big chains, major book and record shops and a slew of fashion stores) also have continuous opening hours Monday to Saturday.

Banks tend to open from 8.30am to 1.30pm and then from 3.30pm to 4.30pm Monday to Friday. They close at weekends but exchange offices usually remain open in the larger cities and in main tourist areas.

Central post offices open from 8am to 7pm from Monday to Saturday (in some cases only until noon on Saturday). Smaller branches tend to open from 8am to 2pm Monday to Friday and from 8.30am to noon on Saturday.

*Farmacie* (pharmacies) are generally open from 9am to 12.30pm and then from 3.30pm to 7.30pm. Most shut on Saturday afternoon, Sunday and holidays, but a handful remain open on a rotation basis (*farmacie di turno*) for emergency purposes. Closed pharmacies display a list of the nearest ones open. They are usually listed in newspapers and you can check out www.miniportale.it (click on Farmacie di Turno and then the region you want).

Many bars and cafes open from about 8am to 8pm. Others then go on into the night serving a nocturnal crowd while still others, that are dedicated more exclusively to nocturnal diversion, don't get started until the early evening (even if they officially open in the morning). Few bars remain open anywhere after 1am or 2am. *Discoteche* (clubs) might open around 10pm (or earlier if they have eateries on the premises), but things don't get seriously shaking until after midnight.

## PRACTICALITIES

★ Use the metric system for weights and measures.

★ Plugs have two or three round pins. The electric current is 220V, 50Hz, but older buildings may still use 125V.

★ If your Italian's up to it, try the following newspapers: *Il Corriere della Sera,* the country's Milan-based leading daily; or *La Repubblica,* a centre-left daily.

★ Tune into state-owned Italian RAI-1, RAI-2 and RAI-3 (www.rai.it), which broadcast all over the country and abroad. Milan-based leftwing Radio Popolare (www.radio popolare.it) is good for its biting social commentary and contemporary music.

★ Switch on the box to watch the state-run RAI-1, RAI-2 and RAI-3 (www.rai.it) and the main commercial stations (mostly run by Silvio Berlusconi's Mediaset company): Canale 5 (www.canale5.mediaset.it), Italia 1 (www.italia1.mediaset.it), Rete 4 (www .rete4.mediaset.it) and La 7 (www.la7.it).

Restaurants open from noon to 3pm and then from 7.30pm to around 11pm or midnight, although the kitchen often shuts an hour earlier than final closing time. In Milan you can expect more generous hours than in the small towns dotted about the lakes (where you should aim to be seated no later than 10pm). Most restaurants and bars close at least one day a week.

Hours for restaurants, bars and shops are not provided in reviews in the course of this guide unless they vary substantially from the above.

The opening hours of museums, galleries and archaeological sites vary enormously, although at the more prominent sites there is a trend towards continuous opening from around 9.30am to 7pm. Many close on Monday. Some of the major national museums and galleries remain open until 10pm in summer.

### SWITZERLAND

Most shops are open from 8am to 6.30pm Monday to Friday, sometimes with a one- to two-hour break for lunch at noon in smaller towns. In cities, there's often a late-shopping day until 9pm, typically on Thursday or Friday. Closing times on Saturday are usually 4pm or 5pm.

Offices are typically open from about 8am to noon and then from 2pm to 5pm Monday to Friday. Banks are open from 8.30am to 4.30pm Monday to Friday, with late opening occurring usually one day a week.

Post office opening times vary, but usually they are at least open from 8am to noon and then from 2pm to 5pm Monday to Friday, and from 8.30am to noon on Saturday.

## CHILDREN

Italians love children, but there are few special amenities for them. Always make a point of asking staff at tourist offices if they know of any special family activities or have suggestions on hotels that cater for kids. Discounts are available for children (usually aged under 12, but sometimes it is based on the child's height) on public transport and for admission to sites.

If you have kids, book accommodation in advance to avoid any inconvenience and, when travelling by train, reserve seats where possible to avoid finding yourselves standing. You can hire car seats for infants and children from most car-rental firms, but you should always book them in advance.

You can buy baby formula in powder or liquid form, as well as sterilising solutions such as Milton, at pharmacies. Disposable nappies (diapers) are widely available at supermarkets and pharmacies. Fresh cow's milk is sold in cartons in supermarkets. UHT milk is popular and in many out-of-the-way areas, it's the only kind of milk available.

For some ideas on places and activities that are likely to win favour with your children, see the Family Travel section (p24). Try not to overdo things and make sure your travel activities include the kids – older children could help in the planning of these.

Always allow time for kids to play, and make sure treats such as a whopping gelato or a slice of their favourite pizza are included in the bag of tricks.

See also Lonely Planet's *Travel with Children* or the websites www.travelwith yourkids.com and www.familytravel network.com.

## CUSTOMS REGULATIONS

Duty-free sales within the EU no longer exist (but goods are sold tax-free in European airports). Visitors coming into Italy from non-EU countries can import, duty free: 1L of spirits (or 2L wine), 50mL perfume, 250mL eau de toilette, 200 cigarettes and other goods up to a total of €175; anything over this limit must be declared on arrival and the appropriate duty needs to be paid. On leaving the EU, non-EU citizens can reclaim any Value Added Tax (VAT) on expensive purchases. Note that this applies to Swiss citizens and residents too.

## DANGERS & ANNOYANCES

It can require patience to deal with the Italian concept of service, which does not always follow the maxim that the customer is always right. While generally courteous and friendly, some people in uniform or behind a counter (including police officers, waiters and shop assistants) may regard you with supreme indifference. Long queues are the norm in banks, post offices and government offices.

### THEFT

Pickpockets and bag-snatchers operate in Milan. You need to be vigilant around train stations, on public transport, in Piazza del Duomo and in the busy shopping streets. You should also pay attention in train stations and around the old city centres of other towns, especially Brescia and Verona. A scam that has been known to occur at stops such as service stations and lookout points involves a tyre being surreptitiously punctured when the vehicle is unattended. A couple of scammers offer to help but, while one distracts the travellers, the other takes items from the car.

In case of theft or loss, always report the incident to police within 24 hours and ask for a statement, otherwise your travel-insurance company won't pay out.

### TRAFFIC

Driving into and around Milan can be nerve-wracking at first, with what seems to have a cavalier dodgem-cars element

DIRECTORY

to it. Motorcyclists should be prepared for anything in the cities. Traffic is dense and the signposting is not always immediately clear. In other cities around the region, things are calmer. Pedestrians should be watchful, as drivers will not always automatically halt for them at crossings.

## POLLUTION

Noise and air pollution, caused mainly by heavy traffic, can be a problem in Milan. A headache after a day of sightseeing is likely to be caused by breathing in carbon monoxide and lead, rather than simple tiredness. On especially bad days, traffic is halved by allowing only vehicles with odd- or even-numbered plates to drive on alternate days. One good piece of news is that smoking is banned in all closed public spaces (including bars, elevators, offices and trains).

# DISCOUNT CARDS

In this book concession prices are generally indicated as adult/senior/child, or adult/concession. At museums and galleries, never hesitate to enquire after discounts for students, young people, children, families or the elderly.

## SENIOR CARDS

In Italy, seniors (aged over 60) who are travelling extensively by rail should consider the one-year Carta d'Argento (Silver Card), available from trains stations for €30 (free for those aged 75 and over). It entitles the holder to discounts of 10% to 15% on national travel and 25% on international trains. In some places, EU seniors have free entry to sights; sometimes only on certain days. Always ask.

## STUDENT & YOUTH CARDS

Free admission to some galleries and sites is available to under-18s. Discounts (usually half the normal fee) are available for some sights to EU citizens aged between 18 and 25 years old. Prices are usually based on age, so a passport, driver's licence or **Euro<26** (www.euro26.org) card may be needed as proof to obtain any discounts.

An **International Student Identity Card** (ISIC; www.isic.org), generally not much use for sights, can be handy for minor transport, theatre and cinema discounts, as well as occasional discounts in some hotels and restaurants (check the lists on the ISIC website); similar cards are available to teachers (International Teacher Identity Card, or ITIC). For nonstudent travellers under 25, the International Youth Travel Card (IYTC) offers the same benefits.

Student cards are issued by student unions, hostelling organisations as well as some youth-travel agencies. In Italy, the **Centro Turistico Studentesco e Giovanile** (CTS; www.cts.it) youth travel agency can issue ISIC, ITIC and Euro<26 cards.

# EMBASSIES & CONSULATES

Several countries have consulates in Milan, of which a selection is listed here. Many countries also have consular services in Lugano.

**Australia** Map pp44–5; ☎ 02 7770 4217; www.aus trade.it; Via Borgogna 2, 20122

**France** Map pp44–5; ☎ 02 655 91 41; Via della Moscova 12, 20121

**Germany** Map pp44–5; ☎ 02 623 11 01; www.mai land.diplo.de; Via Solferino 40, 20121

**Japan** Map pp44–5; ☎ 02 624 11 41; Via Cesare Mangili 2/4, 20121

**Netherlands** Map pp44-5; ☎ 02 485 58 41; Via San Vittore 45, 20123

**New Zealand** Map pp44-5; ☎ 02 7217 0001; Via Terraggio 17, 20123

**Switzerland** Map pp44-5; ☎ 02 777 91 61; www .eda.admin.ch/milano; Via Palestro 2, 20121

**UK** Map pp44-5; ☎ 02 72 30 01; Via San Paolo 7, 20121

**USA** Map pp44-5; ☎ 02 29 03 51; Via Principe Amedeo 2/10, 20121

## FOOD & DRINK

Restaurant listings in this book are in alphabetical order. Restaurants in Italy are nonsmoking. A meal in this guide consists of a *primo* (first course), a *secondo* (second course) and dessert. The budget category is for meals costing up to €20, midrange is €20 to €45 and top end is anything over €45. Most eating establishments have a cover charge (called *coperto;* usually from around €1 to €2) and a *servizio* (service charge) of 10% to 15%.

At budget restaurants in Ticino, you can not expect to fill up for less than Sfr25 per person. Midrange establishments will set you back between Sfr25 to Sfr75 each, while bills in fine-dining restaurants can easily rise to Sfr200 per person. A *tavola calda* (literally 'hot table') normally offers cheap, preprepared food and can include self-service pasta, roast meats and *pizza al taglio* (pizza by the slice). A trattoria is traditionally a cheaper, often family-run version of a *ristorante* (restaurant) with less-aloof service and simpler dishes. An *osteria* is likely to be either a wine bar offering a small selection of dishes with a verbal menu, or a small trattoria. You can sometimes get food to accompany your tipples in an *enoteca* (wine bar). Some of your most satisfying eating experiences in Ticino will happen in *grotti*, rustic,

out-of-the-way eateries, where in the warmer months you can sit outside at granite tables for wholesome local fare.

Bars are popular hang-outs, serving mostly coffee, soft drinks and alcohol. They often sell *brioches* (breakfast pastries), *cornetti* (croissants), *panini* (bread rolls with simple fillings) and *spuntini* (snacks) to have with your drink.

You'll find vegetarian and vegan restaurants in Milan, but elsewhere they are scarce. Many Italians seem to think cheese is vegetarian, so vegans should make sure their dishes are '*senza formaggio*' (without cheese). The good news is that most places usually do some good vegetable starters and side dishes.

Children's menus are uncommon, but you can generally ask for a *mezzo piatto* (half plate) from the menu. Kids are generally welcome in most restaurants, but do not count on the availability of high chairs.

For an introduction to Italian cuisine and wines, see p16 and p274. For information on the opening hours of restaurants, see p303.

## GAY & LESBIAN TRAVELLERS

Homosexuality is legal in Italy and well tolerated in Milan; a little less so in other towns. Overt displays of affection by homosexual couples could attract a negative response in smaller towns. There are gay clubs in Milan but otherwise pickings are slim. The useful website **Gay.it** (www.gay.it, in Italian) lists gay bars and hotels across the country. **Arcigay & Arcilesbica** ( ☎ 051 649 30 55; www.arcigay.it; Via Don Minzoni 18, Bologna) is the main national organisation for gay men and lesbians. Check out the English-language **GayFriendlyItalia. com** (www.gayfriendlyitaly.com), produced by

Gay.it. It has information on everything from hotels to homophobia issues and the law.

# HEALTH

The standard of health care in northern Italy and Ticino is generally good, although the public system can be a little creaky at times. Some planning can save you trouble later. Bring medications in their original, clearly labelled containers. A signed and dated letter from your physician describing your medical conditions and medication, including generic names, is a good idea. If carrying syringes or needles, be sure to have a physician's letter documenting their medical necessity. No jabs are required to travel to Italy. The World Health Organization (WHO), however, recommends that all travellers should be covered for diphtheria, tetanus, measles, mumps, rubella and polio, as well as hepatitis B (see information about the European Health Insurance Card, EHIC, opposite).

If you need an ambulance anywhere in Italy, call ☎ 118. In Switzerland, call ☎ 144. For emergency treatment, head straight to the *pronto soccorso* (casualty) section of a public hospital, where you can also get emergency dental treatment. Pharmacists can give you valuable advice and sell over-the-counter medication for minor illnesses.

## INTERNET RESOURCES

The WHO's publication *International Travel and Health* is revised annually and is available online at www.who.int/ith.

Other useful websites:

**www.ageconcern.org.uk** Advice on travel for the elderly.

**www.fitfortravel.scot.nhs.uk** General travel advice for the layperson.

**www.mariestopes.org.uk** Information on women's health and contraception.

**www.mdtravelhealth.com** Travel health recommendations for every country; updated daily.

## BITES, STINGS & INSECT-BORNE DISEASES

Italy's only dangerous snake, the viper, is found throughout most of the country. Always wear boots, socks and long trousers when walking through undergrowth where snakes may be present. Don't put your hands into holes and crevices, and be careful when collecting firewood. An antivenene for viper bites is available in pharmacies. Keep the victim calm and still, wrap the bitten limb tightly, as you would for a sprained ankle, and attach a splint to immobilise it. Seek medical help, if possible with the dead snake for identification. Don't attempt to catch the snake if there is a possibility of being bitten again. Tourniquets and sucking out the poison are now comprehensively discredited.

Always check all over your body if you have been walking through a potentially tick-infested area as ticks can cause skin infections and other more serious diseases such as Lyme disease and tick-borne encephalitis. If a tick is found attached, press down around the tick's head with tweezers, grab the head and gently pull upwards. Avoid pulling the rear of the body as this may squeeze the tick's gut contents through the attached mouth parts into the skin, increasing the risk of infection and disease. Lyme disease begins with the spreading of a rash at the site of the bite, accompanied by fever, headache, extreme fatigue, aching joints and muscles, and severe neck stiffness. If untreated, symptoms usually disappear but disorders of the nervous system, heart and joints can develop later. Treatment works best early in the illness – medical help should be sought.

Rabies is only found in isolated areas of the Alps. Any bite, scratch or even lick from a mammal in an area where rabies does exist should be scrubbed with soap and running water immediately and then cleaned thoroughly with an alcohol solution. Medical help should be sought.

### HEATSTROKE

Heatstroke occurs following excessive fluid loss with inadequate replacement of fluids and salt. Symptoms include headache, dizziness and tiredness. Dehydration is already happening by the time you feel thirsty – drink sufficient water to produce pale, diluted urine. To treat heatstroke, drink water, fruit juice or both, and cool the body with cold water and fans.

### SEXUAL HEALTH

When buying condoms, look for a European CE mark, which means they have been rigorously tested. Keep them in a cool, dry place or they may crack and perish.

### WOMEN'S HEALTH

Emotional stress, exhaustion and travelling through different time zones can all contribute to an upset in a woman's menstrual pattern.

If using oral contraceptives, remember that some antibiotics, diarrhoea and vomiting can stop the pill from working. Time zones, gastrointestinal upsets and antibiotics do not affect injectable contraception.

Travelling during pregnancy is usually possible, but always consult your doctor before planning your trip. The most risky times for travel are during the first 12 weeks of pregnancy and after 30 weeks.

# HOLIDAYS

Many Italians and Ticinesi take their annual holiday in August. This means that, depending on where you are, many businesses and shops close for at least a part of that month. Milan and cities like Bergamo, Brescia and Cremona can be eerily quiet in August, while lakeside towns such as Como, Locarno and Lugano bustle with holiday activity. Settimana Santa (Easter Week) is another busy holiday period.

Individual towns have public holidays to celebrate the feasts of their patron saints (see p10). Italian national public holidays include the following:

**New Year's Day** (Capodanno or Anno Nuovo) 1 January

**Epiphany** (Epifania or Befana) 6 January

**Easter Monday** (Pasquetta or Lunedì dell'Angelo) March/April

**Liberation Day** (Giorno della Liberazione) 25 April marks the Allied Victory in Italy, and the end of the German presence and Mussolini, in 1945

**Labour Day** (Festa del Lavoro) 1 May

**Republic Day** (Festa della Repubblica) 2 June

**Feast of the Assumption** (Assunzione or Ferragosto) 15 August

**All Saints' Day** (Ognissanti) 1 November

**Feast of the Immaculate Conception** (Immaculata Concezione) 8 December

**Christmas Day** (Natale) 25 December

**Boxing Day** (Festa di Santo Stefano) 26 December

National holidays in Switzerland include the following. Several other local Ticino holidays occur during the year.

**New Year's Day** 1 January

**Easter** Good Friday, Easter Sunday and Monday; March/April

**Ascension Day** 40th day after Easter

**Whit Sunday & Monday** 7th week after Easter

**National Day** 1 August

**Christmas Day** 25 December

**St Stephen's Day** 26 December

# INSURANCE

A travel-insurance policy to cover theft, loss and medical problems is a good idea. It may also cover you for cancellation or delays to your travel arrangements. Paying for your ticket with a credit card can often provide limited travel accident insurance and you may be able to re-claim the payment if the operator doesn't deliver. Ask your credit-card company what it will cover.

If you're an EU citizen (or from Swit-zerland, Norway or Iceland), a European Health Insurance Card (EHIC) covers you for most medical care in public hos-pitals in both countries free of charge, but not for emergency repatriation home or non-emergencies. The card is avail-able from health centres and (in the UK) post offices.

Citizens from other countries should find out if there is a reciprocal arrange-ment for free medical care between their country and Italy or Switzerland (Aus-tralia, for instance, has such an agreement with Italy; carry your Medicare card).

If you do need health insurance, make sure you get a policy that covers you for the worst possible scenario, such as an accident requiring an emergency flight home. Find out in advance if your insur-ance plan will make payments directly to providers or reimburse you later for overseas health expenditures (see car insurance information, p320).

# INTERNET ACCESS

Those carrying notebook computers and mobile phones with internet functions cannot rely on always finding wi-fi. Hot spots remain few and far between, and often require payment. Another option is to buy a SIM card with one of the Italian mobile phone operators, which gives wireless access through the mobile telephone network. These are usually pre-pay services that you can top up as you go.

Many travellers use internet cafes and free web-based email such as Yahoo, Hotmail or Gmail. Internet cafes and centres are present, if not abundant, in all cities and most main towns (don't forget your incoming mail server name, account name and password). Prices hover around €5 to €8 per hour. For some useful internet addresses, see the Resources sections in the destination chapter planners. You must present photo ID (such as passport or drivers licence) to use internet points.

In Ticino, internet centres are equally scarce on the ground and can be more expensive still.

# LEGAL MATTERS

The average tourist will have a brush with the law only if robbed by a bag-snatcher or pickpocket.

If you yourself run into trouble in Italy, you are likely to end up dealing with the *polizia statale* (state police) or the *carabinieri* (military police). The *polizia* deal with thefts, visa extensions and permits (among other things). They wear powder-blue trousers with a fuchsia stripe and a navy-blue jacket. A police station is called a *questura*. The *cara-binieri* deal with general crime, public order and drug enforcement (often over-lapping with the *polizia*). They wear a black uniform with a red stripe and drive night-blue cars with a red stripe. One of the big differences between the police and *carabinieri* is the latter's reach – even many villages have a *carabinieri* post. In Ticino, any brushes with the law will likely be with the cantonal police force. For nationwide Italian and Swiss emergency numbers, see the inside front cover.

As for issues with drink driving, the legal limit in both countries for blood-alcohol level is 0.05% and random breath tests do occur.

## ANTITERRORISM LAWS

Italy still has antiterrorism laws on its books that could make life difficult if you are detained. You should be given verbal and written notice of the charges laid against you within 24 hours by arresting officers. You have no right to a phone call upon arrest. The prosecutor must apply to a magistrate for you to be held in preventive custody awaiting trial (depending on the seriousness of the offence) within 48 hours of arrest. You have the right not to respond to questions without the presence of a lawyer. If the magistrate orders preventive custody, you have the right to then contest this within the following 10 days.

Swiss police have wide-ranging powers of detention without charges or a trial, so be extra careful to stay on the right side of the law. If stopped, you will be required to show your passport, so carry it at all times.

## DRUGS

Italy's drug laws were toughened in 2006 and possession of any controlled substances, including cannabis or marijuana, can get you into hot water. Those caught in possession of 5g of cannabis can be considered traffickers and prosecuted as such. The same applies to tiny amounts of other drugs. Those caught with amounts below this threshold can be subject to minor penalties. You should be equally circumspect in Switzerland.

# MAPS

## CITY MAPS

The city maps in this book, combined with tourist office maps, are generally adequate. More detailed maps are available in Italy at good bookshops, such as Feltrinelli. De Agostini, Touring Club Italiano (TCI) and Michelin all publish detailed city maps.

## DRIVING MAPS

If driving, the Automobile Association's (AA) *Road Atlas Italy,* available in the UK, is scaled at 1:250,000 and includes town maps. Just as good is Michelin's *Tourist and Motoring Atlas Italy,* scaled at 1:300,000.

In Italy, De Agostini publishes a comprehensive *Atlante Turistico Stradale d'Italia* (1:250,000), which includes 140 city maps (the AA Road Atlas is based on this). Perhaps handier for the lakes is TCI's *Atlante Stradale d'Italia* (1:200,000), which is divided into three parts – grab the Nord volume (www .touringclub.com).

Michelin's fold-out Map 353 (Lombardia), scaled at 1:200,000, is good and covers the entire area of this guide, except for Lake Orta and a sliver of territory in the west (for which you'd need neighbouring Map 351, Piemonte & Valle d'Aosta).

Many of these are available online. Check out TrekTools.com (www.trek tools.com).

## WALKING MAPS

Maps of walking trails around the lakes, the Lombard Alps and Ticino are available at all major bookshops in Italy and Switzerland. In Italy, the best are the TCI bookshops. Kompass (www.kompass -italia.it) publishes several 1:50,000 scale maps to the lakes region, including the following titles: *Lago di Como-Lago di Lugano, Lago di Garda-Monte Baldo, Le Tre Valli Bresciane, Lecco-Valle Brembana, Lago Maggiore-Lago di Varese* and *Bernina-Sondrio*.

Most of western Ticino is covered by the 1:50,000 map, *Val Verzasca*, produced by the government body Swisstopo.

## MONEY

The euro is Italy's currency. The seven euro notes come in denominations of €500, €200, €100, €50, €20, €10 and €5. The eight euro coins are in denominations of €2 and €1, and 50, 20, 10, five, two and one cents.

Switzerland's currency is the Swiss franc. The six notes come in denominations of Sfr1000 (which you'll hardly ever see), Sfr200, Sfr100, Sfr50, Sfr20 and Sfr10. Coins are in denominations of Sfr5, Sfr2, Sfr1, Sfr½ (ie, 50 Swiss cents), and 20, 10 and five cents. As a rule, it is pretty easy to use euros in Ticino, although generally you'll get change in francs and the rate used will not necessarily be all that favourable.

A value-added tax of around 20%, known as IVA (Imposta di Valore Aggiunto), is slapped onto just about everything in Italy. If you are a non-EU resident and spend more than €155 (€154.94 to be more precise!) on a purchase, you can claim a refund when you leave. The refund only applies to purchases from affiliated retail outlets that display a 'tax free for tourists' (or similar) sign. You have to complete a form at the point of sale, then have it stamped by Italian customs as you leave. At major airports you can then get an immediate cash refund; otherwise it will be refunded to your credit card. For information, pick up a pamphlet on the scheme from participating stores.

In Switzerland, IVA generally amounts to 7.6% and there is no tax-back program for foreign visitors.

Exchange rates are given on the inside front cover of this book. For the latest rates, check out www.xe.com.

### ATMS

Credit and debit cards can be used in a *bancomat* (ATM) displaying the appropriate sign. Visa and MasterCard are among the most widely recognised, but others like Cirrus and Maestro are also well covered. Check any charges with your bank. Most banks now build a fee of around 2.75% into every foreign transaction. In addition, ATM withdrawals can attract a further fee, usually around 1.5%.

### CREDIT & DEBIT CARDS

Cards are also good for payment in most hotels, restaurants, shops, supermarkets and tollbooths. If your card is lost, stolen or swallowed by an ATM, you can call the following numbers to have an immediate stop put on its use:

**Amex** ( ☎ 06 7290 0347 or your national call number in Italy, 044 659 63 33 in Switzerland)

**Diners Club** ( ☎ 800 86 40 64 in Italy, 058 750 81 81 in Switzerland)

**MasterCard** ( ☎ 800 87 08 66 in Italy, 0800 89 70 92 in Switzerland)

**Visa** ( ☎ 800 81 90 14 in Italy, 0800 89 47 32 in Switzerland)

### MONEYCHANGERS

You can change money in banks, post offices or in a *cambio* (exchange office). Post offices and most banks are reliable and tend to offer the best rates. Commission fluctuates and depends on whether you are changing cash or cheques. Generally, post office commissions are lowest and the exchange rate reasonable. The main advantage of exchange offices is the longer hours they keep, but watch for high commissions and inferior rates.

### TRAVELLERS CHEQUES

Traditionally a safe way to carry money and possibly still not a bad idea as a backup, travellers cheques have been outmoded by plastic.

Visa, Travelex and Amex are widely accepted brands. Get most of your cheques in fairly large denominations to save on per-cheque commission charges. Phone numbers to report lost or stolen cheques:

**Amex** ( ☎ 800 91 49 12 in Italy, 0800 55 01 00 in Switzerland)
**MasterCard** ( ☎ 800 87 20 50 in Italy, 0800 55 01 30 in Switzerland)
**Visa** ( ☎ 800 87 41 55 in Italy, 0800 55 84 50 in Switzerland)

## POST

**Le Poste** ( ☎ 803160; www.poste.it), Italy's postal system, is reasonably reliable. The most efficient mail service is *posta prioritaria* (priority mail). For post office opening hours, see p303.

In Switzerland, the main categories for international post are Economy and Priority. Priority deliveries to Europe take two to four days, and to elsewhere roughly seven days. Economy service to Europe takes four to eight days and to other destinations takes seven to 12 days. For details on the Swiss postal system, call ☎ 0848 454 545 or see www.post.ch.

*Francobolli* (stamps) are available at post offices and, in Italy, at authorised *tabacchi* (tobacconists; look for the official sign – a big 'T', usually white on black).

## TELEPHONE

Direct international calls can easily be made from public telephones by using a phonecard. Generally, it is cheaper to use your country's direct-dialling services paid for at home-country rates (such as AT&T in the USA and Telstra in Australia). Get their access numbers before you leave home. Alternatively, try making calls from cheap rate call centres or using international call cards, which are often on sale at newspaper stands. Skype, VoIP and other internet-based options can be used in some internet cafes.

To call Italy from abroad, call the international access number, Italy's country code ( ☎ 39) and then the area code of the location you want, including the leading 0. When calling Switzerland (country code ☎ 41), the leading 0 in area codes must *not* be dialled.

Italy and Switzerland use GSM 900/1800, which is compatible with the rest of Europe and Australia but not with North American GSM 1900 or the totally different Japanese system (though some GSM 1900/900 phones do work here). If you have a GSM phone, check with your service provider about using it in Europe and beware of calls being routed internationally (very expensive for a 'local' call).

You can get a temporary or prepaid account from several companies in both countries if you already own a GSM, dual- or tri-band cellular phone. You will need your passport to open an account. Always check with your mobile service provider in your home country to ascertain whether your handset allows use of another SIM card. If yours does, it can cost as little as €10 to activate a local prepaid SIM card (sometimes with €10 worth of calls on the card). In

Switzerland, prices start at about Sfr30 for a card with Sfr20 worth of talk-time.

Mobile phone numbers begin with a three-digit prefix such as 330. Toll-free (free-phone) numbers are known as *numeri verdi* and usually start with 800. Non-geographical numbers start with 840, 841, 848, 892, 899, 163, 166 or 199. The range of rates for these makes a rainbow look boring – beware that some can be costly.

Some six-digit national rate numbers are also in use (such as those for Alitalia, rail and postal information). In Switzerland, numbers with the code 079 are mobile phones.

### USEFUL PHONE NUMBERS & CODES

Telephone area codes in Italy begin with 0 and consist of up to four digits. The area code is followed by a number made up of anything from four to eight digits. The area code is an integral part of the telephone number and must always be dialled, even when calling from next door.

In Switzerland, area codes also begin with 0, which must always be dialled. Telephone numbers with the code 0800 are toll-free, those with 0848 are local rate. Numbers beginning with 156 or 157 are always premium rate.

Some useful numbers and codes:

**International access code** ☎ 00
**International direct dial code** ☎ 00
**International directory enquiries** ☎ 176 (Italy), ☎ 18 11 (Switzerland)
**Local directory enquiries** ☎ 12 (Italy), ☎ 18 11, 18 12 (Switzerland)

### PAYPHONES & PHONECARDS

Partly privatised Telecom Italia is the largest telecommunications organisation in Italy and its orange public payphones are liberally scattered about the country. The most common accept only *carte/schede telefoniche* (phonecards). These phonecards (most commonly €2.50 or €5) are available at post offices, tobacconists and newsstands. You must break off the top left-hand corner of the card before you can use it. Phonecards have an expiry date. This is usually 31 December or 30 June, depending on when you purchase the card.

You will find cut-price call centres in the cities. Rates can be considerably lower than from Telecom payphones for international calls. Alternatively, ask about international calling cards at newsstands and tobacconists. They can be hit and miss but are sometimes good value.

In Switzerland, save money on the normal international tariff by buying prepaid cards – Swisscom has them to the value of Sfr10, Sfr20, Sfr50 and Sfr100. Or look for prepaid cards from rival operators.

## TIME

Italy and Switzerland are one hour ahead of GMT. Daylight-saving time, when clocks are moved forward one hour, starts on the last Sunday in March. Clocks are put back an hour on the last Sunday in October. Italy operates on a 24-hour clock.

## TOILETS

Here and there you'll find public toilets in city centres, but more often than not you'll probably want to duck into a cafe or bar. The polite thing to do is order something at the bar, although more often than not no-one will say anything if you don't. Most service stations have toilets.

DIRECTORY

# TOURIST INFORMATION

In Italy, three tiers of tourist office exist: regional, provincial and local. They have different names, but roughly offer the same services, with the exception of regional offices, which are generally concerned with promotion, planning and budgeting.

Generally, provincial tourist offices are known as Azienda di Promozione Turistica (APT). These have information on the town you are in and the surrounding province. Informazione e Assistenza ai Turisti (IAT) offices generally have information only on the town they are in. In Ticino, you'll find useful local offices in Lugano, Locarno and Bellinzona.The Lakes area takes in four Italian regions and the Swiss canton of Ticino, and their tourism websites make a good place to start your web searches. At the website of the **Italian National Tourist Office** (www.enit.it) you can find details of provincial and local tourist offices across the country.

**Lombardy** (www.turismo.regione.lombardia.it)
**Piedmont** (www.regione.piemonte.it/turismo, in Italian)
**Ticino, Switzerland** (www.ticino.ch)
**Trentino-Alto Adige** (www.trentino.to, www.provincia.bz.it)
**Veneto** (www.veneto.to)

# TRAVELLERS WITH DISABILITIES

Italy is not an easy country for disabled travellers and getting around can be a problem for wheelchair users. Even a short journey in a city or town can become a major expedition if cobblestone streets have to be negotiated. Although many buildings have lifts, they are not always wide enough for wheelchairs. Not an awful lot has been done to make life for the deaf and/or blind any easier either.

The Italian National Tourist Office in your country may be able to provide advice and may also carry a small brochure, *Services for Disabled Passengers,* published by Trenitalia (Italian railways), which details facilities at stations and on trains. Trenitalia also has a national helpline for the disabled at ☎ 199 30 30 60. For more information, search on *disabili* at the Trenitalia website (www.trenitalia.com) and click on the English version.

In Milan and Verona, general guides on accessibility are published.

**Accessible Italy** ( ☎ +378 94 11 11; www.accessibleitaly.com) is a San Marino-based company that specialises in holiday services for the disabled, ranging from tours to the hiring of adapted transport. It can even arrange romantic Italian weddings. This is the best first port of call.

Check out **Milano per Tutti** (www.milanopertutti.it) for information on Milan.

For tips on accessibility in Ticino, see www.ticino.ch/turismoaccessibile.

# VISAS

Italy and Switzerland are among the 25 member countries of the Schengen Convention, under which 22 EU countries (all but Bulgaria, Cyprus, Ireland, Romania and the UK) plus Iceland, Norway and Switzerland have abolished permanent checks at common borders. For detailed information on the EU, including which countries are member states, visit http://europa.eu.int.

Citizens of the 27 European Union (EU) member states and Switzerland can travel to Italy (and Switzerland) with their national identity card alone. If such countries do not issue ID cards – as in the UK – travellers must carry a full valid passport. All other nationalities must have a full valid passport and may need visas.

Legal residents (regardless of nationality) of one Schengen country do not require a visa for another. Residents of 28 non-EU countries, including Australia, Brazil, Canada, Israel, Japan, New Zealand and the USA, do not require visas for tourist visits of up to 90 days. The standard Schengen tourist visa is valid for up to 90 days and for travel to all Schengen states.

## WOMEN TRAVELLERS

The lakes area of northern Italy and Switzerland is hardly dangerous country for women. While care should be taken in the big city of Milan (and your guard should never be 100% down), women travellers generally encounter no real problems. Be aware eye-to-eye contact is the norm in Italy's daily flirtatious interplay.

Watch out for men with wandering hands on crowded Milan buses. Either keep your back to the wall or make a loud fuss if someone starts fondling your behind. A loud 'Che schifo!' (How disgusting!) will usually do the trick. If a more serious incident occurs, report it to the police, who are then required to press charges.

Women travelling alone should use common sense. Avoid walking alone in dark streets, and look for hotels that are central. Women should avoid hitch-hiking alone.

# TRANSPORT

## ARRIVAL & DEPARTURE

Flights, tours and rail tickets can be booked online at www.lonelyplanet.com/travel_services.

### AIR

As Italy's economic powerhouse, Milan receives plenty of international flights from around Europe as well as some intercontinental flights to its two airports (Malpensa and Linate).

High season in the lakes area of northern Italy (and Ticino in Switzerland) is from July to August, with May to June as well as September running a close second as shoulder seasons. As things get chilly from mid-October on, low season sets in until Easter. Flight frequencies can drop to the smaller airports in this time, but Milan's airports (including Orio al Serio) remain busy year-round.

### AIRPORTS

Regular intercontinental flights serve Milan's **Malpensa airport** (flight information ☎ 02 7485 2200; www.sea-aeroportimilano.it, in Italian), 50km west of the city. The majority of domestic and a handful of European flights use the more convenient **Linate airport** (flight information ☎ 02 7485 2200; www.sea-aeroportimilano.it, in Italian), 7km east of the city centre.

Ryanair leads a coterie of budget airlines that use the more distant **Orio al Serio airport** ( ☎ 035 32 63 23; www.sacbo.it), 4km southeast of Bergamo's train station. There are daily flights to/from the UK and other European destinations.

## THINGS CHANGE...

The information in this chapter is particularly vulnerable to change. Check directly with the airline or a travel agent to make sure you understand how a fare (and ticket you may buy) works and be aware of the security requirements for international travel. Shop carefully. The details given in this chapter should be regarded as pointers and are not a substitute for your own careful, up-to-date research.

Direct buses link the airport to Bergamo and Milan.

**Brescia airport** (Aeroporto Gabriele d'Annunzio; ☎ 030 204 15 99; www.aeroportobrescia .it), 20km east of Brescia (and around 50km west of Verona), was opened in 1999. Millions of euros have been poured into it, but at the time of writing only a handful of Ryanair flights from London were using it. Its big brother to the east, **Verona-Villafranca airport** (☎ 045 809 56 66; www.aeroportoverona.it), is 12km southwest of Verona, just east of the lakes. This airport has an array of flights. European cities served include Amsterdam, Barcelona, Berlin, Brussels, London and Paris. There is even the occasional intercontinental connection.

Lugano's **Agno airport** (☎ 091 612 11 11; www.lugano-airport.ch) has a few commuter flights. From here, **Darwin Airline** (www. darwinairline.com) operates to/from Rome (Fiumicino), Geneva and Olbia (in Sardinia). **Flybaboo** (www.flybaboo.com) flies regularly to/from Geneva, and **Swiss** (www.swiss.com) to/from Zürich.

## BORDER CROSSINGS

The main points of entry to Italy from France are the coast road from Nice that becomes the A10 motorway along the Ligurian coast (then take the A7 from Genoa north to Milan) and the Mont Blanc Tunnel near Chamonix, which connects with the A5 for Turin and Milan. Rail lines follow roughly the same routes.

From Switzerland, the Grand St Bernard tunnel also connects with the

## ONLINE TICKETS

The internet is increasingly the easiest way of locating and booking reasonably priced seats. This is especially so for flights from around Europe, regardless of whether you are flying with major carriers like Alitalia or low-cost airlines.

There is no shortage of online agents:

**Booking Buddy** (www.bookingbuddy.com)
**Cheap Flights** (www.cheapflights.com)
**Cheap Tickets** (www.cheaptickets.com)
**Discount Tickets** (www.discount-tickets.com)
**Ebookers** (www.ebookers.com)
**Expedia** (www.expedia.com)
**Flightline** (www.flightline.co.uk)
**Flynow** (www.flynow.com)
**Kayak** (www.kayak.com)
**Last Minute** (www.lastminute.com)
**Openjet** (www.openjet.com)
**Opodo** (www.opodo.com)
**Orbitz** (www.orbitz.com)
**Planesimple** (www.planesimple.co.uk)
**Priceline** (www.priceline.com)
**Skyscanner** (www.skyscanner.net)
**Travelcity** (www.travelocity.co.uk)
**Tripadvisor** (www.tripadvisor.com)

## CLIMATE CHANGE & TRAVEL

Climate change is a serious threat to the ecosystems that humans rely upon, and air travel is the fastest-growing contributor to the problem. Lonely Planet regards travel, overall, as a global benefit, but believes we all have a responsibility to limit our personal impact on global warming.

### FLYING & CLIMATE CHANGE

Pretty much every form of motor travel generates $CO_2$ (the main cause of human-induced climate change) but planes are far and away the worst offenders, not just because of the sheer distances they allow us to travel, but because they release greenhouse gases high into the atmosphere. The statistics are frightening: two people taking a return flight between Europe and the US will contribute as much to climate change as an average household's gas and electricity consumption over a whole year.

### CARBON OFFSET SCHEMES

Climatecare.org and other websites use 'carbon calculators' that allow jetsetters to offset the greenhouse gases they are responsible for with contributions to energy-saving projects and other climate-friendly initiatives in the developing world – including projects in India, Honduras, Kazakhstan and Uganda.

Lonely Planet, together with Rough Guides and other concerned partners in the travel industry, supports the carbon offset scheme run by climatecare.org. Lonely Planet offsets all of its staff and author travel.

For more information check out our website: lonelyplanet.com.

A5 and the Simplon tunnel connects with the SS33 road that leads to Lake Maggiore. The SS33 becomes the A26 *autostrada* (toll motorway), which scoots past Stresa on the lake and later melds into the A8 on its way southeast to Milan.

Another approach to the lakes from the Swiss side involves taking the A2 motorway (which runs southeast from Basel and through the St Gotthard tunnel, which will have a parallel railway tunnel, the Gotthard Base Tunnel, possibly by 2015) into Ticino, south via Bellinzona to Lake Lugano. The main rail lines from Switzerland into this part of Italy cross at Domodossola and from Lugano via Como. Minor lines link Locarno and Domodossola, Bellinzona with the east bank of Lake Maggiore and St Moritz with Tirano (in the Valtellina).

From Austria, the Brenner Pass connects with the A22 and parallel rail line south to Verona. Other autostrade and railway lines converge from Eastern Europe through Venice, en route to Verona and Lombardy along the six-lane A4, one of Italy's busiest motorways.

The main passes and tunnels described above are open year-round. Other mountain passes are often closed in winter, and sometimes even in autumn and spring. Make sure you have winter tyres or snow chains if driving in winter.

### BUS

**Eurolines** (www.eurolines.com) is a consortium of European coach companies that operates across Europe with offices in all major European cities. Buses converge on Milan from major cities across

TRANSPORT

Europe. Most national and international buses start and terminate at Milan's **Lampugnano bus terminal** by the Lampugnano metro station (line 1 – the red line), west of the city centre. The bulk of Italian national services are run by **Autostradale** (☎ 02 7200 1304; www.autostradale .it), which has a ticket office at the main tourist office (see p39). It also sells international tickets for **Eurolines** (☎ 055 328 99 39).

## CAR & MOTORCYCLE

When driving in Europe, always carry proof of ownership of a private vehicle and evidence of third-party insurance. If driving a vehicle registered and insured in an EU country (and Switzerland), your home-country insurance is sufficient.

Cars entering Italy and Switzerland from abroad need a valid national licence plate, a sticker identifying the car's country of registration (unless it has the standard EU number plates with the blue strip and country ID) and accompanying registration card.

Ask your insurer for a European Accident Statement (EAS) form, which can simplify matters in the event of an accident. A European breakdown assistance policy is a good investment. The **AA** (☎ 0800 085 72 53 for European breakdown cover; www.theaa.com) and the **RAC** (☎ 08705 72 27 22 in UK; www.rac.co.uk) offer comprehensive cover in Europe. If for whatever reason you don't have such a policy, assistance can be obtained through the **Automobile Club d'Italia** (ACI; ☎ 80 31 16 or ☎ 800 11 68 00 from a mobile phone; www.aci.it, in Italian). Foreigners do not have to join, but instead pay a per-incident fee. The numbers operate 24 hours a day. The Swiss equivalent is the **Automobil Club der Schweiz** (☎ +41 44 628 88 99; www.acs.ch).

You can book a car before you leave home (for multinational car-rental agencies, see p325), but you can sometimes find better deals by dealing with local agencies as you go.

The combination of lakes, plains and mountains in the lakes district is great for motorcycle touring. With a bike you can generally enter restricted-traffic areas in cities too, which can be a significant advantage over getting around with a car.

From the UK, you can take your car across to France by ferry or via the Channel Tunnel on **Eurotunnel** (☎ 0870 535 35 35; www.eurotunnel.com). The latter runs four crossings (35 minutes) an hour between Folkestone and Calais in the high season.

### DRIVING LICENCE & DOCUMENTATION

All EU member states' driving licences are fully recognised throughout Europe. Those with a non-EU licence are supposed to obtain an International Driving Permit (IDP) to accompany their national licence, which your national automobile association can issue. It's valid for 12 months and must be kept with your proper licence.

## SEA

An original approach to Italy's northern lakes could be by sea. The Grimaldi group's **Grandi Navi Veloci** (☎ 010 209 4591, in Spain 902 410200; www1.gnv.it; Moll de San Beltran, Barcelona) runs a daily high-speed, roll-on roll-off luxury ferry service from Barcelona to Genoa (18 hours). An economy-class airline-style seat can cost as little as €16 in winter. A single cabin suite in high season can cost €199. From Genoa, take the train or follow the A7 motorway north to Milan and on to the lakes.

TRANSPORT

## TRAIN

Milan is a major rail hub. High-speed services arrive from as far south as Naples via Rome and Florence, from Venice via Verona in the east, from France via Turin in the west and from major Swiss cities like Zürich and Geneva to the north. An overnight sleeper train also runs from Barcelona.

For longer distances (such as northern Germany, London and Eastern Europe), flying is generally quicker and cheaper, although those who have time and aim to reduce their carbon emission footprint may want to consider the train anyway. The same trip by rail can contribute up to 10 times less pollution per person than by air.

Thomas Cook's *European Rail Timetable* has a complete listing of train schedules. The timetable is updated monthly and it's available from Thomas Cook offices worldwide and online (www .thomascookpublishing.com) for around UK£14 (€16.50). It is always advisable, and sometimes compulsory, to book seats on international trains to/from Italy and Switzerland. Some of the main international services include transport for private cars. Consider taking long journeys overnight as the €20 or so extra for a sleeper costs substantially less than a hotel.

### FRANCE, SWITZERLAND & UK

From Paris, fast direct trains (TGV) run from Gare de Lyon to Milano Centrale station (from €80) and take seven to 7½ hours. Fares depend on demand and how far in advance you book. You can also take a TGV high-speed train to Lausanne, Switzerland, and change there for the Cisalpino. Total travel time is about 10 hours.

Cisalpino high-speed services converge on Milan from Geneva (via Lausanne, Brig and Domodossola) and Zürich (via Ticino). The trip from either Geneva or Zürich takes three hours and 50 minutes (Sfr97 one way).

The passenger-train **Eurostar** ( ☎ 08705 18 61 86; www.eurostar.com) travels between London and Paris. From Paris, you can take TGV (high-speed) trains to Milan.

For the latest fare information on journeys to Italy, including the Eurostar, contact the **Rail Europe Travel Centre** ( ☎ 08448 48 40 64 in UK; www.raileurope.co.uk). Travel times depend in large measure on what connections you make in Paris.

### THE REST OF ITALY

The Alta Velocità (High Speed) services (variously known as AV and/or ESA) that began operation on the new Turin–Milan–Bologna–Florence–Rome–Naples–Salerno line in late 2009 have revolutionised train travel on that route. Nonstop trains between Milan and Rome take three hours (an Intercity train takes 6¼ hours)! With stops in Bologna and Florence, the time is 3½ hours. Already in early 2009, fast trains using standard track had cut traditional travel times (3½ and four hours respectively on the Milan–Rome route). Prices vary according to the time of travel and how far in advance you book.

The partially privatised, state train system **Trenitalia** ( ☎ 89 20 21, Italian-speaking; www.trenitalia.com, www.ferroviedellostato.it) runs most services. Trains in Italy are relatively cheap compared with other European countries.

There are several other types of trains. Some stop at all or most stations, such as *regionale* or *interregionale* trains. Intercity (IC) trains are faster services that operate between major cities. High-speed

TRANSPORT

*pendolini* and other fast services are collectively known as Eurostar Italia (ES), and some make fewer stops than others. Regular ES services run through Milan on the east–west Venice–Turin line. The standard fare on the Alta Velocità from Rome to Milan is €67.50, while the slower IC costs €45. From Venice you pay €29.50 on the Eurostar or €25.20 on the marginally (15 minutes) slower and much more frequent Eurostar City service.

## GETTING AROUND

Trains will get you to the main Lombard towns and some strategic launch pads on and around the lakes. Elsewhere, you'll be relying on a fairly dense network of buses. You can get just about anywhere by bus, although infrequency of some services and the need to change buses at times can make the process a little slow. Ferries ply the lakes, offering not only commuter services but also a range of day-ticket options for day-trippers on excursions. Some handy car ferries cross at several strategic points on lakes Maggiore, Como and Garda.

Clearly, having your own transport provides much greater liberty. Bear in mind, however, that the lakes area is fairly congested. There are plenty of roads leading all over the place but often plenty of traffic on them too. Parking in the main cities is often restricted but not so problematic in smaller towns.

### BICYCLE

Cycling is a popular pastime in Italy. There are no special road rules, but you would be wise to equip yourself with a helmet and lights. With good reason, you cannot take bikes onto the autostrade. If you plan to bring your own bike, check with your airline for any additional costs.

The bike will need to be disassembled and packed for the journey. Make sure you include a few tools, spare parts and a hefty bike lock and chain.

Bikes can be taken on any train carrying the bicycle logo. The cheapest way to do this is to buy a separate bicycle ticket (€3.50, or €5 to €12 on Intercity, Eurostar and Euronight trains), available even at the self-service kiosks. You can use this ticket for 24 hours, making a day trip quite economical.

Some cities (like Bergamo and Brescia) and towns on the lakes have bicycle-hire systems or outlets. Reckon on an average of €10 a day. Outlets are mentioned in the course of the book. Milan and Brescia also have public bicycle systems as a means of public transport.

### BOAT

Regular ferry services began on the main three lakes (Maggiore, Como and Garda) in 1826–27. What was then an essential transport service at a time when poor roads made land travel frustratingly slow, has become a busy and largely tourist-oriented service. Today, ferries crisscross the big three, and Lake Orta, Lake Lugano and Lake Iseo. Timetables are cut back quite drastically in the off-season (November to Easter).

Ferry services on the three main lakes come under the **Gestione Navigazione Laghi** ( ☎ 800 55 18 01; www.navigazionelaghi.it, in Italian). The website contains timetables and pricing for all three lakes. Lakeside ticketing booths and tourist offices also have timetables. Details on individual trips can be found in the relevant destination chapters. A popular option are one-day tickets allowing unlimited travel. On Lake Garda, for instance, such a one-day ticket costs €25.80 per adult and €13.40 per child, with cheaper day tickets for smaller zones available. Check out the Lago Maggiore Express (p70) on the eponymous lake. If you're based at the Swiss end of Lake Maggiore, limited day passes cost Sfr13.80, or Sfr24 for the entire Swiss basin.

From its landing stage on Piazza Motta, in Orta San Giulio, **Navigazione Lago d'Orta** (☎ 0322 84 48 62) runs boats to numerous spots on that lake, including Isola San Giulio. Return fares don't exceed €4, wherever you go.

Operating up to eight ferries daily, **Navigazione sul Lago d'Iseo** (☎ 035 97 14 83; www.navigazionelagoiseo.it) routes go from (south to north) Sarnico, Iseo, Monte Isola, Lovere and Pisogne (and some other smaller stops). Single fares range from €1.90, to €5.75 for the longest routes.

Based in Lugano in Switzerland, **Società Navigazione del Lago di Lugano** (☎ 091 971 52 23; www.lakelugano.ch) operates ferries on Lake Lugano (parts of which sneak into Italian territory) year-round. Passes for one/three/seven days cost Sfr38/58/68. There are reduced fares for children.

## BUS

Getting around the plains towns and to some of the main settlements at the south end of the main lakes is easier by train. To get any further and explore the lake shores and beyond, bus is often the only option for those without their own transport. In the main, services are organised around provincial capitals (eg Bergamo, Brescia, Como, Cremona, Mantua and Verona), which act as hubs for the towns nearby. You will rarely want or be able to scoot from one lake directly to another by bus. Generally, it is easiest to get to your chosen lake by rail and use buses locally.

While most bus services from Milan leave from the main terminal (p319), a handful leave from other points around town. Few of those points will be of interest to the traveller aiming for the lakes. In the bigger towns, the bus station is often handily located near the train station. Sometimes you buy tickets at the station ticket counters (where timetables are posted), but sometimes they must be bought on board. Most of the bus company websites have timetables.

Bus companies operating across the area include the following.

**APAM** (☎ 0376 23 01; www.apam.it, in Italian) Buses around Mantua.

**APTV** (☎ 045 805 79 11; www.aptv.it) Buses run from/to Lake Garda, and connect towns along both shores of the lake. Also connect Mantua with Peschiera del Garda.

**SAB** (☎ 035 28 90 00; www.sab-autoservizi.it, in Italian) Bergamo-based, it operates services around Bergamo province, and to Lake Como, Lake Iseo & the mountains.

**SAF** (☎ 0323 55 21 72; www.safduemila.com, in Italian) Buses from Milan to and around Lake Maggiore.

**SAIA Trasporti** (☎ 800 88 39 99; www.saia trasporti.it, in Italian) Buses serve destinations all over Brescia province and into neighbouring provinces.

**SIA** (☎ 030 377 42 37; www.sia-autoservizi.it, in Italian) Also serves Brescia province and connects the city with the western shore of Lake Garda.

**Sila** (☎ 199 153155; www.sila.it, in Italian) Buses between Milan and Pavia via Certosa di Pavia.

**SPT** (☎ 031 24 72 47; www.sptcomo.it, in Italian) Buses from Como around Lake Como and services to Lugano.

**Trentino Trasporti** (☎ 046 82 10 00; www.tte sercizio.it, in Italian) Buses between Trento & Rovereto & the north end of Lake Garda (incl Riva del Garda and Arco).

In Ticino, on the Swiss side of the lakes, train is the easiest way to get around between the three main cities (Lugano,

Locarno and Bellinzona). Local buses and private trains cover some of the lakeside spots. Otherwise, the country's network of **postal buses** (www.postbus.ch) comes into its own for reaching into the fascinating back valleys that wind off north of Locarno and Bellinzona. Ticket and fare information can be obtained online. Timetables are generally posted at stops.

## CAR & MOTORCYCLE

Italy boasts an extensive privatised network of autostrade, represented on road signs by a white A followed by a number on a green background. An autostrada (A2, represented with the number on red background) also traverses Ticino roughly north–south. If you intend to use the A2 and other motorways in Switzerland, you must buy a one-off Sfr40 vignette on entering the country. This windscreen sticker is valid on all Swiss motorways for a calendar year.

Several motorways converge on Milan (note that all of them can be jammed on Sunday evenings). While touring Lombardy and the lakes area, the one you are most likely to use is the east–west A4, which links Milan with Bergamo, Brescia, Lake Garda and Verona. The A8 leads northwest out of Milan and, in a slightly confusing tangle, becomes the A8-A26 as it approaches the southern end of Lake Maggiore. As the A26, it follows the western shore via Arona and Stresa before it peters out in a smaller route to Domodossola and the Swiss frontier. A branch of the A8 reaches Varese. Once you're about 11km out of Milan along the A8, the A9 branches north to Como and on across the Swiss border, where it continues as the A2 to Lugano, Bellinzona and north through Ticino into the heart of Switzerland. You can pay tolls on Italian motorways with cash or credit card as you leave the autostrada.

You'll be doing most of your travelling on the spiderweb network of *strade*

## DISTANCE CHART (KM)

Note: Distances between destinations are approximate

| | Bellinzona | Bergamo | Brescia | Como | Cremona | Locarno | Lugano | Mantua | Milan | O S Giulio | Pavia | Riva d Garda | Stresa | Varese |
|---|---|---|---|---|---|---|---|---|---|---|---|---|---|---|
| Bergamo | 115 | | | | | | | | | | | | | |
| Brescia | 170 | 59 | | | | | | | | | | | | |
| Como | 60 | 55 | 110 | | | | | | | | | | | |
| Cremona | 208 | 98 | 55 | 155 | | | | | | | | | | |
| Locarno | 20 | 124 | 179 | 69 | 217 | | | | | | | | | |
| Lugano | 29 | 87 | 142 | 32 | 180 | 42 | | | | | | | | |
| Mantua | 278 | 140 | 95 | 225 | 67 | 291 | 251 | | | | | | | |
| Milan | 105 | 52 | 99 | 52 | 101 | 118 | 78 | 186 | | | | | | |
| O S Giulio | 84 | 127 | 175 | 98 | 189 | 64 | 123 | 261 | 87 | | | | | |
| Pavia | 141 | 99 | 135 | 88 | 90 | 153 | 113 | 151 | 41 | 123 | | | | |
| Riva d Garda | 270 | 132 | 79 | 217 | 127 | 263 | 243 | 126 | 180 | 252 | 208 | | | |
| Stresa | 74 | 130 | 177 | 100 | 192 | 56 | 97 | 264 | 89 | 27 | 126 | 254 | | |
| Varese | 64 | 98 | 145 | 33 | 160 | 76 | 37 | 232 | 58 | 63 | 98 | 223 | 65 | |
| Verona | 256 | 118 | 73 | 204 | 113 | 269 | 229 | 45 | 166 | 237 | 194 | 81 | 240 | 208 |

TRANSPORT

## SPEED LIMITS

|  | Italy | Switzerland |
|---|---|---|
| Built-up areas | 50kmh | 50kmh |
| Non-urban roads | 90kmh | 80kmh |
| Highways | 110kmh | 80kmh |
| Autostrade (motorways) | 130kmh | 120kmh |

*statali* (state highways, coded SS), *strade regionali* (regional highways, SR) and *strade provinciali* (provincial routes, SP). The network is especially dense in the plains areas around and south of Bergamo, Brescia, Cremona and Verona. Around the lakes and to the north, the largely hilly and mountainous terrain necessarily means that the road system is thinner. Throughout most of the area, traffic tends to be dense and can be frustrating. Around the lakes and in mountain areas such as the Valtellina, the driving on spring and summer weekends can be a real test of patience as half of Milan's population seems to stream northward.

### FUEL

Italy is covered by a good network of petrol stations. Prices are among the highest in Europe and vary from one service station *(benzinaio, stazione di servizio)* to another. Lead free *(senza piombo;* 95 octane) costs up to €1.11/L. A 98-octane variant costs as much as €1.20/L. Diesel *(gasolio)* comes in at €1.06/L. Prices fluctuate with world oil prices and are marginally higher on autostrade than elsewhere.

### HIRE

Most tourist offices and hotels can provide information about car or motorcycle rental. To rent a car in Italy you have to be aged 25 or over and you have to have a credit card. Most firms will accept your standard licence or IDP for identification purposes. Consider hiring a small car, which you'll be grateful for when negotiating narrow city lanes.

Multinational car rental agencies include the following.

**Autos Abroad** (☎ 0845 029 19 45 in UK; www.autosabroad.com)

**Avis** (☎ 199 10 01 33; www.avisautonoleggio.it, in Italian)

**Budget** (☎ 199 30 73 73; www.budgetautonoleggio.it)

**Europcar** (☎ 199 30 70 30; www.europcar.com)

**Hertz** (☎ 08708 44 88 44; www.hertz.it)

**Italy by Car** (☎ 800 84 60 83; www.italybycar.it)

**Maggiore** (☎ 199 15 11 20; www.maggiore.it)

### PARKING

Parking in most cities in the region can be a trifle complicated. The historic centre of some cities (especially Brescia) is off limits to most traffic, although exceptions are often made for tourists who have hotels in the old centre (in such cases you may be able to enter the city centre long enough to unload, or be given a temporary residents' parking permit by the hotel if it has no private parking area). Milan has instituted the Ecopass, which obliges drivers to pay to enter the centre of town (see p57). Outside that area, it is possible to park in streets (and often on footpaths!) where no special restrictions are in place, or in carparks. Various (and usually quite complicated) restrictions operate in other cities, often with the use of cameras to film unauthorised cars entering city centres (this is especially the case in Brescia). As a rule, it is simplest not to drive in the cities and main towns. In most, you will find street parking away from the centre. Park and walk is the best policy.

TRANSPORT

## ROAD RULES

In Italy and Switzerland, cars drive on the right side of the road and overtake on the left. Give way to cars entering an intersection from a road on your right. It is compulsory for all passengers to wear seatbelts.

A warning triangle (to be used in the event of a breakdown) is compulsory throughout Europe. Recommended accessories are a first-aid kit, spare-bulb kit and fire extinguisher. If your car breaks down and you get out of the vehicle, you risk a fine if you neglect to wear an approved yellow or orange safety vest (available at bicycle shops and outdoor stores).

Random breath tests take place in Italy and Switzerland. If you're involved in an accident while under the influence of alcohol, the penalties can be severe. The blood-alcohol limit is 0.05%.

All vehicles must use headlights by day on the autostrade. It is advisable for motorcycles on all roads at all times.

Speed cameras operate in both countries and fines are increasingly being sent to the home countries of offenders, so beware!

## TAXI

You can usually find taxi ranks at train and bus stations or you can telephone for radio taxis. It's best to go to a designated taxi stand, as it's illegal for them to stop in the street if hailed.

Charges vary. In Milan, for instance, there is a minimum charge ranging from €3 to €6.10, depending on the time of day or night, plus €0.98 per km (rising to €1.47 per km after the first €13.25).

## TRAIN

**Trenitalia** ( ☎ 89 20 21, Italian-speaking; www .trenitalia.com or www.ferroviedellostato.it) runs most of the trains on the Italian side of the lakes area. From Milan, all the main cities are easily reached by train. Brescia, the south-shore towns on Lake Garda and Verona are on the main line connecting Milan with Venice. Other lines link Milan with Bergamo, Cremona, Mantua and Pavia. Bergamo and Cremona are also linked directly to Brescia, as is Mantua to Verona.

Regular trains, Swiss or Italian, connect Milan (Milano Centrale station) with Lugano via Mendrisio and Como (San Giovanni station). A private company, Ferrovie Nord Milano (FNM), has all-stops trains from Milan's **Stazione Nord** (Stazione Cadorna; www.ferrovienord .it, in Italian; Piazza Luigi Cadorna) that terminate at Como's lakeside Como Nord Lago stop.

Hourly trains connect Milano Centrale with Stresa via Arona, on the western shore of Lake Maggiore, on their way to Domodossola and Switzerland. Connecting services run up the east shore. Slower services also run from Milano Porta Garibaldi station. This is also the main departure station for local trains to Varese. Trains run from Milano Centrale to Lecco, up the eastern shore of Lake Como and turn east along the Valtellina valley to Sondrio and wind up in Tirano, a town that sits on a sliver of Lombard

### STAMP IT!

Countless foreign travellers in Italy learn the hard way that their train tickets must be stamped in the yellow machines (usually found at the head of rail platforms) just before boarding. Failure to do so usually results in fines, although the cry of 'I didn't know' sometimes elicits an indulgent response from ticket controllers. So remember: stamp that ticket!

This is not an issue in Ticino.

TRANSPORT

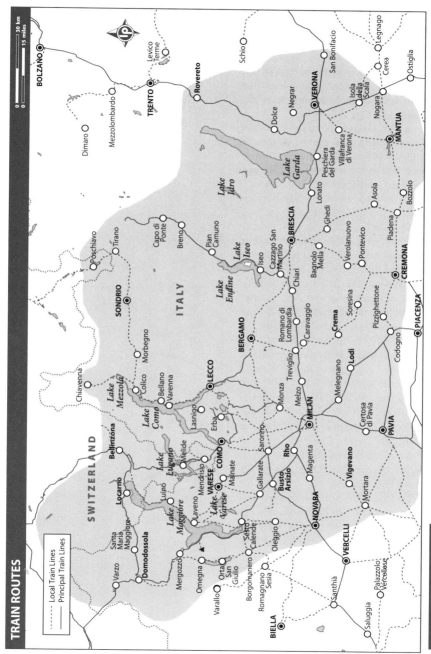

**TRAIN ROUTES**

Legend:
- ----- Local Train Lines
- ——— Principal Train Lines

territory between the Swiss border and the region of Trentino-Alto Adige. The Lecco–Tirano part of this 2½-hour trip is delightful.

An assortment of trains runs up the western shore of Lake Como and from Brescia up along the eastern shore of Lake Iseo as far as Edolo.

With the exception of fast trains operating on the Milan–Brescia–Verona line, and fast(ish) Cisalpino trains running to/from Milan to Switzerland via Stresa and Lugano, pretty much all of the trains in this area are somewhat sluggish *regionali,* calling in at most, if not all stops.

You can buy tickets at the station counter or machines. Within this area, the most expensive ticket you can get is to travel from Verona to Stresa (or vice versa) on a Eurostar City or Cisalpino fast train (this usually involves changing in Milano Centrale). The 2¾-hour trip costs €24.20 in 2nd class. The Milan–Verona run on the Eurostar City fast train is €14.30. Trains from Milan to Tirano and Mantua, respectively a 2½ and two hour trip, cost €8.75 one way. The Cisalpino fast train to Stresa from Milan costs €9 and takes a little under an hour. You need a seat reservation on Eurostar City and Cisalpino services but this can be made when you buy the ticket. On these short trips, it's usually not a problem.

In Ticino, the Milan–Lugano train line continues north to Bellinzona and up the Valle Leventina, to cross the St Gotthard pass into central Switzerland. A branch line connects Bellinzona with Locarno. For timetables and tickets, see **Ferrovie Federali Svizzere** (www.ffs.ch).

Most, but not all, train stations have some kind of left luggage service or lockers.

TRANSPORT

# LANGUAGE

Italian is a Romance language related to French, Spanish, Portuguese and Romanian. The Romance languages belong to the Indo-European group of languages, which includes English, so you might spot some similarities between English and Italian. In addition, as English has borrowed many words from Romance languages, you will recognise many Italian words.

Modern literary Italian began to develop in the 13th and 14th centuries, predominantly through the works of Dante, Petrarch and Boccaccio, who wrote chiefly in the Florentine dialect. The language drew on its Latin heritage and many dialects to develop into the standard Italian of today. It is the national language of schools, media and literature, and is understood throughout the country.

The Lombardy area boasts several dialects of Italian, some with quite marked differences. Milanese, which has a vaguely French ring to it, was by far the most widely spoken of these dialects. Nowadays, most Milanese, whether natives or descendents of immigrants from other parts of Italy, speak little or no dialect. The accent, somewhat nasal, remains unmistakeable, but you are unlikely to hear Milanese spoken. At best, you might encounter it in some proper names (such as restaurants). A century and a half ago, the Milanese novelist, Alessandro Manzoni (1785–1873), struggled to (re)write his great Italian novel in a standardised, Tuscan-based Italian, rather than his native Milanese tongue (and so reach a broader readership throughout a then much divided country). The novel, *I promessi sposi* (The Betrothed), appeared in 1840 and is one of the classics of Italian literature but, in a sense, its author was writing in a somewhat foreign and even artificial tongue.

Among the other related Lombard dialects (spoken from Cremona in the south to Ticino in Switzerland), Bergamasco (the dialect of Bergamo) stands out. You may well hear it spoken and it has a different tonality from Milanese, as well as some different vocabulary (influenced by early medieval Germanic borrowings from their then Lombard overlords).

**LANGUAGE**

The dialects of Brescia and Cremona are similar.

While the Lombard dialects are generally spoken less and less, the marked accent is as strong as ever.

# GRAMMAR

Italian has polite versus informal forms for 'you'. Many older Italians still expect to be addressed by the third person polite for 'you', that is, *Lei* instead of *tu*. Also, it is not considered polite to use the greeting *ciao* when addressing strangers, unless they use it first; it's better to say *buongiorno* (or *buona sera*, as the case may be) and *arrivederci* (or the more polite form, *arrivederla*). We have used the polite address for most of the phrases in this guide. Use of the informal address is indicated by 'inf'.

Italian has masculine and feminine forms of nouns and accompanying adjectives (in the singular, masculine and feminine words often end in 'o' and 'a' respectively). Where both forms are given in this guide, they are indicated by 'm' and 'f'.

If you'd like a more comprehensive guide to the language, pick up a copy of Lonely Planet's *Italian Phrasebook*.

# PRONUNCIATION

Italian pronunciation isn't very difficult to master once you learn a few easy rules. Although some vowels and the stress on double letters require careful practice by English speakers, it's easy enough to make yourself understood.

## VOWELS

Vowel are pronounced shorter in unstressed syllables; longer, in stressed, open syllables:

| | |
|---|---|
| a | as in 'art', eg *caro* (dear); sometimes short, eg *amico/a* (friend) |
| e | short, as in 'let', eg *mettere* (to put); long, as in 'there', eg *mela* (apple) |
| i | short, as in 'it', eg *inizio* (start); long, as in 'marine', eg *vino* (wine) |
| o | short, as in 'dot', eg *donna* (woman); long, as in 'port', eg *ora* (hour) |
| u | as the 'oo' in 'book', eg *puro* (pure) |

## CONSONANTS

The pronunciation of most Italian consonants is similar to that of their English counterparts. Pronunciation of some consonants depends on certain rules:

| | |
|---|---|
| c | as the 'k' in 'kit' before **a, o, u** and **h**; as the 'ch' in 'choose' before **e** and **i** |
| g | as the 'g' in 'get' before **a, o, u** and **h**; as the 'j' in 'jet' before **e** and **i** |
| gli | as the 'lli' in 'million' |
| gn | as the 'ny' in 'canyon' |
| h | always silent (ie not pronounced) |
| r | a rolled 'r' sound |
| sc | as 'sk' before **a, o, u** and **h**; as the 'sh' in 'sheep' before **e** and **i** |
| z | at the beginning of a word, as the 'dz' in 'adze'; elsewhere, as the 'ts' in 'its' |

Note that when **ci**, **gi** and **sci** are followed by **a**, **o** or **u**, the 'i' is not pronounced unless the accent falls on the 'i'. Thus, the name 'Giovanni' is pronounced joh·*vahn*·nee.

A double consonant is pronounced as a longer, more forceful sound than a single consonant. This can directly affect the meaning of a word, eg *sono* (I am), *sonno* (sleep).

## WORD STRESS

Stress is indicated in our pronunciation guide by italics. Word stress generally falls on the second-last syllable, as in *spaghetti* (spa·*ge*·tee), but when a word has an accent, the stress falls on that syllable, as in *città* (chee·*ta*), meaning 'city'.

# ACCOMMODATION

| I'm looking for a ... | Cerco ... | cher·ko ... |
|---|---|---|
| guest house | una pensione | oo·na pen·syo·ne |
| hotel | un albergo | oon al·ber·go |
| youth hostel | un ostello per | oon os·te·lo per |
| | la gioventù | la jo·ven·too |

**Where is a cheap hotel?**
*Dov'è un albergo* do·ve oon al·ber·go
*a buon prezzo?* a bwon pre·tso
**What is the address?**
*Qual'è l'indirizzo?* kwa·le leen·dee·ree·tso
**Could you write the address, please?**
*Può scrivere l'indirizzo,* pwo skree·ve·re leen·dee·ree·tso
*per favore?* per fa·vo·re
**Do you have any rooms available?**
*Avete camere libere?* a·ve·te ka·me·re lee·be·re
**May I see it?**
*Posso vederla?* po·so ve·der·la

| I'd like (a) ... | Vorrei ... | vo·ray ... |
|---|---|---|
| bed | un letto | oon le·to |
| single room | una camera | oo·na ka·me·ra |
| | singola | seen·go·la |
| double room (with | una camera | oo·na ka·me·ra |
| double bed) | matrimoniale | ma·tree·mo·nya·le |
| room with two | una camera | oo·na ka·me·ra |
| beds | doppia | do·pya |
| room with a | una camera | oo·na ka·me·ra |
| bathroom | con bagno | kon ba·nyo |
| to share a | un letto in | oon le·to een |
| dorm | dormitorio | dor·mee·to·ryo |

| How much is it ...? | Quanto costa ...? | kwan·to ko·sta ... |
|---|---|---|
| per night | per la notte | per la no·te |
| per person | per persona | per per·so·na |

LANGUAGE

### MAKING A RESERVATION

Use these expressions in letters, faxes and emails:

| To ... | A ... |
|---|---|
| From ... | Da ... |
| Date | Data |
| I'd like to book ... | Vorrei prenotare ... |
| in the name of ... | a nome di ... |
| for the night(s) of ... | per (la notte/le notti) di ... |
| credit card ... | (...) carta di credito |
| number | numero della |
| expiry date | data di scadenza della |
| Please confirm | Prego confermare |
| availability and price. | disponibilità e prezzo. |

**Where is the bathroom?**
*Dov'è il bagno?* do·ve eel ba·nyo
**I'm/We're leaving today.**
*Parto/Partiamo oggi.* par·to/par·tya·mo o·jee

# CONVERSATION & ESSENTIALS

| Hello. | Buongiorno. | bwon·jor·no |
|---|---|---|
| | Ciao. (inf) | chow |
| Goodbye. | Arrivederci. | a·ree·ve·der·chee |
| | Ciao. (inf) | chow |
| Yes. | Sì. | see |
| No. | No. | no |
| Please. | Per favore./ | per fa·vo·re/ |
| | Per piacere. | per pya·chay·re |
| Thank you. | Grazie. | gra·tsye |
| You're welcome. | Prego. | pre·go |
| Excuse me. | Mi scusi. | mee skoo·zee |

**I'm sorry.**
*Mi scusi./* mee skoo·zee/
*Mi perdoni.* mee per·do·nee
**Just a minute.**
*Un momento.* oon mo·men·to
**What's your name?**
*Come si chiama?* ko·me see kya·ma
*Come ti chiami? (inf)* ko·me tee kya·mee

## SIGNS

| | |
|---|---|
| **Aperto** | Open |
| **Camere Libere** | Rooms Available |
| **Chiuso** | Closed |
| **Completo** | Full/No Vacancies |
| **Gabinetti/Bagni** | Toilets |
| **Uomini** | Men |
| **Donne** | Women |
| **Informazione** | Information |
| **Ingresso/Entrata** | Entrance |
| **Polizia/Carabinieri** | Police |
| **Proibito/Vietato** | Prohibited |
| **Questura** | Police Station |
| **Uscita** | Exit |

| | | |
|---|---|---|
| **beach** | *la spiaggia* | la *spya*·ja |
| **bridge** | *il ponte* | eel *pon*·te |
| **castle** | *il castello* | eel kas·*te*·lo |
| **cathedral** | *il duomo* | eel *dwo*·mo |
| **island** | *l'isola* | *lee*·so·la |
| **(main) square** | *la piazza* | la *pya*·tsa |
| | *(principale)* | (preen-chee-*pa*·le) |
| **market** | *il mercato* | eel mer·*ka*·to |
| **old city** | *il centro* | eel *chen*·tro |
| | *storico* | *sto*·ree·ko |
| **palace** | *il palazzo* | eel pa·*la*·tso |
| **ruins** | *le rovine* | le ro·*vee*·ne |
| **sea** | *il mare* | eel *ma*·re |
| **tower** | *la torre* | la *to*·re |

**My name is …**
  *Mi chiamo …*    mee *kya*·mo …
**Where are you from?**
  *Da dove viene?*    da *do*·ve *vye*·ne
  *Di dove sei?* (inf)    dee *do*·ve say
**I'm from …**
  *Vengo da …*    *ven*·go da …
**I (don't) like …**
  *(Non) Mi piace …*    (non) mee *pya*·che …

## DIRECTIONS

**Where is …?**
  *Dov'è …?*    do·*ve* …
**Go straight ahead.**
  *Si va sempre diritto.*    see va *sem*·pre dee·*ree*·to
  *Vai sempre diritto.* (inf)    vai *sem*·pre dee·*ree*·to
**Turn left.**
  *Giri a sinistra.*    *jee*·ree a see·*nee*·stra
**Turn right.**
  *Giri a destra.*    *jee*·ree a *de*·stra
**at the next corner**
  *al prossimo angolo*    al *pro*·see·mo *an*·go·lo
**at the traffic lights**
  *al semaforo*    al se·*ma*·fo·ro

| **behind** | *dietro* | *dye*·tro |
|---|---|---|
| **in front of** | *davanti* | da·*van*·tee |
| **far (from)** | *lontano (da)* | lon·*ta*·no (da) |
| **near (to)** | *vicino (di)* | vee·*chee*·no (dee) |
| **opposite** | *di fronte a* | dee *fron*·te a |

## EATING OUT

**I'd like …, please.**
  *Vorrei …, per favore.*    vo·*ray* … per fa·*vo*·re
**That was delicious!**
  *Era squisito!*    *e*·ra skwee·*zee*·to
**I don't eat (fish).**
  *Non mangio (pesce).*    non *man*·jo (*pe*·she)
**Please bring the bill.**
  *Mi porta il conto,*    mee *por*·ta eel *kon*·to
  *per favore?*    per fa·*vo*·re

| **I'm allergic** | *Sono* | *so*·no |
|---|---|---|
| **to …** | *allergico/a …* (m/f) | a·*ler*·jee·ko/a … |
| **dairy produce** | *ai latticini* | ai la·tee·*chee*·nee |
| **eggs** | *alle uova* | *a*·le wo·va |
| **nuts** | *alle noci* | *a*·le no·chee |
| **seafood** | *ai frutti di* | ai *froo*·tee dee |
| | *mare* | *ma*·re |

## HEALTH

**I'm ill.**
  *Mi sento male.*    mee *sen*·to *ma*·le
**It hurts here.**
  *Mi fa male qui.*    mee fa *ma*·le kwee

| **I'm …** | *Sono …* | *so*·no … |
|---|---|---|
| **asthmatic** | *asmatico/a* (m/f) | az·*ma*·tee·ko/a |
| **diabetic** | *diabetico/a* (m/f) | dee·a·*be*·tee·ko/a |
| **epileptic** | *epilettico/a* (m/f) | e·pee·*le*·tee·ko/a |

| antiseptic | antisettico | an·tee·se·tee·ko |
| aspirin | aspirina | as·pee·ree·na |
| condoms | preservativi | pre·zer·va·tee·vee |
| contraceptive | contraccetivo | kon·tra·che·tee·vo |
| diarrhoea | diarrea | dee·a·re·a |
| medicine | medicina | me·dee·chee·na |
| sunblock cream | crema solare | kre·ma so·la·re |
| tampons | tamponi | tam·po·nee |

| I'm allergic | Sono | so·no |
| to ... | allergico/a ... (m/f) | a·ler·jee·ko/a ... |
| antibiotics | agli antibiotici | a·lyee an·tee·bee·o·tee·chee |
| aspirin | all'aspirina | a·la·spe·ree·na |
| penicillin | alla penicillina | a·la pe·nee·chee·lee·na |

## LANGUAGE DIFFICULTIES

**Do you speak English?**

*Parla inglese?*  par·la een·gle·ze

**Does anyone here speak English?**

*C'è qualcuno che*  che kwal·koo·no ke
*parla inglese?*  par·la een·gle·ze

**How do you say ... in Italian?**

*Come si dice ... in*  ko·me see dee·che ... een
*italiano?*  ee·ta·lya·no

**What does ... mean?**

*Che vuol dire ...?*  ke vwol dee·re ...

**I understand.**

*Capisco.*  ka·pee·sko

**I don't understand.**

*Non capisco.*  non ka·pee·sko

**Please write it down.**

*Può scriverlo, per favore?*  pwo skree·ver·lo per fa·vo·re

**Can you show me (on the map)?**

*Può mostrarmelo*  pwo mos·trar·me·lo
*(sulla piantina)?*  (soo·la pyan·tee·na)

## NUMBERS

| 0 | zero | dze·ro |
| 1 | uno | oo·no |
| 2 | due | doo·e |
| 3 | tre | tre |
| 4 | quattro | kwa·tro |
| 5 | cinque | cheen·kwe |

## EMERGENCIES

**Help!**

*Aiuto!*  a·yoo·to

**There's been an accident!**

*C'è stato un*  che sta·to oon
*incidente!*  een·chee·den·te

**I'm lost.**

*Mi sono perso/a.* (m/f)  mee so·no per·so/a

**Go away!**

*Lasciami in pace!*  la·sha·mi een pa·che
*Vai via!* (inf)  vai vee·a

| **Call ...!** | *Chiami ...!* | kee·ya·mee ... |
| a doctor | un dottore/ | oon do·to·re/ |
| | un medico | oon me·dee·ko |
| the police | la polizia | la po·lee·tsee·ya |

| 6 | sei | say |
| 7 | sette | se·te |
| 8 | otto | o·to |
| 9 | nove | no·ve |
| 10 | dieci | dye·chee |
| 11 | undici | oon·dee·chee |
| 12 | dodici | do·dee·chee |
| 13 | tredici | tre·dee·chee |
| 14 | quattordici | kwa·tor·dee·chee |
| 15 | quindici | kween·dee·chee |
| 16 | sedici | se·dee·chee |
| 17 | diciassette | dee·cha·se·te |
| 18 | diciotto | dee·cho·to |
| 19 | diciannove | dee·cha·no·ve |
| 20 | venti | ven·tee |
| 21 | ventuno | ven·too·no |
| 22 | ventidue | ven·tee·doo·e |
| 30 | trenta | tren·ta |
| 40 | quaranta | kwa·ran·ta |
| 50 | cinquanta | cheen·kwan·ta |
| 60 | sessanta | se·san·ta |
| 70 | settanta | se·tan·ta |
| 80 | ottanta | o·tan·ta |
| 90 | novanta | no·van·ta |
| 100 | cento | chen·to |
| 1000 | mille | mee·le |
| 2000 | due mila | doo·e mee·la |

LANGUAGE

# PAPERWORK

| | | |
|---|---|---|
| name | *nome* | *no*·me |
| nationality | *nazionalità* | na·tsyo·na·lee·*ta* |
| date/place of | *data/luogo di* | *da*·ta/*lwo*·go dee |
| birth | *nascita* | *na*·shee·ta |
| sex (gender) | *sesso* | *se*·so |
| passport | *passaporto* | pa·sa·*por*·to |
| visa | *visto* | *vee*·sto |

# QUESTION WORDS

| | | |
|---|---|---|
| Who? | *Chi?* | kee |
| What? | *Che?* | ke |
| When? | *Quando?* | *kwan*·do |
| Where? | *Dove?* | *do*·ve |
| How? | *Come?* | *ko*·me |

# SHOPPING & SERVICES

**I'd like to buy …**
    *Vorrei comprare …*     vo·*ray* kom·*pra*·re …
**How much is it?**
    *Quanto costa?*     *kwan*·to ko·sta
**Can you write down the price?**
    *Può scrivere il prezzo.*     pwo *skree*·ve·re eel *pre*·tso
**I don't like it.**
    *Non mi piace.*     non mee *pya*·che
**May I look at it?**
    *Posso dare*     *po*·so *da*·re
    *un'occhiata?*     oo·no·*kya*·ta
**I'm just looking.**
    *Sto solo guardando.*     sto *so*·lo gwar·*dan*·do
**It's not expensive.**
    *Non è caro/a.* (m/f)     non e *ka*·ro/a
**It's too expensive.**
    *È troppo caro/a.* (m/f)     e *tro*·po *ka*·ro/a
**I'll take it.**
    *Lo/La compro.* (m/f)     lo/la *kom*·pro
**Do you accept credit cards?**
    *Accettate carte*     a·che·*ta*·te *kar*·te
    *di credito?*     dee *kre*·dee·to

| | | |
|---|---|---|
| more | *più* | pyoo |
| less | *meno* | *me*·no |
| smaller | *più piccolo/a* (m/f) | pyoo *pee*·ko·lo/a |
| bigger | *più grande* | pyoo *gran*·de |

**I'm looking for …**  *Cerco …*  *cher*·ko …

| | | |
|---|---|---|
| a bank | *un banco* | oon *ban*·ko |
| the church | *la chiesa* | la *kye*·za |
| the city centre | *il centro* | eel *chen*·tro |
| the … embassy | *l'ambasciata* | lam·ba·*sha*·ta |
| | *di …* | dee … |
| the market | *il mercato* | eel mer·*ka*·to |
| the museum | *il museo* | eel moo·*ze*·o |
| the post office | *la posta* | la *po*·sta |
| a public toilet | *un gabinetto* | oon ga·bee·*ne*·to |
| the tourist | *l'ufficio* | loo·*fee*·cho |
| office | *di turismo* | dee too·*reez*·mo |

| | | |
|---|---|---|
| I want to | *Voglio* | *vo*·lyo |
| change … | *cambiare …* | kam·*bya*·re … |
| money | *del denaro* | del de·*na*·ro |
| travellers | *assegni di* | a·*se*·nyee dee |
| cheques | *viaggio* | vee·*a*·jo |

# TIME & DATES

**What time is it?**
    *Che ore sono?*     ke *o*·re *so*·no
**It's (eight o'clock).**
    *Sono (le otto).*     *so*·no (le *o*·to)

| | | |
|---|---|---|
| in the morning | *di mattina* | dee ma·*tee*·na |
| in the afternoon | *di pomeriggio* | dee po·me·*ree*·jo |
| in the evening | *di sera* | dee *se*·ra |

| | | |
|---|---|---|
| today | *oggi* | *o*·jee |
| tomorrow | *domani* | do·*ma*·nee |
| yesterday | *ieri* | *ye*·ree |

| | | |
|---|---|---|
| January | *gennaio* | je·*na*·yo |
| February | *febbraio* | fe·*bra*·yo |
| March | *marzo* | *mar*·tso |
| April | *aprile* | a·*pree*·le |
| May | *maggio* | *ma*·jo |
| June | *giugno* | *joo*·nyo |
| July | *luglio* | *loo*·lyo |
| August | *agosto* | a·*gos*·to |
| September | *settembre* | se·*tem*·bre |
| October | *ottobre* | o·*to*·bre |
| November | *novembre* | no·*vem*·bre |
| December | *dicembre* | dee·*chem*·bre |

| Monday | lunedì | loo·ne·dee |
| Tuesday | martedì | mar·te·dee |
| Wednesday | mercoledì | mer·ko·le·dee |
| Thursday | giovedì | jo·ve·dee |
| Friday | venerdì | ve·ner·dee |
| Saturday | sabato | sa·ba·to |
| Sunday | domenica | do·me·nee·ka |

# TRANSPORT

## PUBLIC TRANSPORT

| What time does | A che ora parte/ | a ke o·ra par·te/ |
| ... leave/ arrive? | arriva ...? | a·ree·va ... |
| the boat | la nave | la na·ve |
| the (city) bus | l'autobus | low·to·boos |
| the (intercity) bus | il pullman | eel pool·man |
| the plane | l'aereo | la·e·re·o |
| the train | il treno | eel tre·no |

**The train has been cancelled/delayed.**

Il treno è soppresso/    eel tre·no e so·pre·so/
in ritardo.              een ree·tar·do

**I want to go to ...**

Voglio andare a ...      vo·lyo an·da·re a ...

| I'd like a ... | Vorrei un | vo·ray oon |
| ticket. | biglietto ... | bee·lye·to ... |
| one-way | di sola andata | dee so·la an·da·ta |
| return | di andata e | dee an·da·ta e |
| | ritorno | ree·toor·no |
| 1st class | di prima classe | dee pree·ma kla·se |
| 2nd class | di seconda | dee se·kon·da |
| | classe | kla·se |

| the first | il primo | eel pree·mo |
| the last | l'ultimo | lool·tee·mo |
| platform (2) | binario (due) | bee·na·ryo (doo·e) |
| ticket office | biglietteria | bee·lye·te·ree·a |
| timetable | orario | o·ra·ryo |
| train station | stazione | sta·tsyo·ne |

## PRIVATE TRANSPORT

**Is this the road to ...?**

Questa strada porta    kwe·sta stra·da por·ta
a ...?                 a ...

| I'd like to hire | Vorrei | vo·ray |
| a/an ... | noleggiare ... | no·le·ja·re ... |
| car | una macchina | oo·na ma·kee·na |
| 4WD | un fuoristrada | oon fwo·ree·stra·da |
| motorbike | una moto | oo·na mo·to |
| bicycle | una bici(cletta) | oo·na bee·chee·(kle·ta) |

**Where's a service station?**

Dov'è una stazione    do·ve oo·na sta·tsyo·ne
di servizio?          dee ser·vee·tsyo

**Please fill it up.**

Il pieno, per favore.    eel pye·no per fa·vo·re

**I'd like (30) litres.**

Vorrei (trenta) litri.    vo·ray (tren·ta) lee·tree

| diesel | gasolio/diesel | ga·zo·lyo/dee·zel |
| petrol/gasoline | benzina | ben·dzee·na |

**(How long) Can I park here?**

(Per quanto tempo)         (per kwan·to tem·po)
Posso parcheggiare qui?    po·so par·ke·ja·re kwee

**Where do I pay?**

Dove si paga?    do·ve see pa·ga

**I need a mechanic.**

Ho bisogno di un    o bee·zo·nyo dee oon
meccanico.          me·ka·nee·ko

**The car/motorbike has broken down (at ...).**

La macchina/moto       la ma·kee·na/mo·to
si è guastata (a ...).    see e gwas·ta·ta (a ...)

**The car/motorbike won't start.**

*La macchina/moto*     la ma·kee·na/mo·to

*non parte.*           non par·te

**I have a flat tyre.**

*Ho una gomma bucata.*   o oo·na go·ma boo·ka·ta

**I've run out of petrol.**

*Ho esaurito la benzina.*   o e·zo·ree·to la ben·dzee·na

**I've had an accident.**

*Ho avuto un incidente.*   o a·voo·to oon een·chee·den·te

**Do you mind if I breastfeed here?**

*Le dispiace se allatto*    le dees·pya·che se a·la·to

*il/la bimbo/a qui?* (m/f)   eel/la beem·bo/a kwee

**Are children allowed?**

*I bambini sono*    ee bam·bee·nee so·no

*ammessi?*          a·me·see

# TRAVEL WITH CHILDREN

**Is there …?**

*C'è …?*            che …

**I need …**

*Ho bisogno di …*   o bee·zo·nyo dee …

| | | |
|---|---|---|
| **a baby change room** | *un bagno con fasciatoio* | oon ba·nyo kon fa·sha·to·yo |
| **a car baby seat** | *un seggiolino per bambini* | oon se·jo·lee·no per bam·bee·nee |
| **a child-minding service** | *un servizio di baby-sitter* | oon ser·vee·tsyo dee be·bee·see·ter |
| **a children's menu** | *un menù per bambini* | oon me·noo per bam·bee·nee |
| **(disposable) nappies/diapers** | *pannolini (usa e getta)* | pa·no·lee·nee (oo·sa e je·ta) |
| **formula (infant milk)** | *latte in polvere* | la·te in pol·ve·re |
| **an (English-speaking) babysitter** | *un/una baby-sitter (che parli inglese)* (m/f) | oon/oo·na be·bee·see·ter (ke par·lee een·gle·ze) |
| **a highchair** | *un seggiolone* | oon se·jo·lo·ne |
| **a potty** | *un vasino* | oon va·zee·no |
| **a stroller** | *un passeggino* | oon pa·se·jee·no |

Also available from Lonely Planet:
*Italian Phrasebook*

# GLOSSARY

**abbazia** – abbey
**agriturismo** – tourist accommodation on farms; farm-stays
**(pizza) al taglio** – (pizza) by the slice
**albergo** – hotel
**alimentari** – grocery shops; delicatessens
**alto** – high
**aperitivo** – before-evening-meal drink and snack
**APT** – Azienda di Promozione Turistica; local town or city tourist office
**autonoleggio** – car hire
**autostrada** – motorway; highway
**AV** – Alta Velocità, high-speed trains that began servicing Turin–Milan–Bologna–Florence–Rome–Naples–Salerno in late 2009

**bambino** – child
**bancomat** – ATM
**battistero** – baptistery
**benzina** – petrol
**bianco** – white
**biblioteca** – library
**borgo** – archaic name for small town, village or town sector (often dating to Middle Ages)

**calcio** – football
**cambio** – money-exchange office
**camera** – room
**campo** – field; also a square in Venice
**cappella** – chapel
**carabinieri** – police with military and civil duties
**casa** – house
**castello** – castle
**cattedrale** – cathedral
**centro** – city centre
**centro storico** – historic centre
**certosa** – monastery belonging to or founded by Carthusian monks
**chiesa** – church
**cima** – summit
**città alta** – upper town
**città bassa** – lower town
**colle** – hill
**colonna** – column
**comune** – equivalent to a municipality or county; a town or city council; historically, a self-governing town or city
**contrada** – district or street (in some towns)
**coperto** – cover charge in restaurants
**corso** – boulevard

**duomo** – cathedral

**ENIT** – Ente Nazionale Italiano per il Turismo; Italian National Tourist Board
**enoteca** – wine bar
**ES** – Eurostar Italia; fast train
**espresso** – express mail; express train; short black coffee
**est** – east
**estate** – summer

**ferrovia** – railway
**festa** – feast day; holiday
**fiume** – river
**fontana** – fountain
**foro** – forum
**funicolare** – funicular railway
**funivia** – cable car

**gelateria** – ice-cream shop
**giardino** – garden
**golfo** – gulf
**grotta** – cave

**IAT** – Informazione e Assistenza ai Turisti; local tourist office
**IC** – Intercity; limited stops train
**inverno** – winter
**isola** – island
**IVA** – Imposta di Valore Aggiunto; value-added tax

**lago** – lake
**largo** – small square
**Lega Nord** – Northern League; political party
**lido** – beach
**locanda** – inn; small hotel
**loggia** – covered area on the side of a building; porch; lodge

**mar, mare** – sea
**mercato** – market

**MM** – Metropolitana Milano (aka *il metrò*); Milan's underground transport system
**monte** – mountain
**municipio** – town hall

**nord** – north

**osteria** – simple, trattoria-style restaurant, usually with a bar

**palazzo** – mansion; palace; large building of any type, including an apartment block
**palio** – contest
**parco** – park
**passeggiata** – traditional evening stroll
**pensione** – guest house
**piazza** – square
**piazzale** – large open square
**pietà** – literally 'pity' or 'compassion'; sculpture, drawing or painting of the dead Christ supported by the Madonna
**pinacoteca** – art gallery
**ponte** – bridge
**porta** – gate; door
**portico** – covered walkway, usually attached to the outside of a building
**porto** – port
**posta** – post office; also *ufficio postale*

**reale** – royal
**rifugio** – mountain hut; accommodation in the Alps
**ristorante** – restaurant
**rocca** – fortress

**sala** – room; hall
**santuario** – sanctuary
**scalinata** – staircase
**stazione** – station
**stile liberty** – 'liberty style', Italian version of art nouveau
**strada** – street; road
**sud** – south

**teatro** – theatre
**tempio** – temple
**terme** – thermal baths
**torre** – tower
**torrente** – stream
**trattoria** – simple restaurant
**Trenitalia** – Italian State Railways; also known as Ferrovie dello Stato (FS)

**via** – street; road
**viale** – avenue
**villa** – town house; country house; also the park surrounding the house

# BEHIND THE SCENES

## THIS BOOK

This 1st edition of the *Italian Lakes* was researched and written by Damien Simonis and Belinda Dixon. It was commissioned in Lonely Planet's London office and produced by the following people:

**Commissioning Editors** Clifton Wilkinson, Paula Hardy
**Coordinating Editor** Kirsten Rawlings
**Coordinating Cartographer** Valentina Kremenchutskaya
**Coordinating Layout Designer** Paul Iacono
**Managing Editor** Bruce Evans
**Managing Cartographer** Herman So
**Managing Layout Designer** Laura Jane

**Assisting Editors** Gabrielle Stefanos, Melissa Faulkner, Alan Murphy, Kim Hutchins, Robyn Loughnane
**Assisting Cartographer** Alex Leung
**Project Manager** Rachel Imeson
**Cover Research** Marika Mercer, lonelyplanetimages.com
**Internal Image Research** Aude Vauconsant, lonelyplanetimages.com
**Thanks to** Mark Adams, Imogen Bannister, Yvonne Bischofberger, Sally Darmody, Janine Eberle, Owen Eszeki, Mark Germanchis, Michelle Glynn, Imogen Hall, Paula Hardy, Lauren Hunt, Nic Lehman, John Mazzocchi, Annelies Mertens, Lucy Monie, Wayne Murphy, Darren O'Connell, Naomi Parker, Julie Sheridan, Caroline Sieg, Glenn van der Knijff

## THE LONELY PLANET STORY

Fresh from an epic journey across Europe, Asia and Australia in 1972, Tony and Maureen Wheeler sat at their kitchen table stapling together notes. The first Lonely Planet guidebook, *Across Asia on the Cheap,* was born.

Travellers snapped up the guides. Inspired by their success, the Wheelers began publishing books to Southeast Asia, India and beyond. Demand was prodigious, and the Wheelers expanded the business rapidly to keep up. Over the years, Lonely Planet extended its coverage to every country and into the virtual world via lonelyplanet.com and the Thorn Tree message board.

As Lonely Planet became a globally loved brand, Tony and Maureen received several offers for the company. But it wasn't until 2007 that they found a partner whom they trusted to remain true to the company's principles of travelling widely, treading lightly and giving sustainably. In October of that year, BBC Worldwide acquired a 75% share in the company, pledging to uphold Lonely Planet's commitment to independent travel, trustworthy advice and editorial independence.

Today, Lonely Planet has offices in Melbourne, London and Oakland, with over 500 staff members and 300 authors. Tony and Maureen are still actively involved with Lonely Planet. They're travelling more often than ever, and they're devoting their spare time to charitable projects. And the company is still driven by the philosophy of *Across Asia on the Cheap*: 'All you've got to do is decide to go and the hardest part is over. So go!'

## SEND US YOUR FEEDBACK

We love to hear from travellers – your comments keep us on our toes and help make our books better. Our well-travelled team reads every word on what you loved or loathed about this book. Although we cannot reply individually to postal submissions, we always guarantee that your feedback goes straight to the appropriate authors, in time for the next edition. Each person who sends us information is thanked in the next edition – and the most useful submissions are rewarded with a free book.

To send us your updates – and find out about Lonely Planet events, newsletters and travel news – visit our award-winning website: **lonelyplanet.com/contact**.

Note: we may edit, reproduce and incorporate your comments in Lonely Planet products such as guidebooks, websites and digital products, so let us know if you don't want your comments reproduced or your name acknowledged. For a copy of our privacy policy visit lonelyplanet.com/privacy.

# THANKS

### DAMIEN SIMONIS

Putting together this book was only possible with the help of others. Among those who helped with ideas and/or with their company were: Daniela Antongiovanni, Sergio Bosio, Paola Brussa, Anna Cerutti, Gianluca Cosentino, Cédric Fahey, Verónica Farré, Alessandra Fasola and Michele, Caroline Heidler, Janique LeBlanc, Edith García López, Emma Lupano, Gisella Motta, Cristina Pasqualin, Stefano Stomboli, Maurizio Trombini and Simona Volonterio. Como tourist office staff were especially helpful. Belinda Dixon was a fine co-author! To all, a heartfelt *grazie mille!*

### BELINDA DIXON

Sincere thanks to the whole Lonely Planet team, especially those who eased the process and made working on this book a delight. Damien, thank you for holding it all together and for excellent advice (not least regarding villas in Como…). And to those who helped along the way, from superb tourist office staff to vineyard owners and olive oil makers, *alla salute!* Also to the AD for calm, kindness and listening to endless traveller's tales.

# ACKNOWLEDGMENTS

All images are the copyright of the photographers unless otherwise indicated. Many of the images in this guide are available for licensing from Lonely Planet Images: lonelyplanetimages.com.

# INDEX

INDEX

INDEX

INDEX

INDEX

## MAP LEGEND

*Note Not all symbols displayed below appear in this guide.*

### ROUTES

| | |
|---|---|
| Tollway | Tunnel |
| Freeway | Pedestrian Mall |
| Primary Road | Steps |
| Secondary Road | Walking Track |
| Tertiary Road | Walking Path |
| Lane | Walking Tour |
| Unsealed Road | Walking Tour Detour |
| Under Construction | Pedestrian Overpass |

### TRANSPORT

| | |
|---|---|
| Ferry Route & Terminal | Train Line & Station |
| Metro Line & Station | Underground Rail Line |
| Monorail & Stop | Tram Line & Stop |
| Bus Route & Stop | Cable Car, Funicular |

### AREA FEATURES

| | |
|---|---|
| Airport | Land |
| Beach | Mall, Plaza |
| Building | Market |
| Campus | Park |
| Cemetery, Christian | Sportsground |
| Cemetery, Other | Urban |

### HYDROGRAPHY

| | |
|---|---|
| River, Creek | |
| Canal | International |
| Water | State, Provincial |
| Swamp | Suburb |
| Lake (Dry) | City Wall |
| | Cliff |

### BOUNDARIES

### SYMBOLS IN THE KEY

**Essential Information**
- Tourist Office
- Police Station

**Exploring**
- Beach
- Buddhist
- Castle, Fort
- Christian
- Diving, Snorkelling
- Garden
- Hindu
- Islamic
- Jewish
- Monument
- Museum, Gallery
- Place of Interest
- Snow Skiing
- Swimming Pool
- Ruin
- Tomb
- Winery, Vineyard
- Zoo, Bird Sanctuary

**Gastronomic Highlights**
- Eating
- Cafe

**Nightlife**
- Drinking
- Entertainment

**Recommended Shops**
- Shopping

**Accommodation**
- Sleeping
- Camping

**Transport**
- Airport, Airfield
- Cycling, Bicycle Path
- Border Crossing
- Bus Station
- Ferry
- General Transport
- Train Station
- Taxi Rank

**Parking**
- Parking

### OTHER MAP SYMBOLS

**Information**
- Bank, ATM
- Embassy, Consulate
- Hospital, Medical
- Internet Facilities
- Post Office
- Telephone

**Geographic**
- Cave
- Lighthouse
- Lookout
- Mountain, Volcano
- National Park
- Picnic Area

## LONELY PLANET OFFICES

**AUSTRALIA**
**Head Office**
Locked Bag 1, Footscray, Victoria 3011
☎ 03 8379 8000, fax 03 8379 8111
talk2us@lonelyplanet.com.au

**USA**
150 Linden St, Oakland, CA 94607
☎ 510 250 6400, toll free 800 275 8555
fax 510 893 8572
info@lonelyplanet.com

**UK**
2nd fl, 186 City Road, London EC1V 2NT
☎ 020 7106 2100, fax 020 7106 2101
go@lonelyplanet.co.uk

**Published by Lonely Planet Publications Pty Ltd**
ABN 36 005 607 983
© Lonely Planet 2010
© photographers as indicated 2010
**Cover photograph** San Paolo, Lake Iseo, Kaos02/
Sime/4Corners Images. **Internal title page
photograph** The Lecco end of Lake Como, Roberto
Gerometta/Lonely Planet Images.

Many of the images in this guide are available
for licensing from Lonely Planet Images:
lonelyplanetimages.com.

Printed by Toppan Security Printing Pte Ltd, Singapore.

**Mixed Sources**
Product group from well-managed
forests and other controlled sources
www.fsc.org  Cert no. SGS-COC-005002
© 1996 Forest Stewardship Council
FSC